D0154076

Evaluating and Assessing the Visual Arts in Education

INTERNATIONAL PERSPECTIVES

Evaluating and Assessing the Visual Arts in Education

INTERNATIONAL PERSPECTIVES

Edited by

DOUG BOUGHTON
University of South Australia

ELLIOT W. EISNER
Stanford University, USA

JOHAN LIGTVOET
The Academy for Art Education, Tilburg, The Netherlands

Teachers College, Columbia University
New York and London

Published by Teachers College Press, 1234 Amsterdam Avenue, New York, NY
10027

Copyright © 1996 by Teachers College, Columbia University

All rights reserved. No part of this publication may be reproduced or transmitted
in any form or by any means, electronic or mechanical, including photocopy, or
any information storage and retrieval system, without permission from the pub-
lisher.

Library of Congress Cataloging-in-Publication Data

Evaluating and assessing the visual arts in education : international perspectives /
    edited by Doug Boughton, Elliot W. Eisner, Johan Ligtvoet.
        p.   cm.
    Includes bibliographical references and index.
    ISBN 0-8077-3511-6 (cloth : alk. paper)
        1. Art—Study and teaching.   I. Boughton, Douglas.   II. Eisner, Elliot
W.   III. Ligtvoet, Johan.
    N85.E9   1996
    707—dc20   95-42090

ISBN 0-8077-3511-6

Printed on acid-free paper
Manufactured in the United States of America

03   02   01   00   99   98   97   96   8   7   6   5   4   3   2   1

CAL
N85
E9
1996

This book is dedicated to the J. Paul Getty Trust,
a philanthropy helping to make the arts
a part of the lives of all people.

Contents

II-B: Museum Policy and Cultural Heritage

Conclusion

International Society for Education through Art
Société Internationale pour l'Éducation Artistique

Preface

This volume is the result of an international conference held at Bosschen-hoofd, the Netherlands, in December 1990. This conference, the first in its kind in the field of art education, brought together 18 of the world's leading scholars in art education, education, and developmental psychology to examine the current state of assessment and evaluation in the visual arts and to identify developments that appeared to them to be desirable. These scholars were drawn from seven countries—Australia, Canada, England, Germany, Hungary, the Netherlands, and the United States—each of which reflects different values and practices of assessment and evaluation in the visual arts.

In planning this conference a number of features were considered essential. First, we wanted a conference that reflected the wisdom and experience of scholars from a variety of nations in order to avoid the parochialism of a single national perspective. Second, we wanted the papers to direct their attention to assessment and evaluation not only in schools, but in museums and cultural centers as well. Each institution, we reasoned, has its own distinctive characteristics and its own traditions, and we wanted the papers to reflect these differences. Third, we wanted a working conference rather than a large international congress in which defensiveness and showmanship might inadvertently be promoted by the size of the audience or the need to protect one's reputation. Finally, we wanted a conference in which substantial time and attention were devoted to the discussion of contentious issues.

All too often time for discussion is restricted at conferences: Most of what is available is devoted to papers being read aloud that could have been read in silence prior to arrival. At Bosschenhoofd, largely because of the conference's small size, participants had the opportunity to read the papers before arriving, thus providing substantial time for discussion. Each presenter was allocated half an hour to summarize the paper. Each group of three papers was allocated an hour and three-quarters for discussion. The result of this structure was a conference that stimulated writers to rethink their views and to modify their papers accordingly within limits that did not make irrelevant their critics' initial analysis.

All discussions were tape recorded and transcribed and were used by the editors to prepare their introductory and concluding comments.

The conference and the papers prepared for it made several notions clear. The field of visual art education is entering a new period in which the invention of assessment and evaluation practices that are congenial to the character of art is an important—indeed a critical—scholarly and professional ambition. The complex and difficult task is to avoid those forms of reductionism that trivialize art and art education, while profiting from the insights, practices, and traditions of those in countries other than one's own. This conference is, we believe, a good example of international intellectual cooperation. It requires discussion of differences in both the form and aims of evaluation and assessment to appreciate not only the features of educational practice in other places, but the features of such practice in one's own culture as well. For example, Great Britain and Holland have long used the practice of moderation to develop consensus on the assessment of student work. (Moderation is the process used to adjust the grades or marks achieved by students in one educational context in order to attain equivalence with similar work of students in another context.) In the United States, where there is a level of sophistication with respect to test construction that Great Britain and Holland have yet to discover, moderation is rarely practiced. Our different traditions tell us both what is possible and what to avoid.

Not only did the conference make some ideas clear, but it also revealed some lack of shared understanding, particularly in the way the terms *assessment* and *evaluation* are used in different countries. While these terms represent the foundation upon which the conference was built, it became clear from the presentations and discussions that assessment and evaluation can mean different things in different countries, and indeed to different scholars.

Evaluation is a generic term that has broad applications and often is used interchangeably with assessment. Assessment, on the other hand, often is used more specifically in England, the Netherlands, and Australia to refer to the procedures used to determine student performance in a national or centralized system of education, usually as an end-point judgment of achievement; for example, the General Certificate of Secondary Education (GCSE) in the UK and the final examination in the Netherlands. In these countries assessment practices employ procedures for the moderation of judgments of studio art performance, often use teams of judges, and may require application of agreed-upon criteria for such judgments. By contrast, in the United States the term *assessment* represents a desire to create practices that more authentically represent a kind of thinking and acting that genuinely matter in education.

While we do not wish to prescribe a single clear meaning for assessment, the reader should be aware of the potential for variation in the specificity of its meaning in different countries. What this book does not provide is a method to assess and evaluate visual art education: The reader will find no prescriptions in it. What the reader will find is a host of further issues, unanswered questions, challenging leads, and sharp differences in conception characterizing the opinions and experiences of scholars who take the assessment and evaluation process seriously. But this is not all. As pointed out above, the terms *assessment* and *evaluation* are used differently in different nations. There is no educational Esperanto in any field, and we believe that although this sometimes causes difficulties in communication, on balance it is an asset *not* to have a standardized language. Standardized language leads to standardized educational practice, and standardized educational practice, like standardized art, is, we think, undesirable.

This volume, and the conference that gave rise to it, is the child of the International Society for Education Through Art (InSEA). This Society, of which Elliot Eisner was President during the period the conference was held, has over 1,500 members in 92 countries. Initiated in 1952, in Bristol, England, under the leadership of Sir Herbert Read and others, it is committed to the creation of an artistically grounded education for the young. It achieves this end by serving its members through diverse publications and conferences held around the globe. This particular conference, however, could not have occurred without the generous financial support of the J. Paul Getty Trust and its Grant Program. The Grant Program provided the resources that made possible not only the conference itself, but this book which resulted from the conference papers and debates. Both the editors and InSEA wish to express their gratitude to the Trust.

There is one person whom the editors wish especially to thank for assistance beyond the call of duty: Kit Grauer of the University of British Columbia who served as InSEA treasurer and who arranged for the disbursement of funds with competence and personal sensitivity. In addition, she distilled the discussions that were recorded, offering the editors a valuable resource for their own analysis and commentary.

Finally, we wish to thank our wives, Thelma, Ellie, and Adriënne, for their forbearance and support while we were engaged or away, trying to create a successful conference and a useful book.

Doug Boughton, Elliot Eisner, Johan Ligtvoet

Evaluating and Assessing the Visual Arts in Education

INTERNATIONAL PERSPECTIVES

Chapter 1

Overview of Evaluation and Assessment: Conceptions in Search of Practice

ELLIOT W. EISNER
Stanford University, USA

There has always been an uneasy relationship between art education and evaluation and assessment. Assessment and its close relations—evaluation and testing—participate in a tradition that puts a premium on predictability, rationality, and precision—features that are not typically associated with the emotional, unpredictable, and ambiguous features of the artistic process. Furthermore, artistic activity, certainly within the context of schools, has been much less concerned with the achievement of specifiable outcomes than with engaging students in the process of making visual images, so much so that pedagogical attention to outcomes was regarded by many as *prima facia* evidence that the teacher did not understand what really mattered in art education.

Evaluation and assessment are also embedded in a scientific tradition as old as the Enlightenment. The measurement of variables and the ability to predict and control outcomes is one index of scientific understanding. Bringing the world—including the human world—under the explanatory and illuminating light of theory was and is one way to demystify it.

Such demystification was the hallmark aspiration of Enlightenment scholars such as Condorcet, Condillac, Descartes, Newton, and Comte (Toulmin, 1990). The philosophical values they promulgated and the impact of their ideas on those committed to the development of a science of education required for its realization the ability to predict and control outcomes. The testing movement in America and elsewhere was imbued with this spirit (Cremin, 1970; Joncich, 1968), a spirit that was regarded by those in art education as inhospitable to the personal, unique, and even mysterious features of artistic creation.

For all of the foregoing reasons, evaluation, assessment, and, especially testing and the arts have never been comfortable bedfellows. Testing typically

Evaluating and Assessing the Visual Arts in Education: International Perspectives: © 1996 by Teachers College, Columbia University. All rights reserved. ISBN 0-8077-3511-6. Prior to photocopying items for classroom use, please contact the Copyright Clearance Center, Customer Service, 222 Rosewood Dr., Danvers, MA 01923, USA, tel. (508) 750-8400.

is predicated on the assumption that the desired outcomes of educational activities are known in advance; artistic creation seeks surprise. Testing aspires for all a set of common correct responses; in the arts, idiosyncratic responses are prized. Testing typically focuses on pieces or segments of information; artistic work emphasizes wholes and configurations. Testing emphasizes the acquisition of products produced by others; the arts emphasize content growing out of one's personal experiences, especially those having to do with matters of feeling. Such matters of emphasis are so fundamental that it seems as though testing and the arts reside in different worlds.

There is another tradition that also has historically separated the arts from evaluation and assessment. That tradition resides not in the aspiration to create a science of education, but in the desire to create a child-centered conception of educational practice. First emerging in the work of Rousseau, especially *Emile*, and manifesting itself especially in those child-centered schools associated with progressive education, that tradition placed primary emphasis on the centrality of process and regarded the arts as means through which children could be liberated from the rule-governed conventions associated with schooling. The arts were believed to have the power to give to each child access to a preverbal imaginative life uncontaminated by prescriptions of correctness. Among art educators the child as artist, almost in the spirit of William Blake, was a dominant metaphor in America, the United Kingdom, and many European countries during the 1930s–50s. This image was not compatible with a view of educational practice aimed at imparting information to children and then testing them to measure the amount of information they retained. Art educators lived their professional lives by different lights.

One result of these differences in conception, both in art education in general and in visual art education in particular, is that art education has not developed the kind of assessment practices and achievement tests that other subjects, particularly mathematics and language arts, have. This might not be much of a liability. Much of what has been created by test makers has reflected a greater concern with statistical precision than with educational significance. Preoccupation with reliability often has swamped concerns for validity, resulting in recent years in a growing dissatisfaction with the educational adequacy of achievement testing. This dissatisfaction began to be most clearly revealed with the emergence of the term *assessment*. Assessment, in the United States, is a term of recent vintage. The older terms, *testing* and *evaluating*, are now being given a less than gentle nudge by this educational newcomer. Why the shift in terminology? What does it signify? Why now?

A clue to answering these questions comes from the adjectives that often are used in conjunction with assessment. These adjectives are *authentic* and *performance*. Authentic assessment implies its opposite—inauthentic assessment. Inauthentic assessment, by implication, is what testing has been. What is it that is inauthentic? Increasingly, there is a strong disenchantment with the dominance of psychometrically developed standardized achievement tests and a growing desire to replace them with procedures that provide a portrait of educational performance that conveys meanings more significant than what optically scored filled-in bubble sheets can provide. The drive is to get closer to "real life," to secure information on performance that really matters.

Similarly, *performance* assessment implies nonperformance assessment. Nonperformance assessment considered literally is, of course, not possible: no performance, no assessment. But considered metaphorically, performance assessment implies that much—even most—standardized testing procedures do not require students to perform. Indeed, some testing agencies have developed multiple-choice tests to measure students' *writing* abilities. The point here is that both the terms *authentic* and *performance*, when modifying assessment, suggest that most existing test practices are educationally feckless. The current aim is to design an approach to assessment that is more relevant to what matters in education than the tests that are now used make possible.

The tradition of practice in the field of testing, in some ways a millstone around the necks of those in some subject areas, does not hang on the necks of those in art education. Art educators have no tradition of testing to abandon. Yet, the absence of tests in art education does not mean that assessment in the arts will be warmly welcomed by art educators. The importance of mystery over certainty, process over outcome, and individuality over uniformity still provides bulwarks against efforts to ask about the consequences of art programs.

On the whole, there is no large appetite among art educators to assess the outcomes, content, or activities associated with teaching of the arts. While we believe art educators are right to resist the reduction of art education to the same bland uniform outcomes so common to many academic subjects, failure to assess art education in ways congruent with the unique features of the arts is a form of professional dereliction. Educators need to determine, as best they can, the results of their efforts, if for no other reason than to protect the young from incompetent teaching and educationally diluted curricula.

There is another reason for the saliency of assessment as well—less noble, but there nevertheless. That reason has to do with accountability. The public expects public institutions to be responsible for the use of the funds it provides. This means accounting for the value they have added to those the funding is intended to serve. The public wants to know if support for public services, whether in schools or museums, makes a difference. Protestations of faith and the expression of heartfelt commitment by art educators for art education will no longer do. The public wants evidence.

Aside from the moral and political justification for assessment, there is an intellectual one. The absence of assessment in art education—or in any other education enterprise—creates an intellectual vacuum that impedes the improvement of pedagogical practice. If there is no way of determining whether pedagogical practices have consequences, there is no basis—save novelty—for changing them. Without assessment there is no good way to understand the relationship between doing and its consequences; in such circumstances it becomes difficult to get smarter about teaching. The political, the moral, and the pedagogical, each in its own way, provide reason enough to pay attention to assessment. Considered jointly these reasons are more than compelling. The contents of this book represent an effort to examine existing practices and to generate the leads needed to invent evaluation and assessment practices that will genuinely serve the educational aspirations of art educators.

FUNCTIONS OF ASSESSMENT

It is important to recognize at the outset that assessment in education has various functions, each distinctive and requiring distinctive tactics and methods. For example, one function of assessment is a kind of educational "temperature taking." Suppose a school, museum, or community center wishes to secure a general picture of the effects it has had on the people it has served. It does not want or need a detailed evaluation of each individual in the program, but a general characterization of a population. To secure this type of information, a multiple-choice test that is simple to administer and score, combined with multiple matrix sampling procedures, may very well be enough for such purposes to be well served.

If, however, one wishes to know whether individuals meet a particular criterion required, say, for admission to a profession or a university, or for promotion, then a "gatekeeping function" needs to be performed by the assessment process. For this function, a detailed picture of individual performance is needed. Temperature taking and gatekeeping are only two functions of assessment. Others include providing pedagogically useful diagnostic information about individuals for those who work with them, determining whether program goals have been achieved, and giving feedback to students. Each of the foregoing functions is best served by using different types of data secured through means that differ in form and focus. Diagnostic functions might require interviews, while a gatekeeping function might require the observation of individual performance on standardized tasks.

Once diverse assessment functions are identified, the press toward a universal, one-size-fits-all approach to assessment diminishes, a more complex view of assessment emerges, and the options one can consider expand. These issues and possibilities are as germane to assessment in the arts as they are to assessment in other fields.

To provide one example of how practices are shaped by function, consider the use of *focus groups* as a way of providing information to curators, museum directors, and museum educators about the extent to which visitors' expectations of museums are met by what the museums provide. In a recent study of art museums (Newman, 1990), visitors were asked if they would participate in a focus group to provide information to museum officials about the degree to which the museum met their expectations. Focus groups are groups that are interviewed by a skilled interlocutor in order to elicit responses that can be discussed by the group as a whole. Such groups often engage in these discussions in a room in which there is a one-way mirror, behind which sit members of the museum staff. Thus, the staff is able to see and hear the discussion. In addition, the focus group discussion is recorded and then transcribed for subsequent analysis. Such a process makes it possible in a way in which structured interviews with individuals cannot, to provide an evaluative picture of what, in this case, museum visitors think of their experience in the museum, how it served their needs, what they found frustrating, helpful, puzzling, and so forth. What we have in this particular assessment practice is a diagnostic function provided *in vivo* by the museum's clients and presented with a vividness that can drive home to museum professionals the degree to which their clients believe they are being well served by the museum.

There are, to be sure, a host of other important functions that this particular form of assessment does not provide, but what it does provide is often extremely useful, particularly because the staff of the museum (or school or center) has the opportunity to see the discussion unfold "in the flesh." Many times our own assumptions are so ingrained that we find it difficult to distance ourselves from our normal practices; we become blind to what is most familiar. The use of a focus group can help us defamiliarize our surroundings, challenge our stock responses, and alter our old habits.

Distinguishing between the functions of assessment is one way to identify their uses, but it is not the only way. Consider what gets assessed.

SUBJECT MATTER OF ASSESSMENTS

Customarily, assessment, like evaluation and testing, focuses on students, clients, museum visitors: those who receive service. The major question is usually: What have they learned from their experience? What have they received from their effort or their visit? Although attention to those who have received services is important, it clearly is not the only important focus in the context of assessment. Two other important candidates are the program that is provided and the quality and manner of its mediation.

A focus on the program, say in the context of schools, could address the significance of the content the program provides, the nature of the activities in which students are engaged, the attractiveness of the materials prepared for students and teachers, and the ease with which they can be used. It could examine the degree to which the content fostered connections between subjects and between subjects and life outside of schools or museums. In short, the content and form of the materials students and teachers use could themselves be subject to appraisal.

In museums, the features of the text associated with an exhibition or individual object could be examined. Is the text readable? Is it riddled with terms such as *oevre* and *genre* and *metier* and *intaglio*, words that the occasional museum visitor is unlikely to understand? Does the text distract visitors? Does it lead them to extra-aesthetic considerations that are unhelpful for experiencing the objects as works of art?

How is the exhibition organized? Does it facilitate comparison and contrast among works? Is it likely to be accessible to the nonspecialist? What about lighting? A place to sit? Guidance in getting around the museum? All of these considerations and more are proper subject matters for assessment and evaluation in a museum.

As important as the assessment of programs is, no programs function without human mediation. In schools such mediation emerges in teaching. In museums it is provided through docentry and in lectures. How that mediation occurs is critical in shaping the impact of the program on clients. Plans and materials are expressions of intentions, but we must not forget that intentions live in the context of interaction, and this interaction occurs in a triadic relationship between a student, a teacher, and the program. These three educational commonplaces define the major parameters of interaction. The student (or museum visitor) brings with him or her an array of expectations, skills, and understandings. These interact with a teacher (or docent or lecturer) who reflects an understanding of some content or process and possesses a repertoire of pedagogical skills. In addition to these skills, the teacher possesses an understanding of the student (or museum visitor) on dimensions relevant to the teacher's educational intentions and the objects or materials available. In many ways, it is the teacher who builds the bridges between the content and the student, and does so in the ways in which the tasks are provided, the explanations given, and the questions raised. It is the teacher who can exploit the students' questions and comments in order to increase the meaningfulness of the encounter. The quality of this mediation, whether in "standard" forms of teaching or in the form of a lecture, is itself a primary subject for assessment. The best and most thoroughly articulated curricular plans can be undermined by poor teaching, and, at times, poorly thought through plans can be saved by excellent teaching.

The point of the foregoing is to underscore the variety of subject matters that assessment practices can address. By no means is assessment limited to student outcomes, although student outcomes, largely measured by achievement tests, historically have been the primary focus of assessment. As attention to content and teaching become increasingly salient in our conception of assessment, the scope and variety of assessment methods are likely to increase. By shifting focus temporarily from what the student has learned or experienced to how the teacher has taught, the form of assessment itself will be changed. Indeed, in many ways attention to the teaching of the visual arts is far closer to a focus on process and performance than the traditional student assessment tasks, which secure information on tests that pay little attention to process and which have no substantive counterpart in the world outside of the classroom.

Thus far this introductory chapter has emphasized the following ideas:

1. Art education historically has embraced a set of educational aims that appear inimicable to the aims reflected in the use of standardized achievement tests. The result has been a paucity of such devices in the field.
2. Although the virtual absence of standardized achievement tests provides no tradition that needs to be abandoned in order to be innovative, attitudes among art educators toward assessment in the visual arts may still be less than enthusiastic.
3. The different functions of assessment need to be appreciated so that a single approach does not, by fiat, define how assessment is to occur and for what purposes.
4. The subject matters of assessment as well as its functions differ. *Program content* and *teaching practices* as well as *student outcomes* should be regarded as critically important commonplaces for assessment.

CRITERIA FOR ASSESSMENT

Given the foregoing, what kinds of criteria might be appropriate for guiding the creation of new forms of assessment in the visual arts? What should we seek to develop? What should we look for? To schematize these criteria—and they should be regarded as heuristics, not as standards—the following criteria for each of the three educational commonplaces are offered.

The Form and Content of Programs

1. *The programs and the materials developed should be user friendly.* The features of the resources that people are to use, whether in the context of a classroom or a museum, are extremely important in shaping users' attitudes about

their use. For example, curriculum materials are developed for teachers that often look more like manuals for the assembly of an M1 rifle than interesting and useful tools for assisting students in the classroom. Frequently precious little attention is paid in the creation of such materials to matters of design, language, layout, visuals, and the like. Too often information is conceptually dense, highly schematized, and uninteresting to read. Similar features often typify the texts that are offered to museum visitors as they prepare to enter an exhibition. The language of the text emanates directly (or seemingly so) from the books that art historians read. It is almost as if the preparers of such material had no idea about the backgrounds of those coming to the museum.

What is needed is a pedagogical conception to provide the designers of materials with the kind of considerations they need to consider in designing what are, after all, pedagogical resources. In the best of all possible worlds such materials would have a "come pick me up" quality about them; they might even be humorous and certainly they should be attractive. Unfortunately, they often appear onerous and unattractive. The development of user-friendly resources is one of the important considerations in facilitating curriculum implementation in school and in providing genuinely helpful information to those who visit museums. A kind of "educational ergonomics" needs to be developed to achieve this kind of aim. At present, we are far from it. Such a criterion should be important when developing or assessing the form and content of programs.

2. *The content of programs should provide tasks and ideas that stimulate and that relate to tasks and ideas beyond themselves.* It is no great achievement to provide tasks and ideas that offer little intellectual or artistic substance to the clients of an organization. In museums that have major collections, the ability to provide work of first caliber is available. But even when such work is available, the mere presence of the work does not ensure that aesthetic experience will be secured and that artistic achievement will be appreciated and understood. What is needed, therefore, is not only the presence of such objects, but the kinds of mediating conditions that increase the probability that the client's encounter with the work will be satisfying and meaningful. Such mediating conditions have been referred to as "silent pedagogy" (Eisner & Dobbs, 1990).

In addition, particularly in the context of schooling, it is important that the content of school programs enable students to make connections beyond the specific content they encounter and use within their classrooms. These materials should enable students to relate what they have learned in the context of their own classroom to the world outside of schools. The major function of schools is not primarily to facilitate learning that is useful within schools, but to foster forms of learning that enable the student to lead a more meaningful and satisfying life outside of school. Therefore, one of the most important criteria for selecting program content and shaping the forms such programs are to take is the degree to which it will have a transfer effect in realms beyond the classroom.

A similar consideration is appropriate, though not as acutely, to art museums. The importance of works of art, beyond their own capacity to generate meaningful experience in visitors, is to enable the visitors to secure forms of understanding and kinds of experience that also can be had in the world outside of the museum. The treatment of light in a painting by Monet is not only about a particular picture painted by Monet but about the ways in which light itself can be seen. The dream-like world of a Magritte says something not only about the incongruity of psychological content within the borders of a picture frame but also about what the mind is capable of generating beyond the gallery. One could give innumerable examples of the carryover effect of art on the human psyche. These carryover effects are significant and can be planned for in the design of programs both within the school and the museum itself.

3. *The forms art programs take should be congruent with their content and aims.* It is not unusual, particularly in schools, for programs devoted to the arts to be "packaged" in a form that is incongruent with art's primary features. For example, the development of curriculum materials, as indicated earlier, that do not display the qualities or spirit associated with the primary content in which the client is to be engaged, often impedes such experience; the form of the program and the materials conflict with the content the program is intended to generate. The creation of materials and programs that are congruent with the content of an exhibition or the intended content of a task in the context of a school is not easily achieved. Yet, it is important. Not only is the medium the message, but the form the medium takes often becomes the primary message, one that frequently overrides the explicit content to be taught. How does one develop a sense of the spiritual, the aesthetic, the contemplative, in a school or museum whose features are incongruent with or even hostile to such qualities? Whether one can always achieve such congruence is doubtful. Nevertheless, it is an important aspiration for those who design programs and materials intended to engage people in art experience.

4. *The content of programs should exploit a variety of sensory modalities and elicit more than one form of cognition.* Humans apprehend the world in a variety of ways. Each sensory modality functions as a kind of information pick-up system that gives one access to the world. Each form of access—visual, auditory, olfactory, gustatory, kinesthetic—provides distinctive kinds of information. It is obvious, for example, in observing infants in their cribs that their

encounters with the world are not only visual, but are tactile, gustatory, olfactory, and more. Infants explore the world through all of their sensory modalities, and this process enables them to form concepts in which the information provided by the object is represented. Similarly, it is important to develop programs that display information in a variety of ways. Not only does each form of representation provide distinctive content (Eisner, 1994), but each individual is likely to have a particular kind of aptitude or proclivity that facilitates access to that information (Gardner, 1983). By restricting the range of forms that are provided, information itself is diminished, and the student's opportunity to learn and experience is reduced. An information-rich environment comes to individuals not simply through text, but through visual images, through auditory forms of information, and through other forms represented by our biological sensory system.

To think about information this way is to recognize that, in a sense, each orifice is a kind of cognitive inlet that has the capacity to stimulate and that provides information that can be displayed in cognition and stored in memory. Indeed, we remember not only the visual, but the auditory, the kinesthetic, the olfactory. Humans have the capacity to take in the world through these modalities, as well as to represent aspects of that world in forms congruent with the form in which the initial information was experienced. The exploitation of such biological resources increases the probability that the meaning of the material will be secured and that a greater sense of equity will be provided.

5. *The tasks within programs should provide for multiple solutions to problems and multiple answers to questions.* One of the great virtues of the arts is the variety of meanings they can convey. Unlike many other fields where precision and correctness are virtues, the arts often celebrate ambiguity and convey multiple meanings. They represent in their embodiment the personal signature of the maker and in their perception the unique ways in which the percipient can experience and interpret the work. These qualities of art ought to be reflected in the kinds of content and tasks that are designed in programs. Rather than conveying to clients that there is only one single correct solution to the interpretation of a work or that there are fixed criteria for the creation of work, it is far more appropriate to design tasks that are congruent with the important features of art itself, one of which is the possibility of diversity.

The creation of such tasks and the provision of such content will, of course, complicate the assessment of outcomes. It is far simpler to determine the match between a student's response and a single correct answer than to interpret and appraise the distinctive qualities of a response on its own terms. Yet, to succumb to the classical conception that standards are to be applied uniformly across all responses is to undermine the values most important in the arts themselves.

The Character of Mediation

1. *When the major means of mediation is a human teacher, significant provision needs to be made for sustained and constructive feedback to the teacher on his or her teaching performance.* It is difficult to underestimate the importance of the teacher in shaping the educational experience of the student. The teacher functions as a gatekeeper, as an interpreter, as a resource person, as someone who helps define the qualities of the environment in which learning is to occur. Because teaching is so crucial to the experience of students, its qualities should be an ongoing object of attention. Yet, paradoxically, teachers often remain insulated and isolated from their colleagues and typically receive little in the way of feedback about their own performance. As a result, most teachers maintain virtually the same array of pedagogical skills that they acquired during their first few years of teaching. Relatively little is done in schools to expand teachers' repertoire or even to help them become aware of the ways in which they function.

Many of the same conditions apply to those who work in museums. Those who lecture and who function as docents typically do not receive the kind of critical feedback that would help them improve their own pedagogical art. Assessment and evaluation in arts education cannot afford to neglect the ways in which teachers function. One way to address this situation is structural. Organizational conditions within schools and museums need to be defined that normalize, as a part of what it means to be a teacher or docent, the provision of such feedback. This will require a reconceptualization of the roles that teachers have within their own institutions. Teachers themselves will need to have a hand in the observation and feedback process.

Although the creation of such structures is a necessary condition, it clearly is not a sufficient one. Having access to colleagues in order to receive assistance in improving one's teaching skills is, of course, helpful, but those who observe need to be able to see what they observe. This means that programs will need to be designed that refine the skills of perception when it comes to teaching so that the insights and feedback provided to teachers are on the mark. The provision of such programs will not be easy: They are complex and subtle. Furthermore, feedback cannot be offered to teachers by following standardized prescriptions for excellence in pedagogy or by applying standards that somehow are intended to suit all forms of teaching.

Teaching, like other arts, bears the signature of its creator, and virtue for one teacher is not necessarily what constitutes virtue for another. The assessment of teaching, like the assessment of the content provided in the programs offered, is a fundamental subject matter for the overall aim, which is, of course, the improvement of the educative conditions in the institution in which art education occurs.

2. *A substantial portion of the information about the quality and effects of teaching should come from the clients the program serves.* One important source of information concerning the quality and effects of pedagogy is those to whom it is directed—the students or clients of the institution. To secure such information procedures need to be employed that not only regularize its acquisition, but do so with a level of depth that is genuinely useful. Too often check-off sheets and other superficial methods are employed that are not particularly helpful to the teacher. The major aim here is to secure from clients information about teaching, and indeed other aspects of the program, that provides insight into what is occurring. The use of focus groups, mentioned earlier, is one way to secure the kind of information that is needed. The use of logs and interviews is another. The major point is that those whom the program is intended to serve are an important source of information about the program and that assessment practices should include them.

The foregoing should not be interpreted to mean that the client's conclusions and evaluations of the program should automatically define the institutional agenda. The information that clients provide is data to be interpreted and appraised, not necessarily followed. Clients' comments need to be heard, not necessarily heeded. Whether they are heeded will depend on far more than their mere presence. It will require interpretive and sensitive minds, precisely what any useful assessment process depends on.

3. *As clients mature they should have increased opportunities to set their own intellectual agenda within the program.* Teaching, like parenting, can foster independence or dependence. In the context of education, the overall aim is to enable the student or client increasingly to become the architect of his or her own education. This means providing a form of teaching that makes more options available as individuals become able to handle them. Ideally, an effective educational program, whether in a school, a community center, or a museum, should make it possible for the client to define his or her own aims and to acquire the skills necessary to pursue them. The objective is to increase the client's autonomy.

There is, of course, a caution that needs to be mentioned. In some forms of progressive education in the 1930s–40s, so much "freedom" was provided to children that they did not know what to do with it; the experience of schooling became unproductive and indeed frustrating. One of the major problems in both teaching and parenting is knowing how many bridges to build, how wide, with how many directional signs. In other words, the wise parent, like the wise teacher, does not provide more guidance than is needed—or less.

This is easier to say than to do, yet it is a critical consideration in any form of effective pedagogy. What a museum, like a school, should seek is the development of a level of confidence and competence that makes it possible for the visitor or student to negotiate the territory. Providing lectures in a museum, for example, in which there is no possibility for listeners to raise questions or to formulate their own line of inquiry is a way of sustaining dependency rather than diminishing it. Similarly, an arts program in a school that never makes it possible for students to define their own artistic agenda fosters dependencies.

Creating incompetence in goal formation and the tactics and strategies needed to achieve goals has been described as a process of "deskilling" (Apple, 1982): the cultivated inability to formulate one's own personal purposes. Unfortunately, many schools contribute to deskilling. The assessment of teaching, and indeed the assessment of the program itself, should address matters of growing independence and try to determine the extent to which both the program and teaching practices contribute to its realization.

4. *Feedback systems employing video portraits of teachers as actors should be used to enhance the quality of information provided about the processes of teaching.* One of the central lessons that the visual arts teach is that not everything that can or needs to be said can be conveyed by words or text. Pictures reveal, they exemplify, they portray, they disclose. This lesson is as important in understanding the contributions of painting and sculpture as in facilitating the improvement of teaching. Teachers need to see themselves teach, and what they see needs to be the subject of critical scrutiny. At present a technology is available—the video recorder—that can make possible such images in a way that was not possible only a decade ago. To the extent to which teaching is a kind of performance—and it always is a kind of performance—the qualities of that performance need to be revealed so that they can be understood and improved upon. A video portrait of a pedagogical performance can be extremely useful as part of an assessment battery focused on mediation. And if mediation issues are extended from human performers to the ways in which exhibitions are hung in museums, then the behavior patterns of clients in relation to exhibitions can also be videotaped and used to understand how the display itself mediates.

Outcomes

1. *The level of client satisfaction with a program is a major consideration in appraising the program that has been provided.* Engaging clients, whether mu-

seum visitors or students, in events and activities that stimulate and satisfy is one of the major desirable outcomes of the museum, the school, or the community center. When satisfactions are intrinsic to the engagement, when the journey is the reward, there is a high probability that similar activities will be voluntarily pursued. When activities are motivated by extrinsic forces, when reinforcers that are not intrinsically connected with the activity itself are employed to provide those satisfactions, the absence of these reinforcers later is likely to decrease the probability that individuals will voluntarily pursue those events and activities (Lepper & Greene, 1978). Thus, understanding the so-called "affective" consequences of engagement in museums, schools, and cultural centers ought to be a major agenda item in the process of assessment.

It is not unusual for assessment to focus on what is referred to as more cognitive outcomes: knowledge acquisition, the development of particular skills, comprehension of bodies of information. While such outcomes can, of course, be important, the major function of schools, and even museums, is not primarily to improve performance within their boundaries, but to influence the ways in which people lead their lives. If programs in schools do not have consequences for the way life is led outside of school, if the ideas and sources of experience they introduce are not extended to daily life, the initial experiences will be limited in consequence. Thus, developing the conditions that provide for satisfaction and assessing in ways that determine levels of satisfaction and, even more, the manifestations of such satisfactions outside of the institution are primary goals of assessment.

At present, there are virtually no research or assessment practices that examine what may be regarded as the external validity or predictive validity of assessment data in the terms described. In academic circles, for example, the validity of assessment data is determined largely by its ability to predict test scores. This hardly is adequate given the aims of education. It is not enough for individuals to perform well on within-school tasks. From an educational perspective, it is not enough for museums to be sources of satisfaction that are limited only to the content of museums. Having one's eyes opened through art within a museum ought to have ramifications for the ways in which the world at large is viewed. Assessment and evaluation practices in schools and museums ought to examine such outcomes. These outcomes, in turn, are likely to be significantly influenced by the satisfactions that have accrued during the initial experience.

2. *The outcomes of programs should be displayed in forms most compatible with the aptitudes of the clients.* In ordinary living, individuals who have, say, visited Paris reveal the qualities of their experience and the meanings secured from the visit in more than one form; some people write, some paint, some create a portfolio of photographs, others tell stories, still others may create poems or

even dramas about their experience. In the so-called "real world," individuals represent their experiences through the forms that they know how to use and the skills that they possess. In schools, the forms that are employed are typically prescribed. One writes about one's understanding of social studies or history. One demonstrates through mathematical computation one's ability to handle numbers. Such expectations are, of course, appropriate, but they are also limiting. One of the important new developments in educational theory that is related to new assessment practices is the realization that human aptitudes matter and that the personalization of experience and its representation are important. Extended, this means that students who experience works of art may wish to reveal what they have experienced in forms that are nondiscursive. Some people may paint the meanings that their encounter with works of art has generated. Others may choose to write poetically about such works. Still others may choose to create a tape recorded narrative. There are a multitude of ways in which meaning can be represented, and the provision of options for students is one way to increase the probability that the meanings that are most important to them will find expression in a form they can know how to use.

Such a practice is riddled with complexities. In the first place, it will make comparability across students very difficult—perhaps impossible. As long as students work on tasks that differ from each other, the ability to make meaningful comparisons across students diminishes. Nevertheless, as an enterprise, education is not primarily a race, with the garlands going to the swiftest, but an enterprise designed to increase personal meaning and to foster development. The provision of opportunities for individuals to follow their bliss, as Joseph Campbell would say, to choose their form of representation, is a cutting edge idea in educational thought, and this lead ought to be pursued in the context of the visual arts. Whether it can be sustained will be determined in the future. Whether students, in fact, have the skills needed to write poetry, create dance, engage in painting or drawing or sculpture with sufficient competence to represent their experience remains to be seen.

It is likely that for many of these forms, the level of competence necessary is not available. Nevertheless, the aspiration to provide such options to students seems sufficiently promising to warrant their pursuit.

3. *Outcomes should be related to several data rather than to a single datum.* In recent years it has become increasingly clear that a more valid, informative, and useful picture of student performance and understanding is likely if judgments are based on a collection of materials rather than on a single test score or performance on a single task. The use of portfolios, for example, has recently become a popular way in which to secure a collection of materials for purposes of appraisal. This strikes us as appropriate and reasonable. Such a

practice shies away from using the end of the semester test or the final project as the sole index of learning. It tends to pay attention to growth and development over time and does so by collecting and assessing the markers that have been created by students during a particular pedagogical period. Such a practice exemplifies and makes vivid comparisons from the past through the present, and this, it seems to us, is likely to highlight and reinforce the recognition of achievement by students, as well as by teachers. We believe that the use of such a practice is generally desirable and encourage its employment in any context—museum or school—in which it can be productively used.

As indicated earlier, the criteria described on the previous pages should be regarded as an array of heuristics rather than a display of discrete standards to be applied uniformly to all situations. Assessment and evaluation in the visual arts need to be undertaken for the reasons advanced earlier, but the forms that assessment and evaluation take need to be appropriate for the function they are to perform and the subject matter they are to address. Once such a multidimensional conception takes root in art education, the field eventually will generate the methods that will give us a much more complete and complex picture of our programs and their effects than we have at present. We are at the threshold of such work and believe that the coming decade will see the fruits of our efforts emerge.

REFERENCES

Apple, M. (1982). *Education and power.* Boston: Routledge & Kegan Paul.

Cremin, L. (1970). *The transformation of the school.* New York: Knopf.

Eisner, E. W. (1994). *Cognition and curriculum reconsidered* (2nd ed.). New York: Teachers College Press.

Eisner, E. W., & Dobbs, S. M. (1990). Silent pedagogy: How art museums help visitors get in touch with exhibitions. *Art Education, 41*(4), 6–15.

Gardner, H. (1983). *Frames of mind: The theory of multiple intelligences.* New York: Basic Books.

Joncich, G. (1968). *The sane positivist.* Middletown, CT: Wesleyan Press.

Lepper, M., & Greene, D. (Eds.). (1978). *The hidden cost of reward: New perspectives on the psychology of human motivation.* Hillsdale, NJ: Erlbaum.

Newman, A. (1990). *Insights: Museum visitors' attitudes and expectations.* Los Angeles: Getty Center for Education in the Arts and J. Paul Getty Museum.

Toulmin, S. (1990). *Cosmopolis: The hidden agenda of modernity.* New York: Free Press.

Part I
EVALUATING ART EDUCATION IN SCHOOLS

Chapter 2

Introduction to the Evaluation and Assessment of the Visual Arts in the Context of Schools

DOUG BOUGHTON
University of South Australia

Unlike in museums, it is in schools that art education is most likely to be subjected to systematic evaluative scrutiny. In countries such as England, the Netherlands, and Australia, procedures for centralized assessment of student outcomes have been long established. In other countries, such as Canada and the United States, there are signs of an awakening interest in assessment procedures that extend beyond the idiosyncratic practices of individual classroom teachers. The recent press of economic-rationalist philosophies promulgated by many Western governments has applied increased pressure on educational authorities to clearly demonstrate the value of classroom practice in measurable terms. While the overall benefits of economic-rationalist philosophies are themselves the subject of much debate, it is clear that one of their effects has been to increase the concern of educators, in many parts of the world, to come to grips with the unique difficulties of evaluating visual arts education in schools.

In this part of the book the problems of evaluating the visual arts in schools are discussed in terms of three foci: evaluating the *content* of art programs, evaluating the *teaching* of art, and evaluating the *outcomes* of art programs. Why is it necessary to differentiate between these subject matters for evaluation? Obvi-

Evaluating and Assessing the Visual Arts in Education: International Perspectives: © 1996 by Teachers College, Columbia University. All rights reserved. ISBN 0-8077-3511-6. Prior to photocopying items for classroom use, please contact the Copyright Clearance Center, Customer Service, 222 Rosewood Dr., Danvers, MA 01923, USA, tel. (508) 750-8400.

ously, relationships exist between them, but it is clear that different evaluative functions must be performed within each focus. For example, to evaluate the content of art programs one must examine the significance and appropriateness of what is taught. The subject matter of art education includes such things as topics, activities, concepts, generalizations, and covert (as well as overt) messages. The key function performed by content evaluation is to assist decision making for those involved in curriculum development, revision, and the comparison of programs. Content evaluation is necessary to enable either formative or summative judgments to be made at various stages of development, testing, or implementation of curriculum materials.

Even if the content of art programs is subjected to rigorous evaluative scrutiny during development and testing, no curriculum materials can ever be teacher-proof. Incompetent teaching can destroy the value of even the most powerfully written programs. Hence the need to examine the quality of teaching as a focus separate from that of content. The difficulties inherent in evaluating art teaching are, in part, shared with evaluating teaching generally and are also, in part, attributable to the nature of the content taught. Defining the nature of art has itself long been problematic for art educators!

Two functions may be performed by the evaluation of teaching. One is a professional development (formative) function concerned with improving teaching performance. The second is a gatekeeping (summative) function required for accreditation, granting of tenure, or dismissal of teachers.

Evaluation of the outcomes of school art programs is a third focus presenting yet another set of challenges for the evaluator. The central task is to determine the extent to which learning has occurred as a consequence of the program, in a way that preserves the integrity of the discipline and reflects the kind of intelligence exercised during art learning. There is no point identifying good content, appropriate learning conditions, and sound teaching practices unless an evaluation of the quality of learning outcomes is undertaken. There is a logical need to determine the degree to which stated course objectives have been met, but there is also a less obvious, but equally useful need, to discover the unanticipated outcomes of art programs.

Overall the evaluation of outcomes serves a wide range of educational needs. It can provide formative information for students and parents and it can yield diagnostic information for teachers, administrators, and curriculum developers. It also can supply summative information for gatekeeping purposes such as university entrance or promotion within course structures.

EVALUATION OF THE CONTENT OF ART PROGRAMS

The issues explored by Felicity Haynes in Chapter 3 and Jean Rush in Chapter 4 are related to the difficult epistemological question: What is the important (assessable) *content* of an art education program? Haynes claims that one important dimension of learning lies beyond the grasp of the evaluator. It is the irreducible core of individual meaning which must precede and give form to the communicated knowledge that is most important, yet defies measurement. Rush, however, argues that the most appropriate content for studio art learning can be clearly specified as *visual concepts* and is identifiable as "tutored images" in the work produced by students. It is clear, as Parsons points out in his response, that the two papers proceed from different premises and arrive at different conclusions: Haynes claims that evaluative endeavor is unable to cope with the complexity, ambiguity, and nuance of artistic learning, while Rush argues the opposite; credible art concepts can be identified from existing art practice, and these can be taught systematically through problem solving processes in the studio.

Haynes begins her paper with a caution to evaluators about the dangers of reductionism, reminding readers that attempts to reduce all human knowledge to quantitative measures are both an error of logic and an example of synecdoche. (Synecdoche is a figure of speech in which a part is used for the whole. A logical fallacy is committed when the part is confused with the whole.) For this reason, one could argue, theory, which may explain part of the truth, cannot be viewed to represent the whole. Haynes's concern with the problems of student assessment practices is driven by the expectation of parents and system administrators that "objective" assessment practices will be applied to student art learning in the context of the Western Australian state education system. The discussion reflects the enormous difficulties of objectivity inherent in centralized summative evaluation exercises, but also points to the necessary complexities one must take into account in the practice of formative assessment.

To avoid the pitfalls of reductionism in evaluation, one should recognize that art education creates multilayered structures of meaning. Haynes proposes a multilayered structure of perspectives for the evaluator, requiring that different forms of evaluation be applied to each. The layers are represented by *cognitive products* (the objects produced by studio practice), *cognitive processes* (inclusive of the processes used in making aesthetic judgments, while recognizing agreed-upon rules and conventions of discourse), and *cognitive states* (direct personal experience of art). The cognitive state of the learner is beyond the reach of assessment practices because the highly personal and emotional nature of aesthetic experience cannot be translated into a communicable form without significantly altering its character.

While Haynes describes the evaluation of learning in art education as a fundamentally problematic exercise, Rush proposes a straightforward approach to the assessment of studio art learning. Rush suggests that the best evidence of students' studio learning is to be found in their artwork. The language of art is a symbol system containing aesthetic properties she calls *sensory, formal, expressive,* and *technical properties.* The teaching of art should focus on these aesthetic properties and promote learning through teacher-generated problems to be solved in the studio. The assessment process involves examination of studio art products to determine whether the results, called *tutored images,* contain evidence of concept acquisition. Students demonstrate their understanding of concepts through their solutions to teacher-generated studio problems. Rush sees problem solving in art education as the most effective way to enable students to understand the kind of creative activity employed by artists in their production of two- and three-dimensional art objects. While acknowledging that professional artists identify and solve their own problems, Rush proposes that student engagement with teacher-identified problems is the most efficient means to enlarge students' expressive options and more quickly acquaint them with studio disciplines. This is subject to the proviso that the teacher is also a practicing artist or working from a curriculum grounded in studio disciplines.

In his response to these papers Parsons accuses both of mistrusting words in connection with assessment and suggests that Rush's proposals are overly restrictive, due to their reliance on formalist studio practices. The main thrust of Parsons's response to Haynes and Rush is that language should play a constructive and necessary role in the interpretation of the results of art education. Done right, he says, "interpretation of this sort is an equal partner with perception . . . and is not something that assessment should avoid." If it is the case in quantum physics that the truth is a matter of alternative interpretation, why should it not also be so for the *cognitive state* (the inaccessible level of aesthetic learning)? Similarly, in response to the Rush model, he suggests that the visual evidence manifested in studio products alone is not sufficient to understand students' art learning. It must be interpreted, and language provides a framework of meaning that makes culturally constructed interpretation possible.

EVALUATION OF ARTS TEACHING

Chapter 5 by Elliot Eisner and Chapter 6 by Pamela Sharp El Shayeb offer different perspectives of the problems inherent in judging the quality of art teaching. While Eisner focuses his discussion more centrally on a conception of evaluation derived from the arts, which he calls *connoisseurship and criticism,* Sharp El Shayeb examines the utility and shortcomings of various scientifically based "criterion list" approaches to art teacher evaluation. Eisner's proposal puts a counter view to traditional scientific conceptions of teacher assessment and supervision, providing a means to overcome the problems of teacher isolation in classrooms. The significant contribution of artistic approaches to the evaluation of classroom life is to directly improve teaching. Sharp El Shayeb, on the other hand, takes an administrative perspective in reviewing some of the conceptual problems associated with definitions of university exit standards, teacher entrance standards, and procedures used system-wide in the professional development of teachers, examining the utility of a variety of performance checklists in summative and formative contexts.

Eisner provides conceptual distinctions that assist in discussions about educational evaluation. He describes key differences between *evaluation, measurement, testing,* and *grading,* and identifies six functions of evaluation, the last of which is his main focus: providing useful feedback to teachers about the quality and character of their work to enable them to improve their pedagogical competence. Eisner's view of teaching is predicated on the belief that no single profile of competencies can represent the ideal. For him teaching is a moral craft, and a performing art, depending on refined sensibility, imagination, flexibility, taste, and highly sophisticated skills, which, at its best, can generate an aesthetic form of experience for both teacher and student. The evaluation model proposed in the paper requires an educational critic in the classroom who is highly experienced in the subject content, is capable of understanding the context, and possesses highly refined perception skills. The act of perception is called *connoisseurship. Criticism,* on the other hand, is the art of disclosure, the main purpose of which is to provide a richly descriptive and vivid, even visceral, view of classroom events so the teacher may reflect in a new way upon the quality and character of his or her teaching. While the major purpose of such evaluative enterprise is to provide the teacher with *descriptive, interpretive,* and *judgmental* statements likely to assist him or her in improving classroom practice, another benefit is the potential to derive general principles (*thematics*) likely to benefit the reader in understanding not only the classroom described but other similar situations. Problems of validation are discussed in terms of three criteria: structural corroboration, referential adequacy, and multiplicative corroboration.

While Eisner proposes an evaluative model aimed at stretching teacher performance to the highest levels of attainment, much of Sharp El Shayeb's discussion is focused on efforts to define minimum performance levels, although she makes the point that lists are not enough to define good teaching. She raises the issues of standards, efficiency, and minimum competencies, all of which are of interest to education system administrators and university art educators. Most U.S. states have written standards for art teaching. Sharp El Shayeb discusses the California State University list and the list developed by the National Art Education Association (NAEA) recommending them as good communicative bases for dialogue between teachers and supervisors, with the proviso that they are carefully used.

Sharp El Shayeb concludes with five recommendations for evaluation appropriate for consideration by system, rather than individual school, administrators. These are: (1) that the evaluation systems selected for use must suit the educational goals; (2) that successful evaluation programs must be demonstrably serious in terms of the time spent in training the evaluators and conducting evaluations; (3) that the evaluation process must be matched to the evaluative purpose; (4) that the evaluative process must have utility (be valid, reliable, and cost-effective); and (5) that teachers must be involved in the process of evaluation so that the quality of evaluative processes will improve.

Rachel Mason's response is critical of the faith placed by Sharp El Shayeb in the use of competency lists as a device to assist in teacher evaluation and expresses disappointment at the lack of effort in the paper to distinguish between "adequate" and "good" teaching. While Sharp El Shayeb's proposals are strong on strategies, images of good teaching are not provided. Mason suggests that the use of lists as a basis for dialogue between trusted connoisseur and teacher is unlikely to succeed because teachers will not be prepared to accept principals or administrators as "connoisseurs of art." In Britain particularly, teacher resistance to accountability is strong.

Mason responds on a point-by-point basis to Sharp El Shayeb's set of conclusions, and at the same time advocates a model of evaluation that casts "supervisor-as-coach" and "teacher-as-researcher." She is disapproving of Sharp El Shayeb's recommendation that school districts be free to choose evaluation systems that may value uniformity of instruction and standardized testing, exhorting teachers to resist such a damaging "labor" conception of teaching. She expresses concern about innate conservatism in the teaching profession in Britain, approving of increased teacher responsibility in the evaluation of teaching only if this responsibility also is linked with curriculum research.

Mason notes that Eisner's proposal to use the methods of art connoisseurship and criticism are generally supported by British teachers, who are largely untouched by the difficulties and assumptions of standardized testing in art. In fact, teachers find the relationship between the evaluation of art teaching and a methodology derived from the arts to be a logical one. Despite teacher enthusiasm, attempts to implement the model in classrooms have provided a number of difficulties, which Mason reports in relation to the four kinds of evaluative statements expected from educational critics.

Teachers experience extreme difficulty constructing vividly descriptive images with words, indicating that training in creative writing is an important prerequisite for individuals who wish to engage in educational criticism. Interpretation requires knowledge of theoretical perspectives not normally acquired by British teachers in the course of their preservice education. Evaluative statements require a degree of subjectivity in the connoisseurship/

criticism model that teachers find difficult to accept; and the degree of generalizability likely to be obtained from thematic statements is questionable, requiring an exhaustive level of description.

Mason raises four general concerns about connoisseurship and criticism in the context of teacher evaluation. She questions the potential for written criticism to affect policy making; she calls for discussion about the way in which negotiations should take place between the evaluator and teacher in order to achieve greater methodological clarity; she questions the right of the evaluator to choose which "legitimate" educational ideology ought to be applied for the purpose of evaluating teaching; and finally she questions the use of "self-centered narcissistic tone and grandiloquent writing style" found in some examples of educational criticism.

EVALUATION OF THE OUTCOMES OF ART PROGRAMS

In Chapter 7 Howard Gardner introduces the problem of assessing student learning by reviewing a variety of possible assessment scenarios in different educational contexts, then illustrates the complexity of the task by outlining some alternative visions of art education found in both the American and other cultural contexts over the last half-century. He proposes a number of "new" ideas concerning assessment that could be more appropriate, not only to the arts, but across the curriculum. These ideas have been developed from the Project Zero work at Harvard and are built upon Gardner's theory of *multiple intelligences*, already widely discussed in the literature.

In addition to traditional *linguistic* and *logico-mathematical* ways of knowing employed in conventional school settings, Gardner and his Project Zero team have identified at least five other relatively independent forms of intelligence, including *musical, spatial, bodily-kinesthetic, interpersonal,* and *intrapersonal.* The intelligence profile varies across individuals, and no single form of intelligence may be regarded as "artistic" or "nonartistic"; however, the exercise of each form of intelligence by any individual may or may not contain an aesthetic dimension, depending on its use. Gardner warns against attempts to measure these five "new" intelligences using canonical means of standardized assessment. In short, it is inappropriate to use the construct of one form of intelligence to assess another. This maxim is at the heart of Gardner's recommendation for assessment of art learning; intelligences, and the practices based on them, must be assessed in *intelligence-fair* ways. An individual educated in an art form must be able to display the behaviors, understandings, and knowledge of the symbol systems associated with that form. The form of assessment used must fairly reflect the amalgam of intelligences employed and the practices used in art.

As a reaction to the restrictive, and frequently inappropriate, information generated by the firmly established habit of standardized testing in the United States, Gardner reports some encouraging shifts in perspective that now value direct observation of student performance in regular classroom contexts rather than in artificial testing situations; collaborative, as well as individual, learning activities; project work with advance notice of the problems to be solved for assessment purposes; and the assessment of performances that are important rather than arbitrarily contrived items.

Following from these new perspectives are ideas about "new" processes for assessment that include providing assessors with sample student responses to given problems. These samples illustrate the potential range of sophistication of response through various levels. The student performance is germane to the art form (as is the case in an apprenticeship context) rather than a pencil-and-paper test that does not directly assess the student's ability to perform in the medium.

Two new vehicles for assessment have been developed with some success in the Harvard ARTS PROPEL project. These are *domain projects* and the *processfolio*. Gardner describes the domain project as a module of work focusing on a concept or practice central to a particular art form, and the processfolio as an evolving cognitive map of artwork in process. Used together these vehicles provide an effective set of evidence for both the teacher and learner to assist in judgments about authentic art learning.

While Gardner's discussion reports his work in the development of intelligence-fair assessment practices that employ tasks and judgment procedures that properly reflect the nature of artistic learning, Diederik Schönau, in Chapter 8, describes the efforts of the Dutch Institute for Educational Measurement (Cito) to improve national assessment procedures through the development of valid assessment criteria, with particular focus on the problems of judge agreement, and the reliability of scoring as applied to studio work.

Since 1981, assessment procedures for final-year studio exams in the Netherlands have undergone considerable development in terms of course design, ideas about examination length, and patterns of judge assessment protocols. Schönau's description of this 10-year evolution provides an interesting insight into the educational and political problems associated with a nationwide assessment philosophy. Ultimately the objective is to construct a system that provides an acceptable degree of judge agreement and at the same time gains acceptance from the teacher-participants. Cito's research indicated that most teachers accepted the practice of jury assessment of work in schools, but that judge training was a problem. In a comparison of the judges' ratings it was found that a greater degree of agreement was achieved between judges using global criteria than was the case with the same judges responding to more structured tasks using seven to nine criteria. Following a comparison of the differences in agreement of five- , three- , and two-judge panels, the researchers concluded that assessment by two judges worked as well as by five, provided discussion followed each assessment session and new schools were consistently visited. However, Schönau states that the introduction of structured assessment criteria as a means to improve assessment of studio art is "problematic, to say the least."

John Steers's response to Gardner and Schönau provides a comparative view of both sets of ideas against a backdrop of the British system of national assessment. He briefly describes the expectations and constraints of assessment efforts in the United Kingdom and concludes that the Dutch model would more closely match the British approach. He judges the ARTS PROPEL model to be too restrictive in that it does not appear to provide the degree of consensus and collaboration British art and design teachers have come to expect in the application of assessment practices. He describes the significant contribution of British teachers to the development of their national assessment procedures, making a case for assessment models that are developed "bottom-up" rather than imposed "top-down." The value of a system designed in collaboration with the teachers who will use, it is that "teacher ownership" is likely to make it work.

Steers discusses the notions of *validity* and *reliability* at some length, and raises the issue of *utility* as a concept that has particular application in national assessment contexts. Utility is the "convenience, flexibility, and cost-effectiveness" of assessment. Gardner's description of assessment, which encompasses consideration of the aesthetic dimension of multiple intelligences, is viewed by Steers as inflexible, inconvenient, and too expensive for use in the United Kingdom. Steers highlights the significance of resource considerations in large education systems, making clear the necessity to negotiate a compromise between the ideal and the possible. In his discussion of the Dutch two-judge model, however, Steers opts for a more expensive "cascade" system of national, regional, and local agreement trials, now used in Britain, as a means to gain increased reliability of moderation practices.

It is interesting to note in Steers's paper the example of "Draft Grade Criteria" in art for GCSE examinations developed by the British Secondary Examinations Council. Steers comments on Schönau's disappointment with the problems encountered by the Dutch in developing specific criterion checklists, suggesting that the British criteria may serve as a simpler model. Further, he suggests these criteria may be more appropriate if used only to resolve disagreement in specific instances, rather than applying them in every case.

In summary, the debates reflected in Part I of this book clearly illustrate the varied perceptions held by writers from different cultural contexts about the roles and goals of evaluation and assessment of the visual arts in school contexts. No clear answers are provided to the evaluative challenges offered by the three foci selected for scrutiny. Each of these—content, teaching, and outcomes—presents unique challenges and difficulties that have been addressed in relatively different ways by educators from different parts of the world. The single clear lesson to be learned is that the intersection of difficulties with language, cultural values, conceptions of art, conceptions of intelligence, and bureaucratic mandates produces extraordinarily complex judgment tasks for educators. The debates that follow provide a useful entry to the conceptual playing field that characterizes many of the major issues arising from the need to evaluate and assess the achievements of students and teachers in visual art classrooms.

I–A
CONTENT

Chapter 3

Zero Plus One: Evaluation and Assessment in the Visual Arts

FELICITY HAYNES
University of Western Australia

> Truth in physical matters can of course never be founded on mathematical and logical considerations alone.
>
> Albert Einstein

> Every ethic looks two ways: it has a public face and a private one . . . no ethic is effective which does not link these; the social duty with the sense of individuality.
>
> Jacob Bronowski, _The Identity of Man_

One thing that characterizes the modern era is an acknowledgment that truth is no longer perceived as some structure of number-like or space-like rules, or as a system of logic. Rather, truth is infinitely complex. At the fifth Marcel Grossman International Conference of the world's leading physicists held in Perth in 1988, it was somewhat daunting to find the majority of scientists present accepting the elusive nature of theoretical constructs and conceding that the means of testing theories inevitably moves further and further beyond the tangible. Statistical mechanics explain such phenomena as heat and pressure in terms of large numbers of interacting individuals. The numbers of such atoms are, relative to us, infinite.

These figurative infinities become actual in quantum mechanics. The essence of modern quantum mechanics is that no complete description of

Evaluating and Assessing the Visual Arts in Education: International Perspectives: © 1996 by Teachers College, Columbia University. All rights reserved. ISBN 0-8077-3511-6. Prior to photocopying items for classroom use, please contact the Copyright Clearance Center, Customer Service, 222 Rosewood Dr., Danvers, MA 01923, USA, tel. (508) 750-8400.

the world can be contemplated. Due to the uncertainty principle, quantum mechanics must treat the world as something that is essentially beyond our full comprehension. Mathematically, quantum theory is presented in terms of infinite-dimensional space. The possibility of theories assuming an identity separate from the physical world becomes more real, and the model proposed by Sir Karl Popper (1972) of a Third World of symbolic human knowledge is one that is readily appreciated by scientists themselves. There is a possible consequent danger of confusing the part with the whole and treating the disembodied theory as if it were the truth from which it evolved, and a means to the end of individual knowledge as if it were the end.

Ironically, while this should mean that measurement is seen as being relative only to some limited system or other, some have used this as an excuse to retreat to the quantifiable as a security blanket. Once one can think of predicates without properties, the predicates can become reified in their own right. This is true of many of our epistemological assumptions inside and outside the school system. Assessment and evaluation take on a different form when they are viewed from the perspective of cognitive products, cognitive acts, cognitive states, or even precognitive states. In this paper I investigate the necessary interaction among the four for assessment and evaluation in the arts.

Two best-selling nonfiction books of the past decade exemplify a process that I contend is distorting society's picture of evaluation of learning in a manner peculiarly inimical to art and to cognitive states, that of regarding one's own coherent world view as the only one. One is Marvin Minsky's *The Society of Mind* (1988), and the other, Rudy Rucker's *Mind Tools* (1987). Each paints a picture of a world in which knowledge and all mental processes can be reduced to logic: the world of artificial intelligence and formal mathematics. The notion of holistically complex, decision-making human beings, individuals reacting to a phenomenal world, collapses before their analytic framework.

I intend first to suggest the ways in which a popular acceptance of this epistemology could have direct consequences for the teaching of school subjects and the arts in particular. In his book, which relates human experiences to a computer-like tree of experience, Minsky (1988) does not once refer directly to the artistic process. Creativity is, as it was with Skinner and Hume, reduced to chance collision of events. What we call a mind, to use Hume's (1740/1888) words, "is nothing but a heap or collection of different perceptions, united together by certain relations and supposed, tho' falsely, to be endowed with a perfect simplicity and identity" (Book I, p. 250).

Rucker (1987) is more modest in claiming to offer no more than the mathematics of information. He seems at first to be simply talking about the five modes of mathematics (number, space, logic, infinity, and information), but in a classic example of synecdoche he states that because these five modes relate to the five basic psychological activities—perception, emotion, thought, intuition, and communication—the latter can be reduced to the former.

Minsky has a Humean agenda before him, in presuming not only that one *can* reduce the five psychological activities to the five modes of mathematics, but that one *should*. In speaking of creativity, he speaks of "the myth that the production of novel ideas artistic or otherwise, comes from some distinctive form of thought" (p. 327).[1] He speaks of the myth that human volition is based on some third alternative to either causality or chance. He speaks of the myth that human minds are self-aware.

Minsky inserts this peculiarly ambivalent quote from John Campbell, without further reference, as an epigraph to Chapter 18.

> Machines—with their irrefutable logic, their cold preciseness of figures, utterly exact observations, their absolute knowledge of mathematics—they could elaborate any idea, however simple its beginning, and reach the conclusion. Machines had imagination of the ideal sort—the ability to construct a necessary future from a present fact. But man had an imagination of a different kind: the illogical brilliant imagination that sees the future result vaguely, without knowing the why or the how; and imagination that outstrips the machine in its preciseness.
>
> Man might reach the conclusion more swiftly, but the machine always reached it eventually and always the right conclusion. By leaps and bounds man advanced. By steady irresistible steps the machine marched forward. (p. 184)

To regard communication as an exchange of bits of information is not necessarily to say that bits are all there is. It is simply that this can be a useful and a systematic way of looking at the world. Bohr's philosophy of complementarity ensures that the opposite way of looking at the world may be as useful.

The two opposing viewpoints here might be called atomism and phenomenalism. The digital, atomistic approach breaks the world into bits. The analogic phenomenal view takes our knowledge of the world to be made up of continuously varying perceptions. The two world views are complementary; each is viable.

Reductionism is the wrong word if it smacks of a Machian determinism. It is a reductionism that is a security blanket. We cannot know infinity so we will build structures to keep infinity out. Rucker (1987) says:

> The computer is so suggestive a model for a human brain that it forces us to look at what it is we actually do. It is quite normal to regard oneself as a finite system that processes information and not as an immortal soul. The soaring cosmic uncertainties that inspired the modern era can now be viewed as simple limitations in human information complexity. (pp. 34–35)

We know that knowledge cannot encompass the whole of reality. One must always be aware of the limitations as well as the advantages of ignoring the possibility of an immortal soul simply because it cannot be measured. One reductionist trick Rucker performs to legitimate his information theory is to reduce the analogue to the digital: "Now for the purpose of understanding the nature of information, we are going to think like digital atomists. I want to build up the notion that the information I can get about something in the world, say a person like you, is an endless string of zeroes and ones" (p. 183).

The acceptance of that model as real has some terrifying consequences for the future of education. The slide from the possibility of reducing the world of knowledge to a digital process to the desirability of doing so is very easy to make. One of the consequences of the model is to reduce the mind to what can be seen and measured as its cognitive products, these apparently having a one-to-one relation with cognitive processes. One means has become mistaken for the end.

The mistake is to forget what the products are assessing and to assume that they are not only necessary but sufficient in education. Members of the art syllabus committee in Western Australia were horrified to receive a note from the Secondary Education Authority saying that because work done at home could not fairly be judged to be a child's own work, the only work to be assessed for grading was time-on-task work completed in the classroom. This seemed to imply that the only thing that counted in art was what could be produced in a 40-minute period or less under the supervision of a teacher.

The price exacted for recognizing the place of any subject in the curriculum is a commitment to showing how that element would satisfy parents' and educationalists' demands for a demonstration of its objectivity, or at least what would count as progress in that area. The slide from seeing assessability as possible, then desirable, then the most important part of the subject, then all there is to the subject, is as compelling here as it was in the case of Rucker. It tends to ignore the possibility of the existence of the multiple intelligences noted by Gardner.

Gardner (1983) examines the characteristic human potential for constructing symbol systems of all sorts as a means of socializing meanings.

> Talk of specific analyzers, of computers, of production systems, or even of modules no longer suffices once one encroaches upon this level of analysis. We must begin to think in terms of more encompassing categories—the individual's experiences, his frames of references, his means of sense-making, his overall world view. . . . Thus, the development of human symbol systems and symbolizing capacities becomes the next, essential part of the story to be related if we are to construct a bridge from intelligences to educational practice. (p. 299)

He proposes only biological limits to all human cognitive achievements and is aware of the limitations of scientific thinking. When he uses the scientific approach to examine students and artists, he at least acknowledges that this is one way of seeing the world, and not the only possible one. For instance, when he notes how the current culture has prompted numbers as the prime means of evaluation, he reminds us of what is left out when this happens.

> It has been the special genius of modern science to combine . . . sensory, logical and linguistic approaches in a new way and to dissociate them from the personal and the religious forms of knowing in which they have hitherto been embedded. . . . What distinguishes contemporary science, whether or not it is practised in a school setting, is a particular use of logico-mathematical thinking in order systematically to investigate new possibilities, to develop fresh possibilities, to develop fresh explanatory frameworks, to test these new frameworks, and then revise them or scuttle them in the light of the results. . . . Like schooling and literacy, science is a social invention to which human intelligences can be marshalled only if the society is willing to accept the consequences. (p. 363)

The maintaining of distance is crucial to most forms of assessment and evaluation in the educational endeavor. In Hobart in 1985, David Aspin delivered a paper called "Assessment in the Arts" in which he correctly criticizes an aesthetic development grid set up by the British Department of Education and Science (DES) for committing the fallacy of composition: "In proposing such grids for the assessment of growth in aesthetic understanding and competence; they [DES] also make a fundamental mistake about the grammar of the ways in which meaning in the arts is embodied and transposed" (p. 2). They speak of "declared objective criteria" and more—"Unless the student has learned the objective criteria of an art form . . . he will be unable to develop his own creative potential" (p. 3).

Aspin went on to argue that while the arts could not be assessed on a normative curve, or on a hierarchy of quantification such as Bloom's taxonomy or the aesthetic development grid, they could be said to be governed by articulable rules of discourse. In my terms he is moving from the cognitive product to looking at the cognitive process, from a more tightly logical system of abstraction to an abstraction of more varied and flexible shared agreements—in Perkins's (1988) terms, toward a pedagogy of understanding.

Aspin outlined the typical features of informed aesthetic judgment in the following ways: They are uniquely noninstrumental in character, and therefore artifacts will create satisfactions of various kinds in the contemplator of the artistic qualities they embody and represent. These satisfactions will be able to be experienced by someone standing in the role of spectator. The making of aesthetic judgments thus requires some conceptual distance between the one making the appraisal and the work being appraised. Being a spectator involves bringing to bear on the work a critical or interpretive apparatus rather than a constructive one. A work will be appraised by its judges applying a set of criteria, working from within some sort of theoretical perspective.

These theories will have been proposed by cognoscenti—those who on the basis of their observation, interpretation, and appraisal of works of art, will have come to some opinion as to what counts as artistic excellence generally for that class of artifact. This process in turn rests on the intersubjective agreements that constitute the particular universe of discourse, the rules and conventions to which talk in and about the arts has to conform if it is to be understood and accepted.

Given this interpretation of aesthetic judgment, it is natural that Aspin should recommend as a minimum for assessing the community appropriate to art that we must first work with pupils and teach the various languages in which meaning in the various worlds of art is created and transmitted; and that we must then work with them on the concept of "getting it right" in creating, communicating, understanding, and valuing products and performances in the arts. Such is the program underlying much of the recent discipline-based art education in the United States and the inductive formalist description required in Broudy's *Enlightened Cherishing* (1972). What is required is a community of scholars who are in agreement and who can develop content for instruction from validated information and practices within the professional art world, particularly from aestheticians, art historians, art critics, and artists (Clark, Day, & Greer, 1987).

I accept this as a valid definition of aesthetic judgment, and also accept that judgment is an important part of what must count as art education, especially if, as with artworks, it sets frameworks within which progress can be evaluated. Even though based on the informational bits apparently required by mathematicians, it has as its foundation shared conventions in the Wittgensteinian sense. For knowledge to be assessable, those conventions must be made explicit, and actions and knowledge must be tested against them. How far the structures need to be formulated in words remains in question, but in some way they need to be communicable. In all of this I concede that creativity favors the well-disciplined mind, that making the standards by which we judge a work of art or student progress helps to communicate the very standards we are trying to teach pupils. By building structures, we can, in Piagetian terms, aid development. Art can be objectively evaluated even if it is not mathematically assessed, and it seems clear that in this social sense aesthetic judgment can be objectively evaluated.

However, knowing about X, or being able to articulate our knowledge about X, while it helps us to know X, is not identical with it. As Brown (1989) points out, discipline-based art educators are contributing little to an account of the sensuous nature of the aesthetic. They may be in danger of forgetting the issue that impelled aesthetic judgment in the first place—that we want students to be capable of aesthetic appreciation in their everyday life, when they are alone and not in danger of being evaluated. Perhaps we also want

them to be talented artists, socially acclaimed, even art critics.
are the specialists, and the baseline is that special mode of knowing.
forms the specialist and layperson alike. In judging whether a person under-stands art well, we can appeal only to those social conventions that have been communicated through some social code, even if it is far more flexible than a code that simply requires a true or false assessment.

Art education largely consists in production, critical appreciation, knowledge of history, and theory, because these are the vehicles through which, rightly or wrongly, we appraise the growth of aesthetic awareness. That we normally speak of art education rather than aesthetic education in the school curriculum is precisely because the art product is one of the main vehicles for assessing the aesthetic state. And, because we are after all engaging in a public process of education, we evaluate whatever cognitive process can be measured through speech or artifacts.

It can be seen that Aspin's criticism of the development grid applies at a lower level to his own explication of aesthetic language. Just as the grid confuses the disciplinary criteria with the products that form them, Aspin confuses the aesthetic judgments with the aesthetic perceptions that preceded them,[2] the cognitive process with a cognitive state. By saying that the objective criteria operate at a different level, Aspin admits that they are necessary but not sufficient. One could argue that they may not even be necessary, that their inclusion necessarily distorts the educational process.

In Western Australia, in 1984, as a result of the McGaw Report, art was excluded from matriculation status because it did not correlate highly with the Australian Scholastic Aptitude Test (ASAT). Those who fought for a higher status compromised by including as a compulsory section an art history component, requiring a 2-hour written examination. High marks in art then correlated more closely with the high ASAT scores (and interestingly enough with first-year exam results in music, Italian, and economics), and art was accepted as a matriculation subject. But was this because the art exam was a better measure of ability in art? The brighter students in physics and chemistry now take up art, where they can get good marks without the slightest aesthetic awareness. They learn the answers by heart and organize their answers intelligently.

For entry into the Curtin University of Technology, students are required to be literate as well as artistic; the essay is a compulsory part of the performance criteria for art. If they know the criteria by which they will pass or not, they can dissociate themselves from aesthetic awareness in the same way that mathematicians dissociate themselves from physical realities. If they do pick up aesthetic awareness in passing, the move will not have been a bad one. But if they can pass well without the aesthetic component, then the mode of assessment will have distorted the nature of the subject. Worse, teachers under pressure will teach to the exam, giving handout lecture notes for students to learn by rote, without any sensitivity to understandings of the words.

Aspin seemed to be speaking of what Gardner (1989) has referred to as the "peri-artistic" bodies of knowledge, in which, after the later Wittgenstein, we are articulating new theoretical structures by making explicit our normally tacit shared conventions. Aspin was talking at the Hobart conference about aesthetic judgment being accountable or objective, not about aesthetic perception; while aesthetic judgment is peculiar to the arts, it is aesthetic perception that is the goal of education, and where the problem of evaluation ultimately sits. Because aesthetic perception is often responsible for changing the aesthetic criteria that form aesthetic judgment, one could argue with Redfern (1986) that there are no universal aesthetic principles or ready-made criteria that can be known in advance and applied automatically. That is to say, as did the physicists to whom I referred earlier, we should not take our current disciplinary guidelines as the whole truth, but merely as the current epistemological guidelines by which we attempt to change their very format—a sort of bootstrapping effect.

Aspin (1986), in the article that grew from his paper, acknowledged that there were key areas in aesthetics not covered by shared agreements. While he states that agreed standards of the so-called "languages" of art should be maintained in teaching, when it came to assessing art:

> we must . . . see that meaning in the arts is plastic and pluri-vocal—heterogeneous both horizontally and vertically in object and genre, and that they [the pupils] must be flexible, openminded and imaginative in seeking meanings.

> our pupils will have to develop the capacity for insight and responsiveness that is appropriate to the various kinds of meaning—some of them non-discursive—that are embodied in the works of art presented to them for their appreciation; and

> pupils' perceptions of the store of possible meanings of a work or awareness of their own capacity to create will be affected not only by the limits of their own powers of precision, performance, judgment and articulacy but also by the fact that products and performances have a life of their own, that grows and enlarges as time passes and experience of them grows—that in some sense, such works are "living beings" towards which, as Arnaud Reid (1986) points out with insight, it is more appropriate to adopt the relationship that Buber called the I–Thou than the I–It attitude proper to mere physical objects of an inorganic kind.

> In the peculiarly holistic and personal mode of knowing appropriate to the arts, the canons of correctness, the criteria of significance and sense defy precise specification in numerical or symbolic terms; the logic of that form of discourse— the peculiar concatenations of noises, marks and signs, the various materials

worked in, the "flavour" of the conventions constituting intelligibility—cannot be set down in the calculus of canonical notation, much less in accordance with the grids or checklists to which some essays in the field of aesthetic assessment have given such pride of place. (1986, p. 48)

He acknowledges the importance of cognitive states in the arts. But he does not speak about the type of assessment one can make or not make of that holistic mode, or of its objectivity.[3] These are the areas that are central to the teaching of art, and we might want to claim that by their very nature they are not assessable. The process of perception that makes us change our disciplinary structures is what we are trying to encourage in schools. And that is the point of teaching arts in schools. Aesthetic appreciation consists of individual holistic cognitive states rather than cognitive acts or products. The acts are consolidated into disciplinary structures that provide true/false answers assessable by public standards for the cognitive products they imply. The individual cognitive states are not yet transmogrified into a normatively assessable component.[4]

We can assume that all human activity occurs relative to a knowledge base. So it is not inappropriate to test for knowledge of art history, design theory, and so on. But we are left with the same gap as that between moral theory and moral acts, between being able to provide reasons for our doing something and being moral. As the epigraph from Bronowski indicates, the public face of ethics is meaningless unless it has the other private aspect. Knowing about utilitarianism or idealism, even knowing about the Kohlbergian stages of development, is a knowledge of cognitive products or processes, which does not necessarily make us more moral.

While we can use psychological or philosophical theory to understand human emotions (and this is a point so trite that it hardly seems worth making), the theory does not work at the same level as the emotions.[5] The aesthetic level is the level of cognition at which a general theory or public conventions connect to the whole individual emotion, experiences, and imagination. It is holistic, not discrete, and hence it might be described as a cognitive state. It is when we try to break it down into assessable criteria, even for the point of the scientific investigation being undertaken by ARTS PROPEL, that it enters the stage of cognitive process or product. It is the mark of the aesthetic state that, while it may depend on rules, it transcends them. The aesthetic state is a point of contact between the disciplinary structure and the infinite complexity of experience on which the disciplines impose their order.

It might be argued that some American researchers are succeeding in pursuing the drive for accountability to lower and lower levels of holistic and personal awareness by making those structures explicit. Project Zero began

24 years ago at Harvard University with the explicit aim of making alternative discourses more accessible. Researchers in the project claim that all human beings are capable of developing at least seven autonomous ways of knowing the world: linguistic, logico-mathematical, musical, spatial, bodily-kinesthetic, interpersonal, and intrapersonal intelligences. The ARTS PROPEL project is searching for assessable criteria for even the more holistic modes of understanding, pursuing one of its founder's claims that pictorial representation is part of a more dense and replete symbol system than words or maths (Goodman, 1984, p. 58). The project researchers are beginning to make explicit the processes by which, say, we can grade a diver's performance on a scale of one to ten and reach common agreement. They have succeeded in redefining knowledge in such a way as to place under scrutiny the current models of evaluation in schools' formal subjects. Howard Gardner's development group continues to study artistic and symbolic development, and David Perkins's cognitive skills group is researching the interaction between cognition and creativity. Perkins (1988) argues that one has to weld thinking to learning in a way that was impossible on a unidimensional assessment of cognitive product. As one learns subject matter, one learns it thoroughly, mindfully, with acute attention to strategy and purposes. As one is learning content, one is making mental models of it, thinking through material actively. Likewise with students. It is accessible in tests by viewing knowledge as constructed and constructive. The logistic true/false dichotomy that is so easy to assess disappears. Structure, metaphor, and irony, rather than theory and fact, begin to take over. But this is often because one is now looking at the "brute facts" of artistic endeavor through many different disciplinary lenses rather than just one. Gardner usually chooses a biologically based cognitive psychologist framework, which is still under negotiation for the shared conventions even of the academic world.

Some progress has been made in making broader evaluative structures explicit. How does one get access to students' perceptual, reflective, and productive skills without words? One way is through student folios and a wide variety of resources such as works-in-progress, self-evaluations, notes, rough drafts, sketches, inspirations from outside sources, teachers' notes and comments, and class journals. The grade given is usually on the basis of "rapid impression subjective marking," the holistic impression of the connoisseurs. In the interests of objectivity, the marking of a visual diary has been done by external examiners in Western Australia, but my feeling is that it is better done by a teacher who knows the student personally. The traditional apprenticeship system for artists under connoisseurs or expert practitioners featuring observation, demonstration, and coaching in context (Schön, 1984) did not require a mathematical assessment. The mere raising of an eyebrow, the correction with the stroke of a brush can be evaluation enough. Contextual, even sometimes directly physical, this form of learning and evaluation is recognized in many current artists-in-schools programs, where "appropriate intelligences are mobilized directly, without the need for linguistic, logical or notational interventions" (Gardner, 1989, p. 72). At least there is a recognition that what is being evaluated here is the understanding of art (Perkins, 1988), an understanding that sees the person as "an adaptive sapient organism" (p. 112) rather than a row of discrete zeroes and ones.

Gardner prides himself on being a scientist and, unlike pure mathematicians like Rucker and Minsky, in contact with a tactile universe, seeking to provide a cogent scientific account of creativity, how humans come to compose symphonies, write poems, invent machines, and construct theories. Even Gardner (1983) admits that given the most optimistic scenario for the future of cognitive sciences, we still cannot reasonably expect an explanation of mind that lays to rest all extant scientific and epistemological problems. But that is to acknowledge the limitations of the scientific discipline he uses to impose an abstracted order on the world. While evaluation of any human performance can take place in a conventionally articulate and assessable manner or be assimilated in a moment's intuition that is not overtly assessable, it is still human evaluation. We can assume that all human activity occurs relative to some knowledge base, even though, as Gardner and Piaget suggest, the base originally may be acquired genetically. So it is not inappropriate to test for knowledge of art history, design theory, and so on. That is an important function of schools. Knowing about moral acts can help us to become more aware and perhaps more moral. It is just that the cognitive structure is not the same thing as or a necessary part of the moral activity itself. This is where the importance of self-awareness comes in. Learning explicitly about the conventions of body language can allow us to manipulate our body language to achieve our social ends.

We acknowledge that we are articulating new areas of cognition, such as semiotics, inner sports, and haptic sculpture, and that the new languages give these previously silent areas of experience identity, presence, and preservation. The danger here, although it represents a healthy recognition of a wider focus of subject matter, is that, like the mathematical theories alluded to earlier, they may take off and assume an independent life of their own. This can happen even when we are moving into the areas of thought and cognition about which we were previously silent and unaware. Gardner (1983) made a distinction between object-related forms of intelligence—spatial, logical-mathematical, bodily-kinesthetic—which are subject to a control exerted by the structure and the functions of the particular objects with which the individuals come into contact, and object-free forms of intelligence—language or music—which are not fashioned or channeled by the physical world. It seems that articulated forms of intelligence can always in principle become disembodied as it were, although it certainly is more difficult with forms of knowing in sculpture or semiotics.

The task is to keep the relatively object-free forms of intelligence in balance and in touch with the object-related intelligence in our classroom methodologies and our evaluation of student success. We can, at whatever cost to our sanity, dissociate our cognitive states from our actions. The theory or cognitive structure does not operate at the same level as the experiential point. The aesthetic state is the point at which a general theory can connect with an individual emotion, experiences, or imagination. It is holistic, not discrete. It is when we try to break it down into assessable criteria that it must take the form of a discipline or at least a shared language, with rules. Without that holistic type of knowing we could not change our social structures and the individual percept that I spoke of in my opening words about the physicists.

We are here engaging in a type of deconstruction where, by standing for a moment aside from the framework of assessment and evaluation, we place into perspective both the values and limitations of assessment. The students who are passing traditional art exams based on true/false statements might make good critics, even curators, but not the best artists.

Employers note with some disgruntlement that school graduates are not trained to adapt to the real world. Their assessment may show them to be informed and to possess the disciplinary structures, but the students do not seem able to apply what they have learned to their daily experiences.

The progress made by researchers in ARTS PROPEL does not succeed in overcoming the difficulty I have been emphasizing in this paper: that there is a critical difference in kind, not simply in degree, between the cognitive state and what can be evaluated. Evaluation of this sort is necessary in education. Heidegger (1966) noted that saying and showing are in no way the expression added to the phenomena after they have appeared—they pervade and structure the openness of the clearing that every appearance must seek out and every disappearance must leave behind. Pushing the frontiers of measurement forward does not imply that eventually all will be reduced to it. The second consequence of my argument is that assessment and evaluation are activities that measure only communicated knowledge, no matter how it is communicated, and that one abstracts that type of knowing to fit a conventional mode, leaving still unmeasured and unmeasurable the holistic cognitive state that is by definition unanalyzable.

There remains an inner state of knowing that precedes and is capable of transforming shared conventions. In *The Politics of Experience*, R. D. Laing (1967) raises the question of what it is that language or artifacts are expressing, in a typical inversion of what we take for common sense.

> The theoretical and descriptive idiom, of which much research in social science consists, adopts a stance of apparent "objective" neutrality. But we have seen how

deceptive this can be. The choice of syntax and vocabulary is a political act that defines and circumscribes the manner in which facts are to be experienced. Indeed, in a sense it goes further and even creates the facts that are studied. The data (given) of research are not so much given as taken out of a constantly elusive matrix of happenings. We should speak of *capta* rather than *data*. The quantitatively interchangeable grist that goes into the mills of reliability studies and rating scales is the expression of a processing that we do on reality, not the expression of the processes of reality. (p. 672)

The nonassessable component is as much part of the subject learned as the accountable. Accountability is more than counting.

Teachers have to be reminded that often what cannot be assessed is still one of the goals they are reaching toward, even in the school situation. In the mathematical sum zero plus one, you can take away the zero and still get one. In art and in all school subjects, you can focus on the assessable without changing students' observable results. If we take seriously Piaget's notion of reflexive construction or Quine's touchstones of reality, we have to acknowledge that even in the public world of schools, zero does count. The ineffable zero is as much a part of the equation as that which can be counted, and, like a dancing duo, zero and one each form a necessary part of aesthetics in the school curriculum.

NOTES

1. The use of the word *thought* might be equivocal here. If thought is being used as Decartes used it to cover "all that is in us, so that we are immediately conscious of it," then I have to disagree with Minsky. If he is making symbolic language a precondition of thought, then Minsky may be right (see Weiskrantz, 1988). On the latter definition, aesthetic knowing may not be a distinctive form of thought as much as a distinctive way of knowing.

2. Aspin has said to me in a phone conversation (July 1986) that he does not believe one can have, as it were, raw aesthetic perceptions. If this is so, Hanson's (1968) theory-dependent perception is reduced to theory-determined perception and there is no space for a relatively direct sense contact with the world that both initially formed our individual world constructions and continually requires us to reform our existing theories.

3. I seek more radical consequences than application merely to the arts. First I want some recognition from educators of what the top physicists are saying. I want to suggest that we now apply the consequences of acknowledging multiple intelligences to other subject areas. It is hard to see why high scores in physics, chemistry, and the two maths should be regarded as the necessary and sufficient criteria for entry into the top medical schools when the final requirement is that they should be able to judge individual, unique, holistic, and very human situations. One of the main problems for student physicians, even if they solve textbook problems well, is that knowledge is not

accessible in diagnosis. It is known that the medical students with the best academic results may make the best medical researchers, but by no means the best doctors. The same thing is true, of course, of professional engineers, dentists, scientists, and musicians.

4. Evaluation and assessment involve a social capacity to code and read symbols. In their attempt to map a neuropsychology of art through investigating aphatics, Gardner and Winner (1981) indicate the complex and interactive nature of holistic (nonassessable) and analytic (assessable) aspects of poetry, music, and visual arts.

5. This point was made as long ago as 1935 by I. A. Richards when he said (quoted in Weitz, 1970, pp. 568, 573) that logic comes in, if at all, only in subordination, as a servant to our emotional response and that the imaginative life is its own justification. However, he wants to keep scientific knowledge and poetic knowledge totally distinct, and not as interactive and interdependent aspects of human knowledge, as I do.

REFERENCES

Aspin, D. (1985, July). *Assessment in the arts*. Paper presented at the meeting of the Philosophy of Education Society of Australasia National Conference, Hobart.

Aspin, D. (1986). Objectivity and assessment in the arts: The problem of aesthetic education. In M. Ross (Ed.), *Assessment in arts education* (pp. 29–53). Oxford: Pergamon.

Broudy, H. S. (1972). *Enlightened cherishing*. Urbana: University of Illinois Press.

Brown, N. C. M. (1989). Aesthetic description and realism. *Studies in Art Education, 30* (4), 212–224.

Clark, G. A., Day, M. D., & Greer, W. D. (1987). Discipline-based art education: Becoming students of art. *Journal of Aesthetic Education, 21*(2), 129–193.

Gardner, H. (1983). *Frames of mind: The theory of multiple intelligences*. New York: Basic Books.

Gardner, H. (1989). Zero-based arts education: An introduction to ARTS PROPEL. *Studies in Art Education, 30*(2), 71–83.

Gardner, H., & Winner, E. (1981). Artistry in aphasia. In M. Taylor Sarno (Ed.), *Acquired aphasia* (pp. 361–384). New York: Academic Press.

Goodman, N. (1984). *Of mind and other matters*. Cambridge, MA: Harvard University Press.

Hanson, N. R. (1968). *Patterns of discovery*. Cambridge: Cambridge University Press.

Heidegger, M. (1966) *Discourse on thinking* (J. M. Anderson & E. H. Freund, Trans.). New York: Harper & Row.

Hume, D. (1740). *A treatise of human nature* (L. A. Selby-Bigge, Ed.). Clarendon Press: Oxford. (Original work published 1888)

Laing, R. D. (1967). *The politics of experience*. Harmondsworth, UK: Penguin.

McGaw, B. (1984). *Assessment in the upper secondary school in Western Australia: Report of the Ministerial Working Party on School Certification and Tertiary Admissions Procedures*. Perth: Government Printer.

Minsky, M. (1988). *The society of mind.* Harmondsworth, UK: Penguin.

Perkins, D. N. (1988). Art as understanding. *Journal of Aesthetic Education, 22*(1), 112–131.

Popper, K. (1972). *Objective knowledge.* Oxford: Clarendon Press.

Redfern, H. B. (1986). *Questions in aesthetic education.* London: Allen & Unwin.

Reid, L. A. (1986). *Ways of understanding.* London: Routledge & Kegan Paul.

Richards, I. A. (1935). *Science and poetry.* London: Kegan Paul, Trench, Trubner & Co.

Rucker, R. (1987). *Mind tools.* Harmondsworth, UK: Penguin.

Schön, D. (1984). *The reflective practitioner.* New York: Basic Books.

Weiskrantz, L. (Ed.). (1988). *Thought without language.* Oxford: Clarendon Press.

Weitz, M. (1970). *Problems in aesthetics* (2nd ed.). New York: Macmillan.

Chapter 4

Conceptual Consistency and Problem Solving: Tools to Evaluate Learning in Studio Art

JEAN C. RUSH
Illinois State University, USA

The best evidence of students' learning in the studio arts is found in their artwork. Students, like other artists, think with images. Creating art, like all thinking, is a search for knowledge and structure. If art is an ordered arrangement of symbols, these visible and tangible configurations evolve from images in their creator's mind. Who can forget, after mixing paint, that blue and yellow make green? If students of art use a particular configuration (green grass), teachers may rest assured that it is part of their conceptual vocabulary.

The symbol system of art is a language whose components may be called aesthetic properties, or visual and tactile concepts. Concepts seem to exist in all of the sensory modes—visual, auditory, kinesthetic, olfactory, and gustatory—as well as in their more familiar numerical and verbal forms. For the purposes of the following discussion, aesthetic properties or visual art concepts may be defined as those Broudy (1988) incorporates in the perceptual activity he calls *aesthetic scanning:* sensory, formal, expressive, and technical characteristics of art objects that viewers can perceive and interpret. *Sensory properties* are also called *visual elements:* They are lines, colors, shapes, textures, and other discrete features. *Formal properties* are *principles of design* that govern how sensory properties combine: balance, rhythm, contrast, emphasis, and other compositional devices. *Expressive properties* are the kinds of meaning conveyed by the sensory and formal properties; Broudy identifies three: mood, dynamic state, and ideas (or ideals). *Technical properties* are characteristics of the media and techniques with which artists shape their images.

Examples of concepts in art are the kinds (rectangular) and qualities (rigid, mechanical) of cut-paper shapes in a collage (sensory concepts), the illusion of depth in a two-dimensional charcoal drawing (formal concepts),

Evaluating and Assessing the Visual Arts in Education: International Perspectives: © 1996 by Teachers College, Columbia University. All rights reserved. ISBN 0-8077-3511-6. Prior to photocopying items for classroom use, please contact the Copyright Clearance Center, Customer Service, 222 Rosewood Dr., Danvers, MA 01923, USA, tel. (508) 750-8400.

the ominous mood of a surreal landscape painting (expressive concepts), and the smooth texture of a polished marble sculpture (technical concepts). When students use visual and tactile concepts to create images that have aesthetic value, they demonstrate their fluency in this artistic language.

Many artists consider creating art to be a problem-solving activity, even though they may not use the vocabulary of problem solving to describe it. Twentieth-century artists associate the terminology of problem solving with the sciences, which many of them see as quantitative in nature and therefore quite distinct from the qualitative and intuitive character of the arts. Problem solving in art is the use of aesthetic properties or concepts to achieve specific artistic objectives in the composition of two- and three-dimensional images.

Both children's and adults' art contains aesthetic properties. Children's images differ in some respects from those of adults because they reflect their creators' immature developmental status. Both children and adults can learn to solve the kinds of problems that characterize creativity in the visual arts.

Studio art instruction that teaches students to act like artists, therefore, not only should incorporate aesthetic concepts but should focus on the operation of these concepts in the creation of visual images. Conceptually focused teaching becomes a process of coaching in which students are encouraged to solve artistic problems just as artists do. Conceptually focused lessons enable teachers to evaluate studio art learning because images made in order to solve problems contain observable concepts and therefore testify to the acquisition of these concepts by students.

When artists create images, they set and solve their own aesthetic problems, and eventually students who become artists learn to do the same. In the United States many elementary and some secondary teachers say they prefer students to set and solve their own artistic problems from the time they first use art materials, about the age of two, a viewpoint called student-centered.

The most extreme student-centered position would be one in which instruction in anything besides the technical skills of media manipulation would be considered an infringement on students' expressive prerogatives. A teacher-centered approach, on the other hand, would be instruction that directs students' attention to artistic problems and the concepts they will be asked to use in solving them, rather than waiting for students to discover the concepts. Conceptually focused instruction would seem to be consistent with the belief of many artists that making art requires not only talent but a level of acquaintance with studio disciplines beyond the reach of the untutored person. From the viewpoint of conceptually focused instruction, designating artistic problems for students to solve is a teaching strategy seen as enlarging students' expressive options.

Teachers using a conceptually focused approach should be knowledgeable in their studio disciplines, by virtue of either being practicing artists or working from a curriculum grounded in those disciplines. Knowledgeable teachers can introduce students to sophisticated aesthetic concepts and their functions in art. During studio art activities, students can employ these selected concepts in order to solve designated problems.

In fact, most approaches to art education in the United States teach standard visual and tactile concepts, although seldom in a systematic way. These concepts are most often called *elements* and *principles of art* or, less commonly, *sensory* and *formal aesthetic properties*. Many teachers also describe the creative process as *artistic problem solving*, even though conceptually focused lessons that pose problems and verify their solution are rare at elementary and secondary levels. Finally, both teachers and the American public highly value the ability of children and adults to be expressive through art media, despite the fact that schools provide little instruction in the recognition and use of the expressive properties identified by Broudy.

CONCEPTUALLY FOCUSED INSTRUCTION

Five assumptions will underlie this discussion of the evaluation of studio art learning.

1. Works of visual art convey meaning to viewers. Artistic imagery is a major component of all world cultures.
2. The language in which art conveys meaning is visual and tactile. Many visual and tactile concepts may be described verbally, but symbol systems of speech, visual imagery, mathematics, and music appear to represent distinct modes of thought (Arnheim 1969; Gardner, 1983).
3. The conceptual content of instruction derives from a worldwide body of existing art, not from the learner. Despite its variety of cultural styles and techniques, the shared aspects of this body of knowledge suggest the existence of an underlying structure that can be called a visual logic or aesthetic code or symbol system.
4. An acknowledged visual logic implies that the arts may be taught systematically. Because the sciences also may be taught systematically does not mean that conceptually focused instruction in art will somehow change the arts into sciences or reduce their value in society.
5. The term *learning* refers to concept and skill acquisition resulting from teacher-generated instruction in a school rather than from student-generated discovery in a nonschool setting.

A studio art lesson or unit that includes concepts drawn from aesthetics, criticism, and history requires conceptual consistency throughout all of its component activities in order to qualify as conceptually focused instruction. Artistic concepts that form lesson objectives should appear in at least three generic lesson contexts: visual analysis, art production, and critical analysis. These three segments are standard in many American and Australian state curriculum guides and perhaps those of other countries.[1]

Visual analysis refers to the introduction of visual and verbal vocabulary. Art production describes the making of images and related activities. Critical analysis provides opportunities to describe and analyze lesson concepts in images by artists and to make recreative, judgmental, and historical or contextual critical assessments of these works.

In visual analysis, prior to students' participation in studio activities, teachers of conceptually focused lessons identify the problem or problems to be solved and suggest hypotheses for doing so. They define visual and tactile concepts that students will apply as they test hypotheses by manipulating art media to make images. Teachers link vocabulary words that label concept attributes with vocabulary images drawn from art or the real world that provide visual definitions. This activity is a form of aesthetic scanning (Broudy, 1988) or systematic aesthetic perception.

In the lesson segment called art production the teacher generally links verbal labels with media techniques before studio activities begin. The teacher may model or demonstrate hypothesis-testing activities and articulate criteria upon which he or she and the students will evaluate the completed work. These evaluation criteria specify the ways in which the lesson hypotheses are to be verified. Verification depends on finding the same aesthetic concepts in completed artwork that the teacher defined in the visual analysis. Upon completion of their artwork, students verify their hypotheses by identifying lesson concepts in their own images and in images made by other students.

Critical analysis is an opportunity for transfer of learning and is therefore best suited to a time after students have demonstrated concept acquisition; that is, after they have completed their studio work. Critical analysis allows students to identify in images of artists, concepts previously learned and used in their own work. While historical analysis is sometimes combined with critical analysis activities, it is a separate activity involving presentation of information about the work (who, what, when, where, and why) as distinguished from the recreative, judgmental, or contextual appraisal of art.

The first two lesson segments must be conceptually consistent if the art production component is to be a problem-solving activity. In problem solving the often-cited antipathy of process and product no longer exists. Process and product become necessarily complementary aspects of art learning.

SOLVING ARTISTIC PROBLEMS

The process known as problem solving also may be called the scientific method. Problem solvers discern a problem and make an educated guess about what might be needed to resolve it; that is, they form hypotheses. This is a conceptual activity, an imaginitive activity, an activity that requires inductive thinking.

Once a hypothesis exists, problem solvers proceed to test it. They try the hypothesis out to see if it works the way they thought it would. They verify the outcomes by means of their own observation. Hypothesis testing is an experiential activity, a perceptual activity, an activity that requires deductive thinking (Kemeny, 1959).

The language used by scientists to describe problems and their solutions is mathematics. The language used by artists is visual or tactile imagery. The existence of mutually exclusive languages or symbol systems may reflect mutually exclusive modes of thought or intelligences (Gardner, 1983).

Differences in these symbol systems produce differences in the ways in which scientists and artists describe problems and also differences in the kinds of problems they address. Gardner's (1983) construct of multiple intelligences implies that capacities such as analysis, synthesis, and a sense of self are more general and overriding, however. His work suggests that, although the languages are different, it is possible to infer that the process of solving problems may be the same (Rush, 1990).

The process adult artists use as they create aesthetic images may be said to parallel the scientific method because artists set and solve their own problems (generate and test their own hypotheses). Broudy (1987) illustrates the scientific method by referring to Dewey's 1910 diagnosis of what might be wrong with a stalled automobile. Broudy emphasizes that "every step in the problem-solving process consists of [an] interplay between concept and percept, between generalization and fact. . . . At each stage of the process imagination suggests patterns of behavior that could be entitled 'If I do this, [then that] will happen'" (pp. 31–32).

> Dewey stressed learning by doing, but the doing was to be problem solving rather than repetition of an assigned task. Doing, for Dewey, was a kind of thinking, and thinking that amounted to anything educationally was a kind of doing— changing an unclear predicament to a line of action by means of hypothesis, prediction or results, and their testing. . . . For this reason a problem-solving strand is needed in the curriculum, not so much to teach concepts and skills but, rather, to test them. (p. 33)

Posing Artistic Problems

Art teachers seldom talk about testing hypotheses, yet most art teachers have come to believe that the problem-solving aspect of art is valuable for students and that portraying art as a mode of thinking helps to justify its inclusion in science-oriented public schools. When students produce artworks that are the result of tuition rather than intuition, the process departs from the scientific method in the following sense: The teacher, rather than the student, designates the artistic problems to be solved and suggests appropriate hypotheses for doing so. Art teachers know from experience that students are unlikely to discover certain concepts and their applications by themselves; research bears out the correctness of this assumption (Feldman, 1980).

What art teachers generally call problems may be considered in the context of this description as hypotheses to be tested: If I do this, then that will happen. Moreover, they are drawn from what Dewey called "warranted assertions" (Broudy, 1981), hypotheses that have been tested over and over again by members of the studio art disciplines until they are commonly accepted as being true. These problems or hypotheses can be simple or complex; they can address sensory, formal, expressive, or technical aesthetic properties.

Imagine that a teacher is asking students to solve certain artistic problems, for example, and is posing the following hypotheses to a student. They exhibit the "if this, then that" pattern characteristic of problem solving in both science and art. These hypotheses are relatively simple, in order to serve as illustrations of the principle. More complex hypotheses would follow the same pattern.

1. *If you use small, medium, and large shapes in your collage, then it will have more variety or visual interest than it would if your shapes were all about the same size.* This is a sensory problem concerning shape and the desirability of incorporating visual interest into a collage. The teacher hypothesizes that variety among shapes will produce visual interest in the resulting composition.
2. *If you paint this small area in the foreground of your still life an intense red, then it will balance the larger area in the background that is a grayed blue-green.* This is a formal problem concerning balance and space in a still life painting. The teacher hypothesizes that a particular color contrast will produce asymmetrical balance and the illusion of depth in the resulting composition.
3. *If you sharpen the contrast between dark and light in your drawing, then it will enhance its surrealistic character.* This is an expressive problem concerning a surrealistic mood engendered within a black and white

value study. The teacher hypothesizes that increased value contrast will sharpen the image and heighten its sense of ambiguity.

4. *If you smooth the clay over the seams in your coil pot, then it will be much stronger.* This is a technical problem concerning the durability of a work in ceramic clay. The teacher hypothesizes that a seamless surface is more durable than one in which the coils are loosely joined.

Early in a conceptually focused lesson, a good art teacher identifies artistic problems for students and makes sure they understand the concepts they could use to solve them. This is a perceptual and critical activity involving description and analysis of visual images. As students advance to more complex problems calling for the creation of more complex images or solutions, their store of visual concepts becomes broader and more intricate as well.

Problems used for instruction are new to the students but not to the teacher. The teacher suggests credible art hypotheses that have instructional value because they are assertions warranted by other artists. These hypotheses concern the application of aesthetic properties or concepts in a particular way for a particular purpose.

Characteristics of Tutored Images

Artistic images that incorporate solutions to problems posed by a teacher during the course of conceptually focused instruction may be called tutored images. Tutored images are therefore a primary source of data for the evaluation of studio art learning. All tutored images display some distinguishing characteristics.

If a group of students all test the same simple hypothesis at one time, in group instruction settings like those in most elementary classrooms, all students will produce outcomes that are similar in some respects. If 25 students in the same class test the first hypothesis listed earlier, for example, then all 25 of their images will contain small, medium, and large shapes. This compositional similarity indicates a conceptual consistency among all class members and is characteristic of tutored images (Rush, 1987, 1989).

There also will be many respects in which shapes will differ from student to student. One student's shapes may represent rabbits, a second student's shapes may be geometric, a third student's shapes may be biomorphic, and so on. Art teachers often view variation among student images as evidence of divergent thinking, and therefore as a desirable outcome of instruction, but variation per se is not justifiable if it indicates lack of instruction altogether.

When a group of students test a complex hypothesis or several hypotheses at once, there will be more noticeable variation among students' artwork than when they test a simple hypothesis. This variation comes from the increased number of options available to each student. Despite increasingly complex images, however, there will be observable conceptual consistencies among students with respect to the hypotheses being tested.

The most variation among tutored images occurs when each student in a class tests hypotheses pertinent to problems unique to his or her own artwork. This latter situation is what is generally meant by individual instruction. Whether instruction is on a group or an individual basis, the role of the teacher remains the same: to identify artistic problems beyond the recognition of the student and to suggest hypotheses for their solution.

Similarities among tutored images made by a number of students may cause observers unfamiliar with conceptually focused instruction to regard the students as restricted in terms of artistic expression (Hamblen, 1988). In contrast, observers aware of the characteristics of tutored images value similarities because, as a reflection of conceptual consistencies, they indicate the presence of lesson content. To a teacher who identifies problems and suggests hypotheses for their solution, conceptual consistencies in student artwork indicate student learning.

Differences among tutored images may be interpreted by some observers as displaying productive novelty and surprise (Eisner, 1987). Dissimilarities reflect hypotheses generated by students in addition to those posed by the teacher. These independent artistic choices form a conceptual context within which lesson content is embedded.

Every art lesson, no matter how elementary, provides the opportunity for practice in setting and solving problems. Generally these independent decisions are less sophisticated than those made by the teacher. As students advance to more complex problems, their ability to identify problems and generate hypotheses increases as well.

EVALUATION OF LEARNING

Evidence of learning is readily apparent in the studio arts because every student makes artistic images. Evaluation of learning is more difficult. It also requires justification among some art educators because of the extent to which they have considered artistic expression an idiosyncratic activity.

A teacher's evaluation of student artwork depends on his or her knowing the nature of the problem the student is addressing and the hypotheses being tested in the attempt to solve it. Students can test artistic hypotheses by applying aesthetic concepts learned earlier in the lesson, in the unit, in the school term, or at home. If these hypotheses are agreed upon by both teacher and student, subsequent observation of completed images can verify the lesson outcome by checking results actually obtained against those predicted.

Students can observe the verification in their own artwork and that of other students. Because the lesson hypotheses are credible ones, teachers can expect that the majority of students who test these hypotheses will verify them. Use of credible hypotheses, therefore, serves an evaluative function for teachers.

Observation of completed artwork also allows the teacher to verify students' understanding of aesthetic concepts used in the hypotheses and their ability to apply them. Student performance is measured against the standard of prior successful testing of the warranted assertion or hypothesis. This is the basis on which all art teachers evaluate student learning.

One of the goals of art education undoubtedly is to produce artists who can set and solve their own problems. In testing credible hypotheses, students manipulate aesthetic properties just as artists do in order to create images that convey meaning. In this way, students learn artistic expression.

There would seem to be at least four reasons why a teacher should use a conceptually focused approach.

1. Some warranted assertions or credible hypotheses of the studio art disciplines are difficult to discover.
2. Teachers can cut short the discovery process and save students time.
3. Students need to learn the problem-solving process as well as artistic concepts.
4. Credible hypotheses provide a basis for the evaluation of learning.

At present few art textbooks or curricula in the United States at any level of schooling show conceptual focus or consistency. The belief that art students learn best when they develop individual creative approaches is widespread among art teachers. Where these curricula are used, however, it is more common to see images produced by young children in conceptually focused programs mistaken for images of older children in child-centered programs than the other way around.

In order to understand conceptually focused studio art instruction, teachers need to see how it differs both from child-centered art education and from the kind of instruction that simply includes the four currently identified content disciplines of the visual arts—aesthetics, criticism, history, and production. Conceptually focused instruction reaches beyond talent, beyond self-expression, beyond media, and beyond subject matter to the nature of imagery and the process of artistic problem solving.

By what criteria ought we judge the amount and quality of art learning taking place as we examine tutored images? Tutored images made in response to conceptually focused instruction by all students, whether children or adults, show two kinds of visual concepts. The first are those designated by the teacher as lesson content. These concepts describe the parameters of the problem to be solved and the hypothesis to be tested in doing so. They appear in the teacher's lesson plan as instructional objectives, vocabulary words, and vocabulary images, and their use by students is required. The second kind of visual concepts are those not singled out by the teacher for particular student attention, but that exist in addition to the instructional objectives. These concepts are a necessary part of the composition or design of the finished artwork, but because they are extraneous to the lesson problem, their use by students is optional. They constitute a visual context within which the instructional content appears.

The hypotheses to be tested appear in the lesson objectives. The means by which these hypotheses are to be verified appear in the evaluation criteria with which teacher and students may critique the images produced during the lesson. These criteria should be specific enough to describe a completed tutored image that corresponds to the parameters of the problem (see Mack & Christine, 1985, for examples of lesson plans).

Concepts learned during visual analysis can be applied five times in one unit or series of lessons.

1. While solving the lesson problem (testing the hypotheses)
2. During the evaluation of student artwork following its production, when learned concepts are identified in the works produced during the class
3. During the critical analysis of exemplar works by adult artists
4. During a second, different problem using the same concepts and skills, if the teacher poses one
5. During a problem subsequently posed by the student that culminates in a spontaneous rather than a tutored image

Conceptually focused studio art lessons contain hypotheses that are well enough defined so that they can be verified by observing the artwork produced by students. All conceptually focused lessons also include the first two kinds of concept applications described above. Providing five opportunities to use lesson concepts within a single conceptually focused unit produces greater concept strength than a lesson in which fewer opportunities occur; repeated concept use is the advantage of a sequential curriculum.

The best evidence of students' learning in the studio arts is found in their artwork. If conceptually focused instruction addresses problem solving and the nature of imagery—its perception, creation, and interpretation—art teachers can begin to define lesson content in terms of the conceptual structure and modes of inquiry intrinsic to the arts disciplines (cf. Greer, 1987). Teachers can inspire students to undertake systematic intellectual inquiry in art by moving from satisfaction with untutored perceptual skills to the educational challenge of serious study.

In the studio arts, researchers have yet to demonstrate the link between visual problem solving and creativity clearly enough for teachers to perceive its value for instruction. Most contemporary American art education programs therefore have overlooked the importance of conceptual focus as a teaching strategy. Only the new discipline-based approach has begun to incorporate conceptual focus and problem solving into some of its emerging elementary curricula.

Conceptually focused lessons allow teachers to coach students in artistic behaviors that are faithful to the real world of art. When teachers pose visual problems to be solved, they give students practice in being artists as they create images that test artistic hypotheses. At the same time, teachers can observe and evaluate student learning.

Art is a language that conveys meaning. When classroom art making is problem solving, students develop the capability to be artistically expressive. Students capable of artistic expression transcend the boundaries of self-expression into the broader creative realm of the artist.

NOTE

1. For example, in Arizona they are called aesthetic assessment, creative art expression, and art in cultural heritage; in California, aesthetic perception, creative expression, and visual arts heritage/aesthetic valuing. In Western Australia they are called art learning, making art, and understanding art.

REFERENCES

Arnheim, R. (1969). *Visual thinking*. Berkeley: University of California Press.

Broudy, H. S. (1981). *Truth and credibility: The citizen's dilemma*. New York: Longman.

Broudy, H. S. (1987). *The role of imagery in learning*. Los Angeles: Getty Center for Education in the Arts.

Broudy, H .S. (1988). *The uses of schooling*. London: Routledge.

Eisner, E. W. (1987). *The role of discipline-based art education in America's schools*. Essay prepared for the Getty First National Conference on Discipline-Based Art Education. Los Angeles: J. Paul Getty Trust.

Feldman, D. H. (1980). *Beyond universals in cognitive development*. Norwood, NJ: Ablex.

Gardner, H. (1983). *Frames of mind: The theory of multiple intelligences*. New York: Basic Books.

Greer, W. D. (1987). A structure of discipline concepts for DBAE. *Studies in Art Education, 28*(4), 227–233.

Hamblen, K. A. (1988). What does DBAE teach? *Art Education, 41*(2), 23–24, 33–35.

Kemeny, J. G. (1959). *A philosopher looks at science.* New York: Van Nostrand.

Mack, S. A., & Christine, D. R. (1985). *CRIZMAC master pack.* Tucson, AZ: Authors.

Rush, J. C. (1987). Interlocking images: The conceptual core of a discipline-based art lesson. *Studies in Art Education, 28*(4), 206–220.

Rush, J. C. (1989). Coaching by conceptual focus: Problems, solutions, and tutored images. *Studies in Art Education, 31*(1), 46–57.

Rush, J. C. (1990, March). *Setting and solving problems: Similarities between science and art.* Paper presented at the Association of Supervision and Curriculum Development, San Antonio.

The Assessment of Studio Work and the Distrust of Language

MICHAEL J. PARSONS
Ohio State University, USA

There are several themes in the papers by Jean Rush and Felicity Haynes. I will identify those that I think most worthy of discussion and indicate the sort of discussion they invite. I will summarize each paper and focus on these themes. I will be as accurate as possible, but I will use my own words and I will be selective. In particular, I will not mention themes that seem noncontroversial or seem not to affect questions of assessment closely. I will reserve doubts and questions until the end.

In her paper Rush describes and advocates a method of teaching art concepts through a largely studio approach, and an associated method of assessment that uses the studio work as evidence. The method begins with the choice of an art concept to be taught. The concept is taught partly by discussion but mostly by getting students to experiment with it in their own work. They test the concept by using it, to see if it works. The teacher assesses their learning by looking at the studio work to see if the concept has indeed been incorporated appropriately. The criterion for assessment is whether the studio work exemplifies the concept in question. Such assessment can be done by examining the work and can be reasonably objective.

The concepts to be taught this way belong to the art medium. They are to be understood and demonstrated in the terms of the medium itself, rather than in natural (i.e., verbal) language. They are a part of the language of art, which is visual and tactile and consists of aesthetic properties and visual concepts. If we use words to help students notice these things (as we do in "scanning"), the words are descriptors that are properly understood only when their referents are grasped visually, or, better still, produced in the studio. This is consistent with the theses of Howard Gardner regarding symbol systems and multiple intelligences: that each medium constitutes a different symbol system and each requires a different intelligence—Rush calls it a "mode of thought"—to work with it. This is why the studio products themselves are the best and most direct evidence of learning. The basic purpose of art education, according to Rush, is to teach such visual concepts for both

54

creative and appreciative use, and students will learn them more readily from instruction than from being left to discover them for themselves.

Turning to Haynes's paper, she argues that, while some learning outcomes in art can be assessed, others cannot; and the ones that cannot are more important. There are, according to Haynes, three broad levels of learning outcomes. Each level is deeper than the previous one. The first level is the one Rush dealt with, the assessment of studio products. This is a substitute for the assessment of the cognitive processes that lie behind the studio products, but Haynes holds that it is not a satisfactory substitute. The second level of assessment is more directly aimed at cognitive processes. These include the processes involved in making aesthetic judgments, and they can be assessed because there are reasonably accepted public criteria for such judgments. However, assessment at this level does not address what is most important about learning in art.

Knowing about art is not the same as knowing art. Talking well about an artwork may not imply a grasp of its aesthetic properties. Meanings in art are articulated in the art medium itself and must be grasped and understood in the terms of that medium. This point about meanings is similar to Rush's point about concepts, and I will henceforth call it the medium-specific view of concepts and meanings. To justify it, Haynes also appeals to Gardner's notion of different, medium-specific intelligences. The general point—and the problem with the second level of assessment—is that putting things into words does not guarantee a grasp of the visual, nondiscursive, meanings of art that are most important.

The third level is the level of direct aesthetic perception and grasp of art, which is where the most important goal lies. This level is personal rather than public, emotional as well as cognitive, holistic, rule-transcending, immediate, and nonverbal. For these reasons, it is in principle not assessable.

Gardner's assessment work with ARTS PROPEL is mentioned here, with some ambiguity. On the one hand, that work brings science closer to the third level by developing or systematizing new assessment methods. On the other hand, there is the danger that whatever assessment touches may be reified and detached from the experience it rests on. The gap between what can be assessed and the immediacy of the aesthetic experience can be bridged. Assessors must always be aware of it.

The paper is deliberately ambiguous about assessment, and its purpose is to recommend that ambiguity to its readers. In the end, as I read it, it is in favor of current attempts to develop methods of assessment in art education, including methods aimed at the level of talk about art and Gardner's work in ARTS PROPEL. These are useful and can be reasonably objective. But assessment is seen as a rather unwelcome price that art education must pay to external authorities.

PURPOSES OF ASSESSMENT

Now to my own comments on these papers. There are a number of striking differences between them, and some surprising agreements. One of the differences is about the purposes of assessment. The papers assume quite different models and motives.

Haynes assumes the model of external evaluation, where assessment is system-wide, is done for summative purposes, and is required by external authorities. Her examples are of national or state exams, and her language is of grades and marks. For her, the motivation for assessment is mostly political: to justify the subject to parents, to compare schools or perhaps teachers, to determine students' future careers, and so on. This is why Haynes is somewhat reluctant to allow its legitimacy and is more concerned with warning against its abuses than with discussing its values.

By contrast, Rush assumes a formative model. She expects assessment to be done by the teacher, in the classroom, for the purposes of helping students and improving teaching. For her, assessment is part of the normal cycle of activities that constitute teaching. The teacher chooses a concept to teach, devises relevant activities, engages the students with those activities, and assesses how well the concept has been learned. Then, presumably, the teacher uses the assessment results to guide the next teaching episode and for general reflection on teaching method. According to this model, assessment has a positive pedagogical value.

These two models are quite different, and the difference accounts for much that is in the papers. I suppose that most of us would have more sympathy with Rush's assumptions, that we should be looking for assessment methods that are useful to the individual teacher. I would even say that this currently should be the primary purpose for the development of assessment methods, because good teaching requires assessment and it is too little present in teaching art today. But it seems important to maintain that there is not an unbridgeable gulf between the two kinds of purpose—the political and the pedagogical.

The difference appears quite marked in these papers, although it is not overtly discussed, and certainly there are those who insist that one must always keep it in mind: that one must be clear about the purpose of evaluation, the audience it is intended for, whether it is summative or formative, and so on.

But I believe that assessment instruments can be devised that serve more than one purpose and that we should aim to do this. In particular, I don't see why feedback that is pedagogically useful to the teacher should not also be useful to policy makers and administrators for a variety of curricular and resource decisions, and to parents and citizens for a general understanding of what is being taught and with what kind of quality standards. This latter purpose, incidentally, seems to me to be an important one, given the continued poor public understanding of education in the arts and their consequent still tenuous place in the curriculum. Several kinds of purposes, including especially pedagogical purposes, can be combined in one instrument, and whether this happens in a particular system is a question of design. Otherwise, we will find ourselves in an unfortunate dichotomizing mind-frame that will prevent us from making progress with developing useful assessment materials.

At the same time, I agree that the specific case of grading individual students in a summative way for gatekeeping purposes seems to demand separate treatment, and I understand that this is a large part of what Haynes has in mind. I understand, too, that this is a particular interest of some of our colleagues in the Netherlands and Britain, where there are summative exams at the national level. I hope that art educators will not take that purpose as the determining one for which we need to develop assessment instruments.

ASSESSMENT OF STUDIO WORK

Another difference between the two papers is their conclusion about the assessment of studio work. Rush thinks it is the best evidence one could use; Haynes dismisses it as superficial. One initial thought about this is that the two authors make different assumptions about what kind of abilities are to be assessed.

Rush is seeking to assess learning that is the result of teaching. She wants instruction to be focused on a chosen concept, and assessment to indicate how far that concept has been learned. Studio products are to be assessed in terms of their use of the predetermined concept, not in terms of their general aesthetic qualities or of the general aesthetic abilities that might lie behind them.

Haynes is less clear about this. Much of the time she speaks as if assessment should be of the general aesthetic abilities of the student, which of course would cover much more than just the results of specific units of instruction. It would pick up, for example, the influence of native ability, family background, socialization, peer interactions, informal opportunities to learn, and previous school learning. Abilities at the third level of holistic experience seem to be very much a product of these other things and only partly a matter of schooling. On the other hand, assessment of critical and historical talk about art may seem to be more about what has been learned from schooling, though not necessarily from specific units of instruction.

At the level in question here, Haynes assumes that assessment of studio works will be of their aesthetic quality, not in terms of some specific learning objectives. Because the assessment of products is a substitute for the assessment of cognitive processes, this means that what is really being assessed are mental processes of a general aesthetic kind. Haynes dismisses the attempt to do this via studio products as reductivist, superficial, and even misleading. She asserts that studio works are a poor stand-in for the aesthetically relevant cognitive processes that lie behind them.

Rush, too, looks at studio work as evidence of the cognitive processes that produced it. But in her case these processes are specifically defined. She is looking for the grasp of particular concepts, and she believes that studio work can be good evidence for them. The concepts are specified ahead of time, and it can be seen whether or not they are used in the work. In other words, Rush has tried to find a way to use studio work as evidence for assessment by focusing the work on particular concepts and examining it only for the use of those concepts. She argues that observing whether students use a concept in their own studio work is the best evidence of whether they understand it. This seems to me a debatable claim, and it is not clear that she has evaded Haynes's charge.

It seems unlikely that one can tell by looking at studio work whether a student has understood a particular concept or has blindly followed the teacher's suggestion. To consider Rush's example: A teacher wishes to teach students to understand the visual interest created by the use of differently sized cut-papers in collage. The teacher encourages the students to use differently sized cut-papers in their work. They succeed. The teacher can tell they succeeded. But the concept has to do with the visual interest created by the different sizes. How can one tell they have perceived the visual interest created this way? Perhaps they were just following the teacher's suggestion to use different sizes of papers. It is hard to see how they could fail in this "use" task provided that they understand what differently sized means, but the "understanding" task demands more.

The same point applies to Rush's other examples: the intense red that will balance the larger blue-green area, and the dark–white contrast that will enhance the surrealistic mood. One can reliably get children to use greater dark–white contrast, but grasping a surrealistic mood is not a behavioral task. Haynes's general point seems to be that any concept worth teaching in art will have an aesthetic (or an understanding) reference. It is the visual interest that counts, not the different sizes; the balance created by the intense red; and the surrealistic atmosphere enhanced by the contrast of light and dark. One cannot assess the grasp of such things by looking at studio products, because the products may well be produced by just following a teacher's suggestions.

MEDIUM-SPECIFIC VERSUS INTERPRETIVE VIEWS OF AESTHETIC UNDERSTANDING

It seems to me—and this is not Haynes's point—that, in this situation, the best way to get at the relevant understandings would be to discuss students' works with them: Ask them why this, what effect that, what they were thinking of when. The work is evidence, but the evidence needs to be interpreted before it can be used. To get to the cognitive processes that may or may not lie behind it, one needs to talk about it.

Rush's View

What is Rush's argument to the contrary: that looking at the studio work is sufficient to tell what grasp of concepts lies behind it? As far as I can tell, the argument relies on what I previously called the medium-specific view of cognition in the arts. The concepts Rush is interested in are specific to the visual medium. They are formulated in terms of the medium; the cognitive processes they represent are manipulations of the medium, or the grasping of its qualities. Words will therefore be irrelevant, or will at least be less valid as evidence. This argument, it should be noticed, does not do all it is required to do, that is, show that studio work alone is good evidence of understanding. But it does imply that my suggestion that conversation would help, is misguided, and perhaps that there are no other possibilities.

If we look again at Rush's examples—the visual interest of the differently sized cut-papers, the balance provided by the intense red, and the surrealistic mood enhanced by the light–dark contrast—we can see that they have been chosen to be medium-specific in this way. They also, incidentally, fit the pattern of what is known as "aesthetic scanning." One has to do with visual elements, one with form, and one with expressive qualities. (I ignored the fourth example, which is from the technical category. It has to do with the added strength that smoothing the clay of a coil pot may bring. Strength here does not seem to be an example of an aesthetic concept, or one that can be tested by looking in the same way as with the other examples. Presumably one would have to try breaking the pot to test its strength. In general, the technical category does not seem to belong with the others.)

Of the first three, it seems fair to say that they suggest a formalist theory of aesthetic concepts. They suggest that whatever is important to understand about art is there in the work to be seen without reference to the world that lies outside the work. Rush's third assumption confirms this explicitly, when she says that the concepts deriving from "a worldwide body of existing art" relate to an underlying visual logic that is a part of the medium. There is little suggestion that artworks might be about something other than the purely visual or might use elements that are not wholly visual. There is no reference to cultural themes, or to audience. The closest Rush comes to this is with the notion of a surrealistic mood, which, according to the example, can be heightened by the use of light–dark contrast. This, I would say, is an example that raises a host of unwelcome issues for Rush, when one stops to look at it.

If surrealism has something to do with the chance encounter of a sewing machine with an umbrella on a dissection table, then it cannot be discussed only in formal and visual terms (such as the light–dark contrast). This is not so much because real things like sewing machines might be depicted; Rush could probably accept that. It is because of the idea of a chance encounter. To grasp the strange character of an encounter, we must know what is not strange, what is culturally normal. Surrealism, in other words, has something to do with the deliberate absence of normal cultural connections. This implies that a surrealistic mood cannot be grasped by cognitive processes that exclude awareness of culturally shaped connections; that is, by processes that include awareness of only visual connections. It may be that greater light–dark contrast will help the mood; but so also will a discussion of the choice of items pictured, of the cultural connections between them, and even of surrealist theories of the irrational and unconscious powers of mind.

The general point is that the medium-specific view of cognitive processes in the arts seems to require a formalist theory of aesthetics. By definition, it restricts those processes to working with the purely visual character of the work, and, by definition, it excludes reference to the cultural world that lies "outside" the work. I assume this is Rush's intention. We are all familiar with the limitations of formalism in general, and I will not go into them here. But I believe restrictions of this kind are too great a price to pay for a method of assessment.

Notice that Rush's system, and the medium-specific view in general, assumes a noninterpretive view of aesthetic perception. It assumes that there is no gap between perceiving visual materials and grasping their significance, because what is to be understood lies wholly in what can be seen directly. In this noninterpretive account, if we talk about visual ideas or elements, we are only describing or naming (as one does in "scanning") qualities that could be grasped without the use of words. Such talk may be useful in directing students' attention, but it is only a crutch for learners. Verbal language, according to this model, is not fundamental to the important cognitive processes, which are perceptual. Assessment can ask for names, but it would do better to go directly to perceptions.

In my view, this is basically where Rush goes wrong, in avoiding the help available in an interpretive view of aesthetic understanding. An interpretive view suggests that to perceive is not necessarily to understand, and that understanding requires more complex cognitive activities. These activities are whatever is required to connect what is visually perceived with aspects of our cultural world in general. A short phrase for this would be connecting what we see with ideas. For example, to see that an encounter is bizarre is to connect it with ideas.

I will give a more concrete example that comes from a paper written by a colleague of mine, Judith Koroscik. Koroscik (1990) tells how she was taken to see Seurat's famous *La Grande Jatte* in the Chicago Institute when she was in junior high school. She was very impressed by the dots with which it is painted, and she stared hard at them, studying them one by one. She was impressed by how carefully they were painted and by how many there were. But she did not see them as meaningful, although she had been told that they were significant. In her paper, she quotes Nochlin's (1989) interpretation of the style.

> [The] historical presence of the painting is above all embodied in the notorious dotted brushstroke—the petit point—which is and was the first thing everyone noticed about the work—and which in fact constitutes the irreducible atomic particle of the new vision. For Seurat, with the dot, resolutely and consciously removed himself as a unique being projected by a personal handwriting. He himself is absent from his stroke. . . . The paint application is matter-of-fact, a near- or would-be mechanical reiteration of the functional "dot" of pigment. . . . In these machine-turned profiles, defined by regularized dots, we may discover coded references to modern science, to modern industry with its mass production, to the department store with its cheap and multiple copies, to the mass press with its endless pictorial reproductions. (pp. 133–134)

Nochlin interprets the work as an anti-utopian comment on modern industry and its effects on us, as well as, later, on the joylessness of a bourgeois Sunday afternoon in the park. Notice how many ideas are referred to in this interpretation. They are historically and culturally specific ideas, available only through a complex network of other ideas, and not to be taken for granted among students, however visually acute. Without these ideas—according to Nochlin—one cannot make sense of the style. It is important to see that these ideas are available only through language; and that seeing them in the work requires both visual and verbal cognitive activities. Koroscik and her junior high school peers, however, eager and impressed, knew no better than to stare at the dots and, knowing that they did not understand, to stare still harder.

Of course, I have chosen an example that formalism plainly cannot deal with. It is obviously no use in this case to stare harder at the dots, whether one is a child in a museum or an assessor looking at student work. An assessment that could get at the cognitive processes needed in these cases would have to use words in some way—essays, discussions, interviews—in conjunction with the works. Of course, the language-based cognitive processes would not replace those that are visually based. Rather, the former would interpret the latter, help make them meaningful. And we would have two kinds of evidence instead of one: the students' work and their words. But if the assessment were well constructed, these would be evidence not about two "modes of thought" but about one understanding, one that was formed by the natural interplay of the visual and the verbal.

Haynes's View

Haynes seems basically to agree with Rush that perception is noninter-pretive, though in a complicated way. She wants to avoid naming and the kind of reductionist, memory-oriented tasks that naming implies. She finds some validity in assessment at her second level of aesthetic response, the level of criticism, art history, and so on, which is where one would expect to find interpretive activities. But she insists repeatedly that assessment at this level is suspect, because she also adopts the medium-specific view. She has a general distrust of words in connection with art. What really counts for her has little to do with words, and everything to do with the visual medium. For her, the problem with assessment at the second level is not that it is fallible, since (one assumes) all assessment is. The problem is that it is aimed at the wrong target. The important learning lies at the third level, which has nothing to do with words.

The anecdote of the ASAT helps us see how she constructs the issue. Adding a written section to the ASAT exam opened up the possibility that bright students in physics and chemistry could earn good marks without "the slightest aesthetic awareness." And, one has to admit, it could have that effect. In my view this would be because the exam was poorly constructed, or had the wrong purposes (gatekeeping). But it seems that for Haynes, writing (and language in general) is inherently misleading for assessment, however the in-strument is constructed. It always offers dangers without presenting further opportunities. I conclude that she has a general distrust of talk about art.

The alternative view, of course, is that talk about art can play a construc-tive, even a necessary, role in interpretation, and, derivatively, in assessment. In this view, which in general I call interpretive, we must interpret a work of art, and for that we must both look at it and talk about it. In Haynes's lan-guage, our cognitive processes must proceed in terms of both the visual me-dium and natural language. We must try to grasp both the internal connec-tions between the visual elements and forms a work presents and also its connections with ideas more generally. The latter kinds of connections are not simply verbal versions of the former.

We can see visually the encounter of a sewing machine with an umbrella, but we cannot see the chance character of that encounter. To grasp that, we must put the visual elements in the context of a different network of mean-ings, a network that makes possible connections with a different range of ideas. That is, we must put something into words. We can then look at the work again and see its internal relations differently, and repeat the process in a cyclical manner. Having looked at the *Grande Jatte*, we can think about the industrial revolution and attitudes toward it in late-nineteenth-century Paris; and we can then return to the dots and consider whether or not they carry a sense of the mechanical and joyless, and so on. What we have in such a case is not two sets of meanings in two different media, but one understanding arrived at by a kind of thinking conducted in both visual and verbal terms.

If this is what interpretation is like, then it seems to me that assessment should follow that pattern. Assessment should actively try to engage the cognitive processes involved in interpretation and to secure evidence about them. To avoid the dangers that Haynes and Rush are rightly concerned with—that assessment might tap into understanding that is only and merely verbal—of course, assessment has to make sure that the verbal tasks are closely related to the visual, and vice versa. This is more difficult than simply banning the verbal, and it is less popular rhetorically. But I believe it responds better to the complexities of art.

So, to repeat myself, if Rush would talk to students about her targeted concept as well as look with them at their conceptually focused work, she would have a more valid assessment. The case of the Australian written exam is less hopeful because (it sounds as if) it was not constructed to relate the visual part of the exam.

The Case for Language

Another point has to do with the particular value of natural language as a medium for interpretation. Why do I insist on the importance of language in this context? Why not some other medium? Why not, for instance, speak of interpreting visual artworks by translating them into music or dance? Or two-dimensional art into three-dimensional? I do agree that each of these media can be regarded as symbol systems in terms of which we can make sense of the world, and that interpretive work in any of them can be valuable. So why focus on the verbal? Is this just the prejudice of a school system already dominated by the verbal, against which we should fight? From the tendencies of their papers, one might expect this to be what Rush and Haynes would say.

But natural language is not just another medium, one more among many. It is much more deeply connected than the others to our world of ideas, to the culturally constructed network of thoughts and expectations with which we make sense of our life. Language represents and embodies for us what the hermeneutic philosophers call our life-world, the horizon of meanings against which we interpret individual events and objects. The life-world consists of our attitudes, assumptions, emotions, institutions, relationships, and expectations, all of these loosely but meaningfully connected together into what we call a culture. What connects them is primarily language. Language connects these things (let us call them "ideas") into networks that are themselves loosely connected; and when we talk about a work, we connect it via those networks with other parts of our life-world.

We call this interpretation, whether of artworks or anything else. This is what happens when we relate student work with the idea of chance encounters and the subconscious, or the Seurat with the effects of the Industrial Revolution, with a repressive morality, with department stores and mass media, and so on. Those connections can be made only with language because the ideas exist only via language. Done well, interpretation of this sort is an equal partner with perception in the achievement of understanding art and is not something that assessment should avoid.

It is then somewhat puzzling that Rush, a supporter of discipline-based art education (DBAE), suggests that approach should be aligned against the constructive role of language in interpretation. In my view, criticism and art history are interpretive activities. They are ways of talking constructively about the significance of art for the purpose of understanding it better. This view makes them fit oddly with the medium-specific view.

If DBAE promotes the teaching of art history and criticism, then it too fits oddly with the medium-specific view. The alternative is to suppose that art history and criticism are not interpretive activities, but are mostly a matter of naming qualities and connections that can be seen directly, without the necessity of words. If that were the case, why would we want to teach them? Similarly, it is puzzling that Haynes adopts this limiting, medium-specific, view of the third level of aesthetic perception and experience, excluding from it the connections of art with the rest of life. She begins her paper by asserting that modern science and math are matters of alternative interpretations, incomplete, fallible, historically constructed. Why not also aesthetic experience? Are its cognitions not equally complex?

PRINCIPLES OF ASSESSMENT

To make this discussion somewhat more concrete, I close by describing some principles undergirding an assessment project we have at Ohio State University. This project is still in its early stages (at the time of this writing it has been going on for about a year-and-a-half) and involves a small faculty team led by Nancy MacGregor and Bill Loadman. We have reached agreement on a number of principles of assessment and have begun to put them into practice.

1. *Promote the improvement of teaching and communication to others.* The first principle is that we want to develop assessment procedures and materials

that are useful for the improvement of teaching and for communicating to others what art education is centrally about. We want our work to be useful to teachers, to help them adjust their curriculum and instruction; and to administrators, parents, and citizens who would like to understand more about the outcomes of art education. We are using various kinds of visual and verbal data for these purposes and many of them are qualitative in nature. Like Haynes, we are concerned with assessing processes that are aesthetically important. But since, unlike Haynes, we take an interpretive rather than a medium-specific view of aesthetic understanding, we do not take this to mean that they are out of reach. We are not automatically suspicious of verbal responses; we regard them as offering a different kind of data for judgment. Consequently we look for exercises that combine the visual and the verbal. Our data include studio work and commentaries on it; and when we ask for verbal responses (whether oral or written), it is always in the presence of actual works. (I was reassured to realize that the assessment exercises developed at ARTS PROPEL—the domain projects and the processfolios that Howard Gardner described—also include verbal discussions, writing assignments, and reflection across examples, even if this is not consistent with the medium-specific view.)

2. *Focus on the outcomes of instruction.* Like Rush, we want to focus assessment on learning that is the result of instruction. We do not aim to assess abilities that are more general than this, that are the result, for example, of social background, parental influence, or schooling in general. This means that many already existing measures are not relevant. Developmental measures, for example, such as my own or those of Abigail Housen, are much too general. If we want to help teachers improve their teaching, we must help them assess the results of their instruction and not something else. We do this by providing examples of quality instructional units that incorporate assessment materials. This means that we must first identify, or clarify, the intended objectives of instruction. Like Gardner, we have found ourselves in practice often having to devise curricular episodes and to teach them, in order to see if our assessment tasks are effective. We regard this effect—of improving curriculum through appropriate assessment—as highly desirable.

3. *Classify learning outcomes.* Another principle is to classify carefully the kinds of educational processes we assess. We have discussed category schemes for such processes at length. For example, we are interested in the transfer of learning. To be able to transfer knowledge from one situation to another is a criterion of understanding. So we develop instruments that call for the transfer of ideas learned during instruction to cases that lie at a varying distance from the original. We rarely ask students to reflect on only one work, whether it is their own or someone else's.

4. *Develop category schemes of cognitive abilities.* These help us decide what should be assessed and how to assess it. For example, some connections are more like facts and others more like principles. On the one hand, one might apply knowledge gained of one work to an interpretation of another; on the other, one might use the knowledge to reason about whether the artist's life or intention is relevant to the meaning of the work. There are distinctions between "meta" levels of knowledge; between, for example, being able to produce a certain effect and knowing how one produces it; or between being able to produce a criticism and knowing the criteria that one uses in it.

There is knowing-that and knowing-how—the knowledge of cases and the knowledge of processes. The latter include especially knowing how to proceed when confronted with an interpretation. There are inquiry skills, knowing how to ask questions and develop answers. And so on. These are important dimensions for assessment procedures.

We are still developing useful categories for the important learning. We believe we must take them seriously if we are to assess—or teach—the important cognitive processes. If we want the materials to assess important learning, we must have sound ideas about the kinds of processes that are required for understanding and interpreting art. In general, we have found helpful concepts in the expert–novice paradigm (Koroscik, 1990), in work on misconceptions (Perkins & Simmons, 1988), and in discussion of models of transfer (Prawat, 1989).

5. *Enable assessment by teachers.* We want assessment materials that can be used by teachers and do not require outside experts. Given the demands of the teaching role, this means that the categories and rating systems must be limited. As we have developed a sense of how to assess particular learning, we try to teach those concepts first to particular classes of students; then we work with teachers in developing and testing the assessment materials in their own classes. This provides a salutary check on our tendency to develop complicated category systems and controls our decisions about levels of abstraction, developmental appropriateness, and so on. It also suggests different ways of teaching and different kinds of curricula, and illustrates the pedagogical cycle that connects assessment with instruction. It generates much data, both quantitative and qualitative, out of which we will construct some easily communicated models. But we are a long way from that yet.

REFERENCES

Koroscik, J. (1990, April). *Novice–expert differences in understanding and misunderstanding art.* Paper delivered at the annual meeting of the American Education Research Association, Boston.

Nochlin, L. (1989). Seurat's *Grande Jatte:* An anti-utopian allegory. *The Art Institute of Chicago Museum Studies, 14*(2), 133–153.

Perkins, D., & Simmons, R. (1988). Patterns of misunderstandings: An integrative model for science, math, and programming. *Review of Educational Research, 58*(3), 303–326.

Prawat, R. S. (1989). Promoting access to knowledge, strategy, and disposition in students: A research synthesis. *Review of Educational Research, 59*(1), 1–41.

FELICITY HAYNES

In general, I agree with the summary of my paper offered by Michael Parsons. I wish to elaborate only to remove what he calls an ambiguity about assessment. It is an ambivalence rather than an ambiguity, for I am more positive about the need for assessment and less mistrustful about talk in education than he indicates in his reply. The nonassessable outcomes of art education are not the *most* important ones. Rather they are important enough not to be discarded, existing as they do as an obverse face to all the formative and summative assessment and evaluation that must take place in the classroom if schools are to have any value as socializing agents.

Without this invisible face being acknowledged, even as a silent presence, the other two levels of assessment become disembodied. Without either level of assessment, teachers become irrelevant to the holistic private face of art, and thus less meaningful to the individual student. For art education to be efficacious, the three levels must continuously interact. They can, as Parsons remarks, be constructively interdependent. Were I to rewrite the paper completely now, I should probably begin with an example from chaos theory, rather than physics, that exchanges the theoretical move toward abstraction for a nonlinear dynamics that is complex and never quite predictable, with the holistic individual playing the part of the butterfly's wing that continuously throws formal and predictive patterns into beautiful new variations.

If I *really* mistrusted words about art education, I should have been forced in the interests of consistency to hum or draw my paper rather than present it in words. However, a diagram or two illustrating the three levels of cognition might have helped add another dimension to the discussion. Those three levels were (1) fairly formal forms of knowledge, which I have claimed usually are used to give grades to cognitive products; (2) the more fluid heuristic realms of meaning used to evaluate ordinary language meanings in the cognitive process; and (3) the personal ways of knowing involved in a cognitive state. To show these in the form of a three-layered mobius strip has the advantage of not being hierarchical, of letting one face become the other almost invisibly, with the realms of meaning providing a constructive interface between the nonverbal and formal levels.

Because we are talking mainly about art education here, the move toward abstraction appears unidimensional, and the mobius strip cannot accommodate Gardner's mutually exclusive symbol systems. So this visual symbol will need to be complemented by another, in which the holistic person at the center makes sense of the world by first constructing a fluid dynamic of linguistic and nonlinguistic shared conventions, which meet and overlap at the base, and then, when principles become more abstract and less concrete, branching off into formal disciplines such as physics, geometry, ethics, history, music, and even perhaps, to concede Parson's final point, potentially aesthetic experience. Some disciplines are more distantly removed from ordinary language than others. For instance $E = mc^2$ does not mean much to the layperson but is essential to an understanding of physics. The independence from reality of the principles at the formal level of forms of knowledge is encapsulated by Julius Kovesi's epigram that one cannot make scrambled eggs out of fried ones, that for well-formed disciplines such as physics and art to communicate they must come down from the peaks of the mountain and talk at a commonsense level. And the point of talking at a commonsense level is to engage at least the cognitive state of the personal individual, which forms the base of all knowing. The Arabic notion of zero as a starting point for number has served us well in the past and should continue to do so.

JEAN C. RUSH

In his attentive response to my paper, Michael Parsons raises questions about certain aspects of my arguments that may be unclear to others as well. I appreciate the opportunity to address two of them in greater detail: the pedagogical usefulness of formal analysis, and language in teaching and assessing performance in studio art.

In addition, readers should see my paper as consistent with, and an extension of, the theoretical framework of an approach to art education called discipline-based, or DBAE. This approach recommends broadening the scope of art instruction to include concepts and skills from four arts disciplines, sometimes within a single lesson: aesthetics, art criticism, art history, and art production or the studio arts.

The discipline-based approach is frequently criticized either for neglecting instruction in the studio arts or for teaching them in a way that stifles creativity, or both. In contrast, as a former painter, I endorse DBAE theory specifically because it has the potential to teach students to behave as artists do. This is not to say that DBAE practice always fulfills its theoretical promise.

Why do its critics and proponents hold such divergent views of DBAE? Critics seem to mistake DBAE prescription for proscription when children make the figurative pictures from pencil, crayon, or tempera paint, and the clay bowls, wire figures, papier-mache masks, and other two- and three-dimensional artworks that characterize elementary school studio art. Critics believe DBAE suppresses self-expression.

I have undertaken here and elsewhere to clarify the conceptual similarities between the best kinds of elementary school art activities and making art, and to show the value of knowledgeable adult intervention in what often is a trial-and-error, noneducational process. I refer readers to two prior articles (Rush, 1987, 1989) in which I explain the configuration of a model art lesson whose format allows students to practice artistic expression while making tutored images.

In discussing the production of images I am not talking about craft, the skillful use of art materials to create a beautiful object as an end in itself, or even about design, the aesthetic intertwining of function and form. Art implies the creation of meaning through the transubstantiation of these same art materials into images with metaphorical dimensions. Acknowledging the long-standing philosophical and pedagogical distinctions between art and craft, and between art and design, is essential to understanding my message.

FORMAL ANALYSIS

Parsons suggests that my arguments rely on what he calls a "medium-specific view of cognition in the arts," a view he interprets as confining concepts to a visual medium, which would indicate a formalist theory of aesthetics. From this he infers that "whatever is important to understand about art" may be seen in the medium "without reference to the world that lies outside the work."

Rather than regarding my approach as medium-specific, I would prefer to call it image-specific, indicating that aesthetic concepts assume a particular configuration when demonstrated in any one work of art. Visual concepts certainly may exist in the mind independently from their particular embodiment in art media. A concept like that of negative space, for example, has thousands of possible configurations, only some of which an artist can use at one time.

I acknowledge that both contextual and intrinsic factors contribute to the appreciation of a work of art. However, appreciation per se is not the focus of my paper, even though Parsons emphasizes appreciation in his response. I am interested in enabling students to use media to produce artistic images. The primary visual identification of any work always rests on its particular formal configuration. This formal configuration expresses essential aesthetic information whose existence must be perceived by a viewer in order to understand the metaphorical content or meaning of the work. The formal configuration reflects the artist's intent. Students who aspire to be artists need to practice manipulating formal elements and principles, what Broudy calls sensory and formal aesthetic properties, because they constitute the grammar and syntax of the language of art. Meaning is embodied in form.

Parsons enunciates a position, which seems widespread among art educators, that equates formal analysis of artworks with the aesthetic stance called formalism. This is an unlikely misidentification for an aesthetician, so I conclude that my analytic approach may give readers the misleading impression that I care only about the elements and principles of form.

If so, it is a misperception I would like to correct. I assumed the grammar and syntax of formal analysis would be appropriate for an examination of the artistic process because, thanks to the Bauhaus, it constitutes an artistic pedagogy shared by all Western societies. As such, I expected art teachers to find it intelligible.

Formal analysis, a kind of pedagogical formalism, as this might be called, constitutes the descriptive, analytic, and critical language with which we speak about the conceptual skeleton within a work of art. Although teachers may find the language of form deficient in some respects, most teachers at all levels of schooling use it for lack of viable alternatives.

The language of form is useful for analyzing art of many aesthetic persuasions besides the formalist. I intend formal analysis to be a vital component of art lessons, but not the only one, and certainly not the vehicle for teaching only formalism. One of the strengths of DBAE is its attempt to acquaint students with many aesthetic points of view.

LANGUAGE AND ART

Parsons also infers from my interest in visual concepts that I would prefer to omit speech from the instructional process. He suggests that "if Rush would talk to students about her targeted concept as well as look with them at their conceptually focused work, she would have a more valid assessment."

Parsons is quite right about the ability of words to enhance the process of visual understanding. In my eagerness to document the validity of visual evidence, I neglected to explain the way in which language should function in the teaching process. In fact, I understated the importance of language because the most noticeable feature of discipline-based art education, and the one most often criticized, is its emphasis on talking about art. Art teachers uncomfortable with formal, critical, historical, or aesthetic analysis as part of the studio process are apt to conclude that increased emphasis on talking means less emphasis on doing.

By using formal analysis, teachers can call students' attention to art concepts in images viewed before and after studio art activities. Analysis can be a group or individual activity. Assessment procedures, particularly critiques (critical analysis of completed student artwork) that move from formal analysis to interpretation, rely heavily on spoken and written language. Some information about art, particularly contextual information, can be conveyed to students only verbally. Koroscik (1990) cites Nochlin's use of perceptual evidence, the "mechanical reiteration of the functional 'dot' of pigment . . . [in which] we may discover coded references to modern science, to modern industry," by bringing out contextual knowledge essential to her interpretation of the meaning of Seurat's image. As Parsons correctly notes, "if the assessment were well constructed, [language and vision would present] evidence not about two 'modes of thought' but about one understanding, one that was formed by the natural interplay of the visual and the verbal."

Parsons, in later conversation relating to my paper, has indicated that part of the negative response to DBAE may be in reaction to what teachers perceive as a "Dick and Jane" approach, that is, reducing the art object or the artistic process to such absurdly simple components that it becomes meaningless. Perhaps it also reminds us of Humpty Dumpty in our fear that the object or process, once taken apart by either design or accident, can never be reassembled into the magical whole—which, as the Bauhaus itself taught us, is greater than the sum of its parts.

Getting from the parts to the whole describes the artistic process; getting from the whole to the parts illustrates the challenge of teaching others to become artists. The first, in my experience, is less difficult than the second, or at least less difficult than trying to explain the second to educators who are not artists themselves.

Even children create pictures, which are one kind of image; but only those educated as artists learn to discern the formal skeleton that supports artistic metaphor. Understanding imagery constitutes the gateway to the studio arts.

The key to creating art is speaking the language: not self-reference, but reference to concepts; not formalism, but formal analysis; not only context, but content; not one style of expression or aesthetic stance, but many.

I recommend neither Dick and Jane nor Humpty Dumpty, but instead encourage students to solve real problems as they create images with metaphoric potential. This kind of studio activity will allow us someday to think of their works as art and of them as artists.

REFERENCES

Koroscik, J. (1990, April). *Novice–expert differences in understanding and misunderstanding art*. A paper delivered at the annual meeting of the American Education Research Association, Boston.

Nochlin, L. (1989). Seurat's *Grande Jatte:* An anti-utopian allegory. *The Art Institute of Chicago Museum Studies, 14*(2), 133–153.

Rush, J. C. (1987). Interlocking images: The conceptual core of a discipline-based art lesson. *Studies in Art Education, 28*(4), 206–220.

Rush, J. C. (1989). Coaching by conceptual focus: Problems, solutions, and tutored images. *Studies in Art Education, 31*(1), 46–57.

I–B
TEACHING

Chapter 5

Evaluating the Teaching of Art

ELLIOT W. EISNER
Stanford University, USA

I start by making some distinctions that are often conflated in discussions of evaluation. These distinctions, which I will describe but not elaborate, are among the concepts *evaluation, measurement, testing,* and *grading.* Evaluation is an activity concerned with appraising the value of some object or process. It results in making a judgment about the merits of something. Measurement, which often is assumed to be a necessary condition for the conduct of evaluation, particularly in education, has no inherent relationship to the evaluative process and is logically unrelated to it. Measurement is an activity aimed at quantifying qualities; it has to do with matters of amount or magnitude as described with reference to some arbitrary standard. For example, if I stand on a scale in Stanford, California, I get a read-out in pounds. If I do the same in Holland, the read-out is in kilos. If I travel to London and weigh myself there, the read-out is in stones. The standard in each locale is an arbitrary one and of no empirical consequence as long as I know the unit being used and have a baseline for comparison. Measurement is a descriptive activity. Evaluation is a normative one. Evaluation begins when I express delight or dismay at what the scale tells me.

Testing is a process designed to evoke a response from some individual or group so that the merits of the response can be appraised. Tests are, so to speak, contrivances used for securing information, but they, too, have no intrinsic connection to evaluation. Evaluation most often occurs without the use of tests, although tests, like measurement, can be used in the process of evaluation.

Grading, like testing and measuring, is another practice that is logically

Evaluating and Assessing the Visual Arts in Education: International Perspectives: © 1996 by Teachers College, Columbia University. All rights reserved. ISBN 0-8077-3511-6. Prior to photocopying items for classroom use, please contact the Copyright Clearance Center, Customer Service, 222 Rosewood Dr., Danvers, MA 01923, USA, tel. (508) 750-8400.

unrelated to evaluation. Grading is a data-reduction process that uses a symbol to represent the results of an appraisal or evaluation. We typically evaluate without grading, although one would hope that grades would not be assigned without evaluating.

I make these distinctions at the outset because conceptual clarity is a virtue when dealing with phenomena as complex as the evaluation of art teaching and because to assume that measuring, testing, or grading is necessary for evaluating is to impose constraints on the evaluation process that are unnecessary.

I turn now to another set of distinctions before addressing the evaluation of art teaching. These distinctions pertain to the functions of evaluation and to the view of teaching that I hold. Any idea about how the evaluation of teaching should occur, whether the subject is art or science, mathematics or literature, is predicated on a vision of what teaching entails. Conversely, evaluation also rests on a vision of what is needed to make defensible value judgments. This vision, in turn, is related to the function evaluation is to serve, and in this area there are several. Without elaboration, I will identify six important functions of evaluation and make the last of these the focus of this paper.

First, evaluation can and does perform a temperature-taking function. For example, in the United States, the National Assessment of Educational Progress (NAEP) is designed to provide the American public with a picture of the educational health of the nation. NAEP *does not* provide an assessment of individual performance. Indeed, it uses a multiple matrix sampling procedure to assess and report the performance of 9-, 13-, and 17-year-old students by cohort, gender, and region of the country. Evaluation as temperature taking is, roughly, like a nation's GNP: It is a broad indicator of the nation's or the states' health.

Second, evaluation also can be used as a kind of gatekeeping. In this function the performance of students is used to determine access to educational opportunity. In France the Bac, in Germany the Arbiteur, in England the A Levels, in the United States the Scholastic Aptitude Test; all of these exemplify evaluation efforts that significantly influence students' educational options. Such evaluation efforts have ramifications not only for students, but for schools and their curricular priorities since schools often are judged by the way their students perform on gatekeeping examinations.

Third, evaluation can be used to assess the quality of educational programs. In America, the North Central Association of Schools and Colleges, for example, provides institutional accreditation by assessing the quality of the programs that institutions offer. Similarly, the National Council of Teacher Education appraises the quality of teacher education programs. The American Psychological Association provides accreditation for university programs awarding graduate degrees in psychology and, of course, most self-study evaluation efforts are designed to strengthen local school programs by focusing the faculty's attention on their quality.

Fourth, evaluation typically is used to assess the extent to which students have achieved a program's goals. In the standard logic of curriculum planning, educational objectives are the targets to which evaluation efforts are directed. The use of criterion-referenced tests are among the more recent technical innovations in the evaluation field and most clearly express a means/ends logic of curriculum planning. The use of such tests reflects a vision of schooling in which a body of content is prescribed by grade level and in which students are promoted to the next grade on the basis of successfully having mastered the material that was taught. The achievement of program goals is the student's passport to the next grade.

Fifth, evaluation often can be and is used as a procedure through which teachers "diagnose" their students' academic strengths and weaknesses. Evaluation in the form of observation, testing, and analysis of the student's classroom work, provides a basis upon which teachers make pedagogical decisions about what might be done next.

Sixth, evaluation can be and sometimes is used as a means through which teachers secure useful feedback on the quality and character of their own work. When used in this way, evaluation is essentially an educational medium. It is intended to help teachers improve their classroom performance. Since teaching is as isolated a profession as it is an important one, providing assistance to teachers in a form that enables them to increase their pedagogical competence is of the utmost importance. Unfortunately, professional norms within schools often make the observations needed to provide such feedback difficult to secure. Teachers often protect their professional privacy and sometimes regard visitors who observe as threatening intruders. Yet isolation from other professionals is not a condition conducive to professional growth, and without such growth the ability to create and mediate programs that have significant educational consequences is likely to be diminished. It is this use of evaluation to which this paper is directed.

In selecting this focus I necessarily will neglect evaluation practices that focus on matters of certification. Those practices, too, are related to the evaluation of art teaching, but I believe that the enhancement of students' art education is intimately, though not exclusively, related to teachers' skills and the substance of the programs they provide. It is the practicing art teacher who carries the educational mission forward, and it is the teacher, therefore, who must receive constructive attention. I believe that of the six functions of evaluation that I have identified, evaluation as feedback and guide is the most directly useful in helping teachers get better at what they do.

THE NATURE OF TEACHING

A word or two about my view of the "nature" of teaching. In a sense, teaching has no nature. That is, teaching is an artifact. It is a created performance shaped by the sensitivity, imagination, and intentions of the teacher. It cannot be skillfully practiced when driven by recipes, controlled by algorithms, or deduced from theories. At their most useful, the guidelines derived from research in the social sciences function as heuristics for the teacher. They are intellectual resources, rules of thumb, not rules.

The implications of this view are important for the evaluation of art teaching. If one believes that a single scientifically derived best way of teaching exists, the evaluative task can be regarded as finding the discrepancy between what the teacher does and the ideal. The task then for the teacher (or the supervisor) is to bring the teacher's behavior in line with the idealized model. If there is indeed a best way, is it not reasonable for every teacher to employ it? Not to do so would be professionally irresponsible.

The vision I hold of teaching, a vision that puts a premium on constructive ingenuity in an array of tasks that have no single best method, moves teaching into the realm of craft. Since the decisions made by teachers have moral consequences for students, teaching is, as Tom (1984) aptly put it, "a moral craft." Teaching, I would add, not only is a moral craft; at its best it is a performing art. It is an art that depends on refined sensibility, imagination, flexibility, taste, and highly sophisticated skills. At its very best, it generates an aesthetic form of experience for both teacher and student.

Given these views of teaching, its evaluation cannot be properly done by using a mechanistic or closed form of assessment. When professional creativity is encouraged, indeed prized, the pedagogical performances of teachers are significantly incommensurate. When incommensurability exists, judgment must be employed, and when judgment is employed, the bases for judgments are of crucial importance. In this particular domain—the domain of judgment—sensibility and perceptivity provide the material for such judgment.

So much for preliminaries. What is the state of research on the teaching of art, and, more specifically, what is the state of the literature on the evaluation of art teaching? It is to these questions that I now turn.

THE STUDY OF TEACHING

During the past 2 decades, considerable attention has been devoted to the study of teaching. This attention is perhaps best represented in the three handbooks of research on teaching—Gage (1963), Travers (1973), and Wittrock (1986). As a result of these publications, a number of ideas have emerged that are relevant to the teaching of art. First, it has become clear that in the assessment of teaching, the subject matter matters (Stodolsky, 1988). Although this may appear to some as obvious, the most influential general orientation to the study of teaching has been characterized by a search for its common features, regardless of the subject. In 1960 Ryans, for example, looked for common personality traits among effective teachers. Bellack (1966) looked for classroom discourse patterns related to student achievement. More recently, Gage (1978) and his associates have focused on process–product relationships. Others have addressed the importance of time on task (Rosenshine, 1976), set induction, checking for understanding (Hunter, 1982), and other features thought to contribute to high levels of student achievement. Like their counterparts in learning theory, many students of teaching have tried to discover the essential features of teaching effectiveness free from the constraints of context, subject, or local conditions.

More recently (Shulman, 1987; Stodolsky, 1988), it has been recognized that what one teaches counts in the study of teaching; teaching poetry and teaching social studies, teaching art and teaching mathematics, impose different requirements for both teacher and learner. Hence, current research strategies have been directed toward what teachers do within a particular discipline or subject field.

This development, as reasonable as it is, does not go far enough. A subject like art, for example, can be used for a wide variety of purposes and can have very different emphases. Art can be geared toward the development of creative thinking skills, the refinement of the perception of works of art, the enlargement of the understanding of art history, or the development of art-making skills. It can be integrated with other subjects or it can be taught alone. Furthermore, to whom art is taught is not an irrelevant consideration in the assessment of teaching skills. Teaching 6-year-olds art may impose different requirements on the teacher than teaching 16-year-olds. Not only does the subject matter; the pedagogical uses of the subject matter as well.

Second, it has become especially clear to those who have tried to reform schools that the context within which teachers work significantly influences what teachers believe is possible (Eisner, 1988). It is difficult to change one's way of teaching if familiar teaching routines create a sense of comfort and if risk of failure with new ones is consequential. It is difficult to modify one's teaching practices if one is not aware of some of the ways in which they undermine the achievement of what one values. Teacher isolation does not afford much of a mirror to those who teach.

The implications here are important for those who wish to use educational evaluation to improve the process of teaching and, through it, the quality of education. They suggest that because context as well as subject counts, context needs to be addressed in efforts to improve teaching. Improved teaching requires attention to more than teaching, a theme to which I will return later.

A third idea that has begun to acquire saliency in the study of teaching relates to the forms of knowledge practitioners possess. Historically, the improvement of teaching, like the improvement of other educational practices, has been predicated on a theory to practice model. The basic assumption has been that the work of university researchers will provide empirically verified research conclusions that teachers can use to improve the quality of their work (Broudy, 1976). Something like an agricultural model, the aim was for basic researchers working in universities to disseminate the results of their efforts to educational middlemen—something like agricultural extension workers—who would then provide guidance to teachers working in schools. It has become increasingly clear that the sources of understanding concerning teaching are not limited to those provided by social scientists. Teachers also know a great deal about teaching, and what they know is not entirely reducible to social science (Atkin, 1989). Hence, a fresh appreciation for pedagogical reasoning has begun to emerge, a kind of modern day discovery of Aristotle's practical knowledge. This new found appreciation has opened the door to a kind of cognitive pluralism that did not exist before in the field of education. Increasingly, students of education are recognizing that there is more than one form of knowledge, more than one way to secure it, and more than one way to "validate" it.

A fourth important idea that has emerged in the study of teaching is that not only does the context count, but that teachers need to have a stake in the policy decisions that affect their professional lives. Almost all of the recent reports on the improvement of American schools assign a new significance to the role of the teacher as a shaper of educational policy (*Tomorrow's Teachers*, 1986). In most enlightened quarters, teachers are seen no longer as passive recipients of policies handed down to them from above, but as professionals who have something important to say about the features of educational policy. This new vision of the teacher's role is summed up in the idea of "empowerment," and although this term has an unfortunate militaristic ring, it does make clear the point that teachers are no longer to be regarded as passive recipients of decisions made elsewhere. This new vision is presumably as potentially significant for those who teach art as it is for those who teach any other subject.

The foregoing sets the stage for the conceptual core of this paper. Thus far I've distinguished among evaluation, measurement, testing, and grading. I've described six different but important functions of educational evaluation. I've provided a conception of teaching as a moral craft and as a form of artistic activity. I have identified research bearing upon the evaluation of teaching, and I have described some of the important ideas that have become salient in the practice of evaluation and the improvement of schooling.

THE EVALUATION OF ART TEACHING

There are at least two tacks that can be taken concerning the evaluation of art teaching. One of these pertains to the evaluation of art teachers, the other to the teaching of art. The former, which I will not discuss, focuses on evaluation as a gatekeeping function. Its mission is to identify those who possess the necessary credentials and skills to be certified to teach. The National Teacher Examination in the United States serves this purpose. It is used to determine eligibility and to provide individuals with access to the profession. The evaluation of art teaching, on which I will focus, attends to the classroom performance of teachers and uses evaluation as a way of assisting art teachers and influencing schools and school district policies so that they enhance rather than diminish the teacher's pedagogical performance.

The form of evaluation that I believe holds the most promise for improving teacher performance is qualitative in character, and the particular approach to qualitative evaluation that I will emphasize is one that my students and I have developed at Stanford University over the past 15 years. It is based on two concepts central to the appraisal of virtually all art forms. These concepts are *connoisseurship* and *criticism* (Eisner, 1991). I first will describe the functions of connoisseurship and criticism and then relate these functions to the pedagogical practices of art teachers.

I start by re-emphasizing that this form of evaluation is intended to help teachers improve the quality of what they do in their classrooms. Since teaching is a complex form of human action and teachers lead professionally isolated lives, a necessary condition that must be created within schools is the teacher's de-isolation. This means having another professional in the classroom observe and provide feedback to the teacher on his or her work. While the presence of another adult in the classroom is a necessary condition for such feedback, it is not a sufficient one. Presence provides the opportunity to see what goes on, but does not guarantee it. To *see* what a teacher does requires a cultivated form of perception. In the arts, those who have achieved high levels of perception in a particular domain are called connoisseurs. Connoisseurship may be thought of as the art of appreciation. Its aim is to enable one to experience the qualities that are displayed by some process or object. The ability to make such observations is learnable. Indeed, many of our own educational priorities in the field of art education are intended to further the student's ability to experience works of art and other visual forms. This effort, in a sense, is designed to increase the student's level of connoisseurship.

In the arts, connoisseurship profits not only from refined sensibilities, but from an understanding of the context and function of the works attended to. Cubist painting, for example, is not only an array of color and form; it participates in a history, is driven by a set of intentions, grew out of a particular tradition, and influenced another one. Futurism participates in a different

set of ideas, reflects another set of artistic aspirations, and is related to a political ideology quite different from those reflected in the cubist works of Gris,
Braque, and Picasso. My point here is that connoisseurship in teaching, no
less than in art, is enhanced by a broad understanding that is brought to bear
on the perception, interpretation, and appraisal of what one sees.

It is difficult to overestimate the importance of connoisseurship in the
improvement of teaching, for it is connoisseurship that gives consciousness
its content. But connoisseurship is a private activity. Connoisseurship is the
art of appreciation. It need not have a public expression. It is criticism that
gives connoisseurship its public face. The function of criticism, wrote John
Dewey (1934), is to re-educate the perception of the work of art. Critics write
about art in order to expand and deepen the viewer's experience with the
work. In educational criticism, the office of the critic is similar. It is to use
what educational connoisseurship provides as content to be transformed into
a public statement about what the critic as connoisseur has seen. When I say
public, I do not necessarily mean broadly publicizing the observations made
about a teacher; I mean sharing them with someone, most often the person
who has been observed. Indeed, educational connoisseurship is not limited to
the activities of the teacher. It can be focused on the class as a whole, on a
particular group of students, or on an individual student. In short, connoisseurship and criticism are ways of seeing and describing what occurs in classrooms and schools as a whole, as well as what an individual teacher does in
the course of his or her work (Eisner, 1991).

The relevance of connoisseurship and criticism to the evaluation of
teaching becomes especially clear if one compares it with more conventional
approaches to the assessment of teaching and to the view of teaching I described earlier. In conventional approaches to assessment, the need to achieve
inter-rater reliability is crucial. As a result, the most common strategy is to
dimensionalize teaching, to specify criteria for each dimension, to train observers to apply these criteria, and to use more than one observer in a classroom in order to demonstrate through correlational and other statistical
procedures that independent judgments made about teaching on these dimensions overlap.

When one's vision of teaching is based on assumptions of the existence
of an absolute standard or one best method, it makes sense to dimensionalize
teaching and to prescribe criteria through which teaching performance can
be appraised. When discrepancies between the teacher's performance and the
idealized criteria appear, an agenda for correction emerges. The training task
is to reduce that discrepancy and to seek isomorphism. When there is believed
to be one best method, the aim of supervision in teaching is to enable teachers
to converge upon it.

But these assumptions about teaching are not ones I embrace. There is no single best teaching method, there are methods, and, like art itself, the particular method employed often is related to a genre within which there are considerable variations. When one adds to this conception the desiderata that teachers should be encouraged to exercise their own educational imagination, the appropriateness of a fixed set of criteria for the evaluation of teaching diminishes even further. What then does this conception leave us with? Is this a recipe for pedagogical nihilism? Are we on the verge of rampant relativism in which "anything goes"?

I think not. While judgment still must be exercised, the quality of judgment is extremely important. The evaluative task is to make such judgments defensible without imposing a mechanical or rigid set of officially sanctioned criteria for teaching. Indeed, the absence of such standards in the fixed sense invites judgment. Before turning to the bases on which judgments about the quality of teaching can be made, I wish to delve more deeply into the meaning of educational criticism, especially its structure.

The Meaning of Educational Criticism

Educational criticism typically takes form in writing, although it can occur in the context of discussions with teachers and others as well. Regardless of the form it takes—written or spoken—it has four dimensions, which for analytic purposes I will describe separately. These dimensions are *description*, *interpretation*, *evaluation*, and *thematics*. The descriptive work of the educational critic is intended to provide a portrait of a classroom and the teacher's performance within it so that the reader can secure a vivid image of what has transpired. In this process literary devices—simile, metaphor, the cadence of language itself, innuendo, prosody, analogy—are used to convey a sense of place and action. The aim of the critic here is to make it possible for the reader to know the scene through the eyes of the critic. Like the work of historians such as Barbara Tuchman and journalists and novelists such as Truman Capote, the educational critic makes it possible for a reader to vicariously participate in the situation described. Consider the following description of an art teacher working in a classroom:

> There are really three "arts-and-crafts" rooms presided over by Don Forrister. The main classroom is located, fittingly, in the school's Vocational wing, whereas to reach the other two—the photography darkroom and the weaving room— requires considerable transit through those right-angled corridors. Forrister's classroom is L-shaped (the lap of the L is an adjoining arts material storeroom), its angularity somewhat softened by the layers of student crafts and artwork that cover the horizontal surfaces and cushion the walls.
> Entering this room is like exiting from the building: one leaves the

nowhere-land of the school plant and slips back into Appalachian hill country. The sense of place returns, thanks largely to the local flavor of objects like the baskets woven of birch twigs, the large, intricately designed Sunday quilt, and the drawings of hill country still lifes. Many of these exhibit the same blend of the aesthetic and the functional seen in the artifacts of the Southern Highlands pioneers.

And the longer one remains, the stronger wafts the aroma of the hills, not only in the distinctive accents of the students, but also in their open and friendly demeanor, a reflection of their elders on the sidewalks of Bryson City. And certainly, the perseverance and care of the students as they tussle with their materials are the qualities one can see fossilized in the artifacts of the mountain pioneers. Does the same fuel that fired the engines of the mountain craftsmen move these students in Don Forrister's classroom? Is it indeed a struggle for economic survival that motivates them? Are the scarlet threads woven into that rug merely to supply a tangential beauty, placed there primarily to catch the eye and only secondarily to please it—not as an end in itself, but as a means of ringing the cash register?

Just what does motivate these teenagers? It is an important question, because the answer can provide a clue to the *educational* meaning and significance of the program's outcome—the character of its impact on the lives of these students. Having spent only four days in the school, I will avoid pronouncements, and instead share my reasons for some strong suspicions. They are based on observations of student comportment, on their informal comments, on mass "whole class" discussions over which I presided, and on interviews with individual students. (Barone, 1983, p. 11)

In the descriptive aspect of educational criticism, the critic's voice is present, not obscured. The aim is not to provide a detached, procedurally objective (Eisner, 1991) account of what has occurred; such an account would diminish the vividness and the sense of the scene, thus reducing forms of understanding and modes of knowing that vicarious participation makes possible. The critical task is to call attention to the pedagogically important features of a complex array, and this requires neglecting aspects of classroom life in order to get to the educational heart of the matter and making it vivid. To accomplish this task, the critic must possess a level of connoisseurship that makes insight possible and the language skills to make insight public through artistically crafted prose. The model of such activity is, of course, found in literature.

Traditional conceptions of objectivity and subjectivity, fact and fiction, are violated in this approach to the educational world. The search for objectivity that has characterized so much work in the social sciences is replaced in this orientation by philosophical constructivism, a view that recognizes that our conceptions of the world are products of the transactions between a world we cannot know in its pristine form and the cognitive structures, including our values, that we bring to the world. In this sense, the worlds we know are the worlds we make (Goodman, 1978). The experience we have is the experience we take. The agent is always active and the line between fact and fiction is harder to draw than we are accustomed to believing. The point here is that the brilliance of the image and the strength of human empathy contribute to our understanding of what has occurred. Good critics of teaching facilitate the achievement of both.

The second dimension in educational criticism is interpretive. By interpretation I mean accounting for what one has given an account of. Given a description of a state of affairs—a portrayal of the way a teacher introduces an activity in an art class or leads a discussion about a work of art—how shall the responses of the students be explained? What accounts for the teacher's approach to these tasks? What is likely to be taught and learned by the methods used and by the emphasis or focus the teacher employs? In trying to account for these events, theories in the social sciences may come into play. To the extent to which they make credible interpretation possible, such theories ought to be used. However, classroom events are always particulars, and theory is always both general and ideal, and, as such, must give way to the press of the particular (Schwab, 1969). No theory is ever adequate for explaining everything about any particular event. Thus, theory is a kind of cognitive map, an amplifier of rationality, a structure intended to expand comprehension. Wisdom in the use of theory consists of knowing when to abandon it in order to account for events in plausible, but atheoretical, terms. Consider the following interpretation:

Interestingly, the Arts Program booklet suggests that it is those once tangential, individually produced aesthetic qualities that today provide the craft products with their functional value:

"In our age of mass production where a certain 'sameness' marks most products, there is a growth market for goods that are unique and distinctive. The craftsman who can design and produce articles that have aesthetic value and bring distinction to their owners, have access to a market with which mass production cannot compete." (Forrister & McKinney)

Thus the "functional" value of today's craft objects may be defined less by their usability than by their ability to persuade a prospective purchaser visually. The mountain folk of yore could have survived the winter under an ugly quilt, but today's Appalachian craftsmen must beware the frigidity of the uninterested consumer.

Recall, however, that Forrister's students are generally not interested in selling their wares, and can therefore give freer range to their own personal aesthetic values in the construction of their objects. Individual self-expression thus seems central not only to the activities of Forrister's future artists but to the craftsmaking as well, and that is surely one of the sources of a profound satisfaction that attracts them to Don Forrister's class.

Here, then, is what we have learned thus far about the Swain program: that there exists within the program major nonvocationally related features, including motivational factors such as a thirst for self-esteem and a need for self-expression; and that these incentives result in program outcomes that are officially unsanctioned and therefore officially ancillary, but that are of central importance to a preponderance of the students. (Barone, 1983, pp. 19–20)

Tom Barone attempts to account for the focus of Forrister's art program and its attraction to students. Implicitly, if not explicitly, it is based on a theory of motivation.

A third dimension to educational criticism is evaluative. As I indicated earlier, education is a fundamentally normative enterprise. The values or models that one embraces in conceptualizing educational aims and in selecting educational events for attention are as contentious as they are crucial. There is no single correct value orientation for defining either the mission of education at large or of educational practice in particular. The educational critic has the responsibility of bringing to bear on educational events those values that he or she regards as justifiable. This means that there will always be selectivity operating on the critic's part in both the perception and the description of classroom events. Although a critic can certainly try to understand the value orientation of the teacher, and while classroom events can be described with reference to their relationship to those educational value commitments, such practices do not obligate the critic to subscribe to the values the teacher embraces. Teachers may be very effective in achieving values that an educational critic rejects. The aim of the critic is not simply anthropological; it is not simply a matter of *describing* values and relating practices to them, but of *appraising* the value of the events that have transpired, and this means making judgments about their educational worth.

Making judgments about teaching practices obligates the critic to justify the judgments made. That is, if judgments are not to be whimsical they need to be grounded in a value orientation. While such grounding does not require a reader to accept the values the critic holds, it does make those values clear.

In many cases it is possible to discern the values the critic brings to the classroom, through an analysis of the language the critic uses and what he or she emphasizes in the critical account. Educational values display themselves in both subtle and not so subtle ways. A prolegomenon on one's value orientation is not always necessary, particularly if the critic's values are well known, as they often are among prominent writers on education such as, for example, John Holt, John Dewey, or Paulo Freire.

The point here is that evaluation that is value-free is an oxymoronic concept. To do evaluation requires the application of values to some process or object. It is the critic's values that count here, and although the critic can and indeed ought to be cognizant of the values the teacher embraces, the critic, as I indicated earlier, has no obligation to accept them. If for some broader reason an artist intentionally creates a third-rate painting, such an achievement does not make the painting first-rate. The efficient achievement of educational goals that are of little worth has no significant educational merit. What's not worth teaching is not worth teaching well.

The fourth dimension of educational criticism is thematics. Thematics is an effort to distill from the observations of particular teachers in particular classrooms certain general principles or naturalistic generalizations (Stake, 1975) that enable a reader to understand not only the situation described, but other situations like it. If you consider, for example, the function of novels and plays as devices that not only make a particular cast of characters vivid, but use those characters as means through which more general conclusions about human beings can be drawn, my point will be grasped. *Macbeth*, for example, is about more than an eighth-century Scottish nobleman. Steinbeck's *The Grapes of Wrath* is not only about a particular family being displaced during the Great Depression in America; it is about displacement, the Depression, and social inequalities. *Death of a Salesman* is not only about Willy Loman, its main character, but about middle age and the loss of livelihood. In short, the universal, in a sense, resides in the particular, and from an analysis of the particular can emerge generic ideas whose import extends well beyond the particular situation from which they were derived. The articulation of thematic notions is what good educational critics achieve. These generalizing structures are presented to the reader not in the form of a formalized deductive logic, but as canonical images (Arnheim, 1990) and general interpretations that can be used to anticipate the future with greater efficiency or to reconstruct or reinterpret events of the past. Generalization is retrospective as well as prospective, and the lessons learned from studies of particular teachers in particular schools often have relevance to other teachers in similar schools. Educational criticism makes those themes apparent and shares them with the universe of readers interested in schooling.

It should be clear from the foregoing that the practice of educational criticism as an approach to the evaluation of art teaching is a highly interpretive activity that depends on acuteness of perception for its content and on the ability to create a form of prose that will carry the meanings that insightful perception has made available. It also requires the ability to exercise judgment and to engage in a form of rational analysis that in many ways is closer to arguments made in law and to analyses and interpretations in political science than to the experimental activities in behavioral psychology. The daily events that constitute life in the classroom are phenomenologically dense and intellectually challenging. The reduction of such phenomena to numerical scores through procedurally objective methods often eviscerates the very qualities and meanings that matter.

The constructive narrative that educational criticism represents is, as I indicated earlier, primarily a vehicle for helping teachers understand how they and their classrooms function. Its major aim is, as Dewey (1934) indicated, to re-educate the public's perception of the teacher's work and the classroom in which it occurs. In addition, educational criticism is useful for assisting policy makers to secure a more complex and authentic picture of the schools their policies are designed to influence. With a more comprehensive view of the factors that affect teachers and students, and a more authentic portrayal of the kind of life students and teachers lead together, there is a greater probability that educational policy will be well founded and helpful.

One other point that I wish to make about the structure of educational criticism is one that I only implied earlier. In characterizing description, interpretation, evaluation, and thematics, I had of necessity to separate them into categories. My aim was to make each as clear as I could on its own terms. In the actual writing of educational criticism, such categories are much less tidy. Interpretation infuses description, just as description infuses interpretation. Evaluation functions in perception just as the search for the general in the cloak of thematics influences the quest for what is significant in the classroom. In other words, the tidy categories that I have employed in order to describe each in its own terms are typically fused and intertwined in educational criticism when it is written, and, indeed, they are fused even in the act of perception.

I mention this because it would be a mistake to suppose that good educational criticism *requires* that each category be treated independently. There are some writers who may wish to approach their work in this way, but such an approach is not a necessary condition, and if treated as a prescription for writing, might hamper the kind of seeing and saying that genuinely excellent educational criticism makes possible.

What the foregoing provides is an approach to the evaluation of art teaching that recognizes the variety of ways in which it can occur, that provides a place for artistry in pedagogy, that does not relinquish judgment in appraisal, and that exploits the capacities of language—figurative as well as literal—to help teachers get better at what they do. This approach is rooted firmly in the traditions of the arts and humanities, and depends on developed sensibilities and the uses of judgment to reveal what is significant about a performance, place, resource, or social configuration. In a sense, educational criticism results in telling narratives about a teacher's work. At its best it helps teachers secure a fresh appreciation of their classrooms, schools, and teaching practices.

The term *narrative* tends to conjure up images of fictitious accounts, "mere" stories. How does one secure a warrant for such stories? How can we come to trust what a critic has to say? It is to matters of what conventionally has been called "validation" that I now turn.

Validation of Educational Criticism

There are three strategic criteria for validating educational criticism. One is called *structural corroboration*, the second, *referential adequacy*, and the third, *consensual validation*. Structural corroboration is achieved by appealing to multiple data sources to support the conclusions or sense of an educational criticism. When an educational critic makes a point about a teacher's ability to stimulate sophisticated forms of visual problem solving among students, the evidence to support this claim is located in the display of situations, teaching acts, and/or the work that students have created. The claim is structurally corroborated by what in the field of law is referred to as circumstantial evidence and in sociology by what is called triangulation. The critic seeks to locate the recurrent events that make his or her observations, interpretations, and appraisals credible. Collectively, the evidence is weighty; the narrative is believable.

In this process interpretation plays an important role because determining what events mean requires more than providing a description of their incidence; it requires a sense of their import. Determining import requires judgment, and judgment depends on the critic's ability to make sense out of what he or she sees.

The second strategic criterion, referential adequacy, refers to the critic's ability to enable the reader (or listener) to locate the classroom referents about which the critic has written or spoken. Recall that the main function of criticism is to re-educate perception, in this case the perception of art teaching. The test of effective criticism is its ability to reveal those subtle but significant aspects of teaching that might otherwise go unnoticed. In this sense, the critic serves as a kind of midwife to perception. After having read a good educational criticism, the reader ought to be able to see (or recall) more than he or she would have without the benefit of the criticism.

This criterion for educational criticism is entirely empirical in character. The term *empirical* comes from the Latin *empiricus*, which means "to experience." The "validity," or, better yet, the usefulness of educational criticism is located in the degree to which it helps the reader perceive and hence experience the presence and meaning of classroom events.

In many ways this process is like good political science. Complex issues of war and peace, for example, require attention to subtleties, profit from insight, and depend on the exercise of judgment. Good political science is not merely a matter of counting the incidence of soldiers or tanks, but it requires strategic and tactical analysis. It requires attention to the tone of political communiques, an appreciation of the language of diplomacy, and a feeling for the social and economic context within which all of this occurs. Such analyses and appraisals are much closer to an art form than to a scientifically verified conclusion. As Goethe said, "Between the general and the particular, the particular always prevails." The task of the critic is to write in a way that makes the particular vivid. Through its vividness it becomes referentially adequate for experiencing the process or object addressed.

Consensual validation is the process of determining the congruence among critics' descriptions, interpretations, and evaluations of a product or process. Closest to practices used in the social sciences, consensual validation is based on inter-judge agreement. If, for example, several educational critics were to observe a classroom, the operational question in this form of validation would be: Do the judges' accounts of the classroom agree? What one seeks here is consensus.

It should be said that while consensus among judges is necessary for consensual validation, it is not the primary index of useful criticism. Consensus tells us about the overlap among judges' views. It is quite possible to have different critical accounts, each of which in its own way sheds light on the qualities and meaning of the situation. What matters most is insight into a work or process. There are literally thousands of criticisms of *Hamlet*. We do not appraise the value of any single critic's work by its congruence with the work of others, but rather by the extent to which it deepens or expands our appreciation of Shakespeare's play. Similarly, three educational critics may give us three different, but nevertheless illuminating, accounts of a single school or classroom.

The Implications of Educational Connoisseurship and Criticism

What does the foregoing mean for the evaluation of the teaching of art? It means several things. First, it means that to adequately evaluate the teaching of art, it must be seen within the context in which it occurs. It is not a matter of assessing a teacher's knowledge on tests or tasks outside of the classroom; the classroom itself is the real test. Second, it means that the individual who observes the teacher needs to be able to see, not merely look at, what the teacher does. This requires a form of educational connoisseurship that can be developed, but does not accrue to someone simply by virtue of experience as a classroom teacher or as a result of being a school administrator. Connoisseurship provides the bases for experience and the material for description, interpretation, evaluation, and thematics. Third, it means that there is no single model of pedagogical virtue that defines teaching ability in art or in any other field. Different teachers of art can be excellent for very different reasons. In the best of all possible worlds, each teacher would confer his or her own signature on his or her teaching performance. Like art itself, teaching is not standardizable even when there are some common features. Fourth, it means that the constructive use of evaluation of teaching depends on the ability to convey what one has seen to a teacher or to a policy maker to deepen the person's understanding of what has transpired. This requires the ability to use language in ways that can capture and reveal idiosyncrasy, provide meaningful interpretation of what has transpired, justify judgments made about the quality of teaching, and locate those themes that might serve others well in generalizing about the particular case to other cases like it. It means that the evaluation of teaching requires the ability to use a critical language that avoids reducing one's observations solely to a set of numbers.

These requirements are formidable. They require training and a recognition and acceptance of the subject-specific, person-specific, context-specific character of a teacher's work. In short, they require a willingness to use an artistically grounded model of human performance, a model that I believe better suits teaching than procedures that seek to foster virtue in teaching through fidelity to a fixed ideal. These requirements also mean that we will no longer have the pseudo comfort of describing teaching through the use of highly reductionistic symbols. The assignment of a symbolic digit or even a set of digits to an array of variables is unlikely to reveal what has transpired and is not likely to be useful to teachers for improving what they do.

The use of the approach I have described is complex and fraught with difficulties, yet I believe we have seriously oversimplified the tasks of improving teaching. We have paid far too little attention to what teachers actually do when they teach. We have used highly reductionistic frameworks for assessment that are typically far too general to be helpful. We have neglected the special demands of the subject matter and the particular pedagogical function for which it is used. We have been so concerned with inter-rater reliability that we have avoided features that threaten it and we have been unwilling to face up to the artistic character of excellent teaching. Indeed the *Handbook of Research on Teaching* (Wittrock, 1986) weighs seven pounds and has over 800 main entries in its index. Not one of those entries is devoted to research on artistry in teaching. This aspect of teaching has been sidelined in the effort to find, as Gage (1978) puts it, a scientific basis for the art of teaching.

There are two other complications that also must be addressed. One pertains to what a broadened conception of curricular goals and content means for the evaluation of art teaching. The other pertains to the impact of context on the evaluation of teaching.

During the past decade visual arts curricula in American schools have been expanded to include not only the creation of art, but the development of critical skills in the perception of art and other visual forms, an understanding of the cultural and historical conditions within which art is created and that it influences, and a focus on questions and issues pertaining to the nature of art itself (Eisner, 1987). Although most clearly referenced in discipline-based art education (Greer, 1984), this model of creating, seeing, and understanding art is present in a wide array of approaches to art education and published in a very large number of state art education curricular frameworks. Each of these four domains also has implications for the evaluation of art teaching. Those who would evaluate an art teacher's ability to help students understand the history of art, for example, must themselves understand the history of art. Those who would evaluate an art teacher's efforts to help students understand aesthetic theory must themselves be conversant with philosophical aesthetics. Those who would evaluate an art teacher's ability to develop his or her students' ability to perceive and describe the qualities of a work of art must themselves be able to see the qualities of the work being described by students. In short, new aims and wider content for art curricula impose new and wider demands on the evaluator. It is difficult—even impossible—to make adequate judgments about the intellectual merits of a content that one does not understand. It is impossible to appraise the relevance of a student's comments about the quality of a visual image that one does not see. Broader content requires a wider array of evaluation skills. Since most art education in the public schools has focused on the development of studio skills, the expansion of curriculum will require the development among teachers of art of an array of skills that few now possess. In short, our new curriculum models have complicated, not simplified, the evaluation of art teaching.

But the implications do not terminate with broader curricular content. They also extend to the context within which teaching occurs. By far the dominant model for the teacher has been and is a single adult working alone with a group of 25 to 35 students in a classroom. Virtually all approaches to the evaluation of teaching, as well as to research on teaching, have been predicated on this model. Although this model is clearly dominant in most schools in America and elsewhere, there is no reason to assume that these arrangements are natural ones. They are artifacts, the products of tradition and habit. Teachers of art like other teachers can work with several colleagues. They can share pedagogical responsibilities, they can employ curriculum models aimed at the integration of several subject matters, they can teach far fewer and far more students than one typically finds in a conventional classroom. As these new conditions emerge in schools, the tasks of teaching will themselves change; new conditions and new contexts for teaching will help redefine the skills of teaching and the forms of craft and art that may be displayed within them. In short, we should not assume that the evaluation of teaching will always occur within the conventional classroom setting that we have for so long known.

To generate a body of research on teaching that uses evaluation practices based on the assumption that traditional teaching conditions are necessary, is to impede rather than to facilitate educational progress. As we invent new ways to carry out our professional mission in schools, we will move ineluctably into the edges of incompetence. The new virtually always requires new skills and sometimes new conceptions. Our evaluation practices should not impede such development; on the contrary they should support teachers who have the courage to redefine their professional roles and take pedagogical risks. The evaluation of art teaching, like teaching in general, ought to be seen as a facilitative process. When it is seen that way, it is more likely to help realize the aims that this orientation to the evaluation of teaching has advanced: Evaluation itself becomes an educational medium, and the evaluator, a teacher who helps teachers grow.

REFERENCES

Arnheim, R. (1990). *Thoughts on art education* (Occasional paper series, Vol. 2). Los Angeles: Getty Center for Education in the Arts.

Atkin, J. M. (1989). *Curriculum action research: An American perspective.* Paper presented at the American Educational Research Conference, San Francisco.

Barone, T. (1983). Things of use and things of beauty: The story of the Swain County High School Arts Program. *Daedalus, 112*(3), 1–28.

Bellack, A. (1966). *Language of the classroom.* New York: Teachers College Press.

Broudy, H. (1976). Search for a science of education. *Phi Beta Kappan, 58*(1), 104–111.

Dewey, J. (1934). *Art as experience.* New York: Minton, Balch.

Eisner, E. W. (1987). *The role of discipline-based art education in America's schools.* Essay prepared for the Getty First National Conference on Discipline-Based Art Education. Los Angeles: J. Paul Getty Trust.

Eisner, E. W. (1988). The ecology of school improvement: Some lessons we have learned. *Educational Leadership, 45*(5), 24–29.

Eisner, E. W. (1991). *The enlightened eye: Qualitative inquiry and the enhancement of educational practice.* New York: Macmillan.

Gage, N. (Ed.). (1963). *Handbook of research on teaching.* Chicago: Rand McNally.

Gage, N. (1978). *The scientific basis of the art of teaching.* New York: Teachers College Press.

Goodman, N. (1978). *Ways of worldmaking.* Indianapolis: Hackett.

Greer, D. (1984). Discipline-based art education: Approaching art as a subject of study. *Studies in Art Education, 25,* 212–218.

Hunter, M. (1982). *Mastery teaching.* El Segundo, CA: T.I.P. Publications.

Rosenshine, B. (1976). Classroom instruction. In N. Gage (Ed.), *The psychology of teaching methods: Seventy-fifth yearbook of the National Society for the Study of Education* (pp. 335–371). Chicago: University of Chicago Press.

Ryans, D. G. (1960). *Characteristics of teachers.* Washington, DC: American Council of Teachers.

Schwab, J. (1969). The practical: A language for curriculum. *School Review, 78*(5), 1–24.

Shulman, L. (1987). Knowledge and teaching: Foundations of the new reform. *Harvard Educational Review, 57*(1), 1–22.

Stake, R. E. (Ed.). (1975). *Evaluating the arts in education: A responsive approach.* Columbus, OH: Merrill.

Stodolsky, S. S. (1988). *The subject matters.* Chicago: University of Chicago Press.

Tom, A. (1984). *Teaching as a moral craft*. New York: Longman.

Tomorrow's teachers: A report of the Holmes Group. (1986). East Lansing: Michigan State University Press.

Travers, R. (Ed.). (1973). *Handbook of research on teaching*. Chicago: Rand McNally.

Wittrock, M. (Ed.). (1986). *Handbook of research on teaching*. Chicago: Rand McNally.

Chapter 6

Good Teaching: Evaluating Art Teaching in the Context of Schools

PAMELA SHARP EL SHAYEB
San Jose State University, USA

What is good teaching in art? What are the standards? What does the evaluation of good teaching in the context of schools look like? As part of a collection of papers dealing with the evaluation of art teaching and with the content and the outcomes of art programs in a variety of settings, this paper focuses on the evaluation of art teaching in the context of schools. Although it is difficult to consider the evaluation of art teaching as an isolated topic, apart from the discussions of content and the assessment of outcomes, these will be set aside as images of good teaching and ways to identify and celebrate it are developed.

Evaluation is a process that involves definition, description, standards, and judgments of value. Although the purposes of the evaluation of teaching range from the making of judgments leading to personnel decisions such as the elimination of incompetent teachers and the identification of master teachers (summative), to the gathering of data and setting of goals to be used in staff development programs (formative), for the purposes of this paper an assumption is made that the common goal of all forms of evaluation is to provide systems for communication between teachers and their evaluators, and to serve as a basis for professional growth. Evaluators can include principals, art supervisors, mentor teachers, and others who have been assigned administrative duties. I begin with a look at teaching in general and at art teaching in particular, continue with examinations of standards for art teaching, uncover problems, elaborate suggestions for the development of effective programs for the evaluation of the teaching of art in the context of schools, and close with a call for increased participation of art educators, including teachers, in the design and evaluation of programs for evaluating art teaching in the context of schools.

Evaluating and Assessing the Visual Arts in Education: International Perspectives: © 1996 by Teachers College, Columbia University. All rights reserved. ISBN 0-8077-3511-6. Prior to photocopying items for classroom use, please contact the Copyright Clearance Center, Customer Service, 222 Rosewood Dr., Danvers, MA 01923, USA, tel. (508) 750-8400.

GOOD TEACHING

What is good teaching in art? What is good teaching in general? Some would argue that good teaching in general is best identified through measures of effectiveness. That is, one knows that good teaching is taking place when most students learn most of what they are supposed to learn (Berliner, 1987).

Measures of effective teaching in art would use student outcomes as evidence of student competencies, to be judged through a variety of means (Gardner, 1989; Wiggins, 1989). Many believe, however, that there is more to good teaching than effectiveness as measured by student outcomes. In her book *The Good High School*, Lightfoot (1983) describes good teaching as a mixture of observable, measurable parts and less tangible, more elusive qualities.

> My first assumption about goodness was that it is not a static or absolute quality that can be quickly measured by a single indicator of success or effectiveness. I do not see goodness as a reducible quality that is simply reflected in achievement scores, numbers of graduates attending college, literacy rates, or attendance records. I view each of these outcomes as significant indicators of some level of success in schools. And I view these as potent, shorthand signs of workable schools, but each taken separately, or even added together, does not equal goodness in schools. "Goodness" is a much more complicated notion that refers to what some social scientists describe as the school's "ethos," not discrete additive elements. It refers to the mixture of parts that produce a whole. (p. 23)

The whole includes people, structures, relationships, ideology, goals, intellectual substance, motivation, and will.

A good school in Lightfoot's study is ultimately dependent on good teaching, and good teaching, like a good school, is situationally determined, embedded in a context, with a history and an evolution. Content and outcomes, whether in art or music or social studies, are only part of the situation and only part of a complex set of aspects that together contribute to the context and definitions of goodness. Good teaching in general is more than effectiveness. Good teachers build programs from knowledge and sensitivity to the context of the school and individual students. They measure their successes in multiple ways, reflecting on student engagement in learning and the general, overall environment of their classroom and school as well as student outcomes.

But what about good art teaching? Surely it can be differentiated from other good teaching, viewed either narrowly as effectiveness, or broadly as a whole. What are the characteristics that differentiate the teaching of art from teaching in other content areas? In a study of art teachers and teaching, Gray and MacGregor (1986) conducted field observations of teaching practice in three geographically separate areas in Canada. The study was subsequently extended to include teachers from the United States as well. For their early work, they selected 32 teachers who had been identified as having a professional impact within their schools, "whose individuality played a role in shaping curriculum and instruction practices in art" (p. 1). Their pictures of these teachers are drawn from three perspectives: the teachers' backgrounds, philosophies, and perceived professional roles; the conduct of classroom activities; and the artifacts of their teaching, which include space, equipment, and products. Analysis of data collected through interviews with the teachers and observations of their classrooms generated summary statements by each of the two researchers. Their joint summary statement regarding the conduct of teachers' classrooms, or the teaching of art, in parallel with Lightfoot's work, had to do with teacher and student relationships, again a characteristic of good teachers in general. They found that the good art teachers got to know their students very well and used their understandings of the students' feelings, thoughts, and life situations outside school to guide classroom interactions.

Teachers' understandings and knowledge of students as individuals also include understandings of student growth in general and in art. Arnheim (1990) writes about a teacher's need to understand growth and to recognize and respect phases of development.

> The growth of the young mind is at best a delicate process, easily disturbed by the wrong input at the wrong time. In the arts as well as elsewhere in education, the best teacher is not the one who deals out all he knows or who withholds all he could give, but the one who, with the wisdom of a good gardener, watches, judges, and helps out when help is needed. (p. 58)

A good teacher knows about physical, psychological, and social growth and development, and understands student responses to changes in themselves and their worlds.

The identification of teachers' knowledge, understanding, and empathy as an indicator of good teaching is found in other research. Flinders (1989) observed that good teachers bend school and classroom rules to adapt instruction to what they know of their own classroom and the realities of their students' lives. Lightfoot's good teachers are responsive to the human context of their teaching. They display a fearless and empathetic regard for students, indicative of deep understandings, and they see students as people worthy of respect. Good teachers build their programs on their knowledge, sensitivity, understanding, and respect for students, and those programs can be as diverse as the students.

Lightfoot adds to knowledge and empathy, however, by suggesting that good teaching also requires that teachers have something to teach. Good art teaching requires that teachers know something about art. Gray and Mac-Gregor (1986) observed teachers using their knowledge of subject matter throughout their teaching, but especially in formal and informal critiques, in which the good teachers responded to sensory, formal, and technical aspects of student work. They also identified teacher knowledge about art through observation of the variety and excellence of artworks and reproductions on display in classrooms and the rest of the school.

STANDARDS FOR ART TEACHING

Good art teaching, like good teaching in general, draws upon knowledge and understanding of art content and of students. Identifying teacher knowledge and skills is only part of evaluation, however. Standards and judgments are also part of evaluation. Judgments of the adequacy of the depth and range of knowledge held by an art teacher as well as of the appropriateness of the teaching will depend on standards for art teaching and the evaluator's conception of the purposes of art education. In setting standards for art teachers, Wilson (1985) begins by presenting his view regarding the purposes of art education, which are to assist students in understanding, constructing, and working with symbolic worlds. To do that, teachers need to master a range of content that includes media, tools, forming processes, composition, subject matter, art forms, cultural contexts, and art theory and criticism. Building on the evaluation of his own preservice teachers, recalled experiences of hiring for a school district, and imagined activities of teachers, Wilson describes what art teachers should be able to do. Using the theater as a metaphor, the art teacher "writes the script (prepares the unit and daily lesson plans), sets the stage (arranges the classroom), rehearses, speaks the lines and acts the parts (presents lessons), criticizes the performance and productions of the student cast" (p. 86).

Others responsible for teacher training and certification have drawn up standards for art teaching: Every state in the United States issues certification for teaching art (Price-Richard, 1989). All states have official documents describing requirements for art teachers and for elementary generalist teachers, and instruments for assessing knowledge and skills of prospective teachers. Many have curriculum frameworks that either prescribe or suggest content for public schools. Universities and colleges seeking accreditation for their teacher preparation programs usually pay close attention to those documents. A committee of professors of art education at California State University (CSU, 1989) has drawn up a set of sample subject-matter competencies for students who wish to become credentialed teachers.

The CSU Competencies

The CSU document, developed to assist in standardization among the 19 campuses of the university, begins with a description of generic competencies, which seem to be essential both within and outside the disciplines. There are 14 generic competencies in three categories. The generic competencies are followed by 34 art competencies in five categories: art production, art history, art criticism, aesthetics, and relationships between the areas of art as well as connections with life and other academic disciplines. Figure 6.1 presents definitions of the categories and examples of competencies from each.

Besides presenting the range of competencies, the 50-page document includes discussions of the principles of assessment in art, general guidelines, assessment design, and methods of information gathering. It is an important document not only for the art educators on the 19 campuses of California State University, but also for school people who may not be familiar with the current literature of art education and the changes that have been made in recent years in thinking about art teaching and the preparation of art teachers. Many generalist educators and administrators do not know what they might expect in their recently credentialed teachers or in which directions staff development programs might move. The competencies will be difficult to measure, perhaps as difficult as some of the more general characteristics that Lightfoot describes (qualities such as openness and willingness can be as elusive as empathy and understanding), but nevertheless the CSU list provides guidelines for securing evidence for assessment and processes for making judgments.

The NAEA List of Proficiencies

Art teachers themselves have defined good teaching and begun to establish standards through a list of proficiencies and behaviors only recently approved by the Delegates Assembly of the National Art Education Association (NAEA, 1990), a group that represents art teachers from across the United States. It is a heroic list of 75 items—grand, courageous, risky, and larger than life. A summary of the NAEA list can be found in Figure 6. 2. This list differs from the professors' list in both content and purpose. The sample competencies suggested by the CSU faculty are focused primarily on what teachers should know; the NAEA list is focused primarily on what teachers should know how to do. The professors suggest that the sample competencies may be useful as a basis for assessing the subject-matter knowledge, understanding, skills, and attitudes of prospective art teachers; the NAEA list is presented as a minimum set of proficiencies for all certified art teachers.

Figure 6.1 Selected Examples of Sample Competencies for the Assessment of Subject-Matter Competency of Prospective Art Teachers

Generic Competencies

Art teachers, like all others, must be prepared to teach beyond their subject matter. They must possess generic competencies which can be applied to the art classroom to help students to learn the general things which they must know, as well as to learn how the specific subject matter may be useful. The following understandings, skills, and values are deemed essential.

    1. Understandings (5 samples in original list)
- Understands that knowledge is not the mere accumulation of facts, but rather its coherence depends upon its organization in such structures as theory, metaphor, and paradigm.

    2. Skills (4 samples in original list)
- Expresses ideas in a variety of forms such as written, oral, symbolic, visual, mathematical, nonverbal.

    3. Thinking Skills (5 samples in original list)
- Recognizes biases and flaws in reasoning and knows how to formulate and justify a given position.

Art Competencies

Relationships

    It is expected that prospective art teachers will be able to see relationships between the areas of art, as well as to see connections with life and with other academic disciplines.
- Students will (8 samples in original list)

Understand how making and responding to art serve as ways of learning.

    I. Competencies in Art Production

    The making of art is concerned with the formal qualities of art, learning to focus on techniques of various media, and learning about art concepts rooted in historical precedent. Creating one's own art should focus on generating ideas and themes and then on integrating those ideas and themes with all that has already been learned about art.

    Students will (8 samples in original list)
- Demonstrate ability to choose a theme/idea and to create several art works expressing that theme/idea.

    II. Competencies in Art History

    The study of visual arts heritage is concerned with the recognition and formation of contexts for art. Such study focuses on the arts within a diverse set of cultural and historical contexts. In this sense, culture means the shared values, attitudes, and beliefs of particular groups of people. Through study of visual arts heritage one gains insights into the process of cultural transmission and the human condition across time, as these are related to the arts.

    Students will (6 samples, each with 2 further definitions in original list)
- Possess knowledge of historical and cultural methodologies and strategies of inquiry in the visual arts.

Figure 6.1 Continued

1. Recognize different strategies of inquiry into the arts developed and utilized by historians, anthropologists, psychologists, and sociologists.
2. Demonstrate ability to use historical, ethnographic, and other sociocultural methods of inquiry to examine art and the societies that produced it (investigation of primary and secondary sources such as documents, interviews, video tapes, diaries, photography, audio recordings, etc.).

III. Competencies in Art Criticism

Art criticism refers to oral and written communication of reasoned opinions and interpretations regarding analysis, evaluation, or appreciation of works of art. The critic makes careful judgments regarding the merits and defects of works of art, remembering that works of art lend themselves to multiple interpretations, that there is no single correct judgment of a work of art, and that boundaries of art are continually expanding in response to opportunities presented by new technology and changing cultures. Art criticism is concerned with the following issues: the value of the work of art, the truth of the work of art, the interpretation of the work of art, the technique of the work of art, and the appreciation of the work of art.

Students will: (7 samples in original list)

• Talk or write about the form and content of works of art using contemporary theories of art and criticism to explain meanings and expressive qualities.

IV. Competencies in Aesthetics

Philosophy of art refers to writings about the nature of art and related concepts such as aesthetic perception and aesthetic valuing. Philosophy of art encompasses a process of critical inquiry in which questions are more important than answers, the search more important than the goal. Philosophers of art explore five major questions: what is art, what is artistic creation, what is aesthetic experience, what is art criticism, and what is the relation of art to other values in a society or culture?

Students will: (5 samples in original list)

• Express openness to varied aesthetic attitudes and willingness to both reflect on and question aesthetic theories.

Note: Excerpts from the *Resource Guide: Subject Matter Assessment of Prospective Art Teachers,* 1989, Los Angeles: California State University. Used by permission.

The range of proficiencies and behaviors in the NAEA list goes beyond Wilson's list. According to the practitioners, art teachers not only provide for Wilson's theater, they produce the show (participate in school budget negotiations), sweep the theater (clean up), and sit on the arts commission (advocate for art education outside the school). The NAEA list is much broader than the professors' list, including such things as community service and professional responsibilities, but it does not include a category suggested by Lightfoot's work, one focusing on the understanding of individual students'

Figure 6.2 Summary of National Art Education Association Teacher Appraisal Committee List of Art Teacher Proficiencies and Behaviors That Could Be Monitored

All certified teachers can reasonably be expected to:

1. Possess comprehensive knowledge about all aspects of art education, including studio production, art history, art criticism, and aesthetics. Use written and graphic art vocabularies. Communicate to students the role of art in terms of life enrichment, careers, and cultural development of diverse societies, particularly those of the students and themselves.
2. Demonstrate an understanding of the artistic development and function of art in the creative and mental growth of the students.
3. Develop plans and course outlines that provide regular, sequential instruction aligned with district and/or state documents employing texts, reference sets, outside resources, and other exemplary curricula. Update lessons, media, and curricula to improve instruction from year to year.
4. Present varied approaches to teaching: encouraging the production of original and imaginative works of art through both traditional and experimental means, and providing for guided and independent practice and inquiry, as well as opportunities for creative process/activity.
5. Ensure that students' tasks are congruent with the objective of a unit or lesson. State objectives and their importance clearly and completely, maintain focus on major objectives/concepts.
6. Present precise and comprehensive information and directions for assignments in a logical, sequential order in a variety of modes: demonstrations, oral, written, and visual examples.
7. Adjust and monitor delivery systems as needed to maintain a high degree of student success: involving students in discussions, adjusting systems to all types of learners, checking students' levels of understanding before setting them to task.
8. Provide meaningful feedback to students as to their measure of success: providing an atmosphere conducive to learning and assessing degrees of success in positive ways, including regular exhibitions of their projects.
9. Attend to classroom management of supplies, provide adequate time for activity and clean-up, provide storage for student work. Establish and enforce classroom rules, including those relating to noise and safety.
10. Assist in community activities that benefit the art program and school: student art shows, service to museums, field trips, artists-in-schools, legislative action, etc.
11. Maintain involvement in current developments in the field through activities such as writing articles, texts, and curriculum materials, reading professional journals, taking graduate courses, professional memberships, and advocacy.
12. Participate in and contribute to the art education profession, through such activities as supervising intern teachers, attending professional meetings, giving workshops, and fundraising.

Note: Summary of National Art Education Association's *Teacher appraisal committee list of art teacher proficiencies and behaviours that could be monitored,* 1990. Used by permission.

lives and the context of their own school. Perhaps in a revised and re-summarized list, a new item 11 might read: "Demonstrate an understanding of and empathy for students' lives outside the classroom, the cultural heritage of the community, and specific characteristics of their own school."

The NAEA list of proficiencies and behaviors is prefaced with a statement suggesting its use. It was not intended that the proficiencies and behaviors on the list become an absolute mandate to state educational and/or governmental agencies or that all behaviors listed must be adopted in their appraisal devices. Rather, the list is intended to be a resource from which agencies can author their own list of behaviors that all certified art teachers should be able to demonstrate. The criteria suggested by the list should suit the unique needs of states/provinces and/or local school districts. It is, however, the feeling of the Teacher Appraisal Committee that the behaviors listed constitute a minimum set of proficiencies that all certified art teachers can reasonably be expected to perform (NAEA, 1990, p. 1).

Others have offered sets of criteria that bridge the CSU and NAEA lists of competencies and behaviors. Based on a report prepared to define guiding principles for the Connecticut Competency Instrument by Armour-Thomas, Saunders (1989) has developed a set of criteria for beginning art teachers that provides basic standards for art classroom management, instruction, and student assessment. It provides concrete standards for art teaching that are clear and general enough to be used by evaluators with little specialized training in art. Professors of art and education develop their own sets of criteria for making judgments of student success through the establishment of course requirements. All of these criteria, listed in course outlines and syllabi, serve to further define the nature and activities of art teaching and suggest standards.

Problems with Checklists

Problems exist, however, with lists such as those described above. Imagine that the NAEA list became a checklist. Would it be reasonable to think that a good art teacher would receive a check for every one of the 75 items on the original list? Suppose the checklist included a scale of from 1 to 5, with 5 being a top rating for each item on the list. Would it be reasonable to expect that a good art teacher would receive a score of 375, or top rating on each item? And how would one determine what constituted a score of 5 on an item? What concrete evidence would have to be found in order to award a score of 5? And could one believe that the list of 75 items was complete and that all were valid measures of good teaching? What aspects have been left out of the list? Eisner (1979, 1982, 1985) has written convincingly over the years on the need for artistic approaches to evaluation and its partner, supervision. He constantly reminds us that lists, scores, averages, and the like, rooted in scientific approaches to evaluation, may not be entirely appropriate for evaluating an enterprise that seems to be more like an art than a science and ought to be evaluated as such.

DEVELOPMENT OF EFFECTIVE EVALUATION PROGRAMS

As not-to-be-checked lists, however, the CSU and NAEA lists and others have a great deal of value, primarily as focus and direction for the initiation of communications among and between teachers and schools. Wise, Darling-Hammond, McLaughlin, and Bernstein (1985) point out that programs for teacher evaluation can provide major communication links between school systems and teachers by identifying concepts of teaching and framing the conditions for their work, as well as structuring, managing, and rewarding the work of teachers. In their study of effective practices in teacher evaluation, they identified four conceptions of teaching and school organization with re-lated approaches to evaluation: as labor, as craft, as profession, and as art. Let's look at these conceptions with the CSU and NAEA lists in mind.

The first conception is teaching as labor. Standards for effective teaching as labor are concretely determined and specified. A supervisor (school admin-istrator) helps the teacher implement the art program in a prescribed manner, adhering to specific routines and procedures. Following standard practice in instructional supervision, the teacher and his or her supervisor confer to es-tablish goals and to identify or devise new strategies. The supervisor observes the teacher in his or her classroom, and they meet later to discuss the teacher's success in meeting the established goals (Drake, 1984). In a supervisory situa-tion, the CSU and NAEA lists could provide starting points for discussion and for the determination and specification of goals.

Conceptions of teaching as craft bring a need for specialized skills and general rules for their application. Teachers are expected to exercise their craft without detailed instructions or close supervision. The principal is a manager who hires teachers with requisite skills and holds them to general performance standards. Preservice preparation and certification are central in conceptions of teaching as craft. Certification, offered through state stan-dards, National Council for Accreditation of Teacher Education standards, and National Association of State Directors of Teacher Education and Certi-fication standards, promises that beginning teachers come to the job with the basic skills and knowledge they will need. Those involved in the design and implementation of certification programs could learn from the CSU and NAEA lists just what skills need to be included in those programs if new teachers are to perform as craftspersons.

Conceptions of teaching as a profession ask that teachers have not only the special skills of teaching as a craft, but also the capacity to make judgments about when the skills should be applied. In distinguishing between craft and profession, Wise and colleagues quote Broudy: "We ask the professional to diagnose difficulties, appraise solutions, and to choose among them. We ask him to take total responsibility for both strategy and tactic. . . . From the craftsman, by contrast, we expect a standard diagnosis, correct performance of procedures, and nothing else" (1956, p. 182). In this context, the CSU and NAEA lists could become a tool for use by teachers in evaluating themselves and their peers as professionals, providing guidelines for the professional development of standards of knowledge and practice.

As an art, teaching might or might not resemble the picture presented by the CSU and NAEA lists. Teaching as an art would require a repertoire of competencies, proficiencies, and skills, but the inclusion of specific items on the list in any one situation would depend on a teacher's insight and imagination, applied in that situation with specific students. As an art, teaching will probably not follow carefully prescribed procedures, but rather yield loosely knit patterns of instructional strategies and student activities, edited and revised to fit the context. The school administrator is seen as both a connoisseur and critic—one who knows about and appreciates good art teaching and is able to help the teacher see what he or she is doing in the classroom, both good and not-so-good (Eisner, 1985). Options and directions for change are up to the teacher as artist. In this context, the CSU and NAEA lists would be useful for directing the perception of evaluators as they look at the range of the characteristics of good teaching in art.

The NAEA list, used not as a checklist, but as a tool for assessment across conceptions of teaching and evaluation, is a most interesting document in that it reveals art teachers' conceptions of themselves. It says, "Here is what we know and do and are willing to be held accountable for." It is not only interesting, but also critically important in the real world of the evaluation of art teaching, for in the real context of schools art teachers are often responsible for their own evaluation. In a booklet of contributions from experienced art teachers to introduce new teachers to the field, Brouch and Funk (1987) suggest that teachers

> Take five or ten minutes at the end of each day to sit back, put your feet up and reflect upon what good things happened to you as a teacher and for the learners you are entrusted to teach. Admit to any failings and think about how you will avoid them in the future. . . . If you have done something exceptionally well, give yourself a giant pat on the back and permit a broad smile of accomplishment. Repeat such goodness frequently. (p. 30)

This gentle suggestion is based on Brouch and Funk's understanding of the contexts of schools in which teachers find that the responsibility for reflecting on their teaching, establishing a system for making change, and providing rewards rests primarily on their own shoulders.

Even in the best of schools, principals readily admit that they have little time to spend evaluating good teachers and that they know little about the teaching of art as a discipline. They do know about teaching in general, however, and rely on their knowledge of and standards for good teaching in general in evaluating art teachers rather than on specific standards for art teaching. They do this based on their best guess that teachers who meet high standards and values of good teaching in general will provide effective instruction in art. Moreover, in the context of the best schools neither summative nor formative evaluation takes place with a great deal of frequency. In a large urban school district in California, the teachers' legal contract with the school district specifies that every probationary teacher is to be evaluated by his or her immediate supervisor in writing once a year, and every permanent teacher every 2 years. Every other year may be enough if evaluation is seen as summative and valuable primarily in maintaining files for personnel decisions. Current literature on evaluation, however, suggests that evaluation can and should play a central role in staff development and as such ought to happen more often than once every year or two. Although standard practice in teacher evaluation, moving in a staff development direction includes a preobservation conference between the evaluator and the teacher, a classroom observation, a written classroom performance report, and a postobservation supervisory conference, such a system does not offer teachers much help or provide a great deal of information to administrators.

Following a discussion of the role criticism might play in the evaluation of teaching as an art, Eisner (1985) describes the distance between the practice of educational criticism and the ways teachers are typically evaluated: The vast majority of teachers have nothing like such (critical) feedback. Most of us try to learn about teaching in the reflections we find in our students' eyes. We sometimes make inferences from their casual remarks or from remarks sometimes made in anger. We reflect on our teaching walking home after class or rehearse before entering it, but basically we conduct our teaching alone. Few of us ever receive reflective, competent educational criticism about that portion of our professional lives in which we engage so often and from which we seek so much satisfaction. As a result, most of us are only partially aware of our strengths as teachers and, perhaps more important, what we do that interferes with our teaching.

The distance between ideals and actual practice in evaluation ought not be ignored. Teachers welcome the kind of interest and attention that Eisner and others describe in the literature on educational criticism. Although many studies show that a lack of specific supervision contributes to low morale, teacher absenteeism, and high faculty turnover, teachers rarely receive more than general comments about their performance in the classroom (Bennett, 1987). Good teaching in art deserves more.

CONCLUSIONS

So what can be done? What is good practice in evaluation in general and what are the implications for evaluating the teaching of art? In their study of teacher evaluation practices, Wise and colleagues (1985) have come to a set of general conclusions and recommendations for evaluating teaching. Their definition of successful programs for the evaluation of teaching is the one adopted as a central premise in this paper: that successful programs for evaluation provide a major communication link between the school system and teachers. On the one hand, it imparts concepts of teaching to teachers and frames the conditions of their work. On the other hand, it helps the school system structure, manage, and reward the work of teachers. Building on their work, I offer a few specific suggestions for developing programs for evaluating the teaching of art.

1. *To succeed, a teacher evaluation system must suit the educational goals, management style, conception of teaching, and community values of the school district.* Wise and colleagues suggest that

> A school district that values uniformity of instruction and emphasizes standardized testing as the measure of goal attainment should not adopt a teacher evaluation process that allows multiple definitions of teaching success. A district that values multiple outcomes of teaching and learning should not use standardized test scores for evaluating teachers. (p. 103)

They recommend that schools not simply adopt an evaluation system because it works for other schools. They also recommend that states not impose highly prescriptive teacher evaluation requirements.

Reflecting on the teaching of art, it seems that schools should examine the differences in goals, styles, conceptions, and values within a school, across subject areas and among those teaching in one subject area as well. Traditionally, multiple outcomes and definitions of success have been valued by art educators, and although the current literature in the field suggests movements toward more structured, discipline-based instruction, a variety of approaches exist in schools, taught well by good teachers, often in adjacent classrooms. Even in schools in which art teachers base their programs on specific district or state guidelines, a wide range of approaches to the implementation of those guidelines can be found. If one of the primary values of evaluation is to initiate programs for teacher change and growth, it would seem important at least to begin evaluation processes with consideration and respect for the whole "jumble." In districts that value uniformity, formal programs for evaluation of art teaching may need to be limited to judgments of good teaching in general, with informal celebrations of differences. In districts that value multiple outcomes, the evaluation of art teaching can go beyond generalities to focus on specific and perhaps unique combinations of activities resulting from individual teachers' choices of content and methodology.

2. *Top-level commitment to and resources for evaluation outweigh checklists and procedures.* Wise and colleagues found that successful programs of evaluation are "distinguished by their seriousness of purpose and intensity of implementation" (p. 120). They recommend that:

1. Districts provide time for evaluators to make reliable and valid judgments and to offer assistance
2. The quality of evaluation itself be assessed
3. Evaluators be trained in observation and evaluation techniques

Simply finding the right checklist is not the answer. Although checklists such as those provided by the NAEA and CSU can focus discussion and provide for shared understandings of criteria, evaluation provides opportunities for discussion to go far beyond sets of criteria. Judgments of good teaching in art involve considerations of varied approaches to art teaching and the actual context of the school—the people, structures, relationships, ideology, goals, intellectual substance, motivation, and will (Lightfoot, 1983). Evaluators of art teaching will need observational skills and time to discuss teaching assumptions and contextual variations. They will probably need to visit classrooms more than once every other year.

3. *The school district must decide the main purpose of its teacher evaluation system and then match the process to the purpose.* The purposes of evaluation range from the making of judgments leading to personnel decisions such as the elimination of incompetent teachers and the identification of master teachers (summative) to the gathering of data and setting of goals to be used in staff development programs (formative). The case studies conducted by Wise and colleagues reinforce conclusions that a single evaluation process can serve only one goal well. Assuming the position that most teachers are competent and pose no problems, the National Association of Elementary School Principals (1988) suggests that evaluation processes "should be fashioned not to winnow out deadwood but to build on the foundation of skills that teachers already possess" (p. 6). The Association recognizes, however, that schools and

principals have a legal responsibility for making and recording official indications of every teacher's level of performance. They, along with Wise and colleagues (1985) and McGreal (1983), suggest that processes of evaluation designed to yield performance ratings be separated from those designed to guide programs for staff development.

The identification of the purposes of evaluation and possible separation of processes would be especially valuable in the evaluation of art teaching. Acheson (1985) suggested that the kinds of goals that teachers set in negotiation with the administrators who make personnel decisions, were "safe" goals rather than goals that might make them vulnerable. This is a time of change in art education—in the past few years we have been asking art teachers to make changes and grow in rather "risky" ways.

The field is asking for more attention to multicultural concerns, for greater infusion of art history and criticism into studio courses, and for substantial programs of student assessment. Separation of personnel decision making from the staff development process might make it possible for art teachers to initiate discussions of change and plans for growth in areas in which they feel less secure.

The establishment of more than one system of evaluation in a school district also would serve art education's need to identify and celebrate excellent teaching. Art teachers often report feeling isolated and undervalued by the larger school community. Our best teachers, inexperienced and seasoned, are often unsung heroes, reflecting alone on the goodness of their teaching, not really knowing what they are doing well or how they could become even better. Wise and colleagues point out the differences in staff needed if schools are to identify their very best teachers.

> The evaluation of excellent teaching, we believe, requires judgments by experts rather than by generalists.
>
> Whereas principals can evaluate for performance improvement (where the need for reliability is relatively low) and can evaluate for termination decisions (where the criteria are the least common denominators of teaching), the judgment of excellence requires an expert. Excellent teaching, we submit, cannot be judged in the abstract as is generic teaching competence. To judge excellence, an evaluator must know the subject matter, grade level, and teaching context of the teacher being evaluated. (p. 108)

Judgments of excellence call for skilled art teacher/evaluators and multiple samples of teaching. They also call for processes of evaluation separate from those designed to identify incompetence.

4. *To sustain resource commitments and political support, teacher evaluation must be seen to have utility, which, in turn, depends on the efficient use of resources to*

achieve reliability, validity, and cost-effectiveness. The actions of the NAEA Teacher Appraisal Committee (NAEA, 1990) came in response to public demands for accountability, for a more fully developed sense of professionalism among teachers, for higher standards for entry and more substance in teacher training programs, and for reforms in certification and teacher evaluation. Acknowledging a general lack of expertise in art education on the part of educational and governmental decision makers, art teachers have recognized the need to assume responsibility for the investigation of these issues and especially teacher evaluation throughout the country and to provide support for changes.

Their work is the result of a collective resolve to provide access to materials and information that will assist educators in the development and implementation of programs designed for the evaluation of art teaching. It is only beginning, however.

Wise and colleagues found that for a teacher evaluation system to be useful to the district and credible to teachers, administrators, and the community, it needed to offer plausible solutions to the major perceived problems or needs of the teaching force. So far, the NAEA efforts have produced only a set of criteria for good teaching, but perhaps that is all that a national organization ought to do. We have seen how the NAEA list (and others) could be used in a variety of ways, depending on differing conceptions of teaching, and we have seen that different programs of evaluation can serve different purposes. To be useful, evaluation programs need to be designed for local needs. They must have utility and efficiency in the local context.

5. *Teacher involvement and responsibility improve the quality of teacher evaluation.* If any evaluation is to be successful, all participants must share understandings of the criteria and processes involved and a sense that these criteria capture the most important aspects of teaching. Evaluators need a knowledge of the subject matter, an understanding of appropriate instructional strategies, an ability to understand and interpret student behavior, a sensitivity to individual teachers, and recognition of suitable outcomes or goals (Acheson, 1985). Many administrators have little knowledge about the specifics of art teaching. As in other areas, art teachers can bring their specialized knowledge of art and of the teaching of art to the design of programs of evaluation and staff development. Teacher involvement throughout the process of evaluation is especially important in the evaluation of art teaching for another reason. Neither the activities nor the results of good art teaching are predictable. Natriello (1983) found that, although teachers' acceptance of evaluations is significantly less when their teaching is characterized as being more complex and less predictable than that of others, when the teachers had a hand in designing and implementing the process of evaluation, their views of evaluations

improved. Teachers in an area as complex and unpredictable as art need to feel that they have had some influence in the evaluation of their teaching if they are to place any value on their own participation or its outcomes.

It is desirable for school districts to involve expert teachers in the supervision and assistance of their peers and for teacher organizations to be involved in the designing and overseeing of evaluation (Wise et al., 1985). Traditional hierarchical evaluation practices, often adversarial, are giving way to more participatory approaches in which administrators and teachers share not only power but also opportunities to improve the quality of teaching. It is time to attend to the complexities of evaluation, to employ methods that best suit the arts, and to join forces as researchers, teachers, and administrators in assuming responsibility for the evaluation of art teaching in the context of schools.

REFERENCES

Acheson, K. (1985). The principal's role in instructional leadership. *Oregon School Study Council Bulletin, 28* (8), 1–25.

Arnheim, R. (1990). *Thoughts on art education* (Occasional paper series, Vol. 2). Los Angeles: Getty Center for Education in the Arts.

Bennett, W. J. (1987). *What works: Research about teaching and learning* (2nd ed.). Washington, DC: United States Department of Education.

Berliner, D. C. (1987). Simple views of effective teaching and a simple theory of classroom instruction. In D. C. Berliner & R. V. Rosenshine (Eds.), *Talks to teachers* (pp. 93–110). New York: Random House.

Brouch, V. M., & Funk, F. F. (Eds.). (1987). *Appleseeds: For beginning art teachers.* Reston, VA: National Art Education Association.

Broudy, H. S. (1956). Teaching—Craft or profession? *Educational Forum, 20,* 175–184.

California State University Working Group on Assessment of Prospective Art Teachers. (1989). *Resource guide: Subject matter assessment of prospective art teachers* (R. D. Reeser, Chair). Los Angeles: California State University.

Drake, J. M. (1984, February). *Improving teacher performance through evaluation and supervision.* Paper presented at the annual meeting of the National Association of Secondary School Principals, Las Vegas.

Eisner, E. W. (1979). *The educational imagination.* New York: Macmillan.

Eisner, E. W. (1982). An artistic approach to supervision. In T. J. Sergiovanni (Ed.), *Supervision of teaching.* 1982 Yearbook of the Association for Supervision and Curriculum Development (pp. 53–66). Washington, DC: ASCD.

Eisner, E. W. (1985). *The art of educational evaluation: A personal view.* London: Falmer.

Flinders, D. J. (1989). *Voices from the classroom: Educational practice can inform policy.* Eugene, OR: ERIC Clearinghouse on Educational Management.

Gardner, H. (1989). Zero-based arts education: An introduction to ARTS PROPEL. *Studies in Art Education, 30*(2), 71–83.

Gray, J. U., & MacGregor, R. N. (1986). *Personally relevant observations about art concepts and teaching activities.* Unpublished manuscript, University of British Columbia, Department of Visual and Performing Arts in Education, Vancouver.

Lehman, P. R. (1988). *What students should learn in the arts.* 1988 Yearbook of the Association of Supervision and Curriculum Development (pp. 109–131). Washington, DC: ASCD.

Lightfoot, S. L. (1983). *The good high school.* New York: Basic Books.

McGreal, T. L. (1983). *Successful teacher evaluation.* Alexandria, VA: Association for Supervision and Curriculum Development.

National Art Education Association. (1990). *Suggested certified art teacher appraisal model* (W. D. Smith, Chair). Unpublished manuscript, Teacher Appraisal Committee, NAEA, Reston, VA.

National Association of Elementary School Principals. (1988). *Effective teachers: Effective evaluation in America's elementary and middle schools.* Alexandria, VA: Author.

Natriello, G. (1983). *Evaluation frequency, teacher influence, and the internalization of evaluation processes: A review of six studies using the theory of evaluation and authority* (Final Report). Eugene, OR: Center for Educational Policy and Management.

Price-Richard, M. J. (1989). *Art education: Certification and teacher education.* Unpublished manuscript, Getty Center for Education in the Arts, Los Angeles.

Saunders, R. J. (1989). How to select an effective art teacher. *NASSP Bulletin, 73*(517), 54–60.

Wiggins, G. (1989). A true test: Toward more authentic and equitable assessment. *Phi Delta Kappan, 70*(9), 703–713.

Wilson, B. (1985, May). Evaluating teaching in the arts: Scenes from a complex drama. In D. W. Baker (Comp.), *Teachers in the arts: Proceedings of a national symposium* (pp. 85–101). Louisiana State University, Baton Rouge.

Wise, A. E., Darling-Hammond, L., McLaughlin, M. W., & Bernstein, H. T. (1985). Teacher evaluation: A study of effective practices. *The Elementary School Journal, 86*(1), 103–121.

Improving the Quality of Art Teaching

RACHEL MASON
Roehampton Institute, London, UK

The following is a response to papers by the American art educators, Elliot Eisner and Pam Sharp El Shayeb. The theme these authors addressed was the evaluation of art teaching. Both papers fell into the theory rather than the practice end of the continuum in that they discussed particular models of evaluation rather than practical prescriptions for use in specific art educational contexts. Whereas both writers rejected the possibility that objective tests and/or measurements can be indicators of effective art teaching, and both opted for qualitative evaluation methods and outcomes, their papers had little else in common. Eisner's paper restated his well-known principles of educational criticism, which he understands as a form of educational evaluation and has developed over the years, and Sharp El Shayeb found some constructive educational uses for the competency model of evaluation, which is being discussed as an approach to dealing with standards for entry into the profession at the present time in both the United States and the United Kingdom.

The response that follows is informed by my personal experience working in art teacher education in a different national system from that of the authors. The first part, which is a response to Eisner, takes the form of a critique of his principles of educational evaluation arising from experiments with it in graduate courses for practicing teachers studying for an advanced degree in art and design education (master of arts) in the UK. The second part, which is a response to Sharp El Shayeb, takes account of her constructive proposals for using lists of competencies to improve the quality of art teaching in general but is an argument against the use of the competency model of evaluation per se. Admittedly, Sharp El Shayeb also rejected this model, but the references to it in her paper touched a raw nerve at a particular point of time in the history of education in the UK when a reflective practitioner model of teacher education was losing ground to the competency model mandated by the central government.

CONNOISSEURSHIP AND CRITICISM

Elliot Eisner's paper restates and enlarges upon his conception of evaluation of teaching as connoisseurship and criticism, which he has promoted consistently over the years. My understanding of the aims, methods, and outcomes is as follows.

An evaluator's role is that of an educator who helps other teachers to grow and get better at what they do. The method is similar to that used in anthropology. An evaluator negotiates entry into the subculture of a school to observe a teacher and collects ethnographic data. On leaving the field, he or she constructs an ethnographic account of life in a classroom, which is humanistic rather than scientific (Edgerton & Langness, 1974) in that it can be highly symbolic, metaphorical, or personal. Here the similarity to anthropology ends. Because the evaluator is, or should be, a connoisseur of the educational action observed, and because evaluation hinges on interpretive judgments about that action's educational worth, the analysis of fieldwork data is closer to literary criticism. The outcome of an evaluation is a written report that is useful because it provides a means to re-educate the perception of the teacher's work and of the classroom in which it appears. In addition, it assists policy makers in securing a more complex and authentic picture of the schools their policies influence.

Eisner's tendency to "aestheticize curriculum thinking" has been roundly attacked by education theorists (Gibson, 1981; Kaelin, 1989; Smith, 1984). Since he offers his artistic perspectives rather than rules as tools for practitioners, I argue that they are no less pretentious than the suggestion that education should be viewed scientifically. His conceptual frameworks supply some valuable insights into evaluation of teaching, and I have made them the basis of some experiments with practicing teachers of art and design. This response to his paper will focus on issues arising out of these experiments.

Experimenting with Educational Criticism

The teachers with whom I worked were bemused by the idea that teaching could be anything other than art, or that evaluation could be quantitative. I put this down to the fact that industrialization is a very recent trend in British public education and the application of so-called scientific management techniques is only just being introduced; also to an anti-intellectualism that characterizes British art and design (Allison, 1986). The teachers I work with differ from American colleagues since they are unlikely to have been subjected to standardized tests either in school or during initial teacher training and would not know how to produce such tests if required.

Second, they are enthusiastic about educational criticism but have difficulty implementing it. The fieldwork aspect is no obstacle. Once Eisner's conceptual framework has been explained, they experience very little difficulty selecting particular educational actions as a focus for investigation, establishing the necessary rapport with teacher-practitioners and negotiating entry into schools; once inside schools they proceed with alacrity to uncover and amass "ethnographic data." But they find writing reports extremely problematic. I propose to consider Eisner's four dimensions of educational criticism separately at this point, bearing in mind that in actual practice they overlap.

1. *Description.* Educational criticism hinges on the construction of dramatic expressive portrayals of educational events that aim both to convey a sense of place and action and to draw attention to pedagogically important features. An evaluation report should be couched in qualitative language and emphasize literary qualities (i.e., be metaphorical and imaginative). It should invite readers to participate vicariously in the situation observed. The art and design teachers I work with experience extreme difficulty constructing vivid images with words. In my opinion, this reflects the poor quality of English language and literature instruction provided in schools and, also, the enormous hold that technocratic or instrumentalist thinking now has on ordinary language in everyday life. Training in literary writing is clearly a prerequisite for educational criticism, and yet it is not a part of my professional responsibility.

2. *Interpretation.* Eisner says this aspect of criticism involves accounting for what one has given an account of; this necessitates knowledge of theoretical perspectives. This is a very real problem. Pedagogy has always been less popular in the United Kingdom than in other European countries. But the scholarly function of education departments in universities and polytechnics has been eroded recently by national directives for teacher accreditation, and courses in "educational foundations" have virtually disappeared. Teachers cannot apply theory to educational criticism unless they know it, but the antitheoretical nature of British teacher training has resulted in a largely pragmatic approach.

3. *Evaluation.* This is where curriculum criticism differs most from anthropology, since it necessitates the connoisseur bringing to bear on the events in question values that he or she thinks are justifiable. The values of the teachers being observed must be taken into account too, but the evaluator's values should prevail in the appraisal and formulation of judgments about an event's educational worth. Arguments must justify the judgments with regard to particular educational value orientations and must be grounded clearly.

   Being in touch with one's inner self is fundamental to this kind of critical exercise, but the teachers I work with find it difficult to allow subjectivity a central role in evaluation and research. They are by no means "passionless persons" entirely submersed in the daily round (Greene, 1978), yet they feel powerless; they do not appear to have a sense of constituting the world they inhabit through the interpretations they adopt or can make for themselves. Greene has written about the need to cultivate "wide awakeness" in teachers. She argues that because teachers are living beings, they suffer objectification like other members of the society; they also are thrust into molds. They play roles defined by others, although their interpretations of these roles must in some manner be grounded in an understanding of themselves. Again, committed rationality also rests on the capacity for self-reflection. Boredom, lassitude, automatism, abstractness; all these erode self-awareness and the desire to make sense. It ought to be possible to bring teachers in touch with their own landscapes. The learning may become a process of the "I" meeting the "I."

4. *Thematics.* Thematics are defined by Eisner as "the articulation of thematic notions" or "naturalistic generalizations" that occur as a consequence of the critic accumulating descriptive evidence and making evaluative judgments. This is a tough nut to crack and one with which I have wrestled for years with reference to phenomenological theory. Granted, phenomenological descriptions are not the same as ethnographic descriptions. Van Manen (1984), for example, says they can be thematic, exegetical, existential, or exemplicative and are likely to involve the researcher in varying examples so that the invariant characteristics of the phenomena come into view. But they deal with a logic of inference that is comparative rather than classificatory, so similar principles must apply. Most important, the patterns and structures (themes) of classroom life that Smith (1984) has noted are "the real heroes" of Eisner's approach, cannot be extracted unless an evaluator is prepared to ask questions and push description to exhaustive levels.

Concerns About Educational Criticism

Next I raise some general concerns about the aims, methods, and outcomes of educational criticism. First, the potential of written evaluation for assisting policy making is limited in educational systems in which administrators and teachers are overwhelmed by paperwork. Since the teachers I work with observe administrators affording higher priority to judgments communicated orally, those teachers question whether written criticism is necessary at all.

To date, I have responded by arguing that the notion of "fixing human action through inscription" (Ricoeur, 1979, p. 75) is central to educational criticism as it is to phenomenological method. Constructing written texts is important because it marks educational events and actions and detaches them from their agents. In doing so, it opens them up to an infinite range of possible interpretations and allows them to develop consequences of their own.

Second, I have some concerns about the exemplars of curriculum criticism that are available to student evaluators in the literature. From my phenomenological perspective the majority are too instrumentalist. They reflect the mistaken tendency of critics to see art as an object not work, and their failure to understand meaning as something that arises in a relationship (Palmer, 1969). I want to argue that evaluators cannot understand classroom events so long as they assume moral superiority and ask all the questions. In addition, the majority of the exemplars are too opaque. Eisner's *Educational Imagination* (1985) includes the following brief commentary on research method:

> In doing educational criticism, an individual typically makes contact with a school—usually a classroom teacher but at times the principal—explains what we are doing at Stanford, and tries to find out if there are teachers in the school who might find feedback on their own teaching useful. If such a teacher is found the person functioning as an educational critic will arrange to visit that classroom for an extended period of time, in some cases on a daily basis for two or three weeks. During these visits the educational critic will directly observe what goes on. Sometimes the educational critic will talk to a teacher to try to find out what kind of information the teacher wants, in which case a part of what the critic would do is observe in light of the teacher's needs. Most of the time, however, the critic allows the emerging conditions of the classroom to suggest what might be important in this classroom and from such observations constructs a theme or focus for critical description. (p. 228)

What I miss in this and many examples of educational criticism is detailed discussion of how negotiation takes place and, more important, how teachers respond.

Third, is educational criticism democratic? Feminist evaluators (e.g., Kirkup, 1986) have raised the question about power and politics in evaluation research. They stress the need for democratic evaluations that provide an information service to the whole community (sometimes referred to as "an honest broker model") and insist that an evaluator has no right to promote personal values and choose which educational ideology she regards as legitimate.

Fourth, there is a problem with the self-centered narcissistic tone and grandiloquent writing style that are problematic in many examples of educational criticism (Gibson, 1981). Should I encourage British teachers to strain after equivalent kinds of qualitative literary effects, given that they lack the necessary writing skills and appear ignorant of educational theory? Perhaps

Smith (1984) was right when he advised evaluators to aim for simple pragmatic reports written in clear, precise prose rather than imaginative impressionistic accounts.

Finally, Willis (1978) has distinguished between aesthetic, personal, and political dimensions of curriculum criticism. How can the necessary balance be achieved?

Contribution of Educational Criticism

In raising the above questions about democracy, authenticity, and descriptive-interpretative writing in Eisner's model of educational evaluation, it is not my intention to deny its significant contribution to theory and practice in the field. On the contrary, my experiments have convinced me that its fundamental premises are correct. Namely, that art educators do experience their classroom teaching as "art," do feel isolated in their classrooms, and can learn from informal evaluative feedback about it from art education critics who are able to establish the necessary climate of trust and mutual respect. (However, as I have said, I think we need more examples in the literature of how negotiation and feedback actually take place.)

My experiments have shown that the ability to use reflective tools to reconstruct personal meaning in narrative form does not come easily to wouldbe art education critics. Likewise, the skills Connelly and Clandinin (1988) point out are needed to relate theory and practice to the everyday domains of the practitioner and theoretician worlds, the domain of theory used by practitioners, and the domain of personal experience are not readily acquired. Where an act of criticism is performed and communicated informally within a classroom, its idiosyncratic, aesthetic nature is less problematic in that the teacher being evaluated can choose whether or not to accept the outcome. Where such a criticism is articulated in writing to a wider public, it takes on new political and social meanings. Moreover, if educational criticism is as good or bad as the critic who performs it, the critic whose mind is impoverished or who has limited perspectives is no good to anyone. Therefore, my concerns about "wide awakeness," "resistance to theory," and "qualitative writing style" are crucial methodological issues.

EXPLORING STRATEGIES TO DEFINE GOOD ART TEACHING

Sharp El Shayeb begins with some general questions about good art teaching. Then, evaluation of art teaching in schools is selected as a focus.

The ensuing discussion is stronger on strategies for identifying good art teaching than on "images" and "celebration."

The definition of the process of evaluation in the introduction is revealing in that it omits any mention of interpretation. After acknowledging that evaluation occurs in different contexts and is administered by different personnel, she identifies communication as a common purpose of evaluation, and professional growth as the outcome of good communication.

The first part of Sharp El Shayeb's paper includes a review of recent research into good teaching with particular reference to art. Objective tests and/or measurements of student outcomes or teachers' subject knowledge are quickly dismissed as indicators of effective teaching. We are referred to literature that stresses that good teaching is situationally determined and that good teachers demonstrate empathy with students as individuals and a concern for the students' growth and development in art and the school context. Further, art teachers' knowledge of their subject can be ascertained by witnessing their critiques of students' work.

Standards in Art Teaching

Next, Sharp El Shayeb introduces the concept of standards crucial to making judgments about teachers' knowledge of teaching and art. Sharp El Shayeb admits that these are dependent on an evaluator's concept of art education. Sharp El Shayeb comments on Wilson's (1985) view of the purposes and content of art education. For Wilson, the purposes are to assist students in understanding, constructing, and working in symbolic worlds. The content is media, tools, forming processes, composition, subject matter, art forms, cultural contexts, art theory, and art criticism. "Using the metaphor of teaching as theater, an art teacher writes a script, sets a stage, rehearses, speaks lines, acts parts and reviews the performance and production of a student cast" (p. 86).

Rubin (1985) has explored the metaphor of teaching as theater in depth and points out that knowledge of the script and routine performance skills are not enough. Good teachers always have an acting personality, or presence, that is "charismatic." They can manipulate a classroom's ambience to counter student fatigue; construct intrigues that sustain attention; devise instructional scenarios that arouse interest.

The point I am making, with reference to Rubin, is that good teachers do much more than merely carry out Wilson's basic theatrical tasks of, for example, preparing units, arranging the classroom, and presenting lessons. They can perform them with skill, dexterity, originality, and virtuosity. Wilson's and Rubin's views of teacher as performing artist relate to only one of four possible conceptions referred to later on. But the ambiguity surrounding the application of the term *good* and the curious reluctance to distinguish adequacy from excellence evidenced at this point are worrying features of the paper as a whole.

The CSU and NAEA Documents.   Sharp El Shayeb notes that Wilson's performance criteria are at odds with official documentation on standards for art teaching currently in vogue in the United States. Accordingly, she singles out two recent exemplars for detailed attention. The first is a set of sample subject competencies for students entering teaching, drawn up by a committee of professors at California State University (1989); the second, a list of minimum proficiencies for all certified art teachers, produced by teacher representatives of the National Art Education Association (1990).

While I appreciate the goodwill and effort applied to their construction and analysis, I am disappointed by the value-neutral, technical mode of conceptualizing art teaching. In particular, I am concerned by their preoccupation with specification of discrete units of teacher behaviors and base-level standards of efficiency. The CSU document has 50 pages and lists 14 generic competencies in three categories: understandings, communication and thinking skills, and values and attitudes. It has 34 art competencies categorized according to the familiar DBAE formula of art production, art history, art criticism, and aesthetics, together with an intriguing new "relationships between areas of art and connections with life and other disciplines." The NAEA document, which is described as "heroic" in conception, lists 75 minimum behaviors and focuses on what art teachers should be able to do in addition to what they should know.

While readers are warned that the competencies are impossible to measure, Sharp El Shayeb finds the CSU document useful as it reflects new developments in art education and helps generalist educators and administrators evaluate the work of both newly appointed and long-serving art teachers. The NAEA statement has more to offer the profession overall because its definition of the teacher's role is broader (it refers to understanding students' home and school contexts, for example) and it reveals art teachers' conceptions of themselves and of what they are willing to be held accountable for.

What I find surprising is the re-emergence of faith in the social efficiency model of improving teaching, given the competency-based teacher education (C/BPTE) movement's meager success in the past. A one-hour browse through an education library in a North American university last summer unearthed numerous teacher training texts dating from the late 1960s and early 1970s extolling the virtues of the competency approach. Historians of American education (e.g., Zeichner & Liston, 1990) have pointed out that it was the single most controversial trend in U.S. teacher education in this century and was afforded unprecedented attention in the professional literature and popular press, yet its effect on actual practice was minimal. Why are teachers colluding once again with a model of educational accountability that is prescriptive (Eisner, 1985), expects very little of them in the way of professional ingenuity, and grossly oversimplifies their work?

Application of Documents. Sharp El Shayeb speaks out against the use of the two checklists to score or measure art teaching proficiency, but insists they have great value as a focus and direction for the initiation of communication among and between teachers and school systems. Wise, Darling-Hammond, McLaughlin, and Bernstein's (1985) four conceptions of teaching and school organization and related approaches to evaluation as labor, craft, profession, and art help her explain why.

When teaching is seen as labor, checklists provide useful starting points for discussion at times when supervisors/school administrators and art teachers confer to establish goals or to make judgments about achieving these goals after classroom observations. When teaching is understood as craft, checklists are useful aids in the design and implementation of certification programs. When teaching is seen as profession, checklists are useful for teachers to evaluate themselves and their peers because they provide guidelines for the professional development of standards of knowledge and practice. When teaching is seen as art, checklists assist in directing evaluators/connoisseurs to perceive the range of characteristics of good teaching in art.

Pragmatism is all very well, but it has little to do with improving teaching quality. In his book called *Artistry in Teaching*, Rubin (1985) says that calls for standardization in teaching generally are linked with fears of underachievement. Notwithstanding instructional weaknesses in the (American) system, the answer is a reduction in attention to standard operating procedures and recipes for good teaching. He believes that the importance of standardization and method has been widely overstated and has resulted in listless rule following and lack of personal incentive on the part of teachers. Instead of focusing on standards, which are at the base level of teaching, his answer is to concentrate on excellence of "artistry."

Sharp El Shayeb's paper does not address the issue of "listless rule following." Instead, she promises increased commitment to and enthusiasm for evaluation on the part of teachers if the CSU and NAEA lists are used as tools for self-assessment and/or collaboratively in staff development. There are several points to be made concerning Sharp El Shayeb's original definition of the function and purposes of evaluation, particularly regarding her claims about its potential to increase communication between teachers and school districts and to encourage teachers' professional growth. First, the assertion that most teachers would welcome the chance to engage in self-evaluation with the assistance of a trusted connoisseur is probably correct; but few teachers I know would willingly award an administrator, or principal, the accolade "art connoisseur." Second, school-focused, collaborative evaluation schemes such as the IT-INSET programs pioneered in the United Kingdom recently (Everton & Impey, 1989) have shown that partnership approaches to classroom evaluation can improve the quality of teaching and learning where inservice and initial teacher education are combined. Nevertheless, my experience in assisting art teachers in self-assessment during a national curriculum development project (Mason, 1990) taught me that they are extremely wary of external evaluators whose experience and training in evaluation and research methods is slight and whose resistance to accountability is strong. Ownership of evaluation outcomes is a further problem. Whereas art teachers may evaluate for professional growth within the privacy of their classrooms and engage in the necessary self-critical discussion about their work with trusted individuals, once evaluation goes public, they view its function as self-promotion (i.e., propaganda), in the British education context at least!

Critique of Sharp El Shayeb's Conclusions

Some but not all the above points are from the conclusion to Sharp El Shayeb's paper, in which five principles for evaluating art teaching are identified. They are:

1. To succeed, a teacher evaluation system must suit the educational goals, management style, conception of teaching, and values of the school district.
2. Top-level commitment to and resources for evaluation outweigh checklists.
3. A school district must decide on the main purpose of its teacher evaluation system and match process to purpose.
4. To sustain resource commitments and political support, teacher evaluation must be seen to have utility, which, in turn, depends on efficient use of resources to achieve reliability, validity, and cost-effectiveness.
5. Teacher involvement and responsibility improve the quality of teacher evaluation.

With regard to the first principle, I believe art teachers should resist the temptation to collude with school districts that value uniformity of instruction and emphasize standardized testing. It should be apparent by now that I consider the conception of education as industry, and teaching as labor, as damaging to individual incentive and insulting to art teachers' intelligence.

Communicating the NAEA or CSU base guidelines to school district personnel who are ignorant of art education but determined to measure it using
prespecified goals and objectives may offer some slight measure of job security; but it wastes everyone's time and has nothing to do with staff development. School districts must treat teachers as individuals and encourage them
to develop their own convictions and educational ideals. They must focus
evaluation on program activities not intents (Stake, 1975) and make extended
use of the services of experienced teacher-researchers (Stenhouse, 1975).

What I am arguing for is a model of evaluation that is formative and
interactive with curriculum development, one in which action and reflection
on action are the joint responsibility of teams of teachers and educational
researchers working together in mutually supportive ways. Of course, this requires that teachers be motivated to take a research and development stance
with regard to their own teaching (Stenhouse, 1975), and that educational
researchers understand themselves as employed by and accountable to the
teachers and, at the same time, responsible for ensuring that their deliberations go public (that is, are subjected to external criticism). This approach to
curriculum development and evaluation mirrors the best practice in student
teaching, where prospective teachers are treated as special cases by supervisors, who encourage the growth and development of their individual aptitudes and skills while ensuring they are made aware of diverse goals for lesson
activities and routes to their accomplishment. Numerous variations of student
supervision and other partnership models of curriculum development/evalua-
tion and research using a range of qualitative methods have been implemented and documented (some more and some less successfully) in the British education system over the past 20 years (House, 1986; Skillbeck, 1984).
Records are available for scrutiny. But the benefits are long term, and the
models are costly to implement. Moreover, community and school district
representatives must participate if they wish their value perspectives to be
included.

So, I agree with the conclusion that seriousness of purpose and intensity
of implementation as evidenced in a school system's willingness to provide
extensive resourcing for evaluation have greater value than checklists and
standardized procedures. Any curriculum development and evaluation program that is collaborative and involves external participants with knowledge
of evaluation and research in one or another of the ways I have mentioned is
demanding of time and expertise. But school districts, principals, and administrators cannot simultaneously call for improved standards and ignore their
responsibilities in this regard. (In this connection it is worth noting that the
IT-INSET programs in the United Kingdom, referred to earlier, received
enthusiastic support from Her Majesty's Inspectorate until their cost was realized.)

I agree with the conclusion that evaluation programs designed to yield performance ratings must be separated from those designed to guide programs for staff development; and that evaluation of excellence in teaching requires the judgments of outstanding practitioners over several visits to schools. But school systems intent on eradicating incompetence should consider other variables that are susceptible to alteration in schooling too, such as use of time by both teachers and pupils, cognitive characteristics of learners, rate of learning, and home environment (Lynch, 1989).

Both the supervisor-as-coach and teacher-as-researcher development and evaluation models I have been advocating depend on close collaboration among schools, school districts (local education authorities), and higher education. At times, when government decision makers are hell-bent on implementing a technical, business orientation to schooling and are calling for simplistic solutions to complex problems, the question of how to sustain resource commitment and support for extended visits to schools and action research is extremely problematic. But while I applaud both the NAEA and CSU professors for their political initiatives at a time when their educational leaders appear to have lost their way, I think detailed illuminative portrayals of excellent practice (Stake, 1975) should take precedence over generalizations about base-level standards.

Finally, regarding the need for increased teacher involvement and responsibility in art teacher evaluation, I agree, provided it is collaborative and connected to curriculum research. Left entirely to its own devices, I worry about an innate conservatism in the profession that manifests itself, in the United Kingdom, in a reluctance to incorporate assessment of pupils' learning into curriculum evaluation and a failure to respond to minority ethnic community interests and concerns (Mason, 1990). Moreover, I believe that planned programs of staff development involving an entire school staff are needed where curriculum reform is recognized as necessitating a change of paradigm or meaning, not just structural change. One leading multicultural education expert (Lynch, 1989) has this to say about multicultural curriculum reform:

> The classroom reality should not be determined by the teacher's beliefs about the nature of the subject and knowledge of the subject and available material alone. A pedagogic profile is inadequate if there is little interdisciplinary work, motivation is extrinsic to pupils and the teacher decides what is to be taught on a combination of these three factors alone. (p. 88)

Since the CSU and NAEA guidelines call for knowledge and understanding of arts within diverse cultural and historical contexts, and the ability to communicate to students the role of art in terms of life enrichment, careers, and cultural development of diverse societies, perhaps American art teachers are more willing than their British counterparts to engage in planned experimentation in this regard. Given U.S. demographic trends and statistics regarding people of color, quoted recently by Banks (1989), this would not be surprising. But a competency-based approach was discussed as the answer to multicultural curriculum reform in the United States as long ago as 1974! Where is the practice to substantiate this claim?

Rubin's (1985) characteristics of good teachers are not that they are skilled politicians or union negotiators, but that they apply imagination and inventiveness to the act of teaching in schools. His solution to instructional weaknesses in the American system is (1) a more rigorous selection of candidates, (2) a reduction in preservice methods courses, (3) more liberal arts training emphasizing intellectual concepts, (4) an increase in field training experience to model teaching, (5) use of schools that want to train potentially outstanding teachers, and (6) continuing training through apprenticeship. While I do not go as far as he does in supporting an apprenticeship model of initial and inservice art education, bland acceptance of standardized operating procedures for evaluation as a means of quality control just will not do.

When the Japanese Ministry of Education was worried about educational standards in 1972, it substantially improved teachers' remuneration and consequently their public status (Arai, 1988). The United Kingdom, in common with many other European nations, has a lengthy tradition of artistry in teaching, supported by both central and local government resourcing and initiatives for initial and inservice training and curriculum development. It has quality control in the form of a national system of art examinations. I have been amazed and perturbed, therefore, by the present government's hasty decision to implement a social efficiency model borrowed from the United States, given its manifest failure to sustain quality art programs in American schools. While I am sympathetic to Sharp El Shayeb's call for administrators and teachers to share the responsibility for evaluating art teaching, she underestimates the role experienced educational researchers and teacher trainers can play in assisting in the exploration of the full range of value perspectives that should be considered in curriculum decision making.

CONCLUSION

In closing, I want to comment on the emphasis on educational theory in the papers by Eisner and Sharp El Shayeb that I understand as the special contribution of American art educators to the international art education debate. But looked at from a British or Japanese perspective, where there are lengthy and effective public traditions of school art connoisseurship embodied in the tacit knowledge teachers acquire through informal apprenticeship systems, there are significant lacks. Cultural traditions such as public discussion and debate about assessment of pupils' work for national art exams in the UK or informal evaluation of project work from schools at regional art teachers' meetings in Japan (Mason, 1994) function to set standards for good art teaching. What North American literature tends to lack are vivid portrayals of good classroom practice of the kind that are sufficiently concrete and detailed to act as exemplars and convince classroom teachers that the author-researchers understand what good practice means.

The special contribution of American literature is to challenge art teachers operating in more traditional situations to stand back from them and take more personal responsibility for curriculum innovation and change. Given the trend toward research and educational accountability worldwide, the papers by Eisner and Sharp El Shayeb are useful and timely. In the UK, for example, where a competency model of art teacher certification is mandatory, Sharp El Shayeb's analysis of ways in which it can be subverted is particularly helpful. Likewise Eisner's promotion and explication of the qualitative models of art education evaluation that are implicit in well-established reflective practitioner traditions of teacher education in the UK can be used to fuel arguments against their possible demise.

Dormer (1994) has cautioned that theoretical knowledge that provides general insights into how fields of action work and how practice might be improved is not the same thing as the practical and/or tacit knowledge that is necessary to make something work. At the present time, there may be a need to safeguard some systems of local knowledge in Western art education and cultures. Given that debates about merit make sense only within an agreed-upon system of values, art educators operating in systems with extensive traditions of apprenticeship in practical knowledge should think twice before importing the theoretical insights of Eisner and Sharp El Shayeb. In electing to operate with principles and theories of evaluation, those art educators risk a danger that their more localized, practical traditions of making things work well may be devalued and lost.

REFERENCES

Allison, B. (1986). Some aspects of assessment in art and design education. In M. Ross (Ed.), *Assessment in art education* (pp. 113–133). Oxford: Pergamon.

Arai, I. (1988). *A view from Japan on US reform movements in teaching and teacher education.* Unpublished manuscript, Joetsu University of Education, Joetsu, Japan.

Banks, J. (1989, September). *Education for cultural diversity.* Unpublished manuscript, Education and Cultural Diversity Conference, University of Southampton, Southampton.

California State University Working Group on Assessment of Prospective Art Teachers. (1989). *Resource guide: Subject matter assessment of prospective art teachers* (R. D. Reeser, Chair). Los Angeles: California State University.

Connelly, F. M., & Clandinin, D. J. (1988). *Teachers as curriculum planners.* New York: Teachers College Press.

Dormer, P. (1994). *The art of the maker: Skill and meaning in art craft and design.* London: Thames & Hudson.

Edgerton, R., & Langness, L. (1974). *Methods and styles in the study of culture.* San Francisco: Chandler & Sharpe.

Eisner, E. W. (1985). *The educational imagination* (2nd ed.) New York: Macmillan.

Everton, T., & Impey, I. (1989). *INSET partnership in training.* London: David Fulton.

Gibson, R. (1981). Curriculum criticism: Misconceived theory, Ill-advised practice. *Cambridge Journal of Education, 11*(3), 190–210.

Greene, M. (1978). *Landscapes of learning.* New York: Teachers College Press.

House, E. (Ed.). (1986). *New directions in educational evaluation.* Lewes, UK: Falmer.

Kaelin, E. (1989). *Aesthetics for art educators.* New York: Teachers College Press.

Kirkup, G. (1986). The feminist evaluator. In E. House (Ed.), *New directions in educational evaluation* (pp. 68–87). Lewes, UK: Falmer.

Lynch, J. (1989). *Multicultural education in a global society.* Lewes, UK: Falmer.

Mason, R. (1990). *Evaluating arts programmes: The arts-in-schools project in Leicestershire.* Unpublished manuscript, Leicester Polytechnic (now De Montfort University), Leicester.

Mason, R. (1994). Artistic achievement in Japanese junior high schools. *Art Education, 4*(1), 8–20.

National Art Education Association. (1990). *Suggested certified art teacher appraisal model* (W. D. Smith, Chair). Unpublished manuscript, Teacher Appraisal Committee, NAEA, Reston, VA.

Oram, R. (1983). In defence of curriculum criticism. *Cambridge Journal of Education, 13*(1), 7–13.

Palmer, R. (1969). *Hermeneutics.* Evanston, IL: Northwestern University Press.

Ricoeur, P. (1979). The model of the text. In P. Rabinow & W. Sullivan (Eds.), *Interpretive social science* (pp. 73–101). Berkeley: University of California Press.

Rubin, A. (1985). *Artistry in teaching.* New York: Random House.

Skillbeck, M. (Ed.). (1984). *Evaluating the curriculum in the eighties.* London: Hodder & Stoughton.

Smith, R. (1984). *The new aesthetic curriculum theorists and their astonishing ideas.* Vancouver: University of British Columbia, Centre for the Study of Curriculum and Instruction.

Stake, R. (Ed.). (1975). *Evaluating the arts in education: A responsive approach.* Columbus, OH: Merrill.

Stenhouse, L. (1975). *An introduction to curriculum research and development.* London: Heinemann Educational.

Van Manen, M. (1984). Practicing phenomenological writing. *Phenomenology and Pedagogy, 2*(1), 36–39.

Willis, G. (Ed.). (1978). *Qualitative evaluation: Concepts and cases in curriculum criticism.* Berkeley, CA: McCutchan.

Wilson, B. (1985, May). Evaluating teaching in the arts: Scenes from a complex drama. In D. W. Baker (comp.), *Teachers in the arts: Proceedings of a national symposium* (pp. 85–101). Louisiana State University, Baton Rouge.

Wise, A. E., Darling-Hammond, L., McLaughlin, M. W., & Bernstein, H. T. (1985). Teacher evaluation: A study of effective practices. *The Elementary School Journal, 86*(1), 103–121.

Zeichner, K., & Liston, D. (1990). Traditions of reform in US teacher education. *Journal of Teacher Education, 4*(2), 3–20.

ELLIOT W. EISNER

Rachel Mason makes a number of points in her response to my article that warrant a response, if for no other reason than to clarify some misunderstandings of educational criticism. Perhaps the single most important misunderstanding is her belief that "the outcome of an evaluation [and educational criticism] is a written report." This belief is central to most of her concerns, since she claims that the teachers with whom she works have no training in literary writing and find it difficult to create the kind of written narrative that she believes is necessary in order to do educational criticism.

The fact of the matter is that it is no more necessary that educational criticism be in written form, than it is for art criticism to be limited to what a critic writes as contrasted to what a critic says about a work of art. While there are special and important values to writing, which Mason correctly points out, it often is more appropriate to engage teachers in a verbal dialogue when the educational criticism is focused on their teaching. In the context of dialogue the educational critic can take into account the teachers' reactions and adjust his or her comments accordingly. Oral communication has a flexibility that a written form does not, and for some situations that flexibility is more important than the virtues of a written statement. In fact, Mason points out that the teachers with whom she has worked have themselves wondered whether "written criticism is necessary at all." Their intuitions are correct.

What is important is that the aims of educational criticism, its several dimensions—description, interpretation, evaluation, and thematics—and its validation be addressed in the work that is performed. But that work can take an oral as well as a written form. The problem, however, that teachers will confront exceeds the problem of knowing how to write a literary text. If individuals doing educational criticism, whether teachers or administrators, do not possess refined levels of educational connoisseurship, their comments are likely to be shallow or miss the mark. If they have no theoretical resources to bring to bear on what they have seen, they will find it difficult to provide the kind of interpretation that exceeds the merely journalistic. In short, simply asking teachers or administrators to do an educational criticism—regardless of how sympathetic they are to aim and form—is not sufficient. They need training in the perception of educational practice; they need to have theoretical constructs with which to interpret what they have seen; and they need to understand the variety of educational values that any particular form of

129

educational practice might reflect. The acquisition of such sensibilities, competencies, and forms of understanding is not an automatic consequence of teaching experience. The doing of educational criticism is complex and difficult, and for some teachers and administrators it will be inappropriate.

Regarding the instrumental nature of educational criticism to which Mason apparently objects, I can only say that the function of educational criticism, like criticism in general, *is* instrumental. Its aim is to create the "wide awakeness" that Mason applauds. Criticism, wrote Dewey, is aimed at the re-education of perception. It is indeed instrumental. In fact, if it has no instrumental utility, it has no utility.

There are three other points on which I would like to comment. The first has to do with Mason's claim that "evaluators cannot understand classroom events so long as they assume moral superiority and ask all the questions." I find the comment odd. Why must one assume that a critic is morally superior? A teacher who is competent can, without assuming moral superiority, provide comments to a student about the student's written essay that can be useful to the student. Furthermore, a teacher has no legal or professional obligation to heed the comments of an educational critic. The critic's comments can stimulate dialogue, and from my perspective that is all to the good. Such comments are particularly important when one considers that teachers receive very little sustained observation and feedback about their work from their peers. The value of getting comments from someone who wishes to be constructive and who is perceptive and articulate about teaching is not an opportunity we have in great abundance in our schools.

The second comment I wish to address is Mason's question, "Is educational criticism democratic?" Her implication is that it is not and that it should be. My response is that the question is itself irrelevant to the enhancement of educational practice. Do we ask whether a tennis coach is democratic, or a literary critic, or a social critic? Would Harold Rosenberg's art criticism be more informative if it was democratic? Or Charlie Chaplin's criticism of modern times in *Modern Times?* Or Pierre Bourdieu's criticism of contemporary culture? I think not. The point is not democracy, but utility, and the criterion for assessing the value of criticism is its contribution to our awareness and to the enlargement of our understanding.

Finally, I wish to comment on what Mason calls the "grandiloquent" writing style of some educational critics and the tendency to aestheticize educational matters. I think we pay much too little attention to aesthetic matters in writing about education. The function of aesthetic considerations in the creation of text and in oral communication is not to gussy up language, but to perform an epistemological function: The *way* something is written or said is a part of its content. That surely must be understood by those of us working in art education. Why it should need further explication is a puzzlement.

I–C
OUTCOMES

Chapter 7

The Assessment of Student Learning in the Arts

HOWARD GARDNER
Harvard Graduate School of Education, USA

THE VARIETIES OF ASSESSMENT IN DIFFERENT EDUCATIONAL CONTEXTS

Some form of assessment ought to be an inherent part of any educational encounter, but the particular forms of assessment may be as varied as the kinds of encounters. In a traditional culture, educational encounters rarely are separated from daily activities. Young children observe their parents at work and are drawn into activities at their current, modest level of competence. The elders evaluate the youngsters "on the fly," posing more challenging tasks for the more able, supporting or punishing those who prove to be less skilled at picking up the requisite skills.

Such arrangements become formalized when an apprenticeship system is adopted. A distance is deliberately introduced between the novice and the master. Over time a graded set of challenges is posed to the apprentice, and the trajectory of progress to a master level is laid out with some specificity. Still, it rarely is necessary to introduce a separate set of tasks simply for the purposes of evaluation. The apprentice's skills at everyday pursuits can be observed readily and evaluated, at least by the master, if not by older students and by the apprentice.

The kinds of support available in traditional and apprentice settings typically recede from view once formal schooling has become the norm. In the

Evaluating and Assessing the Visual Arts in Education: International Perspectives: © 1996 by Teachers College, Columbia University. All rights reserved. ISBN 0-8077-3511-6. Prior to photocopying items for classroom use, please contact the Copyright Clearance Center, Customer Service, 222 Rosewood Dr., Danvers, MA 01923, USA, tel. (508) 750-8400.

former settings, the behaviors desired in competent adults are evident every-where, and the steps toward their attainment are relatively manifest to the learner (although sometimes they may be hidden deliberately by a hermeti-cally inclined guild). In formal schools, in contrast, most of the practices are inculcated in *decontextualized* settings quite remote from where they ulti-mately may be invoked one day. Calculation is taught with a slate at the desk, rather than in the marketplace; reading and writing occur at one's desk rather than in the church, in the law court, or near the fireplace; geography and history are committed to memory from lists, rather than drawn on in the course of discussing a recent event or planning a forthcoming trip. Following a period of input and drill, the students' progress is customarily monitored by a more formal instrument, usually called an examination or test.

Each of these practices has evolved for understandable reasons. It makes sense for parents to model desired behaviors every day in situations where children at some future time will assume their parents' place; it makes sense for masters to lay out a set of steps and to plot the progress of their charges; it makes sense for reading, writing, calculation, and other notationally oriented activities to be presented in efficient form in a school classroom and to be periodically monitored in an orderly manner. And whenever the task of "se-lection" or "promoting" falls upon an institution, the argument for resorting to some kind of an "objective measure" becomes compelling.

Yet these practices also may come to assume an exaggerated life of their own. In traditional China, the Imperial Examinations by which officials were selected became labeled appropriately as "an examination hell." In contempo-rary Japan, students work tirelessly for years to prepare for the highest stake testing—admission to college, which, in turn, will determine their future oc-cupation. And in the United States today, a certain form of examination—the standardized, multiple-choice, machine-scored test—has come to be re-garded as almost sacrosanct; it has become the instrument of choice for nearly every purpose, from teacher certification to obtaining a driver's license (not to mention the selection of an ideal mate). Certainly, other approaches could be envisioned, including ones that might prove less stressful for the candidates and even more appropriate to the stated aims of the assessment.

The full gamut of assessment procedures is encountered across the range of performances and disciplines, including the arts. In certain subcultures in West Africa, all musicians are drawn from a small caste of families. In such settings, children learn to play and sing at the feet of their parents. In most European countries, artistic guilds grew up in the Middle Ages, and the kind of apprentice–master hierarchy associated therewith has survived until this day. Finally, though more gradually than in "canonical subjects," the vaunted standardized test has begun to be used in the arts. Such tests are invoked to assess knowledge across the art forms—for example, sensitivity to different

literary styles, the criteria underlying aesthetic judgments, com.
forms of musical notation, the facts and concepts associated with
of the visual arts, and the like.

VISIONS OF ART EDUCATION

Every traditional society visited by anthropologists features some form
of artistic activity, whether it is tribal music, communal dance, oral verse,
sculpture, or, more typically, several of the above. In all of these cases, the
practice or performance of the art form is primary and may well not be distinguished categorically (or linguistically) from other work or ritualistic activities. In cultures that are literate, artistic performances remain central but often are complemented by activities that surround the performances—
notations, announcements, criticisms, publicity, histories, and the like. Moreover, in the most differentiated societies, the arts come to be seen as a separate
domain of existence—one comparable in scope, if not in prestige, to the sciences, politics, business, or sports.

As the forms of artistic activity multiply, and particularly where schools
have arisen, controversy surrounds the issue of *which* aspects of arts should be
taught and *how* they should be taught. In the United States, for example, art
education was considered a frill, suited for an elite, until the latter part of the
nineteenth century. At that time, Walter Page Smith and other educational
leaders succeeded in making the argument that skills in drawing would aid
individuals in the workplace, making them more competent and the nation's
industrial base more competitive; in due course, courses in drawing and
draftsmanship became part of the standard curriculum. Observational study
of art works, mostly for patriotic purposes, also was mandated but never became an entrenched part of the curriculum (Wygant, 1983).

So long as realistic drawing is the standard, assessment is not problematic. Quite specific criteria for success can be established, and a student's level
of drawing can be ascertained readily. In countries and cultures where such
technical drawing is at a premium, assessment is straightforward and uncon-
troversial.

Toward the middle of the present century, due in large part to the progressive movement in education, and also to influences from Europe, the
practice of draftsmanship became less central (and less valued) in American
art education. Especially in the case of young children, the arts came to be
seen primarily as a vehicle for self-expression, for personal development.
Involvement in the arts remained a positive value, but the meeting of explicit
performance standards was not. The need for formal assessment thus de-
clined in importance; where some form of assessment remained, those works

that were deemed "expressive," "creative," or "powerful" came to be cherished more than those that were "merely" technically competent. To be sure, those bent upon a career in the arts eventually have to be held accountable to some standards of graphic artistry; but given fast-changing fashions in the world of "high art," even the mastery level expected of the average academician is no longer at a premium.

In recent years, in part as a reaction to certain excesses of "progressive" art education, leaders of the field have called for an education that goes beyond "depiction," "production," "making," or "creating." The usual request has been for an interdisciplinary mix, in which history, criticism, and aesthetics are each taught in sequential pattern from an early age (Getty Center, 1984; Smith, 1987). While assessment has not been a particular concern of the approach dubbed discipline-based art education (DBAE), one possible implication is that the kinds of verbal pencil-and-paper assessment instruments used in the conventional curriculum ought to be transported to the arts. For example, art history might be assessed in the same way as music history, American history, or the history of science.

Operating in parallel with the scholastic assessments of artistic learning has been a small set of instruments developed by educators and psychologists to measure artistic accomplishment. Individually, these instruments probe capacities like artistic preferences, skill at drafting, and artistic judgments (for capsule descriptions of the major instruments, see Appendix A at the end of this chapter).

Of particular note is the ensemble of instruments used by the National Assessment of Educational Progress (NAEP) to assess the capabilities of American students. As administered in the middle and late 1970s, students were evaluated in terms of their perception and response to aspects of art; their valuing of the arts; their productive capacities in the arts; and their knowledge about art. As a standardized test, used throughout the country, the NAEP measure relies on short-answer items; yet it also elicits information of a more open-ended sort, such as students' capacities to design art objects. Not surprisingly, given the status of art education in the United States, performances were generally mediocre; also not surprisingly, given the priorities of current education, arts have been dropped from the current NAEP roster of offerings.

Each view of art education harbors within it a particular stance toward assessment. In no case is the association between "view" and "assessment" necessary, but never is it totally accidental. What one values in the arts is what one will teach for; and the resulting assessments tend to reflect the ways in which artistic materials and performances are taught. A mother *could* administer a standardized test to her young children, and a state bureaucracy *could* recommend full-scale musical auditions for randomly selected youngsters; but neither of these scenarios is particularly likely.

A PERSONAL VISION OF ART EDUCATION

In what follows I introduce a number of new ideas concerning assessment, ones that hold promise for engendering a more beneficent and appropriate form of assessment across curricula. These ideas can be considered without reference to a particular view of art education. Yet inasmuch as they developed out of work at Harvard Project Zero—work itself based on a particular vision of the field—it seems appropriate to put forth that vision explicitly here (Gardner 1990a; Gardner & Perkins, 1989; Winner, 1982).

Every normal human being has the capacity to know the world in a number of ways. In general, schools have focused almost exclusively on two ways that seem to be most crucial in the mastery of the literacies—a linguistic way of knowing, prized in reading and in certain humanistic studies; and a logico-mathematical way of knowing, central for mathematical, scientific, and technological studies. Standardized tests, not coincidentally, are especially appropriate for sampling linguistic and logico-mathematical knowing and may even prove particularly congenial to individuals who happen to be strong in these areas. Sometimes, indeed, otherwise ignorant individuals can score well on such instruments, simply because they understand the means by which standardized test items are generated and scored (Gardner, 1983a, 1990b), or because they happen to exhibit a particular, possibly superficial blend of linguistic and logical abilities that is at a premium in such instruments.

Life extends beyond school, however, and once one leaves the scholastic environs, other forms of knowing loom large. In our own investigations, we have isolated at least five other ways of knowing, sometimes termed *multiple intelligences* (MI). Included in this list are musical intelligence (the kind of ability exhibited by a composer, performer, or informed listener); spatial intelligence (the ability to perceive and manipulate large spatial regions, manifested by a pilot, or more local spatial regions, exhibited by a sculptor); bodily-kinesthetic intelligence (the capacity to use one's whole body, or body parts, to solve problems or to fashion products); interpersonal intelligence (knowledge of other individuals and the means whereby one can work effectively with them); and intrapersonal intelligence (comparable knowledge of oneself, and the concomitant capacity to activate such self-knowledge in making judicious decisions about one's own life).

According to the theory of multiple intelligences, humans have evolved as a species to carry out each of these forms of "information processing" with reasonable fluency. However, intellectual profiles differ across individuals, and an individual can be "intelligent" in one area, while showing little or no flair or skill in other intellectual domains. While the subject of considerable debate (see Moody, 1990; Gardner, 1987), the theory also has proved of relevance to several pressing educational problems (Gardner & Hatch, 1989).

Of particular moment for the present discussion are the theory's implications for the assessment of student learning in the arts. First of all, it will be noted that no particular intelligence is *of itself* artistic or nonartistic; nor, contrary to some misinterpretations of the theory, is there a particular "artistic intelligence" (Gardner, 1983b). Rather, individuals and cultures elect whether to deploy a particular intelligence in an aesthetic way. Linguistic intelligence, when used by a poet or playwright, is being deployed in an aesthetic way; but the same "information-processing" capacities used by a lawyer, reporter, or politician, may well not exhibit any symptoms of the aesthetic. Spatial, bodily, and even musical intelligence may be mobilized in aesthetic or nonaesthetic ways, again dependent on the particular means and goals being pursued by the individual in question (Goodman, 1976, 1978). Hence, one intent on assessing *artistic* abilities needs to determine whether a particular intelligence is in fact being used in ways consistent with artistic practice.

A second, crucial point bears directly upon assessment. Upon learning of the existence of a *set* of intelligences, one understandable impulse is to assume that each of these intelligences ought to be assessed, and that they can in fact be assessed in the canonical ways used in standardized intelligence tests. This impulse must be curbed! Precisely because each intelligence works according to its own operations and principles, it is wrongheaded to attempt to assess it using the linguistic-logical amalgam featured in most standardized measures. Intelligences, the practices based on them, and the domains in which they are customarily deployed, *must be assessed in intelligence-fair ways.*

Specifically, if one wishes to assess spatial intelligence, it is inappropriate to use a pencil-and-paper test; depending on the facet of spatial intelligence at issue, it is appropriate to examine an individual's ability to find his or her way around a new territory, to draw a scene accurately, or to arrange (and rearrange) furniture in a room. By the same token, bodily and interpersonal intelligences do not lend themselves to short-answer standard measures; they must be examined in situ, as an individual uses his or her body to solve a problem, or as an individual interacts directly with other individuals. A score of "100" on a written test of leadership proves meaningless if the same individual typically fails in an actual effort to lead his or her peers. And if the individual can lead effectively, scores on a test of leadership are irrelevant.

In light of these considerations, a particular view of art education suggests itself. Individuals educated in the arts need to be able to display the behaviors and understandings associated with the roles central to particular art forms. Musically educated persons need to exhibit those facets of musical intelligence that are central in the creation, performance, and appreciation of music; they also need to draw on other intelligences that figure in musical competence, from the bodily intelligence involved in playing an instrument, to the interpersonal intelligence involved in communicating effectively to an audience. By the same token, individuals educated in other art forms need to display the complex of intelligences featured in the respective forms, ranging from the spatial intelligence at a premium in painting or sculpture, to the bodily intelligence featured in dance, acting, or mime.

Observers sometimes have proposed that the arts are a natural way of existing or knowing for individuals; and that, accordingly, no special training is needed to achieve artistic competence. Indeed, some have even gone beyond this perspective to embrace a Rousseauian approach, contending that education can prove inimical to the arts. While a destructive art education is certainly conceivable, massive amounts of formal and informal evidence document that learning in the arts cannot be counted on to take care of itself: The symbol systems of the arts need to be learned just as surely as the symbol systems of history, mathematics, or science; and one must learn to "read" and "write" in artistic symbol systems, no less than one must learn to read and write for the traditional disciplines of school (Gardner, 1982; Goodman, 1976; Winner, 1982). While learning and performance in the arts clearly must be assessed in appropriate ways, such learning is certainly susceptible to assessment—indeed, no less so than learning in other disciplinary areas.

PROMISING NEW IDEAS IN ASSESSMENT

Recent discussions about assessment have echoed shifts in our conception of intelligence. When intelligence was conceived of as a single capacity, adequately captured by performance on a pencil-and-paper examination, a parallel faith surrounded such standardized instruments. Now, however, skepticism abounds about the adequacy of received definitions of intelligence and traditional measures of this construct. At least to some extent, this skepticism has come to extend to those measures—and particularly those aptitude measures—that purport to assess human beings through their answering of brief "right–wrong" questions or their selection of one item from a set of four.

(It should be noted that, while intelligence tests were conceived in France by Alfred Binet, and christened in Germany by Wilhelm Stern, they have enjoyed their greatest success and their widest proliferation in the United States. By the same token, the kinds of instruments inspired by intelligence tests—such as state-mandated achievement tests and Scholastic Aptitude Tests—also have achieved most currency in the United States. The situation as described in these pages is probably more acute in the United States than in most other countries; yet intimations of the "IQ-standardized test" mentality can be observed in most countries and may perhaps even be on the rise in developing countries.)

As a counter to standardized tests, a growing number of educators and researchers are calling for assessments that look directly at skills, abilities, and intelligences, rather than peering through the often opaque lens of a linguistic-logical measure. Operating under such names as performance-based testing, appropriate testing, authentic assessment, or alternative assessment, these approaches insist on a relatively large and more veridical slice of behavior, whose relevance to a culturally valued practice is self-evident, rather than a matter of faith (Gardner, 1990b; Wiggins, 1989; Wolf, 1988/1989, 1989; Wolf, Bixby, Glenn, & Gardner, 1991).

Consider some commonly cited instances of performance-based testing.

- In a language class, a child is asked to compose an additional chapter to a story begun in a certain style, and is assessed on the originality and appropriateness of the new literary material. Students assess their own efforts and those of their peers, arriving at a set of criteria that could be more broadly applied; they then publish a collection of the best continuations, which is itself reviewed by peers in another school.
- In a mathematics class, students are asked to budget for a family of four for a week so as to satisfy certain dietary preferences and constraints while still remaining "in the black." They are assessed not only on the acceptability of their solution but on the processes in which they engaged, the factors that they took into account, and even the ways in which they worked together.
- In a biology class, students are introduced to certain principles that govern gait in animals of different sizes having bodies of different shapes; using microcomputers for the creation and manipulation of data, they then design their own "speedy animals" and stage simulated races between them. Assessment involves not only attention to which animal proves most rapid but also to the student's consideration of the consequences of the "virtual animal" for ecological balance and prey–predator relationships.
- In a history class, students study a number of important revolutions in the past. They then monitor current revolutions as reported in the news and seek to predict what will happen in the short- and long-run, on the basis of an emerging model of revolutionary change. Finally, they devise a way of confirming or not confirming their predictions and follow the course of those predictions for the next half-year.

In one sense, there is nothing remarkable about such curriculum and assessment pairings. Skilled teachers often have featured such problems and projects in their classes and have even factored student performances with such materials into final grades. Of note is the fact that the inclusion of such items in assessments is no longer seen as a marginal or "extra-credit" endeavor. Instead, states like California and Connecticut have proposed that such items become part of the procedures whereby student progress is monitored regularly and by virtue of which "high stake" decisions about student achievement are made.

At least in an American context, this trend involves a radical shift in perspective:

1. Instead of assessment taking place out of the context of the classroom, under strictly regulated but highly artificial conditions, assessment is built into the regular curriculum.
2. Instead of students working in isolation, with any collaboration being regarded as collusion, there are now clear occasions on which students are encouraged to work together; even in "high stakes" assessment, cooperation becomes legitimate.
3. Instead of tests being kept under lock and key, with any "leaking" being a matter of acute concern, projects and problems are common knowledge, available to all; indeed the problems-to-be-solved may even be published at the beginning of the year.
4. Performances of importance, such as writing extended passages, assessing one's own writing and that of one's peers, or planning dietary and financial survival for a week, come to substitute for arbitrarily contrived items, which have little intrinsic interest and are not in the least engaging.

The actual ways in which assessment takes place also differ significantly in a performance-based system. Assessors are furnished with sample responses to problems, representing different levels of sophistication on each of the dimensions under examination and, possibly, on the "global" response as well. Thus, in the consideration of writing, for example, a teacher is provided with sample passages reflecting different degrees of originality, technical expertise, stylistic fidelity, use of figurative language, and the like. By the same token, in considering students' candidate budgets, the teacher will have the opportunity to look at specimen spreadsheets that reflect different degrees of understanding of the relevant variables, as well as responses that exhibit other virtues (or liabilities) such as ingenuity, fidelity to the needs of individual family members, or convenience for shopping purposes. Such collections of sample performances become the backdrop for assessing the performances of one's own students. For most performances and understandings of import, a scale of four or five levels should suffice to cover the range that one might expect to encounter in a two to three grade span. To produce a more finely calibrated scale represents overkill; in fact, it is misleading to suggest that one can actually score most performances with that degree of precision. On the other hand, it is important to look at a number of different facets of any performance; the notion that a passage of writing, or a budget, or a simulated animal can be adequately summarized on one dimension is ill-conceived.

The movement for alternative assessment is still in its early stages; it is difficult to predict how far it will progress and which kinds of procedures and evaluations are likely to prove most robust. While these methods are being designed for use across a large population, they may turn out to be more revealing for within-class assessments. Whatever their precise fate, it is already possible to discern ways in which these particular innovative tendencies can have an impact in the arts, even as the arts themselves have much to offer those who would design new, more qualitatively oriented forms of assessment.

NEW APPROACHES TO ASSESSMENT IN ARTS EDUCATION: THE EXAMPLE OF ARTS PROPEL

The newly emerging approaches to assessment across diverse areas of the curriculum are especially congenial to the arts. The oldest tradition of assessment in the arts—that employed in apprenticeships—can easily be considered an instance of performance-based or authentic assessment. Far from measuring skills and capacities in contexts remote from their natural habitat, the master in a traditional apprenticeship looks for evidence of student progress in the activities carried out "on the job." Nor are the standards idiosyncratic ones: Indeed, in many vocations and avocations, the standards are sufficiently well defined and consensual so as to allow assessment to take place, at least in principle, by any knowledgeable professional in the field.

Given the robust tradition of performance-based assessments in the arts, the question arises as to why educators do not simply revert to tried-and-true practices of the past. Three principal reasons suggest themselves. First of all, in most art forms, skill in the medium of performance is no longer the overarching goal of education. Even in music, it is increasingly recognized that members of the band or orchestra require knowledge above and beyond the skills of the performing craft. A second reason is that, in most schools, the classroom teacher—and, in some cases, even the art teacher—is not sufficiently proficient to serve as a reliable model for, and judge of, performances of the more talented or capable students. A third reason derives from the demands being made by educational authorities. Whereas, in an earlier era, educational leaders might have tolerated the absence of formal assessment in the arts, or relied on the master's impressionistic evaluation of students' works, current pressures for accountability often require more formal assessments.

So long as the arts are considered a subsidiary or marginal subject, it is possible to ignore these considerations. Indeed, in most school systems in the United States, there has been little assessment beyond that undertaken casually by teachers. But if the arts are to attain a more serious place among the family of disciplines, issues of assessment cannot be short-circuited. The question is no longer, "Shall we assess?" but rather, "*How* shall we assess?"

Many societies all over the world are grappling with these issues, and the answers will be as varied as the societies posing the question, their goals and values in art education, the kinds of assessment pressures and aspirations they experience, and the resources available to them. In what follows, I will describe one contemporary attempt to carry out appropriate assessment in art education. I hope that the discussion proves of more than parochial interest.

In 1985 the Arts and Humanities Division of the Rockefeller Foundation catalyzed a 5-year cooperative effort among three partners: the Educational Testing Service, the largest and best-known educational assessment institution in the world; the Pittsburgh Public Schools, widely considered to be a well-run American urban school system with a special interest and expertise in assessment issues; and Harvard Project Zero, our own research group that has for the past 2 decades conducted basic research in art education. Our charge was deceptively simple: to create alternative forms of assessment that can identify students with potential and/or talent in areas usually missed by standard forms of assessment (Gardner, 1989; Zessoules, Wolf, & Gardner, 1988).

Given the stipulations of the funding, and our own interest and expertise, we decided to initiate a project at the middle and high school level in three different art forms: music, imaginative writing, and the visual arts. During the first years of the project we worked quite intensively with a small group of teachers, developing specimen curriculum materials as well as prototypical assessment techniques. The teachers have been full and equal partners throughout the development cycle. During the current and concluding phase of the project, we have expanded our efforts to work with a much larger group of teachers, including ones with whom the research team has relatively little direct contact.

What has been our guiding conception of art education? From the first, we have sought to meet two important desiderata. On the one hand, we wish to provide every child the opportunity to participate in the arts in a number of ways, assuming various roles and stances. At the same time, we want to ensure that the making, creating, or producing of art remains central, and that "nonmaking" activities, insofar as possible, grow directly out of a student's own artistic productions. As roles central in all art forms, we introduce the trio of Production (making art in the appropriate media of expression); Perception (effecting relevant discriminations in one's own works and those fashioned by others); and Reflection (the capacity to step back and evaluate one's own artworks, or those of others, in terms of goals, means, and effects). To capture this trio of competencies, we coined the acronym ARTS PROPEL.

Questioned at the start of the project about our focus, we doubtless would have spoken about the importance of assessment and about the extent to which assessment "drives" (where it does not exert a stranglehold upon) the curriculum. We soon discovered, however, that even the most sterling assessment devices are useless in the absence of curricular materials of quality that can yield genuine student learning. To put the matter crisply, unless students have learned something worthwhile, there is no point in assessing. The belief, apparently held by many legislators and school administrators, that one can improve performance simply by frequent assessments posits the causal chain *exactly* backwards: Frequent weighing does not in itself make someone heavier. Only first-rate curricula, well taught, can result in student performances worth assessing at all.

In most domains of life, and certainly in that arena called the arts, the projects in which individuals participate constitute a large part of their daily activities. Some projects are dictated entirely from the outside; some projects are generated entirely by the individuals themselves; and most projects represent an amalgam of self- and other-generated components. We have sought to capture this continuum in our own efforts. Our approach to the territory that encompasses assessment and curriculum has centered on the creation, development, and pilot testing of two new vehicles, which we have termed *domain projects* and *processfolios*.

A domain project is a rich curriculum module that ranges in duration from a few days to a few weeks. Each domain project focuses on a concept (e.g., style, composition) or a practice (e.g., rehearsing a piece of music, executing a portrait) that is unquestionably central to an art form. In every domain project, the student adopts all three of the aesthetic stances, having multiple opportunities to *make* works (or parts of works), to *contemplate* works, and to *reflect* about the processes involved in making and critically evaluating works. The domain project also features multiple opportunities for assessment both during the execution and upon completion of the activity: Assessment can and should be undertaken by teachers, by peers, by outside experts and visitors, and, of special importance, by the student himself or herself.

Given our focus here on the visual arts, it is appropriate to describe two sample domain projects in that aesthetic domain. In the "Composition" domain project, students develop an awareness of the basic principles of design. They create designs both by randomly dropping geometric shapes against a plain background and by deliberately arranging them against a comparable background. They compare their patterns and reflect about the different effects achieved. Students are then introduced to certain of the major principles of composition (e.g., harmony through repetition, surprise through contrast), and they discuss these principles as they have been exemplified in paintings by esteemed artists. Finally, students create a composition in which they seek to achieve either harmony or surprise through one or more of the principles discussed earlier. Reflecting on their works, students evaluate the strengths and weaknesses of each one.

In the "Biography of a Work" students first observe a large set of sketches prepared by Andrew Wyeth prior to his completion of "Brown Swiss"; they then survey a companion set of sketches and drafts of Picasso's "Guernica." Following these perceptual explorations, they embark on their own paintings or drawings, and monitor their own "developing" processes. Students, for example, might be asked to make a picture of their room at home, bringing out aspects of their own personality in the way that they portray that room. This domain project features constant dialectic between sketches and final products, and between the preparatory works of major artists and one's own "rehearsals."

Domain projects each feature a set of self-assessment procedures, which can be used during the course of the life of the project. In the case of the Composition project, students have the opportunity to step back and reflect on the strengths and weaknesses of each composition, the expressive effects achieved in each composition, and just *how* these effects are (or are not) fully realized. In the case of the Biography of a Work, students reflect about the changes they have made, the reasons motivating the changes, and the relation between the early and late drafts. The students' drafts and final products, along with their reflections, then are assessed along a variety of qualitative dimensions such as engagement, technical skills, imagination, and critical evaluative skills. While the primary assessment for the domain project occurs within the class, it also is possible to assess these projects off-site; such assessment sessions have been carried out with reasonable success by "external" art educators brought together under the auspices of the Educational Testing Service.

Domain projects are skeletal frames, designed for teachers to absorb into their own regular curriculum. It has been our experience that teachers typically alter the domain projects so as better to serve their own pedagogical goals; and many go on to devise their own domain projects. Such transformations are highly desirable, for they increase the likelihood that the domain projects will continue to be used with conviction and will serve to educate the students. The opportunity to redesign the domain project also involves the teacher as a genuine inventor and mentor, rather than as a passive purveyor of someone else's materials.

As the name suggests, *processfolios* are a variation of a portfolio. In the familiar version of a portfolio, a student assembles the best of his or her work, usually in the effort to gain admission to a selective program, to win some kind of prize, or to secure showing of works. In contrast, our processfolio is oriented to the furthering of the student's own learning. In a portfolio a student records progress on a project: an initial idea, early sketches, false starts, pivotal pieces (where an idea gels), journal entries (in whatever medium seems appropriate), interim critiques and self-critiques, the final product, critiques of that product, and plans for further revisions of the project or for new projects that in some way build upon the works in the processfolio.

In its totality the processfolio represents a kind of evolving cognitive map of work in progress. And when it works well, the processfolio not only documents the student's growth but aids significantly in the student's own reflectivity, by transforming what is usually treated as the less significant "ground" into a dominant and instructive "figure."

In a class that features processfolios, the teacher's role is best thought of as that of an older and more skilled colleague—a coach or a mentor. Teachers may differ in the extent to which they choose to share their own works with students; but in any event teachers should encourage students to pursue their ideas, to carry projects forward, to reflect upon progress, and to draw lessons from experiences. Processfolios make the most sense when the keeper is engaged in original work: The more teachers are themselves engaged in such work, the more likely the processfolios will achieve an important niche in classrooms.

The maintenance of high standards, so crucial to the success of any art education program, is heavily dependent at the outset on the stance that the teacher takes vis-a-vis artistic performance and productivity; with time, students' effects on one another may well become the chief means of conveying and maintaining standards (Berger, 1991). The teacher's role in a processfolio environment differs from his or her role in a classical apprenticeship in that no single model of progress—no set of discrete levels—underlies the instruction; but in the sense that the teacher serves as an exemplar of productive artistry, and as an embodiment of the standards of the community, an ARTS PROPEL classroom does resemble a classical atelier.

While domain projects lend themselves to a number of familiar forms of assessment, the assessment of processfolios is a more challenging and delicate operation. Processfolios can be assessed on a large number of dimensions. Some of them are straightforward: the regularity of the entries, their completeness, and so forth. Others are more complex and subjective, but still familiar: the overall quality of the final products, on technical and imaginative grounds. Of special interest to us are those dimensions that help to illuminate the unique potential of processfolios for students.

- Awareness of their own strengths and weaknesses
- Capacity to reflect accurately

- Ability to build upon self-critique and to make use of critiques of others
- Sensitivity to their own developmental milestones
- Ability to use lessons from domain projects productively
- Capacity to find and solve new problems
- Ability to relate current projects to those undertaken at earlier times and those that they hope to undertake in the future
- Capacity to move comfortably and appropriately from one aesthetic stance or role to another and back again

The goal is not only to assess along a variety of potentially independent dimensions, but also to encourage students to develop along these dimensions. Such an assessment system has the potential to alter what is discussed and what is valued in the classroom.

Recently, the ARTS PROPEL team has attempted to set down those dimensions of production, perception, reflection, and "approach to work" that can be applied to student processfolios and the projects contained therein. The dimensions are summarized in Appendix B. While the taxonomy is tentative, and is likely to be altered in the light of local conditions, it captures well the considerations we deem most important.

Even to list these dimensions is to convey something of the difficulty of the assessment task and the extent to which it breaks new ground. It would be misleading to suggest that we have solved the problems involved in any of these facets of assessment: Indeed, as we sometimes jest, we simply have several years more experience than others in recognizing what does *not* work! It is sobering to note that it has taken a century to take standardized tests to their present, hardly stupefying status; it is unreasonable to expect domain projects and processfolios to mature in a few years time, with the still modest resources we have at our disposal. Still, our progress to date, and our belief that we are assessing in a way that is worthy of the subject matter, emboldens us to continue our work.

CONCLUSION: CREATING AN "ASSESSMENT ENVIRONMENT"

To dwell on issues of reliability and validity, however important they ultimately may be, is to miss the principal point of these alternative forms of assessment. For too long, I would maintain, many educational researchers—and particularly those in the United States—have allowed the psychometric icons of reliability and validity to dominate our view of assessment. In so doing, they—or perhaps I should say we—have lost sight of the reasons for the assessments and the uses to which they typically are put. The movement for alternative assessment, of which ARTS PROPEL is an enthusiastic supporter, marks an attempt to return the horse to its rightful position ahead of the cart; instead of seeking primarily to satisfy interest groups that remain remote from the site of learning, we need to focus on what is worth assessing in ways that are directly useful to the most important consumers—teachers, parents, and the students themselves.

During the early phases of such an effort, issues of psychometric finesse ought to give way to the everyday practicality and utility of candidate assessments. If new measures serve a rough-and-ready end, they can always be perfected; but if they are not in themselves well motivated and of *prima facie* utility, then there is little point in perfecting them.

Our own experience with ARTS PROPEL suggests a different set of priorities. Neither of our new assessment and curriculum vehicles is likely to have any impact unless it becomes a central element in the classrooms in which it is to be used. Unlike many other educational innovations, they cannot just be "plugged in" to a standard curriculum; nor are they "kits" that can be ordered, installed in a brief interval, and periodically serviced. Rather, these assessment materials need to become part of a transformed atmosphere, a new milieu, in which such projects and processfolios occupy comfortable and appropriate roles.

An ARTS PROPEL program makes heavy demands on the classroom teacher. Just as it makes little sense for parents to pressure a child to read, but then return to their regular place in front of the television set, so, too, it is senseless for teachers to mandate processfolios, unless they believe in and make use of similar reflective materials in their own lives. Processfolios are, in essence, "on-line" records of how an individual progresses in a project of importance to him- or herself, one involving originality and personal stake. To the extent that teachers themselves engage in such projects in their own lives, and make those valued activities manifest to students, will students be drawn into the making of processfolios. By the same token, students will return spontaneously to processfolios only if they receive useful feedback on the contents, and only if they themselves find it rewarding to look over their own progress and their own process in a reflective manner.

Just how to bring about the appropriate "assessment environment" so as to create a "processfolio culture" is not an easy question. Such a transformation certainly cannot happen overnight. Teachers must have the opportunity to observe productive instances of such educational environments and must come to feel "in their bones" that such activities can be useful in their own lives. In some cases the adoption of a processfolio mentality involves a simple transfer of knowledge or skill already manifest in other arenas of their lives;

but sometimes teachers themselves must undergo an experience much like what they eventually hope to provide for their students. I believe that instances of success in Pittsburgh came about because teachers in effect became participants in a processfolio culture that we helped to create.

Let me return in conclusion to a line of argument that was begun earlier in this paper. Participants in ARTS PROPEL first believed that we were working only in the area of assessment, but we soon came to the realization that the line between assessment and curriculum was at most approximate and perhaps ought to be increasingly blurred in the future. We next learned that, no matter how inspired in conception, assessment and curriculum on their own have little effect. Teachers must understand, endorse, and ultimately embody the practices and procedures entailed in vehicles like domain products and processfolios. Unless teachers do so, even the best materials will, like many of the well-motivated American reforms of the 1960s, simply sit on the shelf.

Moreover, it may be unrealistic to expect teachers to subscribe *a priori* to an ARTS PROPEL regimen. In many cases, it makes more sense to begin by constructing environments in which teachers themselves have the opportunity to gain hands-on experiences with the materials and to judge their utility firsthand. Such familiarity cannot be gained in one or two "inservice sessions": Indeed, our own experience suggests that it takes about 2 years of informal experimentation before teachers are comfortable with these innovative procedures.

The final link in the chain takes us back to the origins of this paper. Even the best assessments, curricula, and teachers cannot expect to take hold in the face of a community that is hostile or indifferent. Ultimately, education is always answerable to the needs and values of the community—and perhaps that is as it should be. In cases where the community proves unsympathetic to educational goals and procedures—however laudable they may be—it is necessary to inform and educate the community concerning these new practices; otherwise these are doomed to desuetude. And so, in the end, art education—like all other forms of education—comes to reflect the aesthetic and educational values held by the wider community. It is not a far step to extend this point and to indicate that the community gets the kinds of assessment it deserves.

Acknowledgments. ARTS PROPEL has been funded for 5 years by a generous grant from the Arts and Humanities Division of the Rockefeller Foundation. Work described in this paper also has been supported by the Lilly Endowment, the Rockefeller Brothers Fund, and the Spencer Foundation.

APPENDIX A
AN INFORMAL INVENTORY OF ASSESSMENT OF STUDENT
LEARNING IN THE VISUAL ARTS

Tests of Perception

Meier Art Test
    Careful attention to balance and tension of artwork
    Comparative
    Requires sensitivity in looking at images
    Selection of best image
    Similar to Graves and McAdory

Graves Design Judgement Test
    Tests discrimination, sense of balance, and design
    Tests aptitude for appreciation or production of art structure
    Employs intuitive aptitude

McAdory Art Test
    Tests perception and judgment
    Compares four items rather than two
    Similar to Graves and Meier

Education Through Visual End of Course Achievement Test
    Measures perception
    Strong knowledge component

University of Chicago General Examination (Humanities Section)
    Perceptual component

Visual Skills Perception Test
    Includes taxonomy of Visual Art Cognitive Abilities
    Perception, attention, analysis, transformation, synthesis
    Combination of perception and perception test

Tests of Knowledge

Salt Lake City Humanities Test
    Multiple choice
    Matching
    Completion
    Requires specific art curriculum

Knauber Art Vocabulary Test
  Multiple choice
  Requires specific art curriculum

Eisner Art Information Inventory
  Tests four domains of art
  No example available

Test of Comprehension

University of Chicago General Examination (Humanities Section)
  No example available

Tests of Appreciation

Wilson Art Inventory
  No example available

Eisner Art Inventory
  Attitudes about art
  Gathers important data about how attitudes originate and how interests
    are pursued

Inventory of the Arts
  No example available

Tests of Production

Horn Art Aptitude Inventory
  Timed element to drawing an assortment of items (circles, hat, open
    book, etc.)
  Limited inventiveness
  Includes improvisation exercises to invent image from a few lines given

Knauber Art Ability Test
  Tests abilities such as critical ability and observation, sensitivity to light
    and dark patterns in a composition, imagination and design ability,
    creative imagination, and the ability to represent an idea rather than
    mere physical imitation
  Representative view of a student's creative thinking and abilities

Tests of Fundamental Abilities of Visual Art
　　Includes:
　　　• Recognition of proportion
　　　• Dot to dot drawing (imposes limitations)
　　　• Shading
　　　• Vocabulary
　　Limited aptitude test

Selective Art Aptitude Test
　　Includes color perception and design
　　Indicates advanced training and ability

Visual Skill Perception Test
　　Tests production involving cognitive skills of perception, attention, analysis, transformation, and synthesis
　　Fourth-grade level

Scale for General Merit of Children's Drawings
　　Standard of 14 subjects to rate drawings

Kline–Carey Scale
　　Scaled drawings

Free-Hand Drawing Aptitude Test
　　Eight pencil-and-paper tests

Draw a Man Test
　　Measures intellectual maturity

Qualitative Methods of Portrayal

Responsive Assessment
　　Suited to the arts
　　Utilizes substantive and functional structures
　　Portrayal and holistic communication

Connoisseurship
　　Awareness and appreciation of characteristics and qualities of the classroom

Critiques

> Used by art teachers for in-progress evaluation; usually involves whole class, but can be done individually
>
> Involves participant in learning experience

Portfolio

> Advanced placement, college board
>
> Allows for range of work to be evaluated and enables longitudinal view of work

National Assessment of Educational Progress

Preferences, Valuing Art, Art History

> p. 35: questions reflect content of specific curriculum, which can vary from school to school

Perceiving, Describing, Analyzing, Judging

> p. 43: indicates what students consider art and how they judge it
>
> p. 47: recognizing the theme, main idea, and principal features of works of art
>
> pp. 48–49: comparative items are a way of quickly assessing styles according to themes and features
>
> p. 51 (lower right): mood items, thought provoking
>
> p. 53: judgment about qualities of works of art; relies on thinking
>
> p. 58: judgments about paintings by Klee, Gorky, deKooning, and Henri (requires that students have had training in reading artworks)
>
> p. 59: requires student to have visual vocabulary

Production

> p. 68: six quick sketches for a painting (is scored in terms of fluency; an open-ended creative problem)
>
> p. 73: commercial design (imagination within a structure; difficulty can be with organization of ideas)
>
> pp. 74–75: time limited; expressive item that allows for individual differences

Note: The tests above are listed in *The Assessment of Artistic Thinking: Comments on the National Assessment of Educational Progress in the Arts* by H. Gardner and J. Grunbaum, 1987. Paper prepared for the Commission on the National Assessment of Educational Progress. The reader is also directed to *The Eleventh Mental Measurements Yearbook* by J. Kramer and J. Close-Conoley (Eds.), 1992, Lincoln: University of Nebraska, Buros Institute of Mental Measurements.

APPENDIX B
PROCESSFOLIO ASSESSMENT SYSTEM

Currently this system is based on art, music, and writing, and is planned to be expanded to other domains later.

Production: Thinking in the Domain

Evidence: The evidence for assessing work on the dimension of production lies in the work itself. Thus, these dimensions can be scored by an outsider looking at drafts and final works, as well as by the classroom teacher.

A. Craft: The student is in control of the basic techniques and principles of the domain.
B. Pursuit: The student develops works over time, as evidenced by revisions that are productive and thoughtful; pursues the problem in depth; and returns to a problem or theme from a variety of angles.
C. Invention: The student solves problems in a creative manner; experiments and takes risks with the medium; and sets his or her own problems to solve.
D. Expression: The student expresses an idea or feeling in the work (or in the performance of the work, as in music).

Reflection: Thinking About the Domain

Evidence: The evidence for assessing reflection comes from the student's journals and sketchbooks, and from observations of the kinds of comments the student makes in class. Thus, these dimensions need to be scored by a classroom teacher who knows the student.

A. Ability and proclivity to assess own work: The student can evaluate his or her own work; can articulate and defend the perceived strengths and weaknesses of the work; can engage in "shop talk" about the work.
B. Ability and proclivity to take on role of critic: The student has developed the ability to evaluate the work of others (peers, published artists); has a sense of the standards for quality work in the domain; and can engage in "shop talk" about others' work.
C. Ability and proclivity to use criticisms and suggestions: The student can consider critical comments about his or her own work and can incorporate suggestions where appropriate.
D. Ability to learn from other works of art within the domain: The student can use work by artists for ideas and inspiration.
E. Ability to articulate artistic goals: The student has a sense of him- or herself

as an artist, as evidenced by the ability to articulate goals for a particular work or more general artistic goals.

Perception: Perceiving in the Domain

Evidence: The evidence for assessing a student's perceptual skills comes from the student's journal entries and from observations of the student's comments made in critique sessions. Thus, only a classroom teacher can assess a student on this dimension.

A. Capacity to make fine discriminations about works in the domain: The student can make discriminations in works from a wide variety of genres, cultures, and historical periods.

B. Awareness of sensuous aspects of experience: The student shows heightened sensitivity to physical properties of the environment related to the domain in question (e.g., student responds to visual patterns made by shadows, to sounds of cars honking in different pitches, to patterning of words on a grocery list, etc.).

C. Awareness of physical properties and qualities of materials: The student is sensitive to the properties of the materials that he or she is working with in developing a work (e.g., textures of different papers; timbres of instruments; sounds of words).

Approach to Work

Evidence: The evidence for assessing a student's approach to work lies in observations of the student in classroom interactions and in the student's journal entries. Thus, a student's approach to work can be assessed only by the classroom teacher.

A. Engagement: The student works hard and is interested in what he or she is doing; meets deadlines; and shows care and attention to detail in the presentation of the final project.

B. Ability to work independently: The student can work independently when appropriate.

C. Ability to work collaboratively: The student can work collaboratively when appropriate.

D. Ability to use cultural resources: The student knows where to go for help: books, museums, tools, other people.

REFERENCES

Berger, R. (1991). Building a school culture where quality is "cool." *Harvard Education Letter,* 7(2), 5–7.

Gardner, H. (1982). *Art, mind, and brain.* New York: Basic Books.

Gardner, H. (1983a). *Frames of mind: The theory of multiple intelligences.* New York: Basic Books.

Gardner, H. (1983b). Artistic intelligences. *Art Education, 36,* 47–49.

Gardner, H. (1987). Symposium on the theory of multiple intelligences. In D. N. Perkins, J. Lochhead, & J. C. Bishop (Eds.), *Thinking: The second international conference* (pp. 77–101). Hillside, NJ: Erlbaum.

Gardner, H. (1989). Zero-based arts education: An introduction to ARTS PROPEL. *Studies in Art Education, 30*(2), 71–83.

Gardner, H. (1990a). *Art education and human development* (Occasional Paper No. 3). Los Angeles: Getty Center for Education in the Arts.

Gardner, H. (1990b). Assessment in context: The alternative to standardized testing. In B. R. Gifford & M. C. O'Connor (Eds.), *Future assessments: Changing views of aptitude, achievement, and instruction* (pp. 77–120). Boston: Kluwer.

Gardner, H., & Grunbaum, J. (1987). *The assessment of artistic thinking: Comments on the National Assessment of Educational Progress in the Arts.* Paper prepared for the Commission on the National Assessment of Educational Progress.

Gardner, H., & Hatch, T. (1989). Multiple intelligences go to school. *Educational Researcher, 18,* 4–10.

Gardner, H., & Perkins, D. (Eds.). (1989). *Art, mind, and education.* Urbana: University of Illinois Press.

Getty Center for Education in the Arts. (1984). *Beyond creating.* Los Angeles: Author.

Goodman, N. (1976). *Languages of art.* Indianapolis: Hackett.

Goodman, N. (1978). *Ways of worldmaking.* Indianapolis: Hackett.

Kramer, J., & Close-Conoley, J. (Eds.). (1992) *The eleventh mental measurements yearbook.* Lincoln: University of Nebraska, Buros Institute of Mental Measurements.

Moody, W. (Ed.). (1990). *Artistic intelligences: Implications for education in a democracy.* New York: Teachers College Press.

Smith, R. (Ed.). (1987). Discipline-based arts education [Special issue]. *Journal of Aesthetic Education, 21*(2).

Wiggins, G. (1989). A true test: Toward more authentic and equitable assessment. *Phi Delta Kappan, 70*(9), 703–713.

Winner, E. (1982). *Invented worlds.* Cambridge, MA: Harvard University Press.

Wolf, D. (1988/1989). Opening up assessment: Ideas from the arts. *Educational Leadership, 45*(4), 24–29.

Wolf, D. (1989). Portfolio assessment: Sampling student work. *Educational Leadership, 46*(7), 35–49.

Wolf, D., Bixby, J., Glenn, J., & Gardner, H. (1991). To use their minds well: Investigating new forms of student assessment. In G. Grant (Ed.), *Review of Research in Education* (pp. 31–74). Washington, DC: American Education Research Association.

Wygant, F. (1983). *Art in American schools in the 19th century.* Cincinnati: Interwood.

Zessoules, R., Wolf, D., & Gardner, H. (1988). A better balance: ARTS PROPEL as an alternative to discipline-based art education. In J. Burton, A. Lederman, & P. London (Eds.), *Beyond DBAE: The case for multiple visions of art education* (pp. 117–130). North Dartmouth: Southeastern Massachusetts University, University Council on Art Education.

Chapter 8

Nationwide Assessment of Studio Work in the Visual Arts: Actual Practice and Research in the Netherlands

DIEDERIK W. SCHÖNAU
Dutch Institute for Educational Measurement (Cito)

It is a common belief that art educators consider themselves competent to value their own students' studio work. Teachers know what to look for when they assess studio work produced in their classes. They claim to see its quality, even after a quick look, and a request to formulate criteria or to dissect evaluation into constituent pieces makes teachers insecure and irritated. They know what they see. With regard to other teachers' students, they may differ in opinion from their colleagues, but their reaction will depend on the situation and the moment. In judging one's colleague's students, other criteria and social techniques come into play.

In this highly complex field of the evaluation of studio work, little research has been done. We know little about the process and quality of assessment of studio work in schools. Recent discussions of the quality of art education in schools and the call for a more effective art education, especially in relationship to modern technology-oriented society, make it necessary to examine the validity of this "common knowledge." It is desirable, if not necessary, to find ways to make the goals and standards in studio work more understandable and effective, not only for colleagues in the field or for students, but also for administrators, school boards, parents, and society.

One way to enlarge understandability of studio work in the arts is to formulate as clearly as possible the general goals and the more specific objectives of studio work in secondary education. These goals and objectives then should be related to the intellectual, emotional, and artistic capacities and skills of the students and to the general aims of education at a certain school level. One might consider this move from theory to practice the ideal method of curriculum development.

There is, however, another way to come to greater clarity: by developing

Evaluating and Assessing the Visual Arts in Education: International Perspectives: © 1996 by Teachers College, Columbia University. All rights reserved. ISBN 0-8077-3511-6. Prior to photocopying items for classroom use, please contact the Copyright Clearance Center, Customer Service, 222 Rosewood Dr., Danvers, MA 01923, USA, tel. (508) 750-8400.

criteria for assessment. To formulate goals and objectives for studio work is one matter; to formulate criteria that meet the exigencies of a nationwide assessment is another.

In the Netherlands, final examinations in studio work were introduced in 1981. This brought into focus the need for objectivity, that is, the need to safeguard students from the subjectivity of their teachers. One way to solve this problem is to introduce very specific procedures to which all teachers must adhere. The other way is to formulate the tasks as clearly as possible and to develop criteria that leave little freedom for interpretation by the teachers or judges. In the past 10 years, thanks to the nationwide final examinations in studio work in the Netherlands, much information has become available on the quality of assessment of studio work in secondary schools.

Although the classic statement, "Non scholae sed vitae discimus"—we do not learn for school but for life—may still be an educational axiom, sometimes this idea seems to have been taken too literally in the history of art education. Personal growth and the joy of making art certainly are worth striving for in art education, but more is required than enthusiasm, socially acceptable goals, and good craftsmanship. There is a long distance between such general goals and the certainty that one has reached these goals in the most effective and permanent way.

Whatever the function of art in education, the first step will be to develop a curriculum that gives form and meaning to the general goals. The choice of themes and subjects, the exercises with specific materials and techniques, and the presentation and discussion of selected works of art all contribute to the general goals. Or at least, that is what is expected. The problems in the field of curriculum development are well known. The relationship of these elements of the curriculum to the general goals, as well as to each other, is complicated and sometimes ill-defined. This may be because of the qualitative character of art, where little can be translated or formulated in terms of clear-cut criteria.

Certainly it also involves the position of the arts relative to other subjects, which are thought to have a greater instrumental value. The joy of making things visible is considered a goal per se, counterbalancing the one-sided attention paid to cognitive and intellectual skills. It is said that disturbing the child's joy by introducing goals, norms, and criteria will kill creativity, enthusiasm, and motivation, and will make the arts another scholastic exercise.

Another factor involved is the lack of specific training of classroom teachers in the visual arts. On the other hand, art specialists, especially in primary schools, have the basic knowledge and training required, but have little time to build a personal relationship with children. Art literally becomes an extra in normal classroom routine.

Much can be explained by Western society's view of art in general and of art education in particular: Art is a commodity that enriches life in one's spare time. We cannot, however, blame "society" for the situation and leave it at that.

Teachers have a responsibility to their students, to their discipline, and to society. When it is considered important to present children with certain techniques, formal problems, visual phenomena, or works of art, there is an obligation to determine whether these confrontations and exercises are fruitful and worth the trouble. To determine the quality and effect of learning, criteria, standards, procedures, and instruments for evaluation must be developed.

This paper first describes the way in which studio work is assessed in Dutch secondary education at the preuniversity level. Second, the results of research aimed at improving the quality of assessment in the nationwide examinations are presented and discussed.

NATIONWIDE EXAMINATIONS IN THE ARTS: THE DUTCH EXAMPLE

In the National Endowment for the Arts' report, *Towards Civilization* (1988) that assessed the state of art education, the Dutch final examination system was presented as an example of the positive aspects of nationwide final examinations on curriculum reform, as compared with the usual practice of developing curricula first and having tests constructed on the basis of the curricula. The Dutch example shows that it is possible to develop standards, procedures, and instruments for national examinations in the visual arts that are acceptable to most teachers and to national authorities. It shows that a system of nationwide examinations can have a positive influence on curriculum development.

In order to appreciate what has happened in the Netherlands, some insight into the Dutch education system and the way final examinations in secondary education are organized is useful (Van Hoorn, 1987; Schönau, 1989). After primary school (ages 4–12) and a transition class, students in nonvocational secondary education can choose among three levels: a 3-year course preparing for a certificate that is comparable to junior high school level ("Mavo"), a 4-year course on an intermediate level, comparable to senior general secondary education ("Havo"), and a 5-year course, preparing for university ("VWO").

In order to pass the final examination, Dutch students have to pass a school examination, organized by the teachers of their own school, and a national written examination. The latter is administered to all students at exactly the same time in highly controlled situations.

Each examination contributes 50% to the final mark for a specific subject, and both must conform to the examination regulations prescribed for all schools in secondary education. Apart from these general regulations, the school examination is the responsibility of the school and its teachers. It was developed to enable schools to assess subjects considered important by the school or by the teachers. There are Dutch grammar schools, Protestant schools, Catholic schools, public schools, Montessori schools, and so forth, which all want to preserve their own identity. As the nationwide examinations are pencil-and-paper tests, school examinations also provide opportunities for assessing those aspects that cannot be assessed by means of pencil-and-paper tests.

Nationwide Assessment of Studio Work

In 1970, the visual arts (drawing, craft, and textiles) became school subjects with their own final examinations and had to conform to the tradition of written examinations. As studio work was considered too complex to assess nationwide, especially from an organizational point of view, that part of the curriculum had to be assessed at the school by the teacher. In 1978, the Dutch Ministry of Education and Science gave permission to start an experiment on final examinations at the preuniversity level (VWO) and permitted experimenting with nationwide assessment of studio work, but on that school level only. (The preuniversity level of schooling consists of 6 years of high school, beginning at age 12, and achievement of the VWO certificate permits entry to any university in the Netherlands.) The advocates of final examinations in the visual arts, who already in 1970 had argued in favor of the nationwide assessment of studio work, were finally granted their own form of examination.

Introducing this so-called Central Practical Examination (CPE) was not only a political problem. Practical problems arose when permission was given to start an experimental examination. To show that a system of nationwide examination of studio work was worth the trouble, it was necessary to show that it is possible to formulate national, prescriptive criteria and to arrive at common standards that are acceptable to all teachers. The urge to show that a long-cherished ambition was worth the trouble incited teachers in all three visual disciplines to work hard on the formulation of final goals in studio work at the preuniversity level.

Theoretical Basis for Studio Work: Preuniversity Level

The first problem was to formulate general goals for studio work that were specific to the preuniversity level. It was decided that the three disciplines would try to formulate a core curriculum, with the same goals and general criteria for all three disciplines. The aspects that are specific to each discipline, such as the character of the materials chosen or the way materials are employed, were left to the teacher's competence.

To understand the following properly, it is important to know that in 1978 there was virtually no experience with studio work in the upper grades of the preuniversity level. Therefore, the formulation and introduction of an examination program for this level of education was an experiment in more than one respect.

Members of the committee responsible for the examination program, which was oriented toward the characteristics specific to this school level, decided to focus on the intellectual skills considered relevant for future university students. The notions of self-reliance and differentiation became key words in the theoretical underpinning of studio work at the preuniversity level. Self-reliance has to do with the student's independence in choosing the subject of work, in the ways of making the choice visible, and in the materials and techniques used. Differentiation refers to the general aim of enabling students to develop their preferences and talents. Studio work at the preuniversity level, however, is not meant as preparation for admission into art academies or related institutions. It is aimed at the development of communicative skills in visualization and at the stimulation of an inquisitive mind. Each future university student thus can benefit from art as a final examination subject, because the skills and aims involved can be of use in many different academic disciplines.

As a consequence, it was decided that students should produce studio work on the basis of very general, even rather vague, themes or tasks, instead of tasks on which all kinds of limitations and prescriptions are imposed. Students have to start from a theme and make well-defined choices about the content they want to visualize. Next, they must decide which aspects to emphasize. They are free in their choice of materials and techniques.

The Communication Model

To reach these goals, a didactic approach based on a communication model was chosen. In this model, attention is concentrated not on the content of the "message" itself, but on the way this message is "encoded" and communicated. The process of artistic visualization is considered primarily in terms of a communication process, in which the "sender" is using specific techniques and devices to make his or her point clear to a "receiver," that is, the beholder. Students make their choice from a series of possible values, norms, and aims that they want to communicate to others. To make these choices visible, students then can choose a specific way of visualization. Theoretically, there are five different approaches that can be used as a starting point for the actual design or visualization.

1. The aesthetic approach (or quality, as it is called in the literature), in which the student stresses the aesthetic appeal of his or her work
2. The expressive approach, in which the student's own feelings or ideas are essential
3. The informative approach, in which the student is interested primarily in communicating specific information
4. The appealing approach, in which the work is intended first of all to attract the attention of an observer
5. The exhortative approach, in which the observer takes his or her stand with regard to the content conveyed

Essential for the theory when it is adapted to art production at the pre-university level is that students have to concentrate not only on the final result but even more on the process that leads to the final product. The sketches, studies, and experiments must show that a process of visualization has been completed. Typical for studio work at this level is the freedom for students to make a selection from all their work. The collection is composed to make visible the working process and the problems they have encountered, struggled with, and mastered. Also, because of this emphasis on the process, an examination procedure was formulated that involves the work produced in 28 school periods of 50 minutes each.

Understandably, students determine the function and character of their collections based on the judgment criteria. To enlarge this freedom even further, students are offered a choice of four to six tasks, or themes, from which they select one. These tasks are determined by the committee responsible for the nationwide final written examinations in art criticism and art history. Some examples are given in Figure 8.1.

Consequences for Testing

The choices made in 1979 have complicated the assessment of studio work. The starting points were vague, the theory not yet tested, and the candidates' freedom so enormous that it became difficult to formulate criteria that would do justice to the general aims on the one hand and to the collections produced on the other. In addition, the choice that this approach should be applicable to candidates in all three visual disciplines led to omitting criteria not applicable to all disciplines.

When the Ministry of Education and Science gave permission to start an experiment with nationwide assessment of studio work in the visual arts, it stipulated that all teachers and organizations involved would strive to make the assessment "as objective as possible." From the beginning, this nationwide examination had to fit into the national examination system, not only from an organizational point of view, but also in terms of the quality of testing. The

Figure 8.1 Examples of CPE Assignments (1995)

Two-dimensional art (drawing)

1. Make good cheer.
2. A gaze into infinity. (In this task a form of perspective has to be used.)
3. Students are normally provided with a stanza from a well-known Dutch song or poem.
4. Make a design for a series of postage stamps that will be issued in 1995 on the subject of modern architecture. It relates to stamps of 70, 80, and 160 cents.
   Besides the fact that the whole process of designing has to be made visible, the series has to answer the following purposes:
   • text and typography have to be in unity with the image
   • the final design has to be executed on a minimum size of 10 x 15 cm
   • the use of photographs of buildings is prohibited

Three-dimensional art (handicraft)

5. Struggle of (the) ornaments.
6. Resilience (or elasticity).
7. Design and make a small chest in which you can hide something valuable. The chest has to attract attention and/or curiosity to its content. It has to be provided with a "hidden" lock.

Textile art

8. Ready for use.
9. Eaten away.
10. Black pages.
11. A big party is organized on the theme "Make good cheer." Design and make a garment (piece of clothing) that you will wear to that party.

---

tradition of pencil-and-paper tests, in which the influence of the student's own teacher on the final mark has to be as small as possible, was taken as a paradigm. From this point of view the experiment was destined to fail from the beginning, as the way studio work is assessed differs fundamentally from assessment by means of written examinations. There are no "objective norms" or standards that can be applied to studio work. The "subjective" involvement of judges is essential. At best, it is possible to arrive at a certain degree of intersubjectivity between two or more judges.

As it was stipulated in the examination program that a candidate would have freedom in the choice of materials, content, aims, and character of the studio work, the pursuit of objectivity became even more precarious. The designers of the examination program were very much aware of this problem, but decided to first formulate the general goals of studio work at the preuniversity level and then decide by which means the demands of objectivity in assessment could best be met.

At the outset it was impossible to be more specific on assessment criteria than to formulate a list of points indicating the possible choices a candidate could make. Five aspects of the work were to be assessed.

1. A global, first impression
2. The point of view chosen by the candidate with regard to the content to be visualized
3. The goals chosen by the candidate with regard to the way he or she is to visualize the content chosen
4. The way artistic means are used
5. Final judgment

To meet the demand of maximum objectivity and to conform to the tradition of the Dutch examination system, the work was assessed not only by the student's own teacher, but by a colleague from another school as well.

The Central Practical Examination in Practice

In the first year in which examinations at the preuniversity level were administered (1981), the work was judged by the candidate's own teacher and by a jury of five colleagues. Each jury visited about five schools, assessing some 60 candidates (Schönau, 1988a).

The introduction of a jury was based on four grounds. First it was hoped that in this way the influence of different views on the content and quality of studio work would be neutralized. There had never been an assessment of studio work on a nationwide level, and teachers were used to having maximum liberty in the way they taught their discipline and in their definition of "minimum level of competency." Thus, there was no guarantee that all teachers would value the work presented in the same way.

Second, at this first examination there would not be any insight into what levels of quality were possible.

Third, it was known from earlier research by the Dutch Institute for Educational Measurement (Cito) on comparable disciplines that a jury of five persons would be a solid basis for reaching an acceptable approximation of what was considered to be the true score. Employing more judges would not change the final mark or score of the students.

Finally, it was expected that as a side effect the procedure of a jury traveling to different schools would form a unique opportunity for all teachers to come into contact with studio work produced at different schools. In 1981 most teachers visited at least four schools. It was expected that a certain learning effect would occur as a result of this procedure.

The members of the jury were not permitted to confer on the marks given. The marks were averaged, and the final score was averaged with the score given by the student's teacher.

In 1982, a similar procedure was followed, this time with a jury consisting of only three persons. The 1981 data showed that a reduction in the number of judges from five to three had barely influenced the candidate's final mark. The jury's mean score represented only one-eighth of the overall mark given to a candidate, which is based on the school examination and the central examination of both studio work and art criticism/art history.

Since 1983, all studio work has been judged independently by the candidate's own teacher and one colleague who is a subject specialist from another school. This outside reviewer visits only one school, and every year he or she visits a different school. Since the outside reviewers supervise candidates themselves, they have experience with the year's themes and with the level possible. Immediately after the assessment, both teachers compare scores and, if necessary, negotiate the final grade. This procedure, in which only one colleague from another school is involved in the control of quality, is the general procedure for all written final examinations in the Netherlands in which open-ended questions are used. For financial and technical reasons, an assessment procedure for studio work in which only one external judge would be active was the ideal within the existing final examination system. This system has been maintained since 1983.

Through the years, the criteria by which the work is judged have been fine-tuned. Teachers are more experienced with this kind of assessment. The mean differences between judges have been fairly stable over the past few years. Table 8.1 presents the results for 1987.

Judges

An assessment by at least two independent judges works well, provided that after this assessment the judges discuss their scores and reach an agreement on the final grade. This procedure, in combination with the obligation to visit other schools and to discuss the quality of studio work with unacquainted colleagues, has made the experimental examination of studio work in the Netherlands a success. Most teachers involved in the experiment have pleaded for maintaining this kind of nationwide assessment of studio work in the future.

Whether the introduction of national assessment procedures for studio work has led to a rise in quality, not only at the examination level but also at lower levels, has not been investigated. Actually, there is no information avail-

Table 8.1 Results on Studio Work in 1987[1]

	Drawing	Craft	Total[2]
Number of observations	231	100	336
Mean score of the students' own teachers	6.8	7.1	6.9
Mean score of the independent judges	6.7	6.8	6.7
Mean difference in scores between both judges	0.7	0.7	0.7
Percentage of cases where both judges differ ≤ 0.5 point	51%	56%	52%
Percentage of cases where both judges differ ≤ 1.0 point	79%	80%	79%
Pearson correlation on scores between judges	.67	.71	.68

All works were judged by the student's own teacher and an independent judge.

1. This was the last year information was gathered from both the student's own teacher and the external judge.

2. This column includes the results of students in textile art.

Note: All marks are given on a 10-point scale; the mean difference is based on absolute differences between the marks given by the student's own teacher and the outside reviewer. Only five candidates' textile art results were available. These results are not presented separately but are included in the total column.

able on the basis of which comparisons could be made because until 1978 there was virtually no instruction in the arts in the upper grades of the preuniversity level.

The choice for a specific approach to the aims and content of studio work at the preuniversity level has led to cooperation among three disciplines (drawing, craft, and textile arts) that turned out to be too stringent. As a result of the use of a preconceived, theoretical model, the content and aims of studio work were not based on actual practice. On the contrary, teachers adjusted their practice to general aims based on theoretical assumptions and goals. This has led to tensions among the three disciplines, but also between teachers within the same discipline. Whether teachers have experienced a loss in quality of studio work, because of a loss in personal freedom caused by the obligation to adhere to "official" standards and procedures, is not known. Not all teachers are happy with this nationwide assessment of studio work, but it is not clear whether this has to do with the procedures prescribed or with the general theory on which studio work is based.

The relatively favorable results found concerning judging in the visual arts also may be ascribed to the strong tradition of judging studio work at art schools and teacher training colleges. Studio work produced by future teachers is evaluated and criticized on many occasions, formally or informally, in art schools, both by instructors and by fellow students. This experience and training must not be underestimated. This form of assessment is acceptable to most teachers and seldom has given rise to conflicts. The procedure of another teacher and colleague expressing his or her opinion on the quality of other teachers' candidates functions satisfactorily. Independent assessment leads to a relatively high degree of agreement. Inter-rater agreement is around .70. The mean differences are around .7 to .8 of a point on a 10-point scale. In about 80% of the cases, differences between judges are not larger than 1.0 point. Whether such differences are acceptable is a matter of opinion. The agreement between judges of studio work is less than that found for written examinations. The character of studio work makes a comparison with written examinations rather unrealistic.

Subject Specificity

A remark should be made on the theory underlying studio work. After some years of experimenting, it became clear that the paradigm used was not equally useful for all three disciplines. Drawing teachers were going in another direction: They were moving toward a more "artistic" interpretation of the aims and quality of studio work. The general question of "how" a collection is made is being assessed on more specific, more discipline-oriented grounds, and based on the way materials and visual means are applied.

There is also a tension between the weight given to the process character of studio work and the candidate's tendency to concentrate on the final product. Moreover, certain techniques, especially those used in craft and textile art, are time-consuming, at the expense of time spent on studies and experiments.

For future experiments or innovations, the specific characteristics of a discipline must be taken as a starting point for the formulation of an underlying theory. The procedures developed for the examination in question are highly dependent on the general examination system. The choice of an examination that takes up 28 periods had been proposed by the teachers themselves. The main reason for this was the assumption that a long period of examination would ensure proper attention to the process character of studio work. After 8 years of experimenting, it appeared that 28 periods might be more than necessary for showing a candidate's capacities. Other possibilities have not been investigated, but an examination period of several days may be sufficient.

Current practice in the assessment of studio work may not be ideal. Many teachers, especially those entering the field, need more information and instruction on the criteria used and on the weights assigned to each aspect. For instance, what happens when a student ignores certain aspects or options so that the final collection fails to meet certain criteria? Does it mean that those criteria are ignored by the judge, or that the student is "punished," or that less weight is assigned to those aspects? Students and judges should be provided with guidelines for assessment when a collection lacks certain characteristics.

RESEARCH ON RELIABILITY: IMPROVING ASSESSMENT

In 1981 the committee responsible for the design and evaluation of the preuniversity examination program in the visual arts asked Cito to participate in the general task formulated by the Ministry of Education and Science of "developing and validating of objective criteria" for the assessment of studio work. In consultation with the committee responsible for the examination program, an investigation was begun into the possibility of increasing objectivity; that is, reducing judges' subjective interpretation of the criteria on which studio work is to be assessed (Schönau, 1988b).

Since the assessment was introduced in 1981 on the basis of a rather general, nonspecific procedure in which judges paid attention to only the general aims and criteria of the examination program, a more analytic assessment model was proposed. An inventory was made of all possible criteria mentioned in or closely related to the examination program. On the basis of the results of an inquiry of teachers involved in the experiment, these seven criteria were extracted.

1. Was the theme chosen recognizable in the collection?
2. Was the personal point of view of the candidate recognizable in the collection?
3. Was a critical selection made from different possible solutions?
4. Was the form original, given the choices made?
5. What was the relationship between the visual elements and the approach chosen by the candidate?

6. What was the relationship between materials and techniques on the one hand, and the approach chosen by the candidate on the other?
7. What was the relationship between materials and techniques used and the representation chosen?

To have some control over the relationship of these criteria to the preuniversity level at which they were aimed, two criteria were added that do not appear in the examination program but that often are mentioned in the actual teaching of visual arts: the candidate's concentration during the working period and his or her technical skill.

Procedure

Every collection was assessed independently by several judges on all nine criteria. Afterward every judge provided a subjective overall judgment. This final judgment was not based on the mean of all scores on the nine criteria, but was left to the personal interpretation of the judges. Such a subjective judgment on general quality, after the analytic assessment procedure had been completed, would do more justice to the judge's real opinion. This subjective final judgment was used as the final score in the so-called analytic condition.

Judgments were made on a 10-point scale, in which 1 meant "no performance at all" and 10 meant "an excellent performance"; a score of 5.5 meant "the minimal performance necessary to pass the test." This is the most current scale.

As a point of reference in determining whether the introduction of the analytic assessment model would be an improvement, an assessment by a jury followed the procedures and instructions used in 1981. The average of five scores, given independently by five judges using the assessment procedures then current, would represent the "true score" most adequately.

As with assessment of studio work, it is often assumed that a highly qualified judge is capable of providing an evaluation based on first impression. This form of assessment, based on global impression, was included as well. Finally, the student's teacher's grade was taken as a fourth measure.

Thus, there were four forms of judgment.

1. Judgment by jury, as used in the final examination in 1981 (reference group)
2. Judgment by jury based on nine separate criteria
3. Judgment by jury based on global, first impression
4. Judgment by the candidate's own teacher, according to the criteria applied in the 1981 central examination

Table 8.2 Differences Among Three Judgment Procedures

	Global Reference	Analytic Reference	Own teacher Reference
Number of observations	60	60	60
Absolute mean difference	0.65	0.70	0.95
Range of differences	2.6	4.7	2.8
Standard deviation	0.52	0.70	0.74
Correlation	0.74	0.74	0.70

Note: All numbers are based on jury averages, except for the score given by the student's own teacher. Results on drawing and craft are combined.

In the first three experimental conditions, juries consisted of four to seven teachers, depending on availability, whose mean assessment was used in the analysis. In all experimental conditions, scores were assigned by judges independently. All judges were teachers with experience in the final examination at the preuniversity level. For technical reasons, the investigation was limited to arts and crafts only.

For practical reasons, the number of collections was limited to 60: 40 from arts and 20 from craft. All collections were not part of the final examination, but part of the school examination. This means that the students had not devoted as much time to these collections as they might have if the collections had been made during the final examination. Another limitation was that tasks set were different for all schools. Thus the collections showed a wider variety in character and elaboration than those made for the final nationwide examination. The results are presented in Table 8.2.

Results show that use of an analytic assessment model does not come closer to the true score than does impressionistic judgment. On the contrary, it appears that in the global judgment condition, the true score is approached as closely as in the analytic condition, and that the differences between judges are even smaller in the former. Secondary analysis of these scores has made clear, however, that for drawing, analytic judgment is slightly better than global, impressionistic judgment. For craft, however, the results showed the reverse.

These results did not confirm our expectations. Several explanations may be offered: the limited number of collections used, the great diversity in the collections, the lack of familiarity of judges with analytic assessment models, the strict separation of the criteria used in the analytic situation, and the criteria not being specific to the tasks given.

Improving the Tasks

An analytic judgment is more meaningful when all candidates have advance knowledge of the criteria on which they will be judged. As the tasks given in the central examination are rather general, giving students a wide range of possible approaches, a second investigation was carried out (Schönau, 1987).

This research was aimed at investigating how much more objective assessment becomes when all candidates meet more strict and limiting criteria than the criteria used thus far in the actual examination. Additionally, these criteria would be specific to the tasks given. The judges would assess the collections based solely on these well-defined criteria: an analytic judgment.

In order to investigate this hypothesis, 124 pupils from five different schools were asked to produce a collection on one out of four possible tasks given to them. These four tasks were arranged as follows:

1. A task like the ones in the actual national examination, that is, without any additional criteria related to the task
2. The same task, but provided with some specification of the amount and diversity of the studies and pieces of work, and with 15 criteria by which the collection would be judged, including the maximum score obtainable for each criterion
3. A task, in the same tradition as number 1, but instead of a general theme, a passage from the "Futurist Manifesto" from Marinetti, and also without any further specifications or guidelines
4. The same task as number 3, but with additional information on the five criteria by which the collection would be judged, including the maximum score obtainable for each criterion

Thus, four types of collections were available that were judged on their own terms. Collections on tasks 1 and 3, the so-called structured tasks, were judged according to the guidelines used for the central practical examination. These guidelines or criteria are not specific to the different tasks given. Tasks 2 and 4 were judged according to criteria specific to the tasks and known to the students beforehand. Task 2, with 15 criteria, was intentionally much more structured than task 4, with five criteria.

To show that a nonstructured assessment would lead to more disagreement between judges, assessment of the collections based on the structured tasks (2 and 4) was performed by means of the procedures used in the actual

Table 8.3 Results on Traditional (T) Versus Structured (S) Tasks and Judgment

Kind of task	T	S	S	S
Kind of judgment	T	T	Ssum	Ssub
Number of observations	276	164	164	165
Mean standard deviation for each collection	.91	1.05	.91	.86
mean correlation between judges	.64	.48	.58	.57

Ssum: scores are based on mean of all marks given on independent scales.

Ssub: scores are based on 'subjective' final overall mark given by judge, after scoring on independent scales

Note: T = Traditional, according to practice in the actual final examinations

S = Structured, according more specified indications and criteria

Ssum = Mean score on nine criteria in structured judgment condition

Ssub = Subjective final mark given by judges after they had completed their judgment on the nine distinct criteria

Standard deviation on each collection was averaged, in order to establish a mean standard deviation as an indication of inter-rater reliability.

final examinations. A total of 60 collections were judged, 15 from each of the four groups. For practical reasons this part of the investigations was limited to collections in drawing. The results of this research are summarized in Table 8.3.

The results show that analytic judgment of collections produced on the basis of structured tasks does not necessarily result in greater agreement between judges than traditional assessment of nonstructured tasks. The mean standard deviation for each collection is almost identical in both conditions, and the inter-judge reliability is even lower for the structured tasks. It makes little difference whether the final score, based on analytic judgment, is computed by averaging the different marks given on all criteria or whether it is based on a final, subjective opinion of the judge. In the latter case, differences between judges are somewhat smaller. Further, analytic judgment of a structured task produces lower marks than "traditional" judgment on general tasks.

As expected, traditional judgment of structured tasks yields larger differences between judges, although they exhibit more agreement on the ranking of the collections (Pearson product moment correlation coefficient).

The differences found between the two kinds of tasks (1 and 3 versus 2

Table 8.4 Results on Traditional (T) Versus Structured (S) Tasks and Judgment, per Task (1 and 2)

Kind of task	1T	2T	1S	2S	1S	2S	1S	2S
Kind of judgment	T	T	T	T	Ssum	Ssum	Ssub	Ssub
Number of observations	135	141	83	81	82	82	83	82
Mean score	6.7	5.8	5.3	6.2	5.0	6.7	5.4	6.8
Mean standard deviation for each collection	.82	.99	1.13	.96	1.00	.82	.91	.80

Note:

  1T = Task 1, traditional formulation   1S = Task 1, structured formulation

  2T = Task 2, traditional formulation   2S = Task B2 structured formulation

  T = Judgment according to CPE prescriptions

  S = Judgment based on nine independent criteria

  SSum = Scores based on mean of all marks given on independent scales

  SSub = Scores based on "subjective" final overall mark given by judge, after scoring on
            independent scales

and 4) are presented in Table 8.4. Most striking are the differences in means for both kinds of tasks. These are caused not only by the distinction between structured versus unstructured, but also by differences in character or content of both tasks and their respective criteria.

Task 1, which corresponds to the actual tasks given in the final examinations, is judged more negatively in its structured version (task 2). With tasks 3 and 4, the opposite occurs. From looking at the difference in content of both sets of tasks and at the different degrees of structuring, one might conclude that a certain amount of structuring and the provision of a number of criteria raises the level of agreement between judges. We might be wary of this conclusion, however, in view of the small number of collections available for this investigation.

Discussion of the Results

The research done by Cito on the improvement of objectivity in assessment of studio work in the visual arts has led to some interesting insights. Global impressionistic marking, done by experienced judges, is not without value. Assessment based on more explicit criteria does not result in more agreement between judges. Comparing the results presented in Tables 8.2 and 8.3, one might even get the impression that a structured task assessed by analytic judgment leads to more disagreement between judges than traditional assessment on the more general tasks presented in the actual examination. One possible explanation for this effect may be that students and judges were unfamiliar with the research procedure employed. Using structured tasks based on very explicit criteria differs considerably from the actual situation in school, either during lessons or in final examinations, and from the actual examination program. In this type of research, it is difficult to identify the causes of these results. The perfect research situation would employ different groups of students and judges, all of whom were trained in relevant traditions. This, however, is impracticable.

On the basis of these results, the introduction of structured tasks or analytic assessment models for studio work in final examinations is problematic. Structuring a task just for the sake of introducing structure into a general task may even be counterproductive. Task 2 probably was overly structured. It should be added, however, that both candidates and judges had little or no experience with this kind of analytic assessment.

Limitations

The investigations make it clear that it is inadvisable to use a method of assessment for studio work when neither the teachers, nor the students, nor the judges have any knowledge of or experience with the assessment procedures. On the other hand, one can question the way the true score was defined. Here, the true score was based on averaging the marks given by different judges as the best way to minimize errors of measurement.

Individual judges in the reference group probably differed in their approach, their interpretations of the criteria, and the weights assigned to each criterion. A true score can best be rendered by a jury by mutual arrangement, after an individual and independent assessment by each jury member. This is the best way to compensate for different opinions and weights given to the various aspects, because choices are made explicit and great divergences in interpretation of criteria will be corrected through debate.

The results found in these investigations are not in accordance with the results found for final examinations in other disciplines. Cito has done research on the improvement of inter-judge reliability in written examinations for Dutch language (composition and summary) by structuring the tasks and the assessment models. The result was increased objectivity (i.e., inter-judge reliability and/or smaller differences between judges). This gain, however, was relative since the larger the disagreement before the introduction of a specific procedure, the larger the gain. It also depends on the character of the test used. For instance, when pencil-and-paper tests are used in which a given answer may be true or false, it is easier to be more specific about the grounds for determining the correctness of an answer. When assessment is based on qualitative responses of judges, it is difficult if not impossible to speak in terms of "true" or "false." There are no right or wrong answers. Each judgment or mark given for studio work is a mark on a continuum that is subdivided into intervals. Objectivity in terms of true and false, as used in pencil-and-paper tests, is impossible. The only test used in final examinations in the Netherlands that can be compared with the central practical examination for the arts is Dutch composition. The tasks (titles) given to candidates for this test are comparable to those used in the arts. Judges (teachers), however, have few guidelines, and there is less agreement on the aims of this test or of composition in general as compared with the arts. Inter-judge reliability is considerably lower for composition than for the arts.

FUTURE DEVELOPMENTS

Thanks to the Dutch examination system, art educators in the Netherlands have had the opportunity to experiment with a form of centralized assessment of studio work that conforms to guidelines and criteria.

The research done on the assessment of studio work, as part of the experiment, has shown that the first, global impression is a useful starting point in the assessment procedures. The introduction of distinct criteria used independent of one another does not lead to more agreement between judges. These results are based on a particular situation in which the research was done. One cannot experiment with impunity within an existing school practice or suspend temporarily the effects of years of instruction.

It is too early to conclude that the development of more structured tasks and accompanying criteria will lead to more agreement between judges. This hypothesis can be proven only when the research context is as favorable as it was for the research presented here, in which very broad tasks were assessed on general, nontask-specific criteria. It remains to be seen whether agreement will rise dramatically, let alone the question of whether this should determine the way studio work is taught and evaluated at the preuniversity level.

Another aspect, not mentioned thus far, is the acceptability of structured tasks. From the judges' answers to a questionnaire presented immediately after they completed their assessment, it becomes clear that many teachers do not oppose structured tasks. But taking into consideration the results presented and the fact that there is little or no experience with structured tasks on the preuniversity level, it may be concluded that the introduction of (more) structured tasks and accompanying criteria for judgment just for the sake of improving the quality of assessment, is problematic, to say the least.

REFERENCES

Hoorn, M. Van. (1987). Will Cinderella beat the clock? *Canadian Review of Art Education, 15*(1), 27–34.

National Endowment for the Arts. (1988). *Towards civilization: A report on arts education.* Washington, DC: Author.

Schönau, D. (1987). *Het beoordelen van praktisch beeldend werk: Gestructureerde versus ongestructureerde opdrachten* (Tech. Rep. 235) [The assessment of studio work in art education: Structured versus unstructured tasks]. Arnhem: Cito.

Schönau, D. (1988a). *Het beoordelen van praktisch beeldend werk: Het CPE 1981–1987* (Tech. Rep. 285) [The assessment of studio work in art education: The Central Practical Exam, 1981–1987]. Arnhem: Cito.

Schönau, D. (1988b). *Het beoordelen van praktisch beeldend werk: Analytische versus globale beoordeling* (Tech. Rep. 278) [The assessment of the studio work in art education: Analytic versus global judgment]. Arnhem: Cito.

Schönau, D. (1989). Final examinations in the visual arts: Practice and policies. *Visual Arts Research, 15* (1), 1–7.

Evaluation in the Visual Arts: A Cross-Cultural Perspective

JOHN STEERS
National Society for Education in Art and Design, UK

In discursive examination answer style, I intend to compare and contrast the approaches of Howard Gardner and Diederik Schönau to assessment in the visual arts and, when appropriate, to illustrate my points by making some further comparisons with recent art and design assessment procedures in England and Wales.

A brief personal statement may help to explain my perspective. At the age of 16, while still at school in England, I took a national examination in art. Throughout my career in education I have been involved in one way or another with the administration of national art and design examinations for 16- and 18-year-old students and less formal assessment arrangements for younger students. When, in the 1960s, the examination system was extended to include 80% of the 16 and over age group, there were some art teachers who declared that this would lead to the inevitable death of creativity and imagination—views echoed by the Dutch teachers Schönau cites as saying that "introducing goals, norms, and criteria will kill creativity, enthusiasm, and motivation, and will make the arts another scholastic exercise." Twenty-five years later the participation rate in art and design examinations has increased considerably, and there is a consensus view that standards of teaching and learning have improved. The national curriculum being introduced in England and Wales as a consequence of the 1988 Education Reform Act eventually may require all pupils to be assessed in art at ages 7, 11, and 14. Optional examinations will continue to be available for 16- and 18-year-old students. Consequently, for me, assessment in art and design is a simple fact of life, and the key question is not, "Shall we assess?" but "How can we design for the 6 million children in our schools a worthwhile, reliable, and cost-effective assessment system that is both formative and summative in nature?" It may come as a surprise to some North American colleagues to know that in my career to date I have never been asked to take a standardized, multiple-choice, machine-scored test—indeed, I have never seen one.

I have to say to you that my comments are colored by my conclusion that (1) the Dutch model closely resembles the assessment procedures for the examinations that prevailed in England and Wales until the much-needed reforms of the second half of the 1980s; and (2) the ARTS PROPEL model probably would be mistrusted in the United Kingdom unless it was founded on a concept of teacher "ownership" similar to what British art and design teachers have come to expect. If this is an important principle, it is not evident in Howard Gardner's paper. By relating these models to current and recent developments in Britain, I believe that I am comparing them with the results of an unprecedented, sustained national effort in which the professionalism of classroom teachers has played a particularly significant role. Of course, all observers add their own gloss to what they see; for me, an essential guiding concept is that of "professionalism." By that I mean the effectiveness of implementation, in this case by the overwhelming majority of art and design teachers, while, at the same time, "serving the intrinsic values and interests of the profession."

ASSESSMENT CONSIDERATIONS

It is beyond dispute that the assessment of achievement is an intrinsic part of education. It is generally recognized that

> From their earliest years students are subject to assessment: simple gestures, affirmative or negative reactions are all measures of performance. Teachers, as a matter of course, are continually gathering information about the effectiveness of teaching and learning, accumulating records to monitor students' progress and to assist prognosis. (Secondary Examinations Council, 1986a)

There is also a consensus view that assessment procedures should reflect the aims of courses and should enhance the quality of teaching and learning without dominating or distorting them. It is recognized that well-designed assessment procedures should have the qualities of validity, reliability, and utility.

Gardner suggests that overinsistence on these qualities can inhibit the development of alternative forms of assessment. He says, "If new measures serve a rough-and-ready end, they can always be perfected; but if they are not in themselves well motivated and of *prima facie* utility, then there is little point in perfecting them." At present in the United Kingdom there are several nationwide assessment systems operating for various levels of education from 16-year-olds to graduate level. The important point about these systems is that they are continually being refined and updated to improve the quality of assessment, through the combined efforts of all those involved in the system, from classroom teachers to the officers of the examining/validating bodies. It is essentially a "bottom-up" process as opposed to the "top-down" model where the assessment expert hands down from on high a perfectly designed assessment system engraved on tablets of stone. Teacher "ownership" of the assessment systems is seen as a most important attribute. In essence, British experience seems to suggest that many of the so-called alternative forms of assessment proposed by Gardner can be introduced on a large scale without losing sight of key issues such as validity, reliability, and utility—although these terms may not be used in the same strict sense as, for example, when they are used in psychological tests.

The Business and Technician Education Council (BTEC), which is responsible for the assessment of many postschool subdegree courses, defines these qualities as follows:

Validity
The validity of an assessment is the extent to which it serves its purpose. . . . A valid assessment will therefore employ methods—and accord them relative importance—that reflect the aims and objectives of courses and units.

Reliability
Assessments should, as far as possible, be designed and operated so that they give a similar result when taken by students of similar ability under similar conditions. A perfectly reliable assessment is, however, impossible: unreliability may be caused by differences in the conditions for, or the context of the assessment, in the judgments of markers, etc.

Utility
The utility of an assessment is its convenience, flexibility and cost-effectiveness. It is important because centers have to operate within the time and resources available. (BTEC, 1986, p. 2)

These characteristics inevitably will be in tension in most assessment procedures and, consciously or unconsciously, a different weight will be given to each. With these fairly flexible definitions in mind, and despite Gardner's reservations, the qualities of validity, reliability, and utility are used to examine the assessment procedures described in the papers under review and to provide a partial structure for this paper.

It is also axiomatic that any system of assessment should satisfy certain general criteria. In England and Wales, the Task Group on Assessment and Testing (TGAT), a body that was set up by the government to provide initial advice on assessment in the national curriculum, gave priority to the following four criteria, which, in the United Kingdom, seem to have been accepted as self-evident:

- the assessment results should give direct information about pupils' achievement in relation to objectives: they should be *criterion-referenced;*
- the results should provide a basis for decisions about pupils' further learning needs: they should be *formative;*
- the scales or grades should be capable of comparison across classes and schools, if teachers, pupils and parents are to share a common language and common standards: so assessments should be calibrated or *moderated;*
- the ways in which criteria and scales are set up and used should relate to expected routes of educational development, giving continuity to a pupil's assessment at different ages: the assessments should relate to *progression.* (TGAT, 1987, par. 5)

SOME GENERAL COMMENTS

Elliot Eisner (1972) distinguished among *evaluation, testing,* and *grading.* Neither Schönau nor Gardner makes such a clear distinction, although it may be reasonable to assume that the Dutch are concerned primarily with a grading process and the ARTS PROPEL team with testing to "identify students with potential and/or talent" (Eisner, 1972). If this assumption is valid, it does not imply a necessary and fundamental incompatibility of approach, although Gardner and Schönau would probably assign different priorities to each of the following interrelated *functions* of assessment, as defined by Nuttall (1990):

Feedback for the student or teacher
Motivation for the student or teacher
Licensing/qualifications (attestation of mastery)
Selection
Monitoring national (or local) standards
Agent for control of the curriculum

Gardner provides a lucid account of different approaches to assessment and a brief history of art education *in the United States*—this national perspective needs to be stressed because this point is not always explicit in the paper and significant differences are apparent between current general practices in North America and Europe. Schönau, on the other hand, is careful to define his account in terms of "actual practice and research in the Netherlands." It is immediately obvious that one key difference is that nationwide assessment of art has taken place for many years in some European countries, while in the United States such procedures apparently have not been developed. This simple fact provides a strongly contrasting frame of reference for each paper.

Gardner refers to a prevailing view in the United States that "the kinds of verbal pencil-and-paper assessment instruments used in the conventional curriculum ought to be transported to the arts." He asserts that "in the United States today, a certain form of examination—the standardized, multiple-choice, machine-scored test—has come to be regarded as almost sacrosanct." This view is not so prevalent in the Netherlands or the United Kingdom, where there seems to be widespread recognition that such an approach to assessment would be inappropriate, particularly in the arts. Schönau properly emphasizes that in art "there are no right or wrong answers" and, if this is so, it is surely self-evident that, while the use of standardized tests may be cost-effective, such measures must lack validity and reliability.

It is perhaps worth noting that the British government has recognized that, while assessment in the arts is essential, it need not be approached in the same way as for other subjects. Albeit double-edged, paragraphs in the terms of reference for the Working Group for Art in the national curriculum for England and Wales state:

> The Secretary of State intends that, *because of the nature of the subject*, the objectives (attainment targets) and means of achieving them (programs of study) should not be prescribed in as much detail for art as for the core and other foundation subjects.
> The statutory assessment arrangements for art will not include nationally prescribed tests (except in the case of GCSE examinations at the end of Key Stage 4).[1] (Department of Education and Science, 1991, p. i.; emphasis added)

Another difference to be taken into account when comparing approaches to assessment in different countries is the education of the teachers themselves. Gardner says that one difficulty in developing new assessment models is that "in most schools, the classroom teacher—and, in some cases, even the art teacher—is not sufficiently proficient to serve as a reliable model for, and judge of, performances of the more talented or capable students." In countries where prospective teachers are trained only *after* graduating in their chosen speciality this is much less likely to be the case, although in Great Britain the problem identified by Gardner probably does apply to many primary school teachers who have a generalist rather than a specialist background.

VALIDITY

Gardner stresses that "while learning and performance in the arts clearly must be assessed in appropriate ways, such learning is certainly susceptible to assessment—indeed, no less so than learning in other disciplinary areas." This point of view is echoed in the United Kingdom by the TGAT.

There has been some concern about the practicability of identifying and assessing separate profile components for subjects such as art and music, where the pupils' work is seen to be holistic in nature. But we are satisfied that it is possible to devise tasks of a holistic kind which still allow the identification of separate elements for assessment purposes without jeopardizing the coherence of the whole. For example, in music the strands of composing, performing, listening and criticism might be separated. (TGAT, 1988, pp. 20–21)

There is widespread agreement that the assessment process itself should not determine what is to be taught and learned. Gardner makes the interesting point that assessment has not been a particular concern of the recent discipline-based art education movement in the United States, thus begging many questions about the relationship between programs of study and assessment in the United States. Schönau omits any specific reference to how the Dutch assessment system relates to any national art or art curriculum objectives.

These omissions highlight some crucial issues, as surely it is agreed that good assessment procedures are not bolt-on components to be added when everything else is in place. Two points need to be made here: First, as Gardner suggests, assessment should be an integral part of the educational process and must be incorporated systematically into teaching strategies and practices at all levels; second, because assessment can fulfill various functions, this particular aspect—what is it for and who is it for?—has to be considered when the assessment procedures are designed.

Gardner offers some encouraging examples of performance-based testing where assessment is central to curriculum planning for a number of specific projects. The greater difficulty lies in trying to develop a coherent, long-term curriculum plan that integrates teaching and learning strategies with an appropriate assessment model. For better or for worse this is what the national curriculum under development in England and Wales was designed to achieve.

The "radical shift in perspective" that Gardner says is required before his four propositions could be accepted in the American context, would not surprise many British teachers. There was an uproar in the education community when new national curriculum Standard Assessment Tasks (SATs) for English, science, and mathematics were piloted in a third of the country's primary schools. These tests required a shift away from usual classroom practices, similar to those described as desirable by Gardner, toward more formal arrangements, and there were accounts in the national press of 7-year-old children in tears because they could not understand why their teachers were suddenly unwilling to help them. It is clear that the SATs will require extensive modification if they are to be readily accepted by primary school children or their teachers, and this point has been conceded by the government.

ARTS PROPEL provides a further example of the development of specimen curriculum materials linked to "prototypical assessment techniques." Its basic tenets, including the premise that every child is entitled to participate in the arts in a number of ways and that making, creating, or producing art should remain the central activity, with critical studies tending to grow directly out of the student's own practice, correspond closely to the majority view in Britain. Indeed, there is an obvious correlation between the trio *production, perception,* and *reflection* and the *productive, conceptual,* and *critical and contextual* domains proposed in the report on Draft Grade Criteria for the General Certificate of Secondary Education (GCSE) examinations in art and design. GCSE teaching and learning strategies also appear to have close parallels with ARTS PROPEL's domain projects and processfolios. (For example, the rich interplay between the evolution of students' own artwork and their developing understanding of the work of others is finely observed in *Educating for Art* (Taylor, 1986), the outcome of the nationally funded Critical Studies in Art Education project.) The ARTS PROPEL blueprint for a processfolio is an exact description of the requirements for an ideal GCSE folder of coursework. The description of how the art teacher operates parallels closely the dual concept of a *negotiated curriculum* and *negotiated assessment,* which is regarded as central to good GCSE practice.

RELIABILITY

Schönau argues that it is not enough to rely on simple teacher consensus based on a kind of connoisseurship of the culture of art education. In common with the Dutch, the British examination system at the GCSE and the advanced level has moved steadily in the past 10 years from a dependence on the "gut reactions" of experienced external (off-site) examiners to a more open, teacher-controlled system in which increasingly refined assessment criteria are being developed.

In the United Kingdom, teachers have less faith than they once had in the infallibility of the external examiner, and, commensurate with increased teacher ownership of the examination system, there is a greater emphasis on the interactive roles of the teacher and pupil in the assessment process. This involves sharing criteria for assessment, and here parallels can be drawn with Schönau's description of the significance of the notions of "self-reliance" and "differentiation" and the importance of understanding students' "different approaches" in the Dutch examinations. At a later point he advises against using a method of assessment for studio work "when neither the teachers, nor the students, nor the judges have any knowledge of or experience with the assessment procedures." Gardner advocates performance-based testing where "projects and problems are common knowledge." Again, these approaches appear to have much in common with the concepts of a negotiated curriculum and negotiated assessment, which are currently prevalent in the United Kingdom. This approach places considerable emphasis on the importance of the teacher's sharing assessment criteria with the student and taking into account the student's *intentions* as well as the practical outcomes when assessing projects, which might be either student motivated or externally set. Discussions at various stages of a project, aimed at understanding the student's intentions and approach to a particular task, and various forms of student self-assessment can all be taken into consideration by the teacher for both formative and summative assessments. Clearly this form of assessment cannot be undertaken off-site and is dependent on the key role played by the student's own teacher.

Schönau casts some doubt on the importance of defining explicit criteria for assessment when he concludes, "For drawing, analytic judgment is slightly better than global, impressionistic judgment." However, it may be that the real value of well-defined assessment criteria is not to provide a methodical checklist to examine the work of each and every candidate and thereby, as Schönau suggests, to increase objectivity and "safeguard students from the subjectivity of their teachers." Rather, assessment criteria may be of particular value in establishing common ground to resolve relatively rare, serious differences of opinion between assessors, or for a particularly close scrutiny of the work of a student who is exceptional in some way. It is possible that a pragmatic, hybrid solution can offer acceptable reliability—carefully defined criteria can provide a common basis for negotiated assessment rather than an absolute assessment instrument.

Mention has already been made of the working party commissioned in 1986 by the Secondary Examinations Council (SEC), based in London, to draft Grade Criteria for GCSE examinations in Art and Design (SEC, 1986b). The report of the working party provides an interesting performance matrix to compare with the Dutch example (see the Appendix for the key section of the document). The working party accepted as a basic premise that the purpose of developing grade criteria was to specify the skills and competencies in positive educational terms that 16-year-old candidates could achieve and to give more helpful information to the users of certificates about what candidates know, understand, and can do. Consideration of the aims of art and design expressed in the GCSE national criteria led to the identification of three closely interdependent and interrelated domains.

1. A *conceptual domain* that is concerned with the formation and development of ideas and concepts.
2. A *productive domain* that is concerned with the abilities to select, con-

trol, and use the formal and technical aspects of art and design in the realization of ideas, feelings, and intentions.
3. A *critical and contextual domain* that is concerned with those aspects of art and design that enable candidates to express ideas and insights that reflect a developing awareness of their own work and that of others.

Unlike the Dutch, the GCSE working party took the view that the single set of criteria should apply to a broad range of art, craft, and design activity. In common with Gardner's view that "a scale of four or five levels should suffice to cover the range that one might expect to cover in a two to three grade span," the working party drafted four levels of attainment statements. When these four levels were applied to the domains, a total of five profile components were generated for each subsection of each domain. Scores in each of these sections could then be aggregated to produce the final assessment. This approach seems to be consistent with Gardner's views that to try to design a more finely calibrated scale represents overkill but, at the same time, "it is important to look at a number of facets of any performance." Key to the whole GCSE grade criteria exercise were the two aims of making explicit what has been achieved by a candidate and of not overly restricting the methods by which those criteria might be achieved. The working party accepted that this approach involved many compromises, which included tacit agreement that it simply may not be possible to adequately assess all curriculum objectives because the evidence of some objectives can be too ephemeral to be valid.

In the section of his paper captioned "Visions of Art Education," Gardner suggests that the shift toward self-expression and personal development in the mid-twentieth century led to a decline in the importance of formal assessment. While this in one sense may be true, it is interesting to speculate that an emphasis on the "expressive," "creative," and "powerful" qualities Gardner describes also may be evidence of a shift in the *criteria for assessment* away from criteria concerned with "mere" technical competence. The use of these particular descriptors is evidence that evaluative judgments took place but perhaps in a form that more closely paralleled the teaching and learning objectives of the time.

Currently in England and Wales some 250,000 16-year-old students are formally assessed each year by means of the GCSE examination in art and design. Both studio work and associated critical and contextual studies are examined through a combination of the submission of coursework and a controlled test with similar broad starting points to those used in the Netherlands. Such starting points are expected to offer neutral stimuli which avoid ethnic, gender, and other forms of bias.

A significant difference between the English and the Dutch systems is that the assessment of studio work does not usually rely simply on assessment by the candidate's teacher and "one colleague who is a subject specialist from another school." Schönau claims that such procedures "work well" and that "this form of assessment is acceptable to most teachers and seldom has given rise to conflicts." Perhaps it is cynical to suggest that most teachers might well find such a system "acceptable" and that there could be vested interests at work that prevent the applecart from being upset too often. Experience in England and Wales in the past 10 years has generally led to a change, from a system similar to the one Schönau describes to more complex (and expensive) arrangements designed to provide improved reliability.

Assessment for the GCSE is primarily school-based, and this gives rise to two particular factors that should be noted. First is the large scale of the exercise; and second, that classroom teachers are the principal assessors. Therefore a system of "moderation" is essential to the reliability of the examination. Moderation is the means by which the marks of different teachers in different centers are equated with one another and through which the validity and reliability of assessment are confirmed. Moderation usually depends on a cascade system of national, regional, and local agreement trials.

> Moderation can mean sending a sample of all of candidates' work to a moderator; or it can mean a consortium or local group meeting; or it can mean a moderator visiting a center—the latter most common when the product or process is bulky or ephemeral. (SEC, 1986, p. 7)

This system seems to offer a number of advantages in terms of the reliability, validity, and teacher "ownership" of the examination, but it is expensive to administer and may be of questionable utility in countries with geographical areas much greater than the United Kingdom or the Netherlands.

It should be noted that it has already proved necessary in the Netherlands to make use of a second independent assessor for studio work, presumably because of unreliability factors associated with a single visiting assessor. This also has proven to be a problem in England and Wales, although potential detrimental effects mainly have been offset by the opportunities for further scrutiny presented by the moderation system.

It is always reassuring to recognize that others working independently have come to very similar conclusions to one's own, but, of course, it does not offer final proof that one is right. Perhaps it does provide some evidence that a particular line of development is worth pursuing and that the experiment might be worth extending. The introduction of the national curriculum in England and Wales will almost certainly provide an opportunity to see if the best practice developed for the assessment of 16-year-old students through the GCSE examinations can form the basis of sensible assessment procedures for *all* pupils aged 5 to 16. Some of the difficulties that inevitably will be encountered have been identified by both Schönau and Gardner. Perhaps the most intractable of these is the problem of designing a coherent, integrated system of programs of study, attainment targets, and appropriate assessment procedures that are capable of being used confidently by nonspecialist primary teachers as well as specialist secondary level teachers.

Another obstinate problem implicit in the ARTS PROPEL/GCSE model is the need to design fairly generalized assessment procedures that can accommodate student responses across a wide range of practical art, craft, and design activities and associated critical and contextual studies. A negotiated element that takes into account "ephemeral evidence," such as a number of "false" starts or shifts in the student's stated intentions, is one way of dealing with this. The Dutch emphasize that "students have to concentrate not only on the final result but even more on the process that leads to the final product." This closely parallels the British model, where the process, product, and critical studies elements of coursework and a final test increasingly are taken into account for the essentially summative assessments at ages 16 and 18.

Gardner asserts, "So long as realistic drawing is the standard, assessment is not problematic. Quite specific criteria for success can be established and a student's level of drawing can be ascertained readily." This may indicate that it is much more straightforward to design reasonable assessment procedures for limited aspects of a subject rather than to take a holistic approach. For example, it is relatively easy to establish a sequential program of study to introduce basic techniques with, say, print making or clay: Devising statements of levels of attainment to correspond with the program of study does not present an insuperable problem. In art and design the particular difficulty lies in how to design a sequential curriculum and assessment procedure that accommodates the breadth of the subject without fragmenting the nature of the teaching and learning. It is the complexity of the interrelated experiences considered as essential elements in a good art education that presents a major obstacle. Schönau notes, "The only test used in final examinations in the Netherlands that can be compared with the central practical examination for the arts is Dutch composition." In this context it is interesting to note the example of current English language teaching in the United Kingdom, where it is recognized that there are complex relationships between reading, listening, speaking, and writing, and that these skills should no longer be taught or assessed in isolation from one another. It perhaps follows that Gardner's multiple intelligences are equally interdependent and should not be assessed in isolation one from the other.

A final observation about validity: Gardner refers to the instruments used by the National Assessment of Educational Progress in the United States and comments that the standardized tests, which relied on a short-answer approach, resulted in performances that were "generally mediocre." Is it not self-evident that a mediocre test with a poor correlation with the program of study is likely to produce mediocre and essentially *invalid* results?

UTILITY

Reference has already been made to possible differences between Gardner's and Schönau's concepts of assessment and testing, although this problem of definition is of no particular consequence if it is agreed that testing should include "any broad range of assessment instruments with standardized rules of administration and marking which ensure comparability of results" (TGAT, 1987, Preface).

Gardner rightly expresses reservations about the usefulness of tests in the arts that depend on externally prescribed written questions, with written responses marked according to rigid rules. Having set out his theory of multiple intelligences he issues the forcible reminder that

> Precisely because each intelligence works according to its own operations and principles, it is wrongheaded to attempt to assess it using the linguistic-logical amalgam featured in most standardized measures. Intelligences, the practices based on them, and the domains in which they are customarily deployed, *must be assessed in intelligence-fair ways.*

It therefore follows that because each "intelligence" has its own characteristics, it will require different forms of assessment. As each form of intelligence may be deployed aesthetically or unaesthetically, and as each art form, painting, sculpture, music, and so on, uses a range of intelligences and each of these manifests a range of aesthetic criteria, it is clear that a very wide-ranging set of aesthetic criteria must be established that cross all the multiple intelligences.

It is evident that such an elaborate structure presents at least two serious difficulties. First, it is unlikely that the average classroom teacher will be in a position to assume the major responsibility for assessment using such a system. The second problem is related to the first: The utility of such a system—its convenience, flexibility, and cost-effectiveness—must be in doubt for most general purposes.

When considering the utility of the assessment procedures described by Gardner and Schönau, it might be helpful to have a sharper definition of whether the intention is to assess student *performance* or student *ability*. For example, Gardner appears to focus on assessment of the *intelligence* manifested in an aesthetic act, while Schönau concentrates on the intrinsic *aesthetic merit* manifested as a result of the act. Neither Schönau nor Gardner specifically addresses the distinction that is being made in the United Kingdom where, for example, the notions of criterion-referencing developed in the mid-1980s and described above, are now being replaced by concepts of "performance matrices" and "attainment targets." Commenting on responses to its main report, TGAT (1988) stated:

> There has been some misunderstanding about the assessment of "ability". . . . We had intended to confine our proposals to the assessment of "performance" or "attainment" and were *not* recommending any attempt to assess separately the problematic notion underlying "ability". If "ability" were to be assessed, its meaning would have to be carefully defined; and the problem with defining it without making it merely a measure of a particular type of performance is hard to solve. (p. 2)

In the United Kingdom it seems to have been accepted that, for most practical purposes, standardized statements of attainment will meet the needs of most of those who make use of the various forms of assessment set out earlier in this paper.

CONCLUSION

In conclusion, there are familiar unresolved paradoxes evident in the papers under consideration. Gardner's model is curriculum-designer led, tasks are set that are likely to provide measurable data, and specimen graded responses are provided for comparative evaluation. Schönau describes a consensus-based model that offers a greater degree of teacher ownership of the examination system. Gardner advocates structured tasks and the provision of matching structured assessment models. Schönau suggests that such an approach is artificial and in its stead proposes that a better match should be sought between current education and artistic practice. The dilemmas posed by these different approaches are not new. At risk of accusations of chauvinism, perhaps it is not too unreasonable to suggest that recent and continuing developments in Great Britain serve to identify some of the common ground through which a number of important aspects of Gardner's and Schönau's differing approaches might be reconciled.

The final paradox is that while the arts are considered as marginal in education, and not important enough to warrant assessment: It is implied that the way to make them less marginal is to assess them. But as Gardner rightly emphasizes, "even the most sterling assessment devices are useless in the absence of curricular materials of quality that can yield genuine student learning." To this should be added teachers with real understanding of their subject, supported by adequate resources of time and materials. Hostility and indifference to the arts cannot be countered by introducing assessment procedures. The status of the visual arts in education can be improved only by providing evidence of good practice and demonstrating its relevance to the needs of the individual and the wider community. It is tempting to suggest that where there is a high level of consensus about the aims of art education, and where coherent programs of study are supported by an agreed-upon range of appropriate attainment targets, it is probable that appropriate assessment procedures to meet specific perceived needs, rather than assessment for assessment's sake, will emerge without the need for undue anxiety.

NOTES

Acknowledgment. I am grateful to Dr. David Thistlewood, President of the National Society for Education through Art and Design (NSEAD), for discussing with me the draft of this response.

1. The end of each key stage is defined in legislation as corresponding to ages 7, 11, 14, and 16. The national curriculum will introduce Standard Assessment Tasks (SATs) in the "core" subjects of English, math, and science. At the time of this writing, it is not certain whether similar arrangements will apply to modern languages, history, geography, and technology, but it is probable that different assessment arrangements will be introduced for art, music, and physical education, all of which are defined as "foundation" subjects.

APPENDIX
DOMAIN DESCRIPTIONS AND DRAFT GRADE CRITERIA

Domain A: The Conceptual Domain

This domain is concerned with the formation and development of concepts and ideas in art and design. Such development can be systematic or intuitive, but will always involve a creative and imaginative response to an idea, theme, subject, or task. This will include the ability to develop imaginative work as well as working from direct observations. The formation and development of ideas and concepts may either be shown through the production of support-

Reprinted from SEC, 1986b

ing studies or be made explicit in a realized piece of work. This domain relates to candidates demonstrating the ability to

A1   Observe, select, interpret, and record personal responses to firsthand experience.
A2   Select and use reference and resource materials as a means of forming concepts and developing ideas.

Draft Grade Criteria

A1—Candidates should be able to:
Level 1   Make, with guidance, a simple response to firsthand experience.
Level 2   Observe, select, and record and make a personal response to observations, feelings, and experiences.
Level 3   Observe, select, interpret, record, and show consistency in making a personal response to observations, feelings, or experiences.
Level 4   Observe, select, interpret, record, and show a clear and confident personal response to observations, feelings, or experiences.

A2—Candidates should be able to
Level 1   Select, with guidance, and use reference and resource material to contribute to the formation of an idea or intention.
Level 2   Select and use reference and resource material, and consider one or more ideas for development.
Level 3   Select, analyze, interpret, and use reference and resource material independently. There will be evidence of an ability to develop ideas and make reasoned decisions on their application.
Level 4   Select, analyze, interpret, and use appropriate reference and resource material independently. There will be evidence of an ability to make and use judgments when proposing, developing, and interpreting ideas and planning appropriate working methods.

Domain B: The Productive Domain

This domain is concerned with the ability to select, control, and use the formal elements (e.g., form, tone, line, color) and technical aspects (media, techniques, and processes) of art and design in the realization of ideas, feelings, and intentions. The handling of such elements should be seen in relation to the candidate's functional or expressive objectives. It is important to emphasize that it is acceptable for candidates either to specialize in or to provide evidence of activities in a range of media, techniques, and processes. This domain requires candidates to demonstrate the ability to

B1   Select, use, and compose the formal elements of art and design in the systematic, intuitive, or expressive ordering of ideas, feelings, and intentions.

B2   Select, control, and use media, techniques, and processes.

Draft Grade Criteria

B1—Candidates should be able to

Level 1   Use, with guidance, the formal elements of art and design to make basic statements.

Level 2   Select and use the formal elements of art and design to begin to make statements that show a development of ideas and intentions.

Level 3   Select and use the formal elements of art and design to make statements that show an appropriate development and realization of ideas and intentions.

Level 4   Select and use the formal elements of art and design to make coherent and disciplined statements that consistently show the realization of ideas and intentions.

B2—Candidates should be able to

Level 1   Select, with guidance, media, techniques, and processes and show evidence of basic technical control.

Level 2   Select and use appropriate media techniques and processes and begin to show evidence of developing technical control.

Level 3   Select, use, and control appropriate media, techniques, and processes, and show consistent evidence of developing technical accomplishment.

Level 4   Select, use, and control appropriate media, techniques, and processes, and show consistent and developed technical accomplishment in the realization of ideas, feelings, and intentions.

Domain C: The Contextual and Critical Domain

This domain is concerned with those aspects of art and design that enable candidates to express ideas and insights that reflect a developing awareness of their own work and that of others.

Candidates should show evidence of their knowledge and understanding of the differing contexts in which work may be produced (e.g., historical, social, cultural, technological) and a developing ability to make informed critical judgments. Candidates can provide evidence of their engagement in these aspects in a variety of ways: through their own practical work as well as by using other visual, written, and oral forms of response. Candidates will need to develop an appropriate vocabulary to enable them to participate in these activities.

This domain relates to candidates demonstrating the ability to
C1   Provide evidence of their knowledge of contexts and evidence of understanding through analysis and interpretation. Candidates also should provide evidence of their ability to make critical judgments about their own work and that of others.

Draft Grade Criteria

C1—Candidates should be able to
Level 1   Show, with guidance, descriptive evidence of having considered aspects of their own work and the work of others.
Level 2   Provide description and analysis in which they indicate knowledge of the contexts in which the work was produced.
Level 3   Provide description, analysis, and interpretation of their own work and that of others. Evidence also will be provided that shows a developing ability to distinguish between reasoned judgment and personal preference.
Level 4   Provide coherent description, analysis, and interpretation of their own work and that of others. Evidence also will be provided that shows a clear ability to differentiate between reasoned judgment and personal preference.

Aggregation

1.   Domain-level reporting and overall grade are based on aggregating level performance scores. Criteria are described at four levels of performance, with Level 1 as the lowest and Level 4 as the highest.

2.   Consideration may need to be given when a candidate achieves a consistent performance near the borderline of a higher level. Credit may need to be given for such a consistent performance.

REFERENCES

Business and Technician Education Council. (1986). *Assessment and grading: General guide*. London: Author.

Department of Education and Science. (1991). *National curriculum arts working group: Interim report: Annex A terms of reference*. London: Author.

Eisner, E. (1972). *Educating artistic vision*. New York: Macmillan.

Nuttall, D. (1990, March). Talk presented to Chief Examiners for General Certificate of Secondary Education Examinations in Art and Design, Bath, UK.

Secondary Examinations Council. (1986a). *Policy and practice in school-based assessment* (Working Paper 3). London: Author.

Secondary Examinations Council. (1986b). *Report of the working party: Art and design draft grade criteria*. London: Author.

Task Group on Assessment and Testing. (1987). *A report*. London: Department of Education and Science.

Task Group on Assessment and Testing. (1988). *National curriculum: Three supplementary reports*. London: Department of Education and Science.

Taylor, R. (1986). *Educating for art, critical response and development*. London: Longman.

HOWARD GARDNER

The twin experiences of reading John Steers's comments and listening to the discussion of my draft manuscript have helped me to discern some gaps between what I intended to stress in my paper and what was in fact apprehended by my audience. I appreciate the opportunity to clarify my remarks.

"Context" has not been my favorite concept, but I have gained a new respect for its importance. It is not possible to appreciate my portrait of art education, or the program of ARTS PROPEL, unless one bears the American context in mind. In the United States, art education is highly dispersed, with each of the 50 states and many of the 16,000 school districts having their own programs. There is little common practice, and, while there are isolated examples of exemplary programs, few would contend that the broad swathe of programs are of high quality. Until very recently, the word *assessment* has been virtually synonymous with standardized short-answer tests. While in fact there is in the arts little formal assessment of student, teacher, or program performance, the notion of assessment suggests to most individuals a quantitative, externally imposed, streamlined instrument.

It should be evident to readers of this book that most of the countries represented here have strikingly different art education. There is much more consensus within each country about the goals and means of art education. In the absence of traditions of standardized tests, assessment can move more readily in the direction of qualitative evaluations, or portfolio inspection, or written essays on art historical topics, or some combination thereof. In Great Britain, in particular, there is a long-standing tradition of production-centered art education, with portfolio collection, teacher evaluations, and continuity across grade level and even different regions of the country. Thus John Steers can speak legitimately of assessments as codifying practices that have been in place for a significant period of time. Dutch, Australian, and Hungarian colleagues have analogous histories on which to draw.

New artistic initiatives in the United States, such as DBAE or ARTS PROPEL, face a formidable task. Rather than shaping or codifying existing practices, these initiatives must in effect create or catalyze new practices. Assessments carry the heavy burden of both documenting difficult-to-measure dimensions *and* reshaping practices in a fundamental way. Rather than assuming a familiar and supporting context, innovative programs must in part *create* a new context.

In addition to helping to bring about a sometimes radical reorientation, ARTS PROPEL has assumed a number of other purposes. These range from inculcating new methods of teacher education, to creating new assessment and curriculum vehicles, to helping students become more reflective about their own and others' artistic practices. These goals have evolved over the course of the project and will continue to shift as the contexts of American education continue to change.

What has *not* changed in ARTS PROPEL is the heavy involvement of classroom teachers. From the first weeks, a group of classroom teachers has been involved in all aspects of the project. Materials are devised, tried out, assessed, and revised again by the entire project team. Moreover, as teachers become more engaged with ARTS PROPEL, their ownership steadily increases, until domain projects are designed principally or even entirely by the teachers themselves. John Steers is correct in inferring that ARTS PROPEL involves a sharp shift in perspective for many newly involved teachers; however, he is wrong in any implication that the program was conceived in a soil remote from the typical American classroom.

Having clarified the context in which ARTS PROPEL has developed, I wish to turn in conclusion to the relation between multiple intelligences (MI) theory and this curriculum and assessment approach. One of the initial goals of ARTS PROPEL was to devise methods for assessing nonscholastic intelligences—that is, intelligences other than linguistic and logical ones. However, both MI theory and ARTS PROPEL have evolved significantly since the mid-1980s, and no one involved with the project would maintain now that ARTS PROPEL seeks to measure ability, potential, or competence in a particular intelligence or set of intelligences.

ARTS PROPEL focuses on tasks, projects, and works created in particular domains, such as painting or the writing of poetry. By hypothesis, such activities entail various blends of intelligence. However, the goal of ARTS PROPEL is to help students gain mastery in various domains and to learn how to create works of interest and complexity. While MI theory helped to catalyze ARTS PROPEL, the program can be implemented without any reference or subscription to the theory.

In particular, domain projects help students to proceed from the level of a novice or journeyman to a more expert status. The mature "end-states" sometimes can be described as highlighting one or two intelligences, including ones often ignored in school; but the thrust falls on the assessment of evolving skills, independent of the intelligences that they happen to draw upon or exemplify.

For their part, processfolios are records of evolving works within one or more artistic domains. Through their use, we hope to aid students in learning to execute works of art, reflect on their own artistic development, and proceed in increasingly original ways. Processfolios serve as an excellent introduction to the world of work. While domain projects often highlight skill in a particular intelligence, processfolios offer a playground for a wide range of person- and object-related intelligences, interacting fully and flexibly.

Given the flux and uncertain direction of art education in the United States, it is most unclear what is to be the fate of ARTS PROPEL and other cognate experiments in the discipline. One consequence of the Netherlands conference and this resulting book has been to convince me of the utility of a more coordinated national effort in the area of art education. Should that come about, we would find ourselves in the happier position of creating assessments that codified current practices rather than having to fashion assessment that must attempt to catalyze significant changes as well.

Part II
EVALUATING MUSEUM ART EDUCATION PROGRAMS

Chapter 9

Introduction:
What Is in the Museum Is Art

JOHAN LIGTVOET
Academy of Art Education, Tilburg, The Netherlands

Anyone assuming that the world of museums and museum education is neatly laid out in terms of aims, dominant concepts, generally accepted content, approaches, methodology, and philosophy is running the risk of being seen as a foreigner in the museum landscape. Some museums are committed to entertaining the general public, while others are wholeheartedly committed to a challenging, provocative high-art approach. Where some museum programs are academic in nature, other programs and exhibits are designed to raise (social) consciousness. Most art museums are neither one extreme nor the other, but occupy a position in between. Not surprisingly, like all human endeavors, museums come in all colors, shapes, and nuances.

This part of the book deals with issues related to evaluating museum education programs and is subdivided under two headings, "Museum Education and the Audience" and "Museum Policy and Cultural Heritage." Four international experts in the field have prepared papers, and two commentators have responded to the presentations.

What is educational in an art museum? Is it the labels installed on the walls and floors beside the works of art, and if so who will provide the audience with ways to unravel the complexities of meaning expressed in modern art? Is the educational character of an art museum expressed in the way the

Evaluating and Assessing the Visual Arts in Education: International Perspectives: © 1996 by Teachers College, Columbia University. All rights reserved. ISBN 0-8077-3511-6. Prior to photocopying items for classroom use, please contact the Copyright Clearance Center, Customer Service, 222 Rosewood Dr., Danvers, MA 01923, USA, tel. (508) 750-8400.

collection is on exhibit, or is it in the routing we propose the audience to follow? Do art objects in a museum context speak for themselves, or is there a need for assistance in learning to speak and understand their language? These questions puzzle the minds of Folkert Haanstra, Pieter van der Heijden, and Jan Sas in Chapter 10, and Elizabeth Vallance in Chapter 11. Matters of policy and cultural heritage are treated by Bonnie Pitman and Christiane Schrübbers in Chapters 12 and 13. What is taken seriously in an art museum: the collection and the cultural heritage, or the interests and educational needs of the audience, or both? And does the dominant cultural heritage find a place in the museum, or is a multicultural approach considered?

Once we are convinced that art museums have an important role to play in educating the public, we will have to identify methodologies capable of evaluating how well we do the educational job related to the content (artworks) on display in the exhibition. Visitor responses will have to be evaluated, related to the goals set out by the exhibition designers and education staff. The impact of the routing, flyers, guided tours, audiovisual material related to the visitors' level of understanding, and prior knowledge is too important not to be looked into in a systematic way. How high is the museum's threshold of understanding for a broad range of the population? Is the museum equally attractive for all groups in society, and do we all feel ownership of our cultural heritage?

Abigail Housen (1987), as cited in Chapter 12, provides an interesting contextual framework for evaluation studies under which the issues mentioned before could be examined in the intertwined network of demographic, attitudinal, and developmental studies.

STUDYING MUSEUM EDUCATION

In Chapter 10 Haanstra, van der Heijden, and Sas discuss evaluation and research in Dutch art museums, where audience research and exhibit evaluation have been collected for 30 years. Based on research data, three dominant approaches in museum education have been identified.

1. The academic or specialist approach, in which the museum collection and its specializations (and not surprisingly the curator and art historian) are dominant; connoisseurship is a leading principle.
2. The thematic approach, in which a crosscut through eras, styles, or approaches displays ideas or dominant art/idiosyncratic principles. In Holland, cooperation between curators and educators in the process of designing exhibits is common. In most cases, the themes originate from the arts or art history.

3. The approach aimed at increasing social awareness. Here the collection is a medium too, but the themes generally are rooted in society. The educational challenge to be tackled is in "illustrating" properly the societal problems in an appropriate fine and popular art form. Art is a medium for emancipation or improving public awareness. In applying some trendy management jargon, we could refer to this orientation as a "bottom-up approach," whereas the academic notion could be identified as "top-down."

A number of examples of museum projects and their process and product evaluation are discussed by Haanstra and associates. For example, the "Viewfinder" project in the Rijksmuseum (Amsterdam) focused on helping the audience find its route through the museum collection. The Rijksmuseum Art Box—intended for primary school children in their own school prior to a museum visit—was designed and tested for its potential for improving the learning outcomes of the museum visit.

Is there a significant difference in the amount of information requested by an audience visiting a figurative exhibition of old masters compared with an exhibit of modern art? This type of question was tested in the Centraal Museum (Utrecht) and is discussed in the Haanstra and associates paper.

ISSUES IN MUSEUM EDUCATION

Vallance's Chapter 11 describes the way in which the St. Louis Art Museum delivers the "goods" in a variety of formats and approaches, starting in the entrance hall with a confrontational Richard Serra and ending with an Egyptian mummy. Vallance's central question is, How do we know how well our art museum is educating its public? And what does the museum do to understand its clientele? A number of challenges for evaluating the learning effects in different audiences are discussed.

What are measures of success?
What does the audience already know?
How can long-term effects be assessed?

Vallance examines museum evaluation in several ways that could be described as "naturalistic." She approaches evaluation recognizing the merits of devices like "head count" and "focus group" for specific purposes, and relying on tools that require skilled intuition and feeling the heartbeat of the audience.

Given the fact that, in a sense, the curriculum of the art museum is what is on the wall, Vallance underscores that "even the most carefully designed program with the most appropriate publicity will depend for its success on the underlying 'hidden curriculum' of the art museum." The "hidden curriculum" (Eisner & Vallance, 1974) or its didactic application, "silent pedagogy" (Eisner & Dobbs, 1988), is a crucial factor in any educational setting and cannot be overemphasized. Vallance says, "We think we are pretty welcoming, and we work hard to be so."

On the other hand, she recognizes that the elegant structure that houses the St. Louis Art Museum may very well reflect a completely different message to parts of the general public: "It is graced by six Corinthian columns and other architectural elements whose grandeur and austerity—austere at least when compared with the user-friendly zoo down the hill—are softened, we hope, by the motto carved in stone above the doors: DEDICATED TO ART AND FREE TO ALL." It may well be that the "hidden curriculum" in its full scope is so restrictive to learning in art museums that even the finest "curriculum on the wall" has little chance to root in some strata in our society. Such a realization forces one to investigate a number of political and sociological issues, including

Who owns the museum?
Who pays the bills?
Should the artifacts be in the "cultural mausoleum" or do they belong to the society from which they were borrowed, commissioned, or even stolen?
Which decisions are based on what, and for whom?

Issues like power, ideology, and ownership are no longer removed from the educational enterprise, whether in formal or in informal educational environments. The museum setting is no exception.

DECISIONS AND INFORMATION

Consider the pragmatic point of view from which administrators and other decision makers are inclined to draw conclusions. Ron MacGregor accepts his role as respondent to both Haanstra and associates' and Vallance's papers with a title as intriguing as "Chalk and Cheese." Different interpretations of the attributes and character of the art museum are identified in the papers, resulting in different conceptual frameworks for evaluation.

To visualize the contrasting interpretations in the papers and their implications for museum and art education, MacGregor applies three foci under which both papers are reviewed.

1. Political structures in the art museum
2. Social character of the museum
3. Philosophical considerations in art museum education

After pointing out the common topics that both Haanstra and associates and Vallance have considered, MacGregor shows "how it might be that the reader who draws upon only one of the papers for enlightenment is missing something important." MacGregor's rationale for this comparison is in the "all-too-common practice of administrators and decision makers to rely on one kind of information." MacGregor is straightforward in his remarks: "Museum education needs to be represented by both modes of research [Haanstra et al. and Vallance]. . . . Given the sometimes ephemeral nature of museum education goals, a variety of methods of evaluation and assessment seems highly desirable."

EVALUATING AUDIENCE REACTION

Pitman's Chapter 12 is the first in the second set of papers, dealing with issues of policy and cultural heritage. She provides the reader with a brief overview of the recent history of American museum education. The 1980s are considered a turning point in recent history in the way in which museums view the public. Visitor research and evaluation of exhibitions and programs basically address two issues.

1. Who is the audience, or who could the audience be? That is, where do the people come from? How long do visitors stay? What do they need? What are they interested in?
2. How can the quality of the learning experience in art museums, in exhibitions and/or programs, be improved? How do museum visitors learn? What are they learning? What can improve the quality of the learning experience? What do the curator and educator hope the visitor will learn.

Conducting evaluation studies serves a primary goal in Pitman's perspective: to teach museum professionals to install better exhibitions and offer better programs. The implications for shaping museum education policy revealed by her insights are significant. Not surprisingly, the focus group approach, as described by her, shows the installation treated like a product. On the other hand, the focus group approach was applied to study the process rather than the product in the Getty Focus Group experiment conducted by Alan Newman (1991). Pitman discusses this experiment in qualitative research about the perspectives and attitudes of groups of people. Newman used two distinct focus groups in the experiment—the consensus group drawn from the museum staff and the external focus group, a group of visitors and nonvisitors. The Getty Focus Group study taught museum professionals to listen to the educational needs of the visitor and to explore the possibilities of content and installation level to increase learning in a museum environment.

Pitman also explores Abigail Housen's (1987) work for the Institute of Contemporary Art in Boston, in which three methods of evaluation were applied.

1. Visitor demographics and numbers
2. Visitor attitudes and preferences toward art
3. Visitor development in terms of understanding and comprehension

Housen's study of visitors' aesthetic development revealed much about stages of aesthetic development and how museums can use this information. An interesting topic for further development in this area would be comparing Housen's work with and relating it to the outcomes of a similar cognitive developmental study by Michael Parsons (1987).

Pitman also discusses

• A study of visitors' responses to the exhibition "Beneath the Surface" at the Minneapolis Institute of Arts
• The Denver Art Museum's research of art novices' experiences with art objects
• A self-guided tour brochure entitled "Chairmanship: The Art of Choosing Chairs," which was examined for its effectiveness in introducing the visitor to chairs in the museum's permanent collection

Pitman points out in her concluding remarks that all types of museums "are affirming the role of education as an essential component of their mission." The outcomes of evaluation studies are used by the range of museum professionals, from curators to security staff and volunteers. This may be so, but the core of the problem could be in the (lack of) definition of the word *education*, which is used in so many contexts. It may be that *education* as a container concept carries a completely different cargo for an art historian, an educator, and a guard. The same could be the case for concepts like *art*, of course.

REACHING ACROSS MULTICULTURAL BARRIERS

Schrübbers, in Chapter 13, focuses less on the implications of policy following from audience research than does Pitman, but raises fascinating questions about cultural relationships in multicultural educational contexts. She reports on a museum project with Turkish migrant workers in Berlin. Her contribution to this book is close to Haanstra and associates' "social awareness" type of museum program. The Turkish migrant workers, forced to live and work in a situation that is, in a physical and psychological sense, far removed from their cultural and societal roots, often experience alienation.

It takes courage to design and test a pilot project in museum education like the one portrayed by Schrübbers. The potential pitfalls are many and varied: cultural/cross-cultural, economic, societal. The project must account for the different concepts of art used in different cultures. Struggling through the experimental program, Schrübbers was forced to reflect and reconceptualize basic educational notions, over and over. A Western European individual versus a Turkish society—the difficulty was in trying to avoid Western European ethnocentrism.

Schrübbers's paper is of major importance for museum educators considering the introduction of multiethnic and multicultural aspects in museum education. Its value is not in its spectacular results, but in its description of an identifiable process. Fortunately, the number of people advocating intercultural (art) education at the very core of the curriculum has grown rapidly in the past few years. Many research studies and periodicals are published and conferences are organized about this issue. The 1985 InSEA conference "Many Cultures: Many Arts" (Bath, UK) is one example.

At the Bath conference, a South African artist and writer living in Britain drew massive attention by handing out a leaflet titled "The Words About Us." In this handout Gavin Jantjes (1983) challenged the interpretation of the visual arts of Africa promulgated by much of the literature on African art found in British art libraries. Jantjes stated, "Contemporary understanding of the visual arts of Africa has been shaped not by our words, but by the words about us" (p. 15). Again, political and cultural issues are linked to education: power, colonialism, ethnocentrism, oppression.

Regarding museums, their collections, and presentations with respect to interculturalism, there is a formidable challenge ahead for art historians, curators, and museum educators in rewriting the history of art in books, exhibits, and museum art programs. One thing is for sure: The Western concept of the so-called universal character of art is under serious challenge.

A 1989 exhibition in the Centre Pompidou in Paris supports this claim. Its director, Jean-Hubert Martin, explained (Martin et al., 1989) that the title and the concept of the exhibit, "Magiciens de la Terre" (Magicians of the

Earth), deliberately did not include the word "art." Martin concluded that since "art" has such a specific connotation in the West, in a truly international context, "art" could be understood as colonial. Martin's research team traveled all over the world using the methodology of the cultural anthropologist to discover what non-Western societies consider to be art and which artifacts were valued for what reasons in a given context. The product of their efforts, the exhibit in Paris, showed how Western European we are in our minds, art, culture, and perception.

Another issue related to culture and education should be taken into account when reading Schrübbers's paper. Schrübbers entered the profession of museum education with a Western European training in the educational sciences, which cherishes *Bildung*. In her rejoinder, she incorporates a culture-referenced notion, pointing out that there is a whole world of nuances and connotations between the Germanic concept of *Bildung* and the Anglo-Saxon *education*. Concepts and ideas, embodied by words and images, often vary in meaning and connotation because of cultural contexts, although the words may look similar in writing.

WHAT WE NEED TO KNOW AND WHAT WE NEED TO DO TO IMPROVE MUSEUM EDUCATION

In his response to Schrübbers's paper, Stephen Dobbs draws our attention to a number of important issues. One in particular is more than worth mentioning. The global attention toward a less ethnocentric approach to education, art, and culture is difficult to overlook in its consequences to museum education. Non-Western cultures cannot be ignored any longer. Awareness is growing that there is a multiplicity of peoples shaping and representing the world we live in. In this there is an enormous challenge for all of us working in the arts, in education, and in museums.

Enormous challenges await the knowledgeable museum professional who believes that the rich heritage of all cultures should be cherished and available to everyone. We need to step out of our familiar culture and readjust the lenses and templates through which we view cultural phenomena that are different from the ones we grew up with. The core of the dilemma is that education very often equals enculturalization, and it often takes more than a lifetime even to understand one's "own" culture to an acceptable degree. Curators and museum educators very often spend most of their lives becoming specialists, and often see their strength in their specialist view of the world. Is multi- or interdisciplinarity the key to the solution?

In response to Pitman's paper, Dobbs concludes on a hopeful note that museums changed or made decisions to change as a result of the evaluations that took place. Dobbs remains concerned about the follow-up on research and the changes taking place in the field: "A large job remains to persuade administrators and museum educators themselves to use the wealth of data that are available and that may have application to their respective situations." Is this a short-lived trend, or the dawn of museum education?

It is virtually impossible to overlook the current focus group approach in the museums. Dobbs adds that its outcomes as reported by Pitman are similar to the findings of Eisner and Dobbs (1986), which put forth a strong advocacy for the development and improvement of the educational functions in art museums. While both papers reveal hopeful prospects, there is still much work waiting to be done in museum education.

Dobbs elaborates the following priorities as guidelines to improvement:

- Strengthen the research and evaluation component in the professional programs of museum educators (provide inservice assistance for those who lack such training)
- Nurture the development of the evaluation of museum education programs in a greater variety of circumstances
- Determine codes of conduct for the evaluation of museum art education programs
- Further institutionalize resources to professionalize the field of museum education

CONCLUDING REMARKS

The aim of the conference was to identify and analyze current, common, and desirable theory and practice in the evaluation of art education programs. From the start of the conceptualization of this conference, it was clear that its outcomes should be made available to a worldwide audience interested assessment and evaluation in the visual arts. Anyone who is not a novice in this field knows from daily experience that the route of evaluating visual arts programs is filled with contextual and epistemological swamps and roadblocks.

Foreseeable too was the fact that various professional interest groups within museums can have antithetical feelings toward educational considerations. Curators are inclined (and hired) to acquire, to collect, to conserve, and to select art objects for preservation and exhibition. If an art museum is seen as an institutionalized collection of art objects, the real power in the museum rests with the curators. Education, according to this notion, is distilled from and through the collection on exhibit: The curriculum is what is on the wall and what is said about what is on the wall. "I teach through the objects I choose to exhibit; the objects speak for themselves," as Vallance recorded in a discussion with a curator.

Museum educators want to share, to make art objects accessible, to relate objects to everyday life of the present and past, and to demystify art in its elitist connotation. It is too easy to escape into stereotypical cliches, like the curator as art history professor speaking eruditely to his colleagues without ever seeing a student who is struggling to interpret and understand a painting. A similar set of cartoons can be drawn for the museum educator. As long as these caricatures exist, there must be some foundation for these assumptions.

If we see the curator as concerned primarily with the art object, then we should see museum education as concerned primarily with the audience. But who is the audience, or who should it be? Why "seduce" the audience to experience exhibitions, and what means do we use in trying to do so? Are the selected means adequate to our educational goals? Is there an educational justification for opening the museum door to everyone? Is there an educational framework or theory we can adopt in museum education? And what about the relation to formal education? Are there quality programs in museum education available to train museum professionals to the highest possible levels? And what about inservice training?

These and other questions were raised in the papers and the subsequent discussions, revealing that the field of museum education is far from "mummified" but is alive and aware of the challenge that is ahead.

REFERENCES

Eisner, E. W., & Dobbs, S. M. (1986). *The uncertain profession: observations on the state of museum education in twenty American art museums.* Los Angeles: Getty Center for Education in the Arts.

Eisner, E. W., & Dobbs, S. M. (1988). Silent pedagogy: How museums help visitors experience exhibitions. *Art Education, 41*(4), 6–15.

Eisner, E. W., & Vallance, E. (Eds.). (1974). *Conflicting conceptions of curriculum.* Berkeley: McCutchan.

Housen, A. (1987). Three methods for understanding museum audiences. *The Museum Studies Journal, 2*(4), 41–49.

Jantjes, G. (1983, Winter). The words about us. *Art Libraries Journal,* pp. 14–22.

Martin, J., Francis, M., Magnin, M., Marcade, B., & Blanchow, C. (1989). *Magiciens de la terre* [Magicians of the Earth]. Paris: Editions Centre Pompidou.

Newman, A. (1991). What did the focus group reveal? In A. Walsh, Ed., *Insights: Museums, visitors, attitudes, expectations: A focus group experiment* (pp. 112–122). Los Angeles: Getty Center for Education in the Arts & the J. Paul Getty Museum.

Parsons, M. (1987). *How we understand art.* Cambridge: Cambridge University Press.

II–A
MUSEUM EDUCATION AND THE AUDIENCE

Chapter 10

Evaluation Studies in Dutch Art Museums

FOLKERT HAANSTRA
SCO-Kohnstamm Institute for Education Research, The Netherlands

PIETER VAN DER HEIJDEN
Leiden Municipal Museum, The Netherlands

JAN SAS
Amsterdam School of Arts, The Netherlands

Art museums in the Netherlands boast a tradition of visitor research and exhibit evaluation that dates back to the early 1950s. Some major aspects are discerned in this paper, especially regarding methodology and museological implications. In order to establish a perspective from which Dutch research may be viewed, some general problems of methodology are discussed, as well as the changing situation in Dutch art museums during the past decade.

ROLE OF EDUCATIONAL WORK IN DUTCH MUSEUMS

As a rule, it has been education departments that provided the incentive for much of the evaluative research in Dutch museums, and in most cases it was the educational aspects of the museum work that were evaluated.

Haanstra and Holman (1980) conducted a nationwide survey of educational work in museums, in which about half of the approximately 500 museums in the Netherlands stated that they were in some way engaged in educa-

Evaluating and Assessing the Visual Arts in Education: International Perspectives: © 1996 by Teachers College, Columbia University. All rights reserved. ISBN 0-8077-3511-6. Prior to photocopying items for classroom use, please contact the Copyright Clearance Center, Customer Service, 222 Rosewood Dr., Danvers, MA 01923, USA, tel. (508) 750-8400.

tional work. In their conclusion, the authors distinguished among three types of educational approach in museums.

1. The specialist or academic approach, which sets out to throw light on the collection or an area by providing information.
2. The thematic approach, which puts across themes or principles derived from an area in such a way that the collection fulfills an intermediary function.
3. The approach that aims to increase social awareness. In this approach, the collection fulfills an intermediary function, but the themes do not derive initially from the type of museum or the area involved.

Preference for one of these approaches usually matched the backgrounds of staff members. The specialist approach was, on the whole, favored by staff trained in art history; the other two approaches had their adherents mostly among staff members with an educational training. Guided tours were the most frequently mentioned educational activity: over 90% of museums with any educational activity provided these. Runners-up in popularity, albeit at a distance, were lecturing and organizing classes, providing written material for essays and papers, providing tasks and trails in exhibition areas, and organizing teaching programs related to school curricula (60–70% of educationally active museums provided one or more of these services). Only 20–25% of the museums that did any educational work at all mentioned activities such as creative work, special educational exhibitions, kits (museum-in-the-classroom), and longer-term school projects. This survey mapped the years that must be regarded as the heyday of educational work in museums in the Netherlands.

The spreading of culture among the masses was an issue that drew a great deal of attention, and museum education was regarded as an important means for achieving a better understanding and appreciation of art (in the widest sense of the word). It may come as a surprise, therefore, that museum education seems to have been rather restrained in its use of means and methods, as it was in its use of labor: Half of the official educational workers were part-timers, and some 25%, volunteers.

We must bear in mind, however, that the Netherlands has a great many tiny museums, with staffs of one or two and no funds to speak of—museums that must answer negatively to any question regarding activities conducted. Also, not recognized as an educational activity in the strict sense and therefore not contained in the listings of educational work, was (and sometimes still is) the providing of information panels, labels, leaflets, guidebooks, or activities concerning exhibition design, routing, and lighting—in short, Eisner's concept of silent pedagogy (Eisner & Dobbs, 1988).

Lastly, those who maintained that the experience of a work of art should be as self-contained as possible still kept more than a strong foothold. Providing explanations and education in art museums, despite its political support, has never been generally applauded. The head of the communications department of a large art museum declares:

> I have never been too happy with special educational exhibits. Thematic projects in particular do not do justice to the art. It is for this reason and because of the wish in the 1970s that educational goals should govern the museum's policy, that the resistance to educational services originated. (Ganzeboom & Haanstra, 1989, p. 36)

Despite the above reservations about the nationwide spreading of the educational spirit, it is widely argued that the 1970s had a sense of mission about them, a sense that is lacking today. Willink (1987), for instance, concludes that

> These days, art is allowed to be immune to reasoning in its quality, to be regarded as a self-contained phenomenon. Only indirectly helped by knowledge and insight gained through information, the visitor may, no must . . . freely confront the presented work. (p. 74)

This notion of the museum visit as an independent, unhampered experience, somewhat aloof and perhaps elitist, is indeed a radical departure from some views expressed in Haanstra and Holman's (1980) survey (although it remains an open question how much of these views was translated into the frightening educational bombardment that some seem to recall; see above). But at the same time, this point of view appears to be quite seriously distorted by its modern art perspective. The fact that modern art continues to baffle most visitors, whatever educational means and methods are being set loose upon them, has been used too readily as an argument to dismiss any effort to educate any audience in any artistic experience.

In the 1980s, attention did shift toward the individual visitor and away from the museum as a classroom. Educators relinquished their previous concerns. There is still much demand for guided tours, but this activity often is subcontracted to a group of freelancers or volunteers who are available on demand. School groups are no longer the prime concern. Many educators relieved themselves of the task of guiding children through exhibitions by providing information to teachers, who then must organize their classroom activities and museum visit themselves. This also has been caused by a process of political restructuring that made it particularly difficult to establish continuity in museum–school contacts. Economic factors, of course, have played their detrimental role too.

Lack of terminology notwithstanding, Eisner's concept of silent pedagogy has been recognized as an important issue since the early days of museum education and has, over the past decade, been the focus of increasing interest and expertise, although it has been given a myriad of different names. It seldom has been the responsibility of any one staff member, but rather a shared, and hotly debated, responsibility. As a method and a field of study, this kind of pedagogy has been of increasing importance to educational workers in Dutch art museums since the mid-1970s. This may be one reason why evaluation has increasingly become the educators' concern: There is no other obvious way to substantiate the effectiveness of silent pedagogy.

Retrospectively, it can be argued that the "social awareness approach" was typical of the social welfare ideology of the 1970s and was far removed from the strict interpretation of the museum's task of describing objects. Today, it is very much out of fashion and has virtually ceased to occur, except perhaps in ethnological museums with a totally different ambition. The "thematic approach" has lost some of its support, but it has not disappeared. By far the most popular in art museums, however, is the "specialist approach."

Questions of cause and effect are difficult to answer at this stage, and need not concern us here, but this (re-established) preference for the specialist approach runs parallel to preferences for more measurable results, evaluative research with a distinct marketing taste, and attention to the well-being of visitors to enhance their sense of contentment instead of creating optimum learning conditions. In short, museum education increasingly veers toward public relations.

This connection has always existed: The Stedelijk Museum in Amsterdam, for instance, has had a communications department since the 1960s and has never accommodated a separate education department. The efforts of education were always aimed at spreading culture in some way, a dissemination that should result in more visits, better visits, or happier visitors. This link between education and public relations has received much attention lately, and this development has led to the dissolution of education departments or their merging with public relations departments.

EVALUATION APPROACHES IN MUSEUMS

The different views on museums and museum education are mirrored to some extent in research efforts. Most research consists of audience surveys, studies sampling museum visitors with respect to demographic characteristics, reasons for coming, and so forth. In 1979, Screven concluded from his international bibliography of museum research that about 80% of the studies were audience surveys. In 1984, Screven found that this percentage dropped and relatively more behavior studies, experimental research, and evaluation studies were carried out. In Holland this shift is less clear. In Dutch museums approximately 150 audience surveys were conducted in the past 2 decades, more than 40% of them in art museums. As about 15% of the Dutch museums are museums of art, this means that they are popular research targets.

Current visitor surveys serve primarily marketing goals, but one of the reasons for these surveys used to be to find out whether the museums succeeded in attracting all social groups and classes of the population. Most research outcomes indicate that the policy of spreading culture has not been very successful in Dutch museums. The number of museums rose from 243 in 1950 to 630 in 1988, while public interest has increased about tenfold. People of a lower educational level, however, clearly are still underrepresented. Repeated analysis of public studies shows that museums and exhibitions with intensive public guidance actually do attract a slightly lower educated category of people, based on the level of accessibility expected from the collection. More significant is the effect of educational experiments, like the Art Bus, where the collection is literally brought to the public's door (Ganzeboom & Haanstra, 1989).

The audience surveys frequently contain a number of evaluative questions. Sometimes a general opinion about the museum or an exhibition is asked, but most of these questions deal with the kind and quantity of information given; for instance, whether visitors attended the audio-visuals and how they liked them, whether the texts provided were too long, and so forth. The majority of the more detailed evaluation studies in Dutch museums consist of process evaluations, similarly dealing with matters like whether the visitors read the information panels and to what extent they followed a described route in the museum.

Thus most evaluation studies focus on intervening variables or transactions (Stake, 1975) and not on outcomes. This may be partly because, as Overduin (1983) put it, museum educators are preoccupied with educational means, especially new media and methods. The educational goals have received less attention and often are not very clearly formulated. Educational projects that fit the thematic and the social awareness approaches generally had the most explicit goals. The former was exemplified by a series of exhibitions for secondary schools in the Centraal Museum in Utrecht. The general objective was to teach pupils to look critically at pictures and texts. Themes of these school projects sometimes were basic visual elements (like color or perspective) and sometimes treated content, like symbols or the concept reality in art.

Apart from the general opinion questions included in audience surveys, real product or outcome evaluations in Dutch art museums are scarce. In all cases effects are measured directly or within a short period after the museum visit. For this reason, data about long-term effects are lacking.

There are few examples of the strict goal-attainment approach of exhibit evaluation, as proposed by Shettel (1973; Shettel & Butcher, 1968) and Screven (1976). In this approach the term *goal* refers to measurable learning or performance outcomes shown by visitors as the result of exhibit exposure. Screven describes the following steps: The exhibit goals and intended audience are first defined in measurable terms, the exhibit is developed, visitors are exposed to the exhibit, their reactions are measured (for example, by knowledge tests or attitude questionnaires), and results are compared in terms of how well they match the original goals. If this match is poor, the exhibit is modified or adjusted until the goals are satisfactorily achieved.

In the field of educational theory (McDonald Ross, 1973; Popham, Eisner, Sullivan, & Tyler, 1969), this approach was criticized for its behavioristic premises and its restricted means–end model. Alt (1977; Alt & Shaw, 1984), for instance, opposes the passive nature most goal-referenced studies attribute to the visitors as well as the environmentally deterministic manner in which the effectiveness of exhibitions is explained. Most museum educators feel that a rigorous goal-attainment approach ignores the dynamic complexity of museum environments. One could argue that most outcome evaluations in Dutch museums are moderate forms and variations of Screven's approach.

As Screven (1976) admits, an important prerequisite for applying his approach is "that the museum planner must be willing to follow a few rules of the educational game" (p. 272). However, this condition generally is not met. Museum planners in art museums seldom think of educational goals. Many exhibitions are based on personal preferences and the intuition and authority of museum directors and curators. Even if museum educators wanted to evaluate in the theoretically approved manner—that is, by starting with a front-end evaluation of the plans, followed by formative evaluations while assembling the exhibition, using mock-up exhibits, for instance, and a summative evaluation to get the final results—limited time and money prevent them from doing so. This especially holds true for the many small museums. As a practical solution, Sas (1986) proposed a so-called "correcting evaluation study." This aims at a global evaluation of exhibitions in a gallery within a few days after the opening. The exhibition is modified, if possible, to reflect visitors' reactions. For instance, information is added or changed, the routing is adapted, objects are replaced or even added. Although this stage it is too late for a complete modification, major errors are spotted and corrected without the time-consuming and expensive adaptations a complete formative evaluation entails. When a correcting evaluation is carried out, an exhibition is not completed when it is open to the public, although it may seem to be. Summative evaluation was found to confirm the advantages of correcting evaluation, for visitors reacted more positively after the adaptation of exhibitions (Sas, 1987).

Adherents of the "specialist" or "academic" view on museum education stress the informality of the museum and the freedom it offers visitors: That is, the individual establishes his or her own objectives for the visit. One might have expected that this view should involve a goal-free and naturalistic evaluation approach (Wolf, Andis, Tisdal, & Tymitz, 1979). Such an approach is based on the assumption that evaluation should "respond" to the needs, interests, and perceptions of the audience rather than rest upon *a priori* measurement criteria in the absence of input from actual recipients of the evaluation. The evaluation design should not be formulated in advance, and it should not be static. Rather, it continually evolves and is modified as the evaluator interacts with people in and about the museum. The final data interpretations portray similarities and differences in perceptions and experiences, while describing the origins and context of such agreements and discrepancies. Despite the apparent agreement between this evaluation approach and the views of many Dutch museum educators, no examples of this kind of study have been published.

The next section presents some examples of process and product evaluations that have been carried out, and some general results.

EXAMPLES OF EVALUATION STUDIES

In many Dutch museums, employees are unfamiliar with evaluation studies. If evaluation studies are required, paid and free expertise is provided by universities and other educational institutions, market research companies, or municipal offices. Since a great many of the nonpaid studies are carried out by students, these studies frequently are regarded as incidental. An exception to this is the applied research carried out by students of the Reinwardt Academy in Leiden, an institute for the education of museum employees. Here evaluation studies are part of the educational program, but these evaluations lack theoretical claims. Evaluation studies in Dutch museums organized to develop theories on visitor attitudes and visitor behavior are carried out by the University of Amsterdam (Center of Educational Research) and by the Institute of Social Psychology of the University of Utrecht. At the latter institute, Temme (1983) examines the social influence on aesthetic preferences. He also started applied research and in particular evaluations of exhibitions in important Dutch art museums such as the Rijksmuseum, the Stedelijk Museum in Amsterdam, the Van Abbemuseum in Eindhoven, and the Centraal Museum in Utrecht.

Process Evaluation

Kinds of Information. Some research has been done on special educational supplies in museums. In order to offer the individual visitor different kinds of information, the Rijksmuseum introduced the Viewfinder, a leaflet of thematic/exemplary content (Heijden & Kloek, 1985). The viability of this educational tool was tested by formative evaluation research. Extensive laboratory experiments with mock-ups of Viewfinders provided data regarding layout, readability, learning effects, and emotional response to the medium (Sterken & Tuijnenburg, 1985). In situ experiments involving mock-ups, real Viewfinders, and ways of presentation generated much insight into audience reactions, as well as ergonomics and economic and organizational consequences (Sas & Derks, 1984, 1985).

The Rijksmuseum Art Box provides teachers with an opportunity to prepare primary school children in the classroom for a visit to the museum. The effects of this information kit were investigated at the request of the Educational Department of the Rijksmuseum (Temme, Sas, & Derks, 1986). It was expected that the level of preparation would be mirrored in the efficacy of the visit and the time spent in the relevant areas of the museum. Time spent proved to be an indiscriminate measure, however. The efficacy of the visit was occasionally much improved, but this required strict control by the teacher. Where this control was not exercised, group dynamics took over, and the preparation was lost in awe for the impressive building and the excitement of the collective outing. This also happened with groups that had received intensive preparation.

In the Centraal Museum, an Utrecht museum devoted to old masters and modern art, the signposting was examined from an ergonomical point of view (van Bloemendaal & Spierenburg, 1987). Research also was conducted to investigate whether the information in the "old masters" department was sufficient (Derks & van Megen, 1986). The information consisted of labels with the title of the painting, the name of the artist, dates of birth and death and of the painting, the place where the work was executed, and the technique used. Sixty-two percent of the 109 visitors who were interviewed said that the available information was too limited: 36% wanted more biographical information about the artist; 20% of the visitors were interested in the meaning of the painting, and 20% in the historical period to which the work of art belonged. The same questions were raised in the modern art department. When in an experimental exhibition room with modern art no data were given about the exhibited paintings, 82% of the visitors asked for information. When asked what kind of information they needed, 24% wanted to know the name of the artist, an equal number were interested in the year the work was done, and only 13% were curious to know the title of the work. There was hardly any interest in the kind of information people asked for in a figurative painting setting, that is, the intention of the artist, the meaning of the representation, and historical background information.

It was even noticed that an explanation of the meaning of a work of modern art occasioned resistance of the part of visitors (Temme, van Megen, Damoiseaux, Puts, & Zantinge, 1985). Temme (1988) observes that people are convinced that the recurrent question, "What is it?" sounds somewhat silly when the object is a work of modern art. Even the kinds of questions asked seem to be subject to social norms.

Need for Information. The applied research in museums by Temme originates in the uncertainty reduction theory. One of the starting points in Temme's approach is that the more visitors of art museums are uncertain about the quality and other aspects of the objects, the more they seek information. Once they are in a museum, they will try to reduce their uncertainties. This is the reason why, according to Temme, visitors in art museums want information.

Subjects in laboratory research and visitors in the museums mentioned above have been asked if an explanation of the meaning was necessary to enjoy a work of art. Again and again the researchers found that over 80% of the interviewed people considered an explanation of the meaning of figurative paintings conducive to its enjoyment (Temme et al., 1986). Although information is helpful, it does not always result in a greater aesthetic appreciation. Appreciation is affected when there is uncertainty about the artistic quality of the artwork. This influence may be positive or negative depending on the amount or kind of information (Temme, 1983). These results were confirmed by laboratory experiments in which information yielded more effects on "interestingness" than on "pleasingness" (Meel-Jansen, 1988).

In the Amsterdam Stedelijk Museum, a museum of modern art, over 90% of the visitors used information labels. New visitors wanted more information than frequent visitors. They also used the information that was present more often (Temme et al., 1985). The information is expected to be near the works of art (Puts & Cavallaro, 1986). This may seem obvious, but providing substantial information next to artwork is not common in many art museums, for fear of impeding viewing pleasure.

Amount of Information. Another point of interest in the evaluation studies was the amount of information visitors needed. First, the ideal length and structure of labels for paintings were investigated. An experiment in the Utrecht Centraal Museum used reproductions of a seventeenth-century figurative painting and of a contemporary nonfigurative one. In an exhibition room, four identical reproductions of both paintings were shown together with four labels of different lengths. The visitors were asked which label they preferred. Over 85% of the visitors preferred a label with a minimum of 50 words. Thirty percent chose labels of over 200 words. A long label containing subtitles was preferable (Derks & van Megen, 1986).

As a follow-up to this experiment, real paintings were used instead of reproductions to discover the need for text (Puts, Cavallaro, & de Wit, 1988). In the Utrecht Centraal Museum, 12 seventeenth-century paintings were accompanied by information of various lengths. There were four different versions. The shortest consisted of about 15 words and gave the name of the painter, the title of the painting, and its technique. The second version was approximately 50 words and contained, apart from the information given in version one, a few lines about the painter's life, the representation, and the style of the picture. The other versions had a different amount of text (90 to 170 words), but not a different amount of factual information. One conclusion of this investigation is that redundant information has a negative impact on aesthetic appreciation. Text ranging from 15 to 50 words was preferred in most cases. The extended versions three and four were the most instructive ones. The most important conclusion reached was that the time spent in the exhibition room was influenced neither by the length of the labels nor by the number of labels read. The reading time, however, increased with the length of the labels. Hence, in this case the visitors tended to look less at the exhibited pictures.

Whether the visitors actually read all the available information is another question. In the Franklin Institute Science Museum and Planetarium (Washington, DC), for instance, visitors indicated that they preferred labels of over 300 words. Their behavior did not correspond with their preference, however: They never read more than 200 words. When texts of 200 words were presented, the visitors stopped at 150 to 170 words. They never finished the texts (Borun & Miller, 1980). One should compare the information in a museum with that in a newspaper: The reader can decide what and how much he or she wants to read. However, this raises the editorial problem of providing enough of a foothold to enable a positive choice instead of a negative one (i.e., choosing to stop when exhausted vs. not starting at all for fear of drowning in information). The experiments where visitors reacted positively to structuring through subtitles, seemed to reflect this.

Product Evaluation

Remembering Information. In the research projects discussed above, most attention was paid to the media used or to the process of the media used. Only a small part of visitor research in the Netherlands drew conclusions with respect to learning effects. Do visitors actually learn anything from an exhibition?

In a series of research projects at the Amsterdam Rijksmuseum, the question, "How much information do visitors need?" was phrased as, "What do they remember?" Some interesting learning effects were found: After a visit to an exhibition, 75 to 80% of the visitors gave correct answers to questions about the contents of the exhibition. These results differed significantly from the answers given by those who had not yet visited the exhibition (Cavallaro, Derks, & Puts, 1987; Puts et al., 1988; Temme et al., 1986; Temme & Visser, 1980). In other words, this evaluation concluded that the educational efforts of the Amsterdam Rijksmuseum were satisfactory.

This result exceeded anything Shettel (1973; Shettel & Butcher, 1968), Screven (1984), and Rawlins (1978) ever found. In their research, the casual visitor group as a whole learned very little from the exhibits.

Example in Utrecht. In the 1970s, the Centraal Museum organized educational exhibitions for secondary schools. The main objective of these exhibitions was to teach pupils to look critically at pictures and texts and to grasp their meaning. The exhibitions were planned in collaboration with secondary school teachers. The project took its cue from the idea, common among school children, that reality is properly represented in art only when a picture presents a photographic reproduction of what we perceive. This idea often leads people to reject abstract art. The aim of the exhibition was to show that our perception is selective and that reality is a relative concept. The first part of the exhibition demonstrated this by means of examples from everyday life. The second part showed different ways in which artists represent reality, including comparisons between realistic and abstract paintings.

The project was planned to be integrated into the school curriculum. Participating schools received material to prepare classes for a visit to the museum. This material included general information about the exhibition, suggestions for lessons for teachers of different subjects, and booklets for the pupils. Since the guides were unable to take care of all pupils, the teachers acted as guides. There were sessions in advance during which teachers who intended to visit the museum with their class were given museum tours by the educational staff.

This school project, entitled "What is reality?" was evaluated by Haanstra (1979). The evaluation study was concerned mainly with assessing to what extent the desired effects were achieved. Stake's evaluation model (1967, 1975) was used as a guideline. Evaluation data of the school project were collected by questionnaires for pupils and teachers, observations of teachers and pupils during their visit to the exhibition, and an untreated control group design with a pretest and a posttest. About 70% of the schools actually prepared for the museum visit at school and had a follow-up session as well. This applied only to the art subjects; suggested preparatory lessons in other subjects like Dutch history and science were not given. Pupils visiting the exhibition were assisted by various aids such as video, photographs, information panels, and so on. It was observed that most of the pupils only read a few texts and that the majority of teachers gave only occasional explanations. Only one in five teachers did a complete guided tour. Aids that encouraged pupils to play an active part usually were appreciated, but there were no signs of correspondence between the popularity of certain aids and exhibits and their teaching efficacy. Test results showed increased knowledge of concepts dealt with in the exhibition, but the negative attitude toward nonrepresentational art remained largely unchanged.

Hence, the museum educators succeeded in imparting information about the subject, but changing pupils' attitudes proved to be too ambitious a goal. It should be noted, however, that a quarter of these pupils had never visited an art museum before, and half had gone once or twice a year. Moreover, half of the group were taught neither art appreciation nor art history.

EVALUATION STUDIES: DELIBERATE OR INCIDENTAL?

As we pointed out earlier, museum educators have been preoccupied with their media rather than their message. This approach has become disadvantageous, given new and vigorous budget restrictions and museum management that formulates goals in marketing terminology rather than in educational or cultural terms. Our conviction is that this must not become a situation where marketing research supersedes research on experiential learning in museums.

In all but a few cases, university experts have researched and evaluated Dutch art museums; very little research has been carried out by museum employees. An in-house research and evaluation department has not yet been established in the Netherlands, and has been seriously attempted only once.

An obvious advantage of this system is that a high standard for museum research is maintained, with qualified researchers and more sophisticated methods than the volunteer-cum-questionnaire. Research development and reporting on art museum education hold a place in the broader research community.

The main disadvantage is equally obvious: lack of rapport with daily museum routine and risk of discontinuity. There is an occasional tendency among university-based researchers to drift away from the museums' interests toward the benefits of science. This can be corrected easily; it is more problematic to establish a routine of formative evaluation when working with external experts. Factors of time and expense often prohibit this, and not enough experience with evaluation builds up among museum employees.

Although the number of evaluation studies in Dutch museums is limited, they have resulted in substantial empirical data on the effectiveness of certain educational media. Implementation of these results in other museums is a different matter. Sometimes results apply only to the museum where the evaluation was carried out, and replications in other museums are necessary. However, several general conclusions can be drawn, for instance, about the amount and level of information provided. Interviews with educational workers in museums show that they often choose to disregard this knowledge. Sometimes for aesthetic reasons or out of fear of oversimplification, little or no information about the art objects is given. Or inaccessible philosophical or poetic texts are used because they match the design of the exhibition and the personal views of the organizers. The evaluation studies we reported place great emphasis on the overtly teaching role of exhibitions.

These studies will be most fruitful when museum planners consider art exhibitions to a certain extent as teaching devices. If substantial educational guidance for individuals and groups is provided or if special didactic exhibitions are organized, these conditions can be met. That does not mean that in other museums one can do without evaluations. Evaluation should be used regularly by all museums that desire to be responsive to the changing demographic and psychographic characteristics of their public (Wolf, 1986). A more open-ended and goal-free evaluation approach could be useful here to gain insight into the attitudes, values, preferences, and experiences of museum visitors and to stimulate better communication between visitors and art museums.

Data on the actual communication between exhibit and audience are rather limited. In light of new tendencies to design exhibitions in a confrontational manner, like R. H. Fuchs did in his Documenta 8 and in the Hague Museum, or in an evocative manner, employing a great deal of theatrical effects and decorations, like certain heritage museums do, it is all the more pressing that research into the process of communication be conducted. Apart from evaluation of this special learning environment, research ideally should incorporate inquiry into visitor experience of an object's physical context.

REFERENCES

Alt, M. B. (1977). Evaluating didactic exhibits: A critical look at Shettel's work. *Curator, 20*(3), 241–258.

Alt, M. B., & Shaw, K. M. (1984). Characteristics of ideal exhibits. *British Journal of Psychology, 75*, 25–36.

Bloemendaal, M. van, & Spierenburg, M. J. (1987). *Van paardestal tot kunstpaleis. Publieksonderzoek.* Utrecht: Rijksuniversiteit Utrecht, Vakgroep Sociale en Organisatie Psychologie.

Borun, M., & Miller, M. (1980). *What's in a name? A study of the effectiveness of explanatory labels in a science museum.* Washington, DC.

Cavallaro, A., Derks, L., & Puts, L. (1987). *Kunst voor de beeldenstorm: Een onderzoek naar het effect van de educatieve begeleiding.* Amsterdam.

Derks, L., & Megen, E. van. (1986). *Stal wordt museum: Museum onderzocht*. Utrecht: Rijksuniversiteit Utrecht, Vakgroep Sociale en Organisatie Psychologie.

Eisner, E. W., & Dobbs, S. M. (1988). Silent pedagogy: How museums help visitors experience exhibitions. *Art Education, 41*(4), 6–15.

Ganzeboom, H., & Haanstra, F. (1989). *Museum and public: The public and the approach to the public in Dutch museums; renewed analysis of existing data on public, renewed questioning of educational staff*. Rijswijk: Ministry of Welfare, Health and Culture.

Haanstra, F. (1979). *De evaluatie van een educatieve tentoonstelling* [The evaluation of an educational exhibition]. Amsterdam: Kohnstamm Instituut.

Haanstra, F., & Holman, B. (1980). *Museums and the guidance they give their visitors*. Amsterdam/The Hague: Staatsuitgeverij.

Heijden, P. van der, & Kloek, W. (1985). Kijkroutes: Een nieuwe vorm van educatieve begeleiding in het Rijksmuseum [Viewfinders: A new form of educational guidance in the Rijksmuseum]. (With a summary in English). *Bulletin van het Rijksmuseum, 33*, 3–17.

McDonald Ross, M. (1973). Behavioral objectives: A critical review. *Instructional Science, 2*, 1–52.

Meel-Jansen, A. Th. van. (1988). *De kunst verstaan: Inleiding tot de psychologie van de beeldende kunst*. Assen/Maastricht: Van Gorcum.

Overduin, H. (1983). *Voermannen: Gastvrouwen en educatoren: De geschiedenis van het educatieve werk in Nederlandse musea*. Reinwardt Cahier, Nr. 3. Leiden: Reinwardt Academy for Musicology.

Popham, W., Eisner, E., Sullivan, H., & Tyler, C. (1969). *Instructional objectives*. Chicago: Rand McNally.

Puts, E. T., & Cavallaro, A. (1986). *Wat Amsterdam betreft: Publieksonderzoek Stedelijk Museum*. Utrecht: Universiteit van Utrecht, Instituut voor Sociale Psychologie.

Puts, L., Cavallaro A., & Wit, L. de. (1988). *Onze meesters van het landschap: Educatieve begeleiding en bezoekersgedrag nader onderzocht*. Utrecht: Universiteit van Utrecht, Instituut voor Sociale Psychologie.

Rawlins, K. (1978). Educational metamorphosis of the American museum. *Studies in Art Education, 20*(1), 4–17.

Sas, J. (1986). Zijn uw tentoonstellingen een succes? *Museumvisie, 10*, 127–128.

Sas, J. (1987). Veroverde het beeld het publiek? P. Hagenaars (Eindred.). *Museum & Onderwijs: 50 jaar Jan Cunen Museum*, pp. 33–36, 39.

Sas, J., & Derks, L. (1984). De Kijkroute: Onderzoek naar een nieuw museummedium. *Museumvisie, 8*, 74–76.

Sas, J., & Derks, L. (1985). Hoe loopt de Kijkroute in het Rijksmuseum? [How does the Viewfinder work in the Rijksmuseum?]. (With a summary in English). *Bulletin van het Rijksmuseum, 33*, 34–40.

Screven, C. G. (1976). Exhibit evaluation. A goal-referenced approach. *Curator, 19*(4), 271–290.

Screven, C. G. (1979). Bibliography on visitor education research. *Museum News, 57*(4), 56–59.

Screven, C. G. (1984). Educational evaluation and research in museums and public exhibits: A bibliography. *Curator, 27*(2), 147–165.

Shettel, H. (1973, August). Exhibits: Art form or educational medium? *Museum News*, *52*, 32–41.

Shettel, H., & Butcher, M. (1968). *Strategies for determining exhibit effectiveness* (Final report. AIR E 95-4168FR). Washington, DC: American Institutes for Research.

Stake, R. E. (1967). The countenance of educational evaluation. *Teachers College Record*, *68*, 523–540.

Stake, R. E. (Ed.). (1975). *Evaluating the arts in education: A responsive approach*. Columbus, OH: Merrill.

Sterken, J. Ph., & Tuijnenburg, J. (1985). Cognitieve en emotionele effecten van Kijkroutes bij kunstvoorwerpen [Cognitive and emotional effects of Viewfinders in respect of works of art]. (With a summary in English). *Bulletin van het Rijksmuseum*, *33*, 18–33.

Temme, J. E. V. (1983). *Over smaak valt te twisten: Sociaal-psychologische beïnvloedingsprocessen van esthetische waardering* [Accounting for tastes: Social psychological influence processes on aesthetic appreciation]. (With a summary in English). Dissertation, Rijksuniversiteit Utrecht.

Temme, J. E. V. (1988). Sociaal-psychologische determinanten van het (niet) deelnemen aan culturele activiteiten. In A. M. Bevers et al. (Eds.), *In ons diaconale land: Opstellen overcultuurspreiding*. (pp. 132–152) Amsterdam: Boekmanstichting/Van Gennep.

Temme, J. E. V., Megen, E. van, Damoiseaux, H. M. F., Puts, E. T., & Zantinge, J. H. (1985). *La Grande Parade. Publieksonderzoek 1985*. Utrecht: University of Utrecht, Institute for Social Psychology.

Temme, J. E. V., Sas, J., & Derks, L. A. C. (1986). The cognitive and affective effects of educational guidance in museums. *Poetics*, *15*, 511–526.

Temme, J. E. V., & Visser, A. (1980). Educatieve begeleiding geëvalueerd [Evaluations of educational texts]. (With a summary in English). *Bulletin van het Rijksmuseum*, *28*, 178–189.

Willink, J. (1987). Van vorming naar werving. *Metropolis M, 8* (5/6), 74–80.

Wolf, R. L. (1986). Museums in their blackberry winter. *Museum Studies Journal, 3*, 16–20.

Wolf, R. L., Andis, M., Tisdal, C., & Tymitz, B. L. (1979). *New perspectives on evaluating museum environments: An annotated bibliography*. Washington DC: Smithsonian Institute.

Chapter 11

Issues in Evaluating Museum Education Programs

ELIZABETH VALLANCE
St. Louis Art Museum, USA

The art museum where I work is a grand, elegant Beaux-Arts structure confidently dominating a hill in an urban park, not unlike many American art museums of the turn of the century in its setting, style, and public demeanor. It is graced by six Corinthian columns and other architectural elements whose grandeur and austerity—austere at least when compared with the user-friendly zoo down the hill—are softened, we hope, by the motto carved in stone above the doors: DEDICATED TO ART AND FREE TO ALL. We are a free art museum (the first one in our part of the country), publicly funded since 1907, supported by taxes that our constituents willingly increased less than a decade ago. We offer many, many educational programs, most of them free; our changing special exhibitions are advertised in the most popular media. We welcome all citizens to enjoy the arts from virtually all the world's cultures and all eras of the history of art. We think we are pretty welcoming, and we work hard to be so.

The first thing a visitor to our museum sees on entering the main doors, however, is an enormous rusty assemblage of industrial-looking steel, parts propped against each other, numbers stenciled in white on one side, bearing nearly no relation to what most visitors expect when they decide to go see great art. This is a piece of sculpture by the American artist Richard Serra. It is called "Joplin." The label affixed to the wall many feet away tells us only that much, and that it is on loan from an anonymous lender since 1977. The piece is a large object in a huge public space; it consists of three plates of rolled steel, 8 feet square, and to us who live with it daily it looks at home in the two-story vaulted Sculpture Hall. Enormously heavy and requiring several industrial forklifts to move it, "Joplin" is there to stay for as long as the lenders entrust it to our care.

This last piece of information is not good news to a lot of our visitors.

Evaluating and Assessing the Visual Arts in Education: International Perspectives: © 1996 by Teachers College, Columbia University. All rights reserved. ISBN 0-8077-3511-6. Prior to photocopying items for classroom use, please contact the Copyright Clearance Center, Customer Service, 222 Rosewood Dr., Danvers, MA 01923, USA, tel. (508) 750-8400.

"Joplin" is audacious and confrontational; it is not the public's favorite work in our varied but mostly more traditional collection. What *is* noteworthy, however, is the frequency with which this piece provokes comment. Nearly every day museum staff members hear comments about it, directed specifically to the volunteers at the Information Desk at the other end of this large space, or directed to the guards greeting the public at the front doors, or overheard by staff members as visitors talk—and most grumble—among themselves about this large and unavoidable work.

Usually rhetorically but sometimes genuinely seeking a reply, visitors ask total strangers whether that thing is really art or when the museum plans to remove that rusty pile of metal, or variations on those two general comments. The work provokes comment.

A decade-and-a-half ago, in celebration of the American Bicentennial, 10 sculptors were selected by national competition to create and install sculptures in the public spaces that are the rest stops along the Nebraska stretch of Interstate 80. Eight of these sculptures ultimately were completed and all were, as it happened, nonrepresentational "abstract" pieces. The uproar among the public over this project was substantial, despite the fact that the funding for the project was almost entirely private and the taxpayers' dollars issue was largely moot. The project had many supporters, including especially groups that had formed in the small towns nearest each of the rest stops, and of course the project ultimately was completed. But it was not completed without protest, expressions of outrage, and general consternation by people mystified at the absence of traditional symbols of the Nebraska prairie, such as covered wagons or Indian teepees. Years later I talked with many of the people involved in this project, and one seasoned art administrator observed that the Interstate 80 project had been "the greatest art education project we could have devised": It got people talking about art.

Is the Richard Serra sculpture at our museum a successful piece? Can it be considered "educational," and if so, does it count as part of the "educational program" of an art museum? To what extent was the Nebraska project really "educational": Did it change anyone's thinking? The issue gets more complicated each time I address it.

Personally and professionally, I tend to believe that provoking dialogue about art is and should be one of the missions of an art museum, and that if we are responsible for two friends trying to define art as they confront a perplexing pile of rusting steel, our installation has served at least a minimal educational purpose. The secret glee with which museum staff members endure the outrage about the Serra suggests to me that we have at least a tacitly educational purpose in leaving that unpopular work there to confront our taxpaying public. We are challenging, in a safe and comfortable environment, people's expectations; we invite them to react and to explore their own reactions. While no label proclaims this work a masterpiece, its sanctioned presence in our building challenges the viewer to determine why it is there.

But a challenging work of art can be a provocation that is more or less enjoyable, more or less intimidating, more or less enlightening, and ultimately more or less fruitful as an educational encounter. Whether this work or any part of the collection is enriching to the visitor depends on a great many things. How do we know how well our art museum is educating its public? That is the topic of this paper, and it encompasses many challenging issues that I seek to address in these pages. The problems of evaluating art education programs in museum settings are many; this paper will stake out some of the territory and point the way to inquiry that will benefit both museums and their publics.

WHAT IS A MUSEUM EDUCATION PROGRAM?

The question is less simple than it seems. Obviously, the education programs of any museum—art museum, zoo, natural history museum, or botanical garden—include those programs run by the education department (or by such trained educators as may appear under departments of other names), such as public programs, family programs, public affairs departments, and other programmatic structures. These programs typically include lectures, classes, tours, film programs, special workshops for teachers and families, symposia, festivals, and the production and distribution of instructional/interpretive materials about the collections and exhibitions. Professionals responsible for such programs in art museums include art educators, art historians with pedagogical leanings, curriculum specialists, teacher educators, educational writers, and support staff accustomed to dealing with the public.

But our museum's educational program includes the installation of the Serra sculpture at the main entrance. The curatorial decision to challenge the public with this work did not involve the education department, yet the piece alone provokes at least as much comment as does any lecture we could organize on any topic. It serves a kind of educational function, as does the arrangement of objects in any gallery or the schedule of major special exhibitions over the course of time. An art museum's decisions as to what to place on view for public access are themselves, in effect if not in explicit intent, art-educational decisions. Indeed, as one curator once said to me, "I teach through the objects I choose to exhibit; the objects speak for themselves."

Not all objects really do speak for themselves to people who do not speak their language, however, and even the most traditional curators know this: Wall text and extended object labels are, for most visitors, any art museum's most consistent and most accessible curriculum, always available to guide the visitor through any sequence for as short or as long a time as the visitor wishes. Without a guided tour or a very knowledgeable friend, the visitor's prior knowledge and the label information are the only complements to the objects themselves. The art education program most readily accessible to most people is that provided on the walls of the building by the pictures and by what we say about them in print.

Other aspects of art museums have an educational impact, of course. The public relations department of any museum exists to educate the public about all the museum's resources. The public image of any museum depends both on what it offers to the public and on how the information about those offerings is conveyed to the public; the image of a museum as a welcoming, accessible, comfortable place reaches many visitors first through flyers and advertisements and only eventually through a personal visit and participation in formal programs. The spirit and tone of the museum's gift shop (serious scholarly books or more lighthearted products? varied enough to appeal to everyone?) can communicate much about the museum's interest in making the public feel welcome. So can the attitude of the museum guards and the general friendliness of the museum staff to the public. The easy accessibility of rest rooms, drinking fountains, places to sit, places to eat elegantly or quickly—none of these things is truly "educational" in our usual sense of the word, but all do communicate a message to the public about exactly how easy or difficult it is to enjoy art in a museum setting. There is, I think, a strong hidden curriculum built into the amenities and traditions of any art museum. To the extent that they encourage visitors to stay and learn, they can be considered a part of the educational program.

For the purposes of this paper, we must narrow our scope a bit and settle on a definition of art education that museums could readily accept as the province of educators. Art museum directors differ greatly in their interest in deliberately "educational" programs—some holding to the minimal "art speaks for itself" assumption, others vigorously upholding the importance of communicating about art to a broad public—but we will include the museum director and the curators among the people who create "programs" that can usefully be evaluated for their educational value. Therefore, for our purposes we will consider the problems of evaluating both the explicitly educational programs *about* art and the form and context of the art installation themselves. Several issues arise.

CHALLENGES TO EVALUATING MUSEUM EDUCATION

The most regular challenges to evaluating museum education are

1. Identifying appropriate measures of success
2. The fluid nature of the audience

3. The extremely varied art background of the audience
4. The difficulty of assessing the long-term effects of visual memories and of sheer enjoyment

I will address each in turn and later discuss some of the recurring problems they reflect.

Measures of Success

Our museum reaches more people per capita with its education programs than any other art museum on the North American continent. This is one measure of success. It is persuasive for some purposes: Funding agencies like to know that programs they support will reach a broad audience, and our taxpayers like to know that we are reaching a lot of them. This measure is an extreme phrasing of the most basic measure of success we all use: head count. All of us in the museum education business count heads in lectures, gallery talks, and family festivals; we count tickets sold for film series and registrations for classes and lecture series.

We worry when numbers drop, we rejoice when they climb, until they climb past a level that can allow high quality. We do not always aim for high numbers: Many programs are designed to be small and are specifically limited in attendance. But overall we play the same numbers games played by art museums generally, which are compared in terms of exhibition space, cafe revenues, memberships, cost per visitor, number of corporate contributors, number of new acquisitions, and many other aspects, including, of course, total annual attendance.

None of these measures in itself indicates quality; together, however, they reflect something of the relative standing of the museum in its community and among other museums. We are especially pleased when the numbers are distributed across a broad range of the population, including the inner city, the rural parts of the county, and the suburbs. As a public museum, we look for diversity in zip codes, and we worry when any particular program seems to be attracting only the same regular hard-core audience over and over: A successful program reaches people from many parts of the socioeconomic structure and attracts both new people and repeat customers.

Underlying the measures of success we routinely use are efforts to identify our actual and "targeted" audiences and what we hope they will gain from the experience. This is a question that quietly divides education and curatorial staffs in many museums: Educators, who tend to be populists in such matters, often seek to attract a wide audience from the general public, connoisseurs and novices alike.

Curators seem more prone to seek audiences of peers, to develop in-depth programs aimed less at beginners and more at the aficionados and collectors in the community. One curator I know defines "education" largely in terms of scholarly symposia, routinely forgetting to consider teacher workshops, teacher materials, tours, and free public lectures until reminded of them. Together our departments' programs cover the full range of possible museum audiences, although the standards of different levels of audience vary considerably. A knowledgeable symposium audience may expect innovative new scholarship on a subject, while the drop-in public audience to a free gallery talk expects concise overviews of assorted subjects.

Without overestimating the scholarly background of the one or underestimating the depth of curiosity and experience of the other, it is important to ensure that the programs are appropriate to the audience level. Evaluating these education programs must take these variations into account and establish the measures of success that address the full range.

We use more substantive measures of success for formative evaluation and for long-term planning when we can. Measures that we track after our programs include relevance to classroom teaching (for teacher workshops), preparation by the lecturer, clarity of presentation, degree to which the program conformed to expectations established by publicity materials, extent to which the program stimulated interest in participating in follow-up programs, whether the program attracted first-time visitors, whether these people intend to return, and whether they would recommend the program to a friend and why. A number of museums evaluate more permanent educational resources, such as wall text or special exhibition installations, by gathering systematic public reaction to draft editions or to trial installations: This is typical in the production of printed gallery guide materials, and I have seen pilot installations tested for public reaction at children's museums.

But many of our usual measures of success are intuitive and anecdotal. Rarely does a museum education department evaluate exactly what was learned in an educational program—we tend to look for more elusive measures such as enthusiasm, return visits by "new regulars," new commitments in the form of memberships. It is unusual really to know what our audience learned; pre- and posttests are antithetical to the informal environment we create for most programs. As a consequence, the measures of success applied to the more fleeting museum education programs revolve around numbers, audience feedback, return visits, and sometimes revenue generation. Numbers do reflect the "attractiveness" or popularity of programs, and are a valid if not exactly "instructional" measure that pertains directly to our goals of demystifying the arts and attracting people who had not experienced art before.

But numbers by themselves, of course, cannot tell us if our program provoked even as much discussion among our audience as Serra's "Joplin" regularly does, or whether the dialogue among participants was more informed after our program than it was before. Our assessment of the dialogue-inducing effects of the program may be based on overheard comments or on participants' compliments to us afterward (but more on this "skewed positive" later).

Museum education programs do not assign grades, and thus do not routinely assess skill or concept development, and they do not participate in the creation of national or group norms. Compared with the school setting, which at least is rooted in nationwide traditions of grades, assessment, and standardized tests, museum education programs are isolated, independent, and highly reflective of the educational standards of museum education directors, some of whom are content with stable high numbers, and others of whom worry about subtleties within them.

The Fickle Audience

Unlike school, attendance at art museums is completely voluntary (school children coerced into visits there by zealous teachers might dispute this, but generally it holds true). Attendance also may be sporadic. A recent in-house study indicated that 8% of visitors to our art museum were first-time visitors, another 17% had visited the museum once or twice in the past 2 years, and 47% were "regulars," visiting more than five times in 2 years; only 22% had visited more than 15 times in 2 years—a relatively high visiting rate, but it averages to only seven times a year. Our audience, in short, is quite erratic. Except for programs that specify age limits and/or require preregistration, it is difficult to predict museum audiences for events before they actually happen. Furthermore, since museums lack the sanctions of grades or degrees, they have little besides intrinsic interest in the program to keep "students" coming back. To many museum educators, the constantly changing audience is part of the excitement of programming: It demands that we keep our programs fresh, that we be prepared for a wide range of backgrounds in our students, and that we get very good at estimating approximate size of public programs so that we can order the right number of gallery stools or festival supplies.

That it is permissible to pick and choose among programs is, I think, part of the great appeal of museum education programs for people who seek visual enrichment but cannot make regular commitments in already-busy lives.

The roving nature of our audience also has a circular effect on programs: Since people will select among programs, each program (or part of a program) must be self-contained, valid on its own without weeks of background lectures or years of studio training. We develop programs that are designed to appeal specifically to the occasional visitor, and they do.

The constantly changing audience poses problems especially for evaluating the most fluid and "open" programs—including the exhibitions themselves, the printed text and all amenities, *and* the drop-in programs. It is difficult to capture a museum audience, as any exhibition planner knows. An exhibition of an American "western" artist may attract 100,000 visitors, while only half that number return to a related exhibition a year later. Minority-group audiences may attend one special exhibition of African art in enormous numbers but not the next.

The audience is free to be fickle, a phenomenon that is probably more evident in comprehensive art museums, whose collections cover a wide range of cultures or time periods, than in more specialized museums focused on specific subjects with loyal audiences interested in those collections. With the audience coming and going from program to program, and educators trying endlessly merely to *identify* the audience, much of the evaluation effort focuses on demographics: The transient nature of our audience leads us back to descriptive head count measures of effectiveness.

The result is that we can more readily assess our ability to anticipate the market than we can the instructional effectiveness of the program itself. In my experience, this is the most deceptively risky feature of program evaluation in museums. It is too easy to be complacent about a program that attracted a large crowd.

What the Audience Already Knows

The evaluation of art education programs is difficult enough in a school setting, where students are generally of the same age and curricular history, and where the teacher can reasonably assume what the prior art learning of students has been. Evaluation of art museum education programs—from installations to labels to organized programs—is made more difficult because (1) we do not know in advance what our audience knows about art, and (2) the range of knowledge in any given audience group is likely to be quite wide.

In informal surveys of some of the drop-in Gallery Talks at our museum, I have asked visitors to assess their degree of familiarity with art or art history: The questions are phrased in a friendly fashion, and I tend to believe my audiences when two-thirds (63%) say they know "something" about art through an occasional course or travel, while those knowing "nearly nothing" and "a lot" about art are almost equally split (19% and 14%, respectively). We have not asked the same question of gallery visitors in general, but they are likely to have a similar profile, with a lot of them knowing at least a little about art, and people on both extremes of the scale as well.

What do these visitors already know, and what would they like to know about art? We wish we knew. Curators who assume that art speaks for itself, and who assist the visitor with only minimal information about the piece, seem to assume either that visitors are quite capable on their own of making sense of the works, or that helping visitors understand what they are seeing is not the museum's responsibility.

The other extreme is the museum where every object label is an essay on the history of art. In my view, this is the preferable extreme because it at least gives the visitor the choice of reading or not, but this practice also makes assumptions about the visitor's prior knowledge: in this case, that considerable information is needed and that the object does not work well on its own. (An interesting mix of assumptions about what visitors know and need was evident in an exhibition entitled "The Eloquent Object," showcasing masterful contemporary American crafts with beautiful and sometimes witty objects, with burdensome labels that suggested that the curator did not really trust the audience to appreciate the eloquence of these eloquent objects.)

The range of knowledgeability of museum audiences makes it tempting to focus our substantive evaluation efforts on those programs with regular or well-defined audiences more than on others. Our teacher workshops, for example, attract teachers in a variety of disciplines, and some workshop topics attract very coherent audiences: elementary art teachers, for example, or high school math teachers. In these cases, and in the cases of studio classes that meet on a consistent schedule, it is useful to assess the teaching: These "students" have come to us to learn a specific skill.

Classroom teachers know at the end of a workshop whether they can use in their teaching what they have just learned; studio students know whether they have progressed in using watercolor; our museum teachers can see whether children in Saturday classes are basing their work on what they have seen in the collection. These participants' assessments of the programs are useful in practical ways: They tell us whether the topics we have chosen are pertinent to our population's interest, whether the instruction was effective, and generally whether our educational goals were met.

In these programs, which more closely approximate the school setting, we do know the audience's purpose. When we do not, we accommodate this ignorance by aiming at the middle—in our label copy (we compromise by providing details on *some* pictures), in our special exhibitions (we treat these as new interpretations and provide interpretive text in relatively clear non-scholarly language), and in our programs (we target our lectures at the interested-but-not-fellow-scholar audience, and we define a lot of terms we would not define to our peers). We mean these middle-ground solutions to provoke commentary and dialogue among all levels of visitors, but one thing we do not know is how the different levels of visitor knowledge interact with the sorts of curricular programs we provide.

Does our minimalist label on the Serra sculpture stimulate real exploration among novices, or does it only frustrate these people by its assumption that no more information is needed? If a scholar compliments us on a public lecture, how can we know whether the first-time visitor has also understood it? We have few reliable ways of knowing whether our aim at the middle ground was accurate.

Delayed Effects: Memories and Follow-up

One of the most effective long-term art education programs at our museum was a mummy that we never owned. For many years, a mummy with a bare toe visible was on view in our galleries, on loan from another institution; children loved it. And for years, the most frequent question asked at our Information Desk was, "Where's the mummy?"—by those same children, now grown and bringing their own children to the museum to see this long-remembered artifact. One of those former children, a very successful businessman in the area, began his lifelong love affair with art after seeing that mummy in our galleries. This man, now a major art collector himself, recently donated another mummy "to the children of St. Louis" in thanks for his own early education into the delights of visiting the art museum. Another generation of children is now being initiated into the arts in the same way, and is as delighted.

We know from focus groups that even people who do not visit the museum more than once every 10 years or so have very strong visual memories about particular things they have seen here.

People return to the museum decades after a single visit and inquire about an object they remember in considerable detail. A woman telephoned us from a thousand miles away recently, describing a painting she had seen here 50 years ago as a child, wondering if we had a slide of it; her description was so accurate that although the painting had not been on view for years and was remembered by no present staff, we were able to trace it through catalogues as a piece that had been de-accessioned long ago. People remember paintings they love sheerly for the subject matter, with no idea of the country, time period, style, or artist involved.

Do these enduring memories count as evidence of effective art education? What *do* we want people to retain, years later, from their encounters with art in museums? Those of us who delight in the enriching power of remembered images are charmed and rewarded when someone remembers and still enjoys an image; others who wish our visitors learned more might bemoan the nearly totally non-art-historical nature of that memory. A challenge for evaluating museum education programs is the lack of agreement on the long-term outcomes we seek, a problem exacerbated by the fact that many of the people we see in the museum on any one day we will never see again: We will never really be able to assess *their* long-term learning. Adults coming to us now, long after their earlier visits, may well be responding to effective educational moments long ago, or to effective new PR about the museum, or to influences quite beyond our control such as pressure from a visiting relative. While they are difficult to measure, the long-term positive effects of a museum visit are exactly what most of us hope to create. Some of the questions we ask occasionally in visitor surveys try to assess what has been effective in bringing people into the building—a particular exhibition, a lecture, a lunch date, the need to unwind—and we can ascertain whether they are frequent or first-time visitors, but without an in-depth interview it is difficult to assess whether a prior museum visit has had a long-term effect on a visitor's interest in art.

Most of now running educational programs will never know how enduring an effect these programs have had on how many people. This brings us to our last, and most amorphous, challenge in assessing such programs.

Hardest to measure, because the effects will by definition be seen elsewhere, much later, is the effectiveness of museum programs in helping visitors to enjoy art generally and to make a point of exploring it on their own. I hope someone in my audience a few months ago will remember something interesting about Rufino Tamayo a year from now, but I would fulfill a major mission if a member of my Gallery Talk audience later visits the Rufino Tamayo Museum in Mexico, or was a first-time museum visitor that evening and now tries to visit an art museum when he or she is in another city on unrelated business.

Our goals in museum education are immensely broad and all-encompassing: In other words, we hope our visitors will learn something about our collection, and find something delightful there that they would have overlooked otherwise, but most of all we hope they will forever love art a little more, and see it better, because of what we have offered. We hope our audience will be strengthened in its role as participants in the history of the world's cultures. But it is hard to know if we have succeeded.

What is the "sheer enjoyment" that can come from an effective museum education program, and how would we ever measure it? What most makes a museum experience enjoyable? Museums spend millions in experimental efforts to find out. Each museum has its own atmosphere, its own level of coherence somewhere on a continuum ranging from sophisticated to fun, its own quality of welcome and comfort. Some museums take pride in a quiet scholarly atmosphere, in being a refuge from the storm, other-worldly and peaceful. Others seem to delight in being informal, colorful, a recognizable part of everyday life, accessible in every sense of the word.

Yet what is enjoyment for one visitor may not be for another. Visitors expecting quiet scholarship may be insulted by colorful fun; visitors accustomed to feeling at home in friendly welcoming museums may feel intimidated in solemn refuges. But when a museum experience is enjoyable—when an encounter with art is a pleasant surprise, or confirms high expectations, or offers an "aha" insight, or helps to place a work of art into a context that makes sense, or takes place on a day that is comfortably paced and in pleasant surroundings—the immediate and long-term spinoffs may be substantial. The visitor may become a regular visitor; she may send friends from out of town; he may vote for a tax increase in a future funding election; she may attend a lecture series and discover a better-focused interest in art than she had before; he may organize his children's school to participate in the museum's programs; she may correct misconceptions about the museum voiced by a co-worker over coffee; he may join the museum membership program or become a volunteer. She may come back to learn more. He may come back just to see more. They may send their children to art classes, at our museum or elsewhere. All these spinoffs would be measures of success of some kind; all would be hard to quantify.

SPECIAL PROBLEMS

The challenges to evaluating museum education programs, then, include the difficulty in identifying meaningful measures of success, the fact that our audience is transient and hard to pin down, the fact that our students' comfort and familiarity with art vary enormously, the likelihood that some of the strongest effects of our programs may be so long term and ephemeral that we might never be aware of them, and the related difficulty of knowing whether our "graduates" ever become art consumers generally.

In short, we work in a very open system, with few controls on our student population or on what they learn from our programs. These challenges to effective program development and evaluation in turn pose special problems for evaluating museum education programs. These problems include the following:

1. We only rarely have a clear sense of what our goals are for any specific program. Most museums offer a variety of programs in various formats to attract varied age groups, and the overall goal of these programs is to "reach" the broadest possible audience with appropriate programs. But I know of no instances where the educators set specific goals in advance aside from the usual ones of "good turnout" and "nice (read: varied) crowd." Museum educators' general goals of providing accessible art information to a broad audience are passionately felt and argued for in many forums.

But program to program, I believe we settle too often for numerical success and a feeling by the instructor of having covered the content appropriately. We have not been in the business of developing goals. As a result, our evaluation efforts have lagged behind those in schools.

2. The spontaneous responses to programs tend to be *mostly positive.* The fact that our audience has, by its very (and completely voluntary) presence, made a commitment to learn something and to be open to new ideas predisposes visitors to enjoy the program and to tell us so.

A program has to be pretty poor, or somehow offensive to someone, before we will hear a complaint. It is easy to overestimate the instructional effectiveness of our programs by attending to explicit audience reaction. (Anecdotal evidence of public response to the art itself tends to be skewed more to the negative. It is curious how many people will approach a guard, or an Information Desk volunteer, to comment on how much they dislike a particular work of art—the Serra sculpture, for instance—or to wonder aloud how anyone can really consider that circle of stones on the floor—Richard Long's "Mississippi Circle"—to be art. In a day I spent in a guard's uniform overhearing comments in the contemporary art galleries, most indicated puzzlement or rejection. Rarely do visitors convey their love of any particular piece to our staff.)

3. We estimate program success to some extent by the size and return rate of our audiences, and yet this practice also tends to *overemphasize the positive:* We notice when participants return and become "regulars in our programs" (we recognize them in crowds and see their names recurring on registration lists), but without specifically tracking the nonreturns, we have only a very vague sense of how many people do not come back for more. Nonreturning participants simply do not come back; it is difficult to notice the absence from a program of a person who had attended a related program earlier.

4. It is extremely *difficult to follow up* on our programs to gauge the impact they might have had on people's subsequent relationship to art. Aside from new regulars that we can identify in our own programs, we do not know whether a program has made any difference at all to most participants' future interactions with art. Are we educating better art consumers? How would we know?

5. Even the most carefully designed program with the most appropriate publicity will depend for its success on the underlying *"hidden curriculum"* of the art museum: the messages conveyed by the solemnity or openness of the setting, by the comforts available to tired visitors, by the sparseness or usefulness of the object labels and other interpretive text, and by the ease or difficulty of finding one's way around the building. An excellent program in

an unwelcoming museum will surely have a different reception than the same program in a museum that is open and accessible to all.

A great educational program of exhibitions and other programs can be lost on the public if the PR department does not promote it. Parents finding nothing in the museum shop but scholarly books may decide not to bring their children back for a second visit. Overzealous or unfriendly guards may make a family feel unwelcome near valuable paintings and discourage subsequent visits until the children are older.

No museum education program can fairly be divorced from its context, and the contextual factors are even more difficult to assess than the straight programmatic ones.

6. It is more tempting, because it is easier, to assess the *prior public appeal* of a program than to assess its eventual instructional effectiveness. Our tendency to emphasize head count and other quantitative measures skews our attention to the size of a program's "draw"—the crowd that appears at the start of the program—and away from concerns with its real quality once it is completed. Family Days at our museum are usually enormous: Thousands of people come for a Sunday afternoon of activities focused on a special exhibition, and it is plain in watching them and overhearing their conversations that they are enjoying themselves. As an effort to portray the museum as a friendly, accessible public place, the event clearly succeeds.

Are people really learning about the paintings featured in the exhibition? Probably. But we are less sure about the instructional effectiveness than we are about appeal. In some cases we assume that the "delayed effects" of a few strong memories and the sheer enjoyment of being there will suffice as educational goals for the day. Does this assumption ever violate our real purposes?

7. Many of the most appropriate instruments for assessing the effectiveness of museum education programs would *violate the informal nature of the learning* that we seek to foster. Pre- and posttests of art-historical knowledge, intensive visitor interviews, pop quizzes, and even careful ethnographic observational data could intrude on the comfortable visits we hope our visitors will have, and we can engage in these activities only occasionally for special purposes. Portfolio assessment *is* available as an evaluation tool for studio art classes, but on the whole our visitors come too erratically for us to be able to track them easily.

8. Do we know *what constitutes a fruitful dialogue* about the Serra sculpture? Serious art educators know what they mean by effective discussion of aesthetics, or by criticism. But what of the many visitors who do not stop long

enough to really discuss the piece, and merely pass by it with a nice comment? Are we overestimating the power of this provocative piece when we assume it is serving an educational function if it provokes a comment? Is *any* conversation about art better than none at all? How do we know?

I suspect that museum educators take a lot for granted about how well our programs work. We are, I think, fairly well in tune with the public, and we do have a good sense of what the "average visitor" can handle in terms of content level and intensity of program. Over time, we learn what seems to attract both first-timers and repeat visitors to our programs; any three museum educators describing the qualities of an effective public talk would agree remarkably well. We live daily with the uncertainties and frustrations posed by the four "challenges" I've discussed here and have adapted well to the need to create programs that stand alone and are appropriate to wide ranges of participants.

We know, as any teacher does at the end of the day, whether the program has been "good" or disappointing, using qualitative measures and sheer professional judgment. And we do not believe all of our programs are equally good: we make distinctions routinely and can assure any potential funder about which sorts of programs are most likely to be worth an investment. We think we know what we are doing.

But the problems in evaluating museum education programs are many, and they reflect basic questions yet to be answered about the purposes of our programs. Museums lag behind formal educational settings in being able to assess their educational programs reliably using standards shared by similar institutions. As public or quasi-public institutions with no captive audience, art museums revel in "capturing" what they can of their publics, and their evaluation methods reflect this first-level need. But as museums mature in their roles as educational institutions, and learn to balance their interpretive functions more equitably with their responsibilities to display art well, they will discover the need to better document their considerable successes in the important business of complementing school learning with informal and life-long learning in the arts.

Regular and reliable evaluation of programs, when it comes, will attest to the coming of age of art museums as educators.

Chalk and Cheese

RONALD N. MACGREGOR
University of British Columbia, Canada

One of the more arresting comments I have read on differing traditions in research appeared in an article by Michael Huberman (1987). The American tradition, Huberman observed, is to look at a large number of individual trees and infer from that the presence of a wood. The European researcher, having closely observed the wood, concludes that it is, after all, a wood.

It is an amusing distinction, which deserves to be valid but is not, to judge by the two articles to which I have been asked to respond. For it is the Europeans, Haanstra and associates, who analyze the structure and attributes of the trees, while Vallance, the American, offers an essay on the singular character of the wood.

More cogent than national distinctions, however, is the difference in the authors' approach to the problem of interpreting the attributes and character traits of the art museum, which results in two dissimilar papers. Rather than between trees and woods, the difference is between chalk and cheese.

The two papers are not entirely dissimilar, any more than chalk and cheese may be. But they imply the adoption of quite different conceptual configurations for evaluation. In this response, I first will identify some of the common topics the authors have considered, then attempt to show how it might be that the reader who draws upon only one of the papers for enlightenment is missing something important. My justification for doing so lies in the all-too-common practice of administrators and decision makers to rely on one kind of information. While this response may not alter that practice, at least it cannot be said that the point was never made. I am less concerned with assessing the relative merits of the two papers, and of running the risk of sounding either condescending or finicky, and more concerned with speculating on the implications for the larger professional arena of art education, of some of the statements the authors have made about museum education.

COMMON TOPICS

Three groups of attributes are discussed in both papers. The first group is concerned with structures and mechanisms governing the administration of the art museum, and is characterized by evaluations that are political in intent. The second group is audience-oriented and stems from the social character of the museum. The third group takes as its focus those intrinsic values and personal considerations that make the notion of an art museum tenable in the first place. Whatever evaluations are made within this group are likely to make use of philosophical positions and their effects on practice.

Political Structures in the Art Museum

The political structure of the art museum is both a consequence and a cause of degrees of empowerment among its members. Both papers allude to the common division of responsibility between curators and educators, phrased by Haanstra and associates as information of a specialist/academic nature on the part of the curator, and consciousness raising around themes, for which the educator uses the artwork in an intermediary role. The opportunity to develop these quite different agendas is, however, seldom equally distributed. In a study of seven Canadian art museums of various sizes, Campbell (1989) found that directors tended, as a result of background and professional inclination, to see curatorial considerations as the prime determinant for the museum's programs. Educators, for the most part, were required to develop their programs out of what the curators had already put together. For practical purposes that may make little difference.

There is enough material in almost any exhibition for an educator to exploit in constructive ways. But it does mean that the educator constantly feels the necessity of going the extra mile and of fitting into a program originally designed to render superfluous any formal educational component. As Vallance's curator remarks, he would have "the objects speak for themselves."

Haanstra and associates are cautious in interpreting evidence of disparity between curatorial and educational responsibility. "Providing explanations and education in art museums," they write, "despite its political support, has never been generally applauded." Museum educators, in their more pessimistic moments, might go so far as to claim that whatever political support there seems to be for the museum's educational mandate, often can be dismissed as lip service, and the applause is often more lukewarm than even educators care to admit.

At the bottom of the art museum's pyramid of power are the docents. When one compares their situation with that of any classroom teacher, it is remarkable how little responsibility they have in planning, developing, and evaluating their own activities. Vallance makes the point that museum education programs are isolated, independent, and reflective of directorial standards. Some years ago, Cuyler (1980) reported that, in three major art museums that she surveyed, not only were there no formal statements of goals, or descriptions of the roles to be taken by those participating in educational planning, but there was no clear system, or set of standards, that educators or docents might follow. As a result, those with history backgrounds interpreted the exhibit as historians, ex-literature majors took a narrative approach, and one might speculate that a docent with an interest in accountancy might provide a dollars-and-cents appraisal of what was on show.

Museum education programs have come a long way since 1980, and Cuyler might not find the same lack of articulation in many programs today. Nevertheless, the education of docents still has a patchwork character, as a study by Duthie (1990) shows. In interviews with six docents, Duthie found marked deficiencies in what one might call conceptual clarity and justification in their accounts, but much personal commitment and desire to communicate their own sincerity to others. In an elementary school, one might expect commitment and sincerity among the teachers, but one would also expect a recognition that there exists a body of work to be interpreted for educational rather than personal goals. Where that interpretation presents difficulties for the teachers, it is likely that they would communicate their problems to the principal; school board advisors might be called in to clarify the intent of the program; the staff would have a right to feel that, as a result of their concerns, material would be adapted or deleted until its users found it acceptable.

I do not have the sense, from either of the two papers or from my own experience, that art museums in general act in that way. The docent, then, must always feel that, however evaluation of the museum's activities is carried out, it is largely without the docent's perspective. If all the docents in all the art museums of the world were to decide not to come to work tomorrow, it might cause some gnashing of teeth among those teachers who had arranged visits to the museums, but it would affect neither what was being displayed in the museum, nor how it was displayed, nor what was to be displayed subsequently. This is, I suggest, as close to a definition of powerlessness as it is possible to come to, and it is no wonder if the docent's self-image is decidedly low-key.

The Social Character of the Museum

In the sixteenth century, when cabinets of curiosities were one more means to display the affluence and entrepreneurial skills of their owners, audiences were limited to friends and those whom it might be advantageous to impress. Catering to a general audience was not an issue. Today, museums range from massive public institutions to specialized (often relatively private) collections. These latter pose no audience difficulty, since they are frankly restrictive. But as Vallance has pointed out in some detail, the audience for a public art museum is actually several audiences who differ in their reasons for visiting. The one thing they have in common is the potential to be a returning patron. Haanstra and associates indicate that not only are the audiences varied, but the art museum accommodates them differently. They refer to studies equating level of education and attendance, that seem to reveal that there is more for educated viewers in the art museum than for less educated viewers.

Given the social history of art and its often elitist prerogatives, this disparity is not surprising. As a measure of contrast, visitors to London's Museum of the Moving Image form a much broader cross-section of the general population. Like any other visual arts, film is represented by a range of products, from the relatively inaccessible to the frankly undemanding. But undemanding art in art museums has never attracted the wide audience that undemanding movies have.

At one time, steel engravings of contemporary events were popular sellers, appearing in ornate frames in public buildings or tacked up over the fireplace in farm kitchens. The advent of the camera eliminated the need and the audience for these. Museum art became more difficult, while the movies, with their promises of relaxation, romance, and a happy ending, built a huge and enduring public following.

The art museum educator regards this popular audience as one still worth pursuing, if for no reason other than that given rather disarmingly by Vallance: head counts. Arts in Schools programs are one of the most direct ways to recruit viewers, even if, as Vallance implies, these youngsters may feel more coerced than wooed. A significant part of the social family of the museum, school populations ought to feel particularly welcome, since their support in later life may be crucial to the museum's prosperity.

In Nancy Johnson's (1981) study of what children learned in an art museum, contemplation of the works occupied a relatively small part of the students' time. Instead, if one is to judge from Johnson's account, they learned that the art museum is a repository for beautiful objects; that people go to a good deal of trouble to keep the place clean; that persons are supposed to have feelings about artworks; and other aspects of what Johnson calls "aesthetic socialization." Vallance has noted that many of the museum's patrons remember particular works, or details from them, that are unrelated to the artistic importance of the works but simply strike a personal chord. Johnson makes a similar point about the entire art museum visit: People carry away different and rather fragmented impressions of what an art museum exists for, unless (although Johnson does not develop this point) they have the opportunity to "fill in the gaps" through regular visits, and until art museum staffs become sensitized to the unintended messages they may be giving.

Haanstra and associates make a distinction between information gathering and aesthetic responding, and quote a figure of 82% for viewers who look for more information when the art museum provides none. They also refer to a project built around the title, "What is reality?" as a result of which student information changed although attitudes did not. Herein lies one of the distinctions between an art museum and one devoted to historical artifacts or anthropological material. While a museum of history would no doubt regard it as a nice bonus if a viewer responded aesthetically to their collection of seventeenth-century muskets, their prime concern is informational. They would be quite distressed if their visitors went away with their senses awakened, but their knowledge bases unenhanced. Indeed, it is the curse of some modern museums that the artifacts themselves are often buried under overlays of back-screen projections, built environments, audio effects, and derivative lighting, the whole creating something close to information overkill.

The art museum wishes to place the focus squarely on the work in such a way that the viewer gleans more than information from it. Out of contemplation comes enlightenment. The art museum educator is caught between putting words into the mouth of the viewer (who may, in any case, spit most of them out) and not providing enough to hold the viewer's attention.

As for the argument that the work ought to speak for itself, the Derks and Van Megan (1987) study quoted by Haanstra and associates appears to show that viewers want to know who created a work and when it was completed, but otherwise contains little evidence that viewers were able to derive much from the works themselves.

Certain art museums justify their social role by catering to the widest possible milieu, mounting blockbuster exhibitions assembled at enormous cost, and relying for their success on large numbers of anonymous visitors. Most institutions, however, require the support of a local community to keep afloat. Even if members of the local population do not make extensive use of the art museum's services, there must be a perception among them that the museum serves a useful function. A public relations arm within a local museum would, I suspect, have an easier time defining that usefulness as social activity than it would in making a case for scholarly visibility on the strength of the museum's contents.

Philosophical Considerations in Art Museum Education

Vallance and Haanstra and associates speak as one on the nebulous goals of art museum education programs. Haanstra and associates say, "The efforts of education were always aimed at spreading culture in some way . . . [for] more visits, better visits, or happier visitors." Vallance comments, "We hope they will forever love art a little more, and see it better, because of what we have offered." While there is nothing intrinsically wrong with having undefined or very loosely defined goals, they cut little ice with administrators and financial directors whose reactions are geared to the sound of turnstiles clicking and who look for accountability among the employees.

Based on Haanstra and associates' findings, it seems likely that factors of time and expense preclude long-term interaction between art museum personnel and professional evaluators. Therefore, whatever evaluation of education programs is conducted, must rely on internal agents. Perhaps it is the prospect of internal evaluation that has resulted in an apparent neglect of formal goal setting within many institutions. It may be assumed (the argument would go) that we know what we want, so we do not have to be too specific in saying what it is.

Contrary to that premise, most evaluation studies show that the participants in an enterprise are often least certain of their own aims and those of others within the institution. Before looking at what people do, a necessary first step is to clarify what they think they are doing. Often, the discrepancy between the two bodies of data provides the meat of the evaluation.

The 1986 study conducted by Eisner and Dobbs in 20 American art museums evidently left those authors less than confident about the museums' ability to conduct their evaluations internally.

> The skills necessary to do research and evaluation in museum education have not been well developed. The result is a dependency on others to do the kind of evaluation and research that would prove useful for improving museum education programs or for justifying expenditures on museum education programs to museum boards. (p. 57)

I am surprised that Vallance feels that evaluation instruments and interviews would "violate the informal nature of the learning" that goes on in art museums and "could intrude on the comfortable visits we hope . . . visitors will have," particularly in light of her earlier comments on the Serra sculpture, wherein she spoke of provoking dialogue about the artworks. Perhaps provocation of dialogue should extend to the art museum's operations in general. I should think that one might identify informants among the museum's regular clientele who would be happy to provide regular feedback on the relative merits of exhibits and on the museum's policies in general. There might even be some competition among the museum's clientele to be one of these informants. They might not mirror the views of all museum visitors, but it is overly optimistic to think that any evaluation can do that.

One group that readily could be recruited to provide information is the museum classroom unit, including the visiting teacher and students, and the art museum staff. If nothing else, it might forestall the distressing trend noted by Haanstra and associates of museum educators abdicating responsibility for school visits. "Many educators relieved themselves of the task of guiding children through exhibitions by providing information to teachers, who then must organize their classroom activities and museum visit themselves." That is an effective prescription for putting oneself out of business.

It would be interesting to know on what evaluative criteria such decisions were made and what effects they have had on subsequent school use of art museums. Is this a step toward "curatorializing" the role of the educator: operating at one level removed from public contact and therefore making implementation of ongoing modification of an exhibit's format, in the way Haanstra and associates have outlined, less likely?

DIFFERENT SOURCES, DIFFERENT INFERENCES

The purpose of evaluation surely must be to provide grounds for further decision making. Normally, the evaluator presents a case that the decision maker uses to validate a future course of action. Were I as decision maker given the body of material assembled by Haanstra and associates, how might I react and how would I set my priorities?

Haanstra and associates give me cause for concern. Case by case, they provide evidence that the art museum educator occupies a peripheral and nebulous position in the museum hierarchy. They note a downplaying of the thematic and consciousness-raising approaches taken by educators, and an increased tendency to have the educator act as part of the public relations arm of the museum. They suggest that museum educators "have been preoccupied with their media rather than their message."

They report that evidence of long-term learning as a result of exposure to museum education programs is lacking, while reflective statements by persons who have been exposed to art museum learning are unavailable. They allude to the difficulties of making specific learning gains with students who, in 50% of cases, have visited an art museum only once or twice a year, while a further 25% did not achieve even that level of involvement.

I have some difficulty interpreting one or two of the studies reported by Haanstra and associates. Specifically, in the study by Derks and Van Megan (1986), why were respondents presented with old masters works accompanied by basic biographical and contextual information, while modern works were virtually textless, and then asked similar questions regarding the kind of background they would like to have on each group. It hardly seems like a common baseline from which to launch comparisons.

Nevertheless, on the evidence that Haanstra and associates have given in their paper, I would be unlikely to make any major commitment to an art museum education program and would put my emphasis instead on the art-

historical, curatorially inspired elements of the museum's offerings. The return on an investment in museum education seems altogether too much of a
hit-or-miss affair.

Presented with Vallance's report, however, my response might be different. True, it comes largely without empirical support, save for a few general
references to information collecting. Instead, it presents a picture of evaluation conducted "off the cuff": becoming a guard for a day, for instance. There
is a sense in Vallance's paper that relevant questions define themselves out of
the flow of events, and good practice consists of being constantly reflective
about incidents and comments. If all art museums are like the one described
by Vallance, with many one-time visitors, should not the educational emphasis be on orienting the visitor as quickly as possible to the location of the best
(or best-known) works, so as to make the greatest impact in a limited time? If
visitors come once, does that mean they have equally transitory experiences in
other museums? If they do collect museum experiences from different places,
might the education of the visitor be predicated on information on what is
available in other places (regionally? nationally?) and how it has relevance,
historical or social, for what the local unit contains? Out of such fragments,
programs may grow.

In my self-appointed role as decision maker, I might be inclined to wonder, as Vallance does, where museum education begins and ends. If art museum education is not first and foremost about art, but is instead about raising
consciousness using art as a vehicle, on what grounds is it the special business
of the art museum educator? Still, Vallance's evocation of an enterprise that
is humane, participatory, and stimulating for the community persuades me
that, even if we do not know exactly what is going on, it is worthwhile to
accept the ambiguity, renew the contracts, and divert some of the budget to
education projects.

Reality seldom presents itself in the black-and-white terms that I have
described. Part of the compensation for being only a paper decision maker is
that one can select data to fit the case. It is not a distortion of reality, though,
to suggest that the information presented in the two papers is different in
content, different in character, and different in the inferences one can draw
from it. Although I have simplified both cases, I have not misrepresented their
spirit. A real decision maker, given the material from only one paper, in all
likelihood would form a different set of conclusions than if presented with
the other.

In education, this happens frequently. New programs are introduced despite the existence of contrary studies that suggest that the innovation is controversial, if not downright suspect, from the start. But the situation here is a
little different: It is not that the authors draw upon different sources in order
to promote one position; instead, each draws upon one kind of data collecting

and one style of presentation. It may be, as Haanstra and associates state, that there are no naturalistic studies to balance the experimental studies they have summarized. Vallance's reflective approach is certainly evidence of how such naturalistic inquiry might be pursued.

Museum education needs to be represented by both modes of research. That chalk and cheese are quite different in structure and function does not work to the disservice of either, so long as one does not try to have one serve for both. Given the sometimes ephemeral nature of museum education goals, a variety of methods of evaluation and assessment seems highly desirable.

CONCLUSION

A few years ago, one of the Pacific Northwest states adopted as a slogan for its tourist brochures: Relax in a state of excitement. It could serve equally well to describe the desired effect of museum visiting, the push-and-pull between reverie and mental challenge that generates productive dialogue and brings about understanding. In the day-to-day mechanics of organizing tours, publishing brochures, and conducting workshops, it is easy for educators to equate being busy with having a fundamental role to play in the development of relationships between the public and the art museum. The papers by Vallance and by Haanstra and associates have raised sufficient questions about the roles currently filled by museum educators to suggest that it is inadvisable to accept that equation. The articulation of the political, social, and philosophical place of art museum education is as yet incomplete. For the good of that field, it is not something that can safely be put off for much longer.

REFERENCES

Campbell, N. G. (1989). *The role of the curator and the educator in selected Western Canadian art galleries.* Unpublished master's thesis, University of British Columbia, Vancouver.

Cuyler, F. (1980). *The docent's interpretation of stated gallery philosophy: A comparison of docent training programs in three Canadian art galleries.* Unpublished master's thesis, University of Alberta, Edmonton.

Derks, L., & Megan, E. van. (1987). *Stal wordt museum: Museum onderzocht.* Utrecht: Rijksuniversiteit Utrecht, Vakgroep Sociale en Organisatie Psychologie.

Duthie, L. (1990). *What it means to be a docent: Narratives of art gallery experiences.* Unpublished master's thesis, University of British Columbia, Vancouver.

Eisner, E. W., & Dobbs, S. M. (1986). *The uncertain profession.* Los Angeles: Getty Center for Education in the Arts.

Huberman, M. (1987). How well does educational research really travel? *Educational Researcher, 16*(1), 5–13.

Johnson, N. (1981). Aesthetic socialization during school tours in an art museum. *Studies in Art Education, 23*(1), 55–64.

FOLKERT HAANSTRA, PIETER VAN DER HEIJDEN, AND JAN SAS

According to Ronald MacGregor, decision makers would conclude from "Evaluation Studies in Dutch Art Museums" that it would be unwise to make any major commitment to an art museum education program. By summarizing some important outcomes we hope to convince the decision maker that this conclusion is not justified.

Relating the outcomes of audience surveys to the nature of the collections of the museums and to the educational efforts of the museums indicates that museums with an intensive educational activity attract a somewhat less educated public than might be expected on the level of accessibility of the objects. The relationship is not strong, but nevertheless an effect of educational work on the social composition of the audience is present (Ganzeboom & Haanstra, 1989).

We know from several studies in the Netherlands as well as in other countries that many people come to museums to learn something and that they appreciate that information is given in the displays. In most museums, including art museums, the educational staff provides a large part of this information, whether in passive presentations (texts, leaflets, and so forth) or in active presentations (guided tours, lectures, and so forth).

The shift in educational efforts in many Dutch museums toward passive presentation does not mean the educational staff is putting itself out of business. On the contrary, the growing attention on individual visitors often mirrors a more integrated and more influential position in the museum. More time is spent on the collaborative preparation of exhibitions, which increases the accessibility and the educational value of the event.

The effects of certain educational media have been demonstrated in a number of evaluation studies. Reasons for the limited use of these methods, especially in museums of modern art, have to do with views on the role of museums, not with a lack of effectiveness of educational activities.

We conclude that outcomes from a more qualitative "museum-fair" evaluation approach would be more convincing to most members of the museum staff than a strict goal-attainment approach. An instrument that could be useful in this sense is the so-called learner report: a self-report about personal learning experiences based on a learning theory of the Dutch cognitive psychologist De Groot (1974). It has been used in various educational situations, for instance, in an evaluation of art education in secondary schools in the Netherlands (Van der Kamp, 1984).

REFERENCES

Ganzeboom, H., & Haanstra, F. (1989). *Museum and public: The public and the approach to the public in Dutch museums; renewed analysis of existing data on public, renewed questioning of educational staff.* Rijswijk: Ministry of Welfare, Health and Culture.

Groot, A. D. De. (1974). To what purpose, to what effect? In W. A. Verreck (Ed.), *Methodological problems in research and development* (pp. 16–49). Amsterdam: Swets & Zeitlinger.

Kamp, M. Van der. (1984). Self-assessment as a tool for the evaluation of learning outcomes. *Studies in Educational Evaluation, 10,* 265–272.

II–B
MUSEUM POLICY AND CULTURAL HERITAGE

Chapter 12

Taking a Closer Look: Evaluation in Art Museums

BONNIE PITMAN
Bay Area Discovery Museum, USA

At least since the nineteenth century, when museum pioneers like John Cotton Dana and Benjamin Ives Gilman challenged the institutional status quo with their views of what education in the museum setting was, and ought to be, museum professionals have debated the nature and purpose of the museum's educational function and the status of museum education. The dialogue about museums as educational institutions has thrived throughout the history of American museums. This dialogue has not, however, been a repetition of the same concerns. Rather, it is symbolic of museum professionals' wish to ensure that museums, as educational institutions in the broadest possible sense, provide a public service that reflects both the currents of change in society and the traditional purposes and values of museums.

In its report *Museums for a New Century*, the American Association of Museums' Commission on Museums for the New Century (1984) affirmed a number of fundamental museum education principles. The Commission also made recommendations for future action. Commission members returned often to the themes of public service and education, seeking to assess and clarify the role of museums in our society. The Commission reported that American museums

> through their collections and their programs, offer rich encounters with reality, with the past, and with what exists and with what is possible. They stimulate

Evaluating and Assessing the Visual Arts in Education: International Perspectives: © 1996 by Teachers College, Columbia University. All rights reserved. ISBN 0-8077-351-6. Prior to photocopying items for classroom use, please contact the Copyright Clearance Center, Customer Service, 222 Rosewood Dr., Danvers, MA 01923, USA, tel. (508) 750-8400.

curiosity, give pleasure, and increase knowledge. Museums acquaint us with the unfamiliar, coaxing us beyond the safety of what we already know. And they impart a freshness to the familiar, disclosing miracles that we take for granted. Museums are gathering places, places of discovery, places to find quiet, to contemplate and to be inspired. They are our collective memory, our chronicle of human creativity, our window to the natural and physical world. (p. 17)

An important section of the Commission's report was a call for research into the nature of museum learning. It suggested that the instructional potential of exhibitions be taken advantage of by museums, and that institutions commit themselves to scholarly research, emphasize adult education, and integrate education into all museum activities. The report proposed that this should be accomplished through a restructuring of the organization of museums.

Since 1984, there have been significant changes in all of these areas, and the result has been an improvement in the ways museums view their public dimension. Learning in museums is different from learning in traditional educational environments. Museums communicate messages not only through objects, but through accompanying interpretive resources offered in the galleries and in public programs. Learning for the museum visitors spans a range of experience. Education offers visitors an opportunity to understand new information and to become more aesthetically sensitive and curious about art.

In 1992, the American Association of Museums (AAM) published a report entitled *Excellence and Equity: Education and the Public Dimension of Museums*. The AAM Task Force based its preparatory discussions on this important premise: All areas of museum activity must be understood as contributing to museums' public responsibility. "Museum education" was considered to be too specialized a term to encompass the multifaceted educational role of museums. Trustee and staff values and attitudes, exhibitions, public and school programs, publications, research, evaluation, and decisions made about collection and preservation are all aspects of the educational messages museums convey to their public.

The AAM publication *Excellence and Equity* affirmed the importance of museums redefining themselves as educational institutions. The public service of museums derives from their collective contribution to their audiences. While every museum has individual qualities and local and regional significance, together museums constitute a pluralistic group of institutions working toward shared goals. Individual museums must, however, ensure that they are as accessible as possible to a broad audience and that they do not exclude any audiences by default.

Museums today have added to their traditional responsibilities of collecting and preserving works of art, the presentation of new exhibitions and programs designed to attract and inform their diverse audiences. Professionals in America's museums are making decisions related to the allocation of resources that affect the quality of the learning experience for museum visitors. To make these decisions effectively, they need to know more about the people who do and do not use the museum. As a result, evaluation of museum visitors and nonvisitors has come to play an increasingly significant role in management decisions. Such evaluations aid management in assessing the effectiveness of an educational program or of an exhibition that is analyzed, using the criteria of a learning experience. Evaluations help to identify specific ways to improve service to visitors.

The development and utilization of visitor research and evaluation of exhibitions and programs have come from a need to answer questions about two issues.

1. *Who is the audience, and/or who could the audience be?* That is to say, where do people come from? How long do visitors stay? What do they need? What are they interested in?
2. *How can the quality of the learning experience in art museums, in their exhibitions and/or programs, be improved?* How do museum visitors learn? What are they learning? What can improve the quality of the learning experience? What does the curator or educator hope the visitor will learn?

It is generally agreed that museums fulfill their educational mission through the effectiveness of their exhibitions and programs. Evaluation studies are therefore a primary means through which museum professionals find out about their audiences and understand audience responses to exhibitions and programs. Such studies aid professionals in learning how to prepare better exhibitions and programs.

BRIEF HISTORY OF VISITOR EVALUATION IN THE UNITED STATES

Museums have been studying their visitors since the early part of this century, and art museums have had a significant role in these studies.

In 1916, Benjamin I. Gilman wrote an article on "Museum Fatigue" about visitors' experiences at the Boston Museum of Fine Arts. The evaluation project argued that visitors' fatigue could result from poor exhibition installation, which required special physical effort to see both the objects and the labels. In particular, the article cited crowded cases as inducing visitor fatigue. Accompanying Gilman's text were photographs that documented visitors crouching and twisting in order to see the cases and respond to the evalu-

ation questions. The result of the evaluation led Gilman to make specific recommendations for changing the design and layout of the cases at the Museum
of Fine Arts. Specifically, Gilman recommended that objects and labels be
placed so that they could be seen more easily.

Gilman's research set the stage for much of the work that was to follow.
Dr. Ross J. Loomis, Professor of Social Psychology at Colorado State University, in his book, *Museum Visitor Evaluation: New Tool for Management* (1987),
gives a fine summary of the development of this field, both in America and
internationally.

There have been numerous visitor research studies conducted by art museums that indicate a strong interest among museums in how both visitors
and nonvisitors are affected by museums and exhibitions. The American Association of Museums has a Standing Professional Committee on Visitor
Evaluation. Professional journals, including *Visitor Behavior, The Museum Education Journal, Museum News*, and *Curator*, publish summaries of these studies.

Art museums do study their present and future visitors. These studies
have yielded insights into what motivates people to become involved with
art. The studies have suggested methods to improve exhibition designs and
resources as well as programs.

Dr. Loomis was commissioned by the Getty Center for Education in the
Arts to review studies completed by museums that participated in a focus
group project. Loomis (1987) identified seven categories of evaluation research trends that were used by the art museums in his sample. The 12 museums included in Loomis's review provided 64 manuscripts. Loomis noted that
the studies often had more than one purpose or topic and used more than
one evaluation technique. The six approaches (two of Loomis's categories are
combined in this paper) to visitor evaluation employed by art museums include the following:

1. *Marketing and Image Studies:* Frequently conducted by market research
   firms, these studies assess visitor awareness and image of the museum, and
   visitor satisfaction with the museum experience. They describe visitors in
   terms of demographic, psychological, sociological, and economic characteristics. These studies frequently utilize surveys, panel studies, and focus
   groups.
2. *Member Surveys:* Focused on the museums' membership, these programs
   identify reasons for joining museums. They investigate the types of benefits to be offered and compare not only members and nonmembers, but
   those people who are not renewing membership. Results of these studies
   influence decisions on the management of the membership programs.
3. *Visitor Surveys:* These studies tend to be demographic descriptions of art

museum visitors. The data range from straight attendance data (who came and when) to more detailed analysis of why visitors decided to come to the museum, how they heard about the museum, and what they thought of the exhibition or program. These surveys frequently are used to assess the potential for growth in certain areas.

4. *Special Exhibit Evaluations and Exhibition Evaluations:* These two types of evaluations, which Loomis identified separately in his study, are closely related. Evaluation studies of exhibitions provide data on specific installations, including information on special exhibitions or permanent collections. Various evaluation techniques are integrated to analyze who visitors are and how they are affected by the installations. These studies use summative and formative evaluations, including multiple evaluation methods; they describe visitor reactions as well as pre/post visit surveys.

5. *Evaluation of Interpretive Aids:* Often analyzing the effectiveness of labels, these studies also examine gallery guides, audio tours and video disks, and other interpretive resources used in the gallery. They seek to identify techniques to assess the effectiveness and to improve the quality of a particular interpretive component within an installation. Among the many studies of significance to the art museum field has been the work at the Denver Art Museum and the J. Paul Getty Museum. These studies will be discussed in this paper.

6. *Program Evaluations:* These evaluations consider an enormous range of museum activities, from teacher workshops and curriculum resource units, to docent tours, preschool classes, adult lectures, and outreach activities. Program evaluations usually study programs offered to a specific audience (teachers, fourth graders, parents) or to types of programs such as classes, tours, or an outreach unit. These evaluations frequently are required by funders and help to demonstrate the effectiveness of a program or project. Program evaluations also provide useful information to the staff on ways to improve the quality of the program and to learn what their audiences are willing to attend and to financially support.

Visitor research and evaluation result in an improved understanding of the museum's audience. The research also suggests to staff strategies to improve the quality of learning that occurs in exhibitions and programs. Several of these evaluation strategies will be described in this paper. Fulfilling the responsibility for public education in its broadest sense requires that museum professionals continually assess education services. It also requires that research discoveries be shared with a larger audience. Museum professionals—directors, curators, educators—understand the value of increasing their knowledge of how visitors and nonvisitors respond to exhibitions and programs. Professionals utilize this information as they plan future exhibitions and programs. Evaluation is therefore also a management tool that can affect both programmatic and financial decisions.

EVALUATION STUDIES OF EXHIBITIONS

Museums have sought both to understand and to aesthetically stimulate visitor experiences. Evaluations of exhibitions, whether of a blockbuster exhibition or of a small installation of chairs from a permanent collection, have been an important component of the work conducted in art museum evaluation. Evaluation studies have been charged with goals such as the necessity to understand which visitors are coming and what they are learning. The studies also attempt to understand visitor attitudes toward the museum and how effective the museum has been in organizing an environment that presents aesthetic works and creates an opportunity to learn. There have been numerous studies of this type, and they have utilized a variety of evaluation techniques.

Three evaluation projects are summarized in this section: (1) the Getty Focus Group project, which provided a comparison, utilizing the same methodology, among 11 art museums of visitor and nonvisitor responses to the museum; (2) the Institute of Contemporary Art (Boston) study, which examined different exhibitions and used three types of studies: demographic, attitudinal, and aesthetic development; and (3) the Minneapolis Institute of Arts study, which focused on an exhibition from the Institute's permanent collection and evaluated visitors' understanding of the meaning of the works of art. These three studies have been selected because they provide opportunities to review different methods of exhibition evaluations.

The Getty Focus Group Experiment

A 2-year research study, sponsored by the Getty Center for Education in the Arts and the J. Paul Getty Museum, studied visitors in 11 art museums using "focus group research" methodology. Completed in 1989, this extensive project produced some significant insight on visitors' needs and expectations. The Getty project compared the perceived images, public relations, and quality of interpretation in the galleries of participating museums. The project is also important because its findings have led to specific changes in exhibition installations and orientation areas in several of the participating museums.

The museums in the project are from different regions of the country and exhibit varying sizes and types of art collections. Among the participating institutions were the Art Institute of Chicago, the Seattle Art Museum, the Denver Art Museum, the Dallas Art Museum, the J. Paul Getty Museum, and the Museum of Fine Arts in Boston. Institutions such as the Mystic Seaport in Connecticut, Colonial Williamsburg in Virginia, and the Toledo Art Museum also used the focus group methodology. Alan Newman Research of Virginia conducted the entire Getty project.

Newman refers to the goals of the study as having an emphasis on *process* rather than *product*. The Getty project was designed to study visitor reactions to art museums, as well as to "stimulate interdisciplinary communication among museum professionals." Specific objectives of the project included identifying staff expectations and assumptions about the museum visitors' experiences and characterizing the public's expectations of the museums. Then visitors' experiences at the museums were documented and analyzed.

Focus group research is qualitative. It provides information on the perceptions and attitudes of a group of people. Newman used two types of focus groups in this project: "consensus groups" and "external focus groups." The staff of the museum—the director, senior staff members, curators, educators, and some of the museum's trustees—formed the consensus group. Consensus-group meetings provided an opportunity for the staff to articulate their assumptions about visitors and nonvisitors, and to discuss goals for enhancing the museum experience.

The external focus groups at each museum were arranged in pairs: They consisted of one group of visitors who had attended the museum and a group of nonvisitors. The focus group methodology selects participants randomly, according to criteria that are agreed upon by the museum. In the Getty study, groups of 10 to 12 adults, plus the moderator, Alan Newman, met in a conference room with a two-way mirror. The mirror allowed museum personnel to observe and video tape the proceedings. The participants in each group were aware that their session was being observed and recorded. Newman directed the group conversation based on an outline agreed to by the client museum.

Each external focus group met with Newman to discuss their backgrounds, their interest in art museums, and their expectations about a visit to the museum. The groups were given an assignment, which had been developed by the staff; the assignment included visits to specific galleries in the museum. Participants were asked to record their observations, questions, and reactions in a notebook. One week after their visit, the two external focus groups reconvened to discuss their experiences and to compare these experiences with their expectations.

The museum's consensus group also met with Newman after the external focus group sessions. The staff heard Newman's summary and compared their reactions with the visitors' experiences in the museum. In most of the museums involved in the Getty Focus Group project, this was the first of many staff meetings held to solve problems identified by the visitors.

Newman summarized the focus group's findings in a paper titled "What

Did the Focus Group Reveal?" The text was presented in 1989 at a conference of the 11 participating museums. In 1990, the paper was developed into a publication and video tape, and subsequently it was published in *Insights: Museums, Visitors, Attitudes, Expectations: A Focus Group Experiment* (Walsh, 1991).

In his summary, Newman articulated a number of keys points. The consensus groups generally agreed that staff want visitors to

- Have a positive, meaningful, and educational experience and to leave with a desire to return.
- "Connect" emotionally with objects of significance.
- Have an educational experience that will engage their intellectual curiosity and encourage further learning about the artists or period in history.
- Feel comfortable and welcome.
- Recognize that they are looking at original works of art created by artists.

The external focus groups expressed similar feelings. They wanted to find the museum visit meaningful and rewarding and to want to return. Newman's research revealed the following issues:

- Both visitors and nonvisitors found the museum visit educational because it "promoted an understanding of, or interest in, history or culture."
- The objects in the collections are the primary focus of the museum experience. Visitors were impressed by the beauty, variety, size, and intricacy of the objects in the collections. Almost everyone found a particular work of art that reached out to him or her.
- Museums are reflective places. They provide opportunities for a visitor to reflect and view the world from a renewed prospective.
- There was a distinct difference between the ways visitors and nonvisitors in the external focus groups viewed their initial visit to the museum. Nonvisitors suggested that they were intimidated by museums and had not attended museums previously. Intimidation resulted from a belief that museums serve the upper classes only, or the perception that galleries are unsuitable for families. Other reasons for intimidation included perceived guard discourtesy and lack of museum orientation or information.
- The absence of general awareness of the museum, especially among nonvisitors, was cited as a key reason for not attending.
- Generally, the external focus group had little knowledge of the permanent collection.

Newman reported that there was general agreement by all the participants in the study (i.e., both visitors and nonvisitors) that art museums must improve the educational quality of the museum experience and that this can be achieved through better orientation, information, and direction.

- *Orientation* helps visitors to move around the physical layout of the museum, locates important works of art for visitors, and provides information on educational events. While museums offer these resources, suitable orientation often is not easily accessible to visitors. The focus groups commented favorably on orientation films, video disks, and so forth, because such orientation services, being visual and verbal, are easy to locate.
- *Information* about the works of art is an essential aspect of the museum educational experience. Information was requested by both first-time and repeat visitors. The focus groups expressed dissatisfaction with the type of information presented on labels because it frequently provided insufficient data about objects. Often, instead of providing data about an artist's life, or facts concerned with the historic or artistic significance of an object, labels offered donor information. The focus groups commented that labels were frequently too small or too difficult to read. Brochures, guided tours, and audiovisual materials, from video disks to slide shows, were requested. The groups also requested information on the kinds of programs and tours provided by museums. If programs and tours were available, visitors wanted prompt information.
- *Clear directions* can help to reduce intimidation and promote learning. Moving through a museum can be a complex task if a visitor is trying to locate a specific gallery or is in search of an object in the collection. Maps are often confusing and difficult to follow. Participants frequently turned to guards, who were reported as being neither easily available nor "friendly."

Newman's paper, summarizing 2 years of research, 770 pages, and 132 hours of transcripts, involving more than 220 visitors and 115 professionals, resulted in an assessment of art museums' effectiveness in serving visitors. The research has been extremely helpful to the participating museums. Since the conclusion of the Getty project, the participating museums have addressed specific concerns that were identified by the focus groups. Some museums have reorganized admission desks, provided new labels in galleries, trained security staff and docents, and reinstalled entire galleries. Practical consequences of the focus group's study will be ongoing for many years. The Toledo, Denver, and Seattle Art Museums have continued to use the focus group methodology to evaluate how effective gallery presentations and membership benefits and services are in serving museum audiences. One of the important outcomes of the Getty Focus Group study has been that art museum professionals have more clearly understood the value of listening to the needs of their audiences. These professionals have learned that there are specific and practical steps that can be taken to improve the effectiveness of installations, programs, and the museum environment.

The Institute of Contemporary Arts, Boston

Abigail Housen, Director of the Graduate Program in Art Education at the Massachusetts College of Art in Boston, has completed a number of evaluation studies with different art museums. Like other researchers, Housen has combined diverse evaluation methodologies.

For the Institute of Contemporary Art (ICA) in Boston, Housen (1987) produced a study that included three evaluation methods.

1. Understanding who visitors are (demographic studies focused on numbers)
2. Analyzing what preferences visitors have in art and/or the type of interpretive materials preferred (attitudinal studies)
3. Evaluating visitors' level of understanding and comprehension (developmental studies)

The ICA pilot study examined a selection of exhibitions that were part of the ICA's "Currents" program dealing with issues in contemporary art and encompassing media such as paintings, sculpture, photography, and video. Artists such as Elizabeth Murray, Susan Rothenberg, and Karl Baden have shown their work in the ICA "Currents" exhibitions. The study focused on how to improve the educational value of these exhibitions.

Housen's evaluation study utilized a questionnaire for the collection of demographic data. Visitors were queried about their age, sex, and the number of times they had visited the museum. Interviews were used to conduct an attitudinal study, with open-ended questions soliciting information about the visitors' responses to the exhibition. Visitors were asked about the extent of their use of educational materials. They also were queried about their impression of the museum.

In terms of gathering developmental data, the visitors' level of aesthetic understanding was analyzed in terms of five stages of aesthetic development. Data were collected through open-ended, interview-structured questions. Responses were tape recorded, transcribed, and clinically coded by two expert coders. An Aesthetic Development Scoring Manual, based on a profile of ratings selected from the interviews, classified the visitors' aesthetic style.

The results of the ICA study include the following:

- Respondents requested additional educational information to aid them in their understanding of contemporary art.
- Respondents strongly endorsed the idea of a resource center that would allow visitors to structure their own learning.

The developmental data gained in the study helped the museum to select the types of written and audiovisual resources that were most effective. For example, the ICA understood more clearly what types of learning activities would be effective for visitors at Housen's levels of aesthetic development II, III, and IV.

The study resulted in the decision by the ICA to include journals and books in its general orientation area. The information on the audience and the visitors' new understanding of the levels of aesthetic development was integrated into the ICA's outreach programs for high school audiences unfamiliar with contemporary art. Topics such as "Access to Contemporary Art" and the holocaust were discussed.

The Minneapolis Institute of Arts

The Minneapolis Institute of Arts (MIA) completed a study of the response to an exhibition titled "Beneath the Surface." The exhibition included four sections: Personal Symbols, Cultural Symbols, Religious Symbols, and Symbols of Harmony. The study explored whether selected viewers, in this case, visitors with art backgrounds or "art experts" and "art novices" (visitors with little or no formal background in art) were able to understand the meaning of a work of art through the artist's use of symbols, subject matter, and composition. The MIA wanted to learn whether its untraditional methods using labels without jargon, some interactive components, and part–whole structure, were distinctive in their departure from the more formal presentations usually found in fine arts museums (Gudeman & Johnson, 1989).

The goals of the MIA included

1. Assessing both the entire exhibition and the following seven aspects identified in the exhibition:
     - As a source of learning
     - As a source of enjoyment
     - In terms of the selection of art
     - In terms of thematic panels

- In terms of labels
- The installation arrangement
- The location of the exhibition

2. Assessing the interactive interpretive components of the exhibition to study whether such components were used and if they helped visitors to understand the works of art. The exhibition offered such resources as
    - Conflicting interpretations by critics and notebooks for visitors' use in recording their interpretations
    - Three reference books about symbols in Western and non-Western art
    - A short video in which Red Grooms interprets his work
    - A magnifying glass to be used by visitors in examining the Hans Holbein woodcuts

3. Determining the path used by visitors to move through the exhibition and studying whether "partial viewing" affected visitors' understanding of the works of art (This evaluation goal was put forth by the museum's design staff.)

4. Analyzing the demographic profile of the visitors and determining their general assessment of the exhibition

The MIA study method employed a three-page exit interview questionnaire, which included a map of the exhibition. The questionnaire was completed by 114 randomly selected adult visitors. A statistical analysis was performed by computer. The MIA study yielded the following results:

- There was no significant difference between the ratings of the seven attributes by the art experts and those by the art novices, although the exhibition was designed for the art novices. Visitors indicated their "expertness" if they answered positively that they produced, studied, or collected art or visited museums.
- Study of the utilization of the exhibition's seven interpretive resources—reference books, comment folder, video, and so forth—revealed that 88% of visitors utilized labels, and 34% used the comment book. Other resources were used by 45%–55% of visitors.
- Visitors were asked to draw a path on a map indicating the path they took. Analysis of the maps indicated that visitors took different pathways through the exhibition. The most common path took the form of a "great circle" around the gallery's perimeter.

The Minneapolis Art Institute has continued to document, through further studies, the responses of art novices and to detail the interpretive resources that are most effective.

EVALUATION STUDIES OF INTERPRETIVE RESOURCES

A second area of visitor research has focused attention on specific interpretive resources such as labels, brochures, and video disks. These studies provide more intensive assessments on who visitors are, how they learn, and what types of learning occur. Frequently, these projects are formative evaluations and thus include opportunities to refine a particular interpretive unit and assess it again. A summary of a study of specific interpretive resources conducted at the Denver Art Museum (DAM) follows.

The Denver Art Museum has an extensive record of audience research projects of all sizes. Under the leadership of Patterson Williams, Director of Education, and with the support of the National Endowment for the Arts and the J. Paul Getty Trust, the museum has worked with professional evaluators, most frequently with Ross Loomis. In addition, the museum has trained the staff to conduct small evaluations. The range of evaluation activities is significant because the DAM has evaluated the effectiveness of gallery guides, slide lectures, exhibition labeling systems, and specific programs with schools. The DAM also has studied the attitudes of museum members and of the general community in relation to the museum.

Numerous articles and papers have documented the work at the DAM and the museum's efforts to understand the expectations and characteristics of its visitors. As part of this research, the DAM has learned about the different levels of interest people have in art. This has resulted in a more complete understanding of the needs of art novices and experts when visiting the museum, and the types of interpretive resources that will be helpful and will be utilized by these visitors.

Since the fall of 1986, the DAM has been investigating experts' and novices' experiences with art. The museum has studied what visitors value from the experience and what prevents a person from being engaged by a work of art. The museum's research, especially with art novices (visitors with moderate to high interest in art but little or no formal background), focused on designing interpretive goals to improve the quality of visitors' experiences with art objects.

One DAM project, which concerned both art novices and experts, evaluated labels (McDermott, 1987). These labels, used for works of art in the Native American and the Asian galleries, were designed to provide human interest and a cultural context. The DAM tested different formats for the labels, such as hand-held paddles hidden in pockets and traditional wall labels. The museum's project teams were composed of an educator, a curator, and an editor; they worked on labels for the Asian and Native American galleries. The DAM research resulted in an understanding of general patterns of visitor interest. It was found, for example, that art novices are clearly interested in being transported back in time. They want to understand the conditions under which people lived. Novices also want to comprehend the artist's creative process.

Williams (1989) has defined several content characteristics of a "human connection label." These are that the label

- Describes the people who are behind the work as artists, craftspeople, patrons, and users.
- Articulates the perspective of these people, especially their way of prizing an object.
- Offers, when possible, first-person testimony (quotes and photographs).
- Describes, in very concrete ways, the daily life and/or ways of thinking of the artist or owner of the work of art.
- Features baseline human information about the makers or users; that is, it provides answers to questions such as: Why was the work created? What did the art mean to people? How did it fit into their lives?

As part of the DAM's research about cultural context labels in the Asian gallery, an evaluation was conducted to determine if the labels were being used, in what ways, and whether the audience actually made the "human connections." Two evaluation instruments were utilized: (1) unobtrusive behavioral observations, and (2) personal interviews. The sample was validated against the demographic studies and against other visitor studies conducted by the museum.

Williams (1989) provides helpful guidelines for preparing human connection labels. These guidelines make the following points:

- Effective label content requires knowledge and expertise from both curators and educators. Professionals must communicate with each other so that the visitor benefits.
- A review process, allowing for honest criticism of content from the perspective and interest of the visitor, is necessary.
- The identification of a specific target audience and a written statement of content and stylistic goals help reduce problems among the label team and provides a focus for audience research and evaluation.

A different study at the DAM, called "Chairmanship: The Art of Choosing Chairs," studied a self-guided tour brochure of chairs in the museum's collection (Krulick, Ritchie, & Curry, 1989). Working closely with Curator David Curry, the staff conducted taped interviews to capture Curry's knowledge of and enthusiasm for the objects. The experiment included a small special exhibition of the chairs in the museum's permanent collection, and it was accompanied by a brochure. The introductory label encouraged visitors to take the brochure, which illustrated the 10 chairs and was written in the first person, with excerpts from Curry's transcript. The brochure came with a reading list and a reader assignment. Curry's humorous, informed, and affectionate descriptions of the chairs helped the reader to attend to the objects. Additionally, the brochure was easy to use. The conversational tone, which reflected the curator's point of view, made it distinctive from the museum's other brochures. The information and insights about the objects were useful and challenging to the users.

The DAM discovered early in the study that the brochure was too large to be easily used. This was corrected in the revised version described above. Also, the participatory format could have benefited from formative testing, since many readers overlooked this part of the brochure, finding it too difficult to use.

The evaluation of the brochure was done by a small sample of visitors who had a moderate to high interest in art and included a questionnaire and a group interpretation. The brochure was positively received and was considered a valuable resource for interpreting the exhibition.

The DAM evaluation reports and papers have been included in several editions of the annual *Sourcebook*, published by the American Association of Museums. In addition to those cited earlier, *Sourcebook* articles include a cluster analytic study of visitor characteristics and expectations (Loomis & McDermott, 1980) and a focus group study of "average adult visitors," which was incorporated into the planning of the reinstallation of the Native American collection (Malins, 1985). The articles cited above, which were published by the DAM, suggest the scope of the museum's evaluation research and document the improvements made in exhibitions and programs. The DAM studies are important chronicles of project teams that included an educator, curator, and editor. Together, these teams worked to bridge the gap between the art expert staff and the art novices who visit the museum. Furthermore, the DAM has shared this information with the museum field.

CONCLUSION

With the new century a few years away, we are in the midst of a major change in the way museums are serving as educational institutions. The effective use of evaluations of visitors of art museums is helping to achieve an understanding of how museums, in a new era, can fulfill their responsibility of public service by achieving higher standards for exhibitions and programs.

The argument for museums as educational institutions no longer needs repeating. All types of museums are affirming the role of education as an essential component of their mission. The educational function is accepted as an upper-management responsibility. The broad acceptance of the educational role of museums also has enhanced the utilization of evaluation studies. The application of information gained in evaluation studies is used by many staff members, including curators, educators, designers, and security staff, and by volunteers.

Just as in the past the term *education* too often referred to limited activities related to specific programs, evaluation studies were perceived to have limited goals and application. Today, as the summaries of the various studies demonstrate, art museums are developing an institution-wide commitment to sharing knowledge with the public in the most effective way possible.

While there was once an inherent tension between the concerns of collecting and presenting art, and the responsibility of public access, curators and educators are now developing partnerships that address their mutual concerns and interest. The nature and purpose of collecting are also in transition. The "meaning" of objects and the ways art museums communicate with their public are undergoing changes. The need to provide a historical, cultural, and aesthetic context for the artist and artwork is transforming the types of resources provided to visitors.

Museum visitor evaluation has developed insights on who visitors of art museums are, how they learn, and how people can broaden their understanding of the meaning of works of art. Today, evaluation studies not only help us to know who is visiting museums, but aid us in discovering how people move through the galleries and how they acquire information and perceive works of art.

This paper focuses on evaluation studies that have dealt with exhibitions and related interpretive materials. However, most museums regularly evaluate their public and school programs. The data are collected through questionnaires and interviews, and observations of participants, all generally conducted by staff members. These evaluations help museum educators assess the effectiveness of a particular program, identify their audience, and gather information on how to improve museum programs. The information gathered from these studies is used to make decisions on the management of programs. Such information also affects timing, frequency, and effectiveness of public relations. Because this research has been widely documented and focuses on a specific type of programming, it is not covered in this paper. Demographic studies, image assessments, and membership studies, among other types of research, were not reviewed, because this paper addresses research that has helped art museums perceive the needs of their audiences, focusing on learning in the galleries. These evaluations, as well as many others not documented in this paper, have produced data that have led museum staffs to change the ways art museums provide services to their visitors.

Evaluations cannot produce formulas for labels or identify the ideal number of objects to include in an installation. Evaluation research identifies patterns of behavior, increases our understanding of how visitors interact with objects and labels, and tells us what types of interpretive resources are effective. There is a need to continue to develop ways to study object-based learning. Knowledge gleaned from studies analyzing the manner in which visitors learn from objects will provide opportunities for evaluators in the 1990s to continue to innovate and investigate. The results of these and other evaluation studies will help us to make decisions about how to improve our effectiveness in communicating with the public.

There is a coherence to the research work being conducted today. The issues and questions are not unlike those asked by E. S. Robinson (1928) almost 70 years ago when he was evaluating museums.

What does the "average" man do in a museum? He wanders aimlessly, but not blindly. His attention is drawn to this and distracted from that. He must have glimmering interests which might be fanned into overt enjoyment. Yet this casual visitor is the main mystery, and if he is to be dealt with effectively, there needs to be added to the talking about him and thinking about him a deliberate observation of his behavior. (p. 7)

REFERENCES

American Association of Museums. (1992). *Excellence and equity: Education and the public dimension of museums*. Washington, DC: Author.

Commission on Museums for a New Century. (1984). *Museums for a new century*. Washington, DC: American Association of Museums.

Gilman, B. I. (1916). Museum fatigue. *The Scientific Monthly, 12*, 62–74.

Gudeman, R., & Johnson, K. (1989). A goal-referenced study of exhibition effectiveness. *Visitor Behavior, 3*(4), 7–8.

Housen, A. (1987). Three methods for understanding museum audiences. *The Museum Studies Journal, 2*(4), 41–49.

Krulick, J., Ritchie, M., & Curry, D. P. (1989). A self guide experiment: Chairmanship: The art of choosing chairs. In *The Sourcebook 1989* (pp. 169–178). Washington, DC: American Association of Museums.

Loomis, R. J. (1987). *Museum visitor evaluation: New tool for management*. Nashville, TN: American Association for State and Local History.

Loomis, R. J., & McDermott, M. (1980). Cluster analytic study of Denver Art Museum, visitor characteristics and expectations. In *The Sourcebook 1980* (pp. 163–177). Washington, DC: American Association of Museums.

Malins, S. (1985). Conclusions: An excerpt from report on focus group research: A qualitative investigation of the average adult visitor in relation to Native American art and its museum installation. In *The Sourcebook 1985* (pp. 185–196). Washington, DC: American Association of Museums.

McDermott, M. (1987). Through their eyes: What novices value in art experiences. In *The Sourcebook 1988* (pp. 133–162). Washington, DC: American Association of Museums.

Newman, A. (1991). What did the focus group reveal? In A. Walsh (Ed.), *Insights: Museums, visitors, attitudes, expectations: A focus group experiment* (pp. 112–122). Los Angeles: Getty Center for Education in the Arts & The J. Paul Getty Museum.

Robinson, E. S. (1928). *The behavior of the museum visitor* (Publication of the American Association of Museums, New Series, no. 5). Washington, DC: American Association of Museums.

Walsh, A. (Ed.). (1991). *Insights: Museums, visitors, attitudes, expectations: A focus group experiment.* Los Angeles: Getty Center for Education in the Arts & the J. Paul Getty Museum.

Williams, P. (1989). Making the human connection: A label experiment. In *The Sourcebook 1989* (pp. 179–191). Washington, DC: American Association of Museums.

Chapter 13

Turkish Families Visiting Berlin Museums

CHRISTIANE SCHRÜBBERS
Berlin Museum of Communication and Transport, Germany

The following museum education project took place in 1987 in three West Berlin museums. Its aim was to work with Turkish families, parents, and children of 5 and 6 years of age. Starting from deliberations marked by intercultural aspects, we wanted to see how familiar the Turkish Berlin population was with their cultural and historical surroundings, to increase their analysis of their own existence between two cultures, and to help them interpret the objects in the museum, recognizing their personal situation as migrant workers living in a quite different civilization from their own.

For this work it was natural to choose participants with a well-established Turkish identity and to perform the project in Turkish. So the tour through the chosen museums was planned by me and carried out by a Turkish woman, Nüket Kilicli, who was socialized in Turkish and German culture, and fluent in both languages. She advised me when I designed the project; moreover, she was the active person in working with the participants, speaking and explaining only in Turkish.

The project was developed by the Intercultural Department created by my office, the Museumspädagogischer Dienst Berlin (Museum Educational Service of [West] Berlin).

The first aim of the project was to determine how Turkish people in Berlin see and experience the museums. The second goal was to discover new ways for museums or exhibitions to generate interest among this group by establishing suitable museum educational activities.

This project focused on a very specific case—museum encounters of Turkish and German people, members of two extremely different cultures. I will first outline our planning and theses, then explain the substance of the project, and finally discuss our evaluation. I will conclude with how these theses can be applied in practice.

Evaluating and Assessing the Visual Arts in Education: International Perspectives: © 1996 by Teachers College, Columbia University. All rights reserved. ISBN 0-8077-3511-6. Prior to photocopying items for classroom use, please contact the Copyright Clearance Center, Customer Service, 222 Rosewood Dr., Danvers, MA 01923, USA, tel. (508) 750-8400.

DESIGN OF THE PROJECT

At first we formulated four conditions for our project, each of which I will discuss in the text that follows.

1. Native language: Research would be conducted in Turkish.
2. Personal motivation: The participants would come individually and voluntarily, not as a result of membership in an organization.
3. Variety of museums: Different genres of museums would be tested.
4. Variety of methods: Different museum educational methods would be considered.

Who Speaks Turkish?

Turkish migrant workers in Berlin are of the second and third generation. The first generation of migrant workers began coming in the 1960s at the age of about 20 in order to work. At the time our project took place, most of these immigrants had already retired, some returning to Turkey and some remaining in Germany. The second generation in our study were the children of the first generation. Most were born in Turkey; many lived there until about 15 years of age, moving to Germany with their parents or seeking work and schooling for themselves. At the time of our project, this generation were the active workers. The third generation were the children, born in Germany, of the second-generation workers. At the time of our project, they were in kindergarten or elementary school. The native-language competence of these immigrants was diminishing, without being replaced by German linguistic competence. The problem of partially competent bilinguals was already evident in the schools.

We expected a social and a cultural language barrier. Socially, referring to typical biographies, Turkish migrant workers came predominantly from rural regions, had at best five years of schooling, and were unskilled workers. Culturally, our participants had been socialized in Turkey until about age 15, had not visited a Berlin museum, and had no previous experience with the institution "museum."

In our project, participants entered a strange field in which they should not only acquire knowledge but have an emotional experience as well. Their bashfulness in the strangeness of the museum and the unfamiliar topics of art and history should at least be calmed by their linguistic competence. An analysis of the Turkish population shows that children before starting school master their mother tongue. However, between about 1970 and 1980 Turkish children who learned their mother tongue before attending school had to speak and write German in school. They coped with the situation by learning some German, and unlearning some Turkish, leading to a degree of illiteracy in both languages. We wanted to conduct our museum project purely in Turkish, without complications, that means as well, being well integrated in Turkish culture and individuation.

How Do We Find Participants?

From previous projects we knew that advertising media, including posters, newspaper articles, and radio reports, had little or no effect on the number of Turkish museum visitors. The personal recommendation of an event is the most effective advertising. We wanted to avoid organizations, so we decided to visit the parents' meetings in various kindergartens and introduce ourselves and our museum program. We focused specifically on adult programs. Turkish children had the best chances of integration via German schools. Young adults and elders got few or no offers for integration in the cultural arena. Our direct contact with kindergartners' parents motivated the adults. Their participation in our project was bolstered by the expectation that their children would learn more as well, an attitude that later began to interfere with the project.

Which Museums Do We Visit?

Visits to three museums were desirable to enable participants to develop a growing intimacy within their group and to become comfortable together. The three museums should be different in genre (art, culture, history). They should be linked to the history of the town, since migrant workers living abroad may want an orientation in order to feel more at home. We wanted to assemble locales that would foster a relationship between object and museum goer in a specific way, defined by distinguishing features of the Turkish visitors.

We chose the Charlottenburg Castle, the residence of Prussia's first queen, a splendid building from the late seventeenth century; the Berlin Museum, a museum of the history of Berlin, in a baroque building from the early eighteenth century; and the Georg-Kolbe Museum, the sculptor's former studio, constructed in cubistic design in about 1928.

The Charlottenburg Castle seemed to be the easiest and most attractive stepping stone. It is a tourist's place par excellence; it bewitches by its shimmering gold and baroque decorations in our grey and dull city. In addition, the castle is a building in which a bit of Turkish history is reflected. The topic of our excursion would be the analysis of the stranger and the strange in the period of Illumination.

The Berlin Museum was the second most accessible museum. We assumed that it would attract less interest compared with the castle, but some interest since it shows the history of the city in which our program's participants settled. We chose as the topic, bourgeois childhood and toys of the nineteenth century.

The Georg-Kolbe Museum was planned to conclude our course. We realized from the beginning that this museum would be problematic. In Turkish culture, sculpture is nonexistent except for works imported from the West in the early twentieth century, statues of ltürk, and memorials of the Unknown Soldier. Furthermore, nude sculptures like Georg Kolbe's are considered amoral by religious Turks. Nevertheless, this "difficult" museum was included in the sequence of museum visits. We were curious to know if it was possible to offer our selection of German and Western European art and culture to Turks and to even partially communicate its importance to them. We hoped to gain the group's confidence and take the risk of visiting the Kolbe Museum. The Kolbe Museum is a very social place; its garden is ideal for children's and family programs. In this former studio we wanted to talk about postures and gestures, especially about hands.

Which Methods Do We Choose?

We developed some basic procedures prior to conducting the project. The following five were most important:

1. *Personal care of the group.* Personal talk is important to this group. In the periods of preparation and implementation, we wanted to gain respect and authority. We knew that this personal aspect is often more important than the thematic. Interpersonal connections, in addition to the docent tours in the museums, included introduction of the project and of ourselves during the parents' meetings; personal invitation letters to each museum visit; attentive conversation for welcoming and parting; and reminders of future museum visits at the end of each activity. All these interactions were conducted in Turkish.
2. *Analysis of objects and ensembles.* This point is self-explanatory and does not need any comment. (I expand on this point in my rejoinder to Dobbs.)
3. *Narrative projection.* In each museum we offered a guided tour on the explicit topics described above. In addition, there was an implicit message in these topics referring to the situation of the group: to be strange/be a stranger in the local dominant culture. We looked at the objects and collections once and then again to elicit personal annotations. For example, after seeing and examining a Chinese tapestry, we asked, "How do you judge and which preconceptions do you have of China in particular and of strangers or people from abroad in general?" While looking at toys, we

asked, "What toys did you have as a child? What kind of childhood did you have (rural, middle class, or proletarian)?" Narrative projection means taking as the starting point of interpretation their personal situation as a migrant worker, and the associations and reminiscences that come to mind while looking at the objects.

4. *Biographical method.* Our most important work arose from the composition of our groups, formed by pairs of parents and children. During the guided tours, we planned to initiate repeated conversations between parents and children, as well as conversations among parents and children as separate groups, asking questions about their personal history. We wanted parents, while looking at the museum exhibits, to tell their children about the culture and life of their native country. Thus, they would become information conveyers of Turkish culture and history and partly interpreters of German museum objects. We stressed their competence as museum visitors and their individuality as Turkish Berliners.

5. *Playing activity.* We wanted to close each of our excursions with a playing activity. That should shift the participants' experiences to a different level and make them likely to remember the play. First, it should be fun. Through play, we wanted to learn which activities could be offered to this group: Would they think of the play as nonsense or improper in a museum setting, or, on the contrary, as useful and comfortable?

SUBSTANCE OF THE PROJECT

Charlottenburg Castle

Almost 300 years ago, on the eve of diplomatic relations between Europe and the Osman Empire, Turkish people lived in this castle as servants. Some became reputable and prosperous. The "Turkish threat" had ceased to exist, and melding of the two cultural blocks started to be possible. The Illumination turned toward the strange and the strangers. Brandenburg experienced an economic upswing due to immigrants (who sometimes were expelled), strangers, and most of all the Hugenots. For the intellectuals, the strangers were welcomed bearers of new ideas, a different culture, and special achievements.

The following museum pieces were considered and analyzed:

- The Chinese Room, with its tapestry of everyday scenes
- A portrait of Queen Sophie Charlotte, who was known as a philosopher and marked by the ideas of the Illumination and tolerance against the strange and the strangers

- A portrait of a Prussian lady-in-waiting dressed as a sultana
- A portrait of a Saxon couple acting on stage as protagonists in Voltaire's theater piece "Mahomet"

Information about the pieces was provided and comments were offered on the topic of the strange. The participants were invited to reflect on their personal situation of being strangers and their own judgment of strangers. Contemplating on the Chinese Room, we explained the historical differences in the judgment of the strange. In front of the portrait of the sultana, we discussed conceptions and preconceptions, past and present. In front of the portrait "Mahomet," we talked about the role of religion in tolerance. In the castle ballroom, a role play based on historical material had been planned on the topic: "The sultan sent his ambassador to the Prussian king." Our plan could not be realized, however, because of the curator's concern for the fine wood floor and gold ornamental walls, which we suspected might have been damaged by the children had we proceeded.

Berlin Museum

We visited the displays of middle class toys from 1860 to 1930 and a children's room designed by the architect van der Velde in 1910. There was no guided tour, but an orientation structured by questions: Which are familiar? Which do you have, too? Which do you not understand? During the ensuing discussion, we talked about various courses of socialization of childhood in Germany and invited the children to interview their parents about their childhood and their toys. At the end of our activity we played an old board game, sitting on the floor of the exhibition room.

Georg-Kolbe Museum

This relatively small museum contains mainly sculptures by the artist himself. He lived in Istanbul for a year and conceived a war memorial and a portrait of Enver Pascha. The focal point of our excursion was the sculpture "Call of the Earth" of a woman stopping her dance to listen. The children were asked to imitate the posture of this and other sculptures. Later we examined the figures' hands and their gestures. We talked about various hand expressions, for instance, for praying. At the end all made gestures with their hands, which were then modeled in plaster.

EVALUATION OF THE PROJECT

We evaluated our project using the qualitative method. We collected observations, which we first compared among themselves and then related to the initial conditions and expectations. Our data are not representative of quantitative research. Certainly we worked with a restricted sample to describe typical results, which could serve as a base for advanced projects with refined methods. The following data were collected:

Interest in different museums
Interest in different topics
Efficiency of different methods of transmission

Interest in the Museum

The Charlottenburg Castle did not produce the interest we expected. The baroque splendor did not elicit the anticipated enthusiasm, but on the contrary weighed on the participants. The children had difficulty comprehending the large, dark colored, and badly illuminated paintings. The information that 300 years ago Turks, the first migrant workers to settle in town, lived as servants in this castle, astonished the adults. However, it did not cause an attachment that could lead to intimate conversations.

A more successful pedagogical offering in the Charlottenburg Castle should not include families as a target group. Rather, those who have a more formal interest, students of German language and history, for instance, would find interesting material here.

Interest in the Berlin Museum was much greater than expected. The building itself was not prominent, so the topic got all the attention. This museum should surely offer a family program.

In the Georg-Kolbe Museum, the objects at the center of attention seriously hindered the activity of the participants. Our initial fear was confirmed. The adults positioned themselves in the room in a way that helped to overlook the sculptures; the children were shy. Even with questions and other offers to talk, they did not relax. The final play, however, was met with enthusiasm.

In this target group the general interest in visiting museums is very low due to economic, social, and cultural reasons. Adult Turkish migrant workers are bound to a rigid timetable. Many work 6 days a week. Our program, which began each Saturday at 3 P.M. was the start of the weekend for some visitors; therefore, participating in our excursions was a certain sacrifice. Turkish families spend their scarce free time visiting other members of the family or friends, which is considered a social duty. Unusual additional activities such as our project are seen more as a stress than recreation. Lastly, we found the energy we had to give to personal care of the participants was excessive. We had to spend too much time in fostering the participants' motivation. Even under the most ideal conditions, it would not be feasible to carry on this project given the energy required to undertake the personal care of the participants. Taking all this into consideration, we developed no standard program out of this pilot study.

Interest in the Topic

Strangeness as the starting point of our conversation in the Charlottenburg Castle was a difficult topic. We constructed our guided tours using methods of oral history that we still find suitable. But they could not sufficiently sustain our work, since we were not familiar enough with the specific features of Turkish socialization. A prominent difference is, for example, the definition of a person by the group, normally the family. Our suggestion to the participants to speak about themselves in front of strangers was certainly wrong, as we saw in Charlottenburg Castle. Still, it worked in the apparently exceptional situation of regarding the toys in the Berlin Museum. The participants were so open that they carried on a very lively discussion in the group. Moreover, some delicate questions were touched upon, such as: How much time do the parents spend with their children? How much money do they spend on toys? What kind of childhood did they have? Was there enough money for living? Were there toys? Some participants confessed that all these questions had never before been the subject of conversation among the family. They hinted that before they entered the museum, they would not have imagined talking to their children in such an open manner in other people's presence. Facing the objects in the showcases, dolls and bears and construction kits and mini-household utensils in a puppet house, the adults got into a vivid exchange of reminiscences.

Little can be said about the Georg-Kolbe Museum, the naked human being, and its gestures. We were deliberately provocative in exploring a taboo. And we learned during the work that it was not possible to overcome such deep-seated feelings through our means.

The Effect of the Various Transmitting Methods

1. *Personal care.* It was evident on repeated occasions that personal care in this target group is very important. Members of this group measure the value of a project more by means of who is recommending it than by its content. Through recommendation, the person initiating the project is granted respect and authority, and the event is attended. The motivating force of interest is weaker in Turkish socialization than in Western European culture. As a habit, individuals subordinate themselves and their activities to the code of the group. Rating this weakness, or lack of personal motivation in museums, it seemed to us that the return for our work was low, and that education and shaping (*Bildung*) are difficult to achieve.
2. *Analyzing the content of objects and collections.* The explanations of the objects

and collections were given by the docent. The attempts at working collectively at learning were not backed by the participants. I suggest that they were familiar with a style of frontal teaching, so that they did not adopt our liberal style of group teaching.

3. *Narrative projection.* This term indicates a method of object contemplation in which the object and the associations of the contemplator grow together. The object becomes the projection surface of the contemplator's reminiscences. Talking about it, he or she builds up a different relationship to the reality. I already touched on the fact that this method was unsuccessful with the topic of strangers, but worked well with the topic of toys.

4. *Biographical access.* This point cannot be separated from the previous one. We intended to use biographical access mostly in the discussions between parents and children. Here, too, we had difficulties, because participants apparently adhere to the old-fashioned model of education: When elders talk, children hold their tongues. A deep respect for the elder or the teacher is part of good manners. Parents perceived the project as a school lesson for the children, so they remained silent. A father complained that his child had been acknowledged less often than others during question sessions. This showed us that participants had expectations that we were unable to change either by our presentation or by our working style.

We gained little ground in another area as well: A father had difficulty finding transportation to a museum visit. The docent proposed that to save time, rather than going by bus he get a ride in another father's car. Both men refused the proposal on the grounds that their own difference of social status would not allow it. Clearly, in the course of our series of museum visits, we were unable to realize our intention of increasing intimacy in the group.

5. *Playing activity.* Playing activities made it clear that the parents were unaccustomed to playing with their children. Still, both the board game and the modeling with plaster were very popular. Even in the strained atmosphere of the Georg-Kolbe Museum, the play activity was successful.

FINAL DISCUSSION

Museum education for groups not belonging to the traditional visitor groups requires intense preparation. This is even more valid for participants of foreign cultures. The research starts by analyzing the museum exhibits to choose the subject of the project. The first question is: Do we choose it or not? The following question can be: How do we transmit it?

A survey of museum programs for Turks in the Federal Republic of Germany quickly revealed that topics of everyday life are much more accessible than topics of art and art history. This result awaits theoretical reflection.

Evaluation of Museum Art Education Programs

STEPHEN M. DOBBS
Marin Community Foundation, USA

The papers by Bonnie Pitman and Christiane Schrübbers present very different strategies for exploring the issues of evaluation of museum art education programs. Schrübbers has written about a certain target audience's museum experiences that were the subject of an experimental study in 1987 in three West Berlin museums. The narrative is focused entirely on the design, operation, and findings of a specific intervention. The other paper, by Pitman, is a more general treatment of the topic of evaluation, but also focuses on some efforts to carry out research and evaluation activities in art museums that have become aware of the possible fruits of such labors. In this response paper I will spend the first part reviewing Schrübbers's report, the second part looking at Pitman's paper, and the final section developing some further observations about the evaluation of museum art education programs.

COMMENTS ON SCHRÜBBERS'S PAPER

West Germany, like several other industrialized countries, draws heavily upon foreign nations to supplement its labor pool. For many years the largest contingent (some 50%) has come from Turkey. These Turkish migrant workers are the subject of Schrübbers's study, which evaluated how this population sees and experiences different kinds of museums in West Berlin. The project included an effort "to discover new ways . . . to generate interest," to determine the relative impact of various museums and exhibits, and to try out different museum educational methods. At the outset it was clear that the project managers were faced with a formidable target: The Turkish workers are primarily rural-born, unskilled laborers who have little schooling, whose language competence in Turkish is limited but such diminution has not been compensated with increasing familiarity with the German language, and who work long hours and 6-day weeks, allowing little leisure time within a rigid schedule.

Furthermore, the cultural differences between Turkey and Germany provided additional challenges (and vexations) for any effort to reach out to the worker group. Most participants had never previously been in a museum. If one wishes to look at a project in which the aspiration to reach across multicultural barriers was diligent in the face of numerous handicaps, this is it.

The implications of such an effort should not be lost on other nations, including the United States, which also have experienced a floodtide of immigration in recent decades, with all of the cultural opportunities and conflicts attendant upon the rapidly changing demographics of industrialized democracies. It may be difficult to imagine a more problematic scenario than acculturating Turkish migrant workers to the museums of the nation in which Western art history first took scholarly root. At least in the United States, the outreach to the Hispanic community, for example, often features a glittering array of blockbuster exhibitions (such as "Mexico: Splendors of Thirty Centuries" at the Metropolitan Museum of Art in New York) or special arrangements designed to attract middle class and professional minorities (such as the "Murals of Teotihuacan" show at the M. H. de Young Museum in San Francisco, which included public access to the conservation process).

Perhaps it is also ironic that the fortunes of the subject population have fallen so far, in the disparity of sophistication between the target audience and the German institutions offering cultural content. The great Ottoman Empire once held Europe in awe, but after its disintegration and formal end with World War I the attractions and even the visibility of Turkish culture on the world's stage have been few and far between, save an occasional museum's nod toward Anatolian kilims (textiles) or the like. It is difficult to read the report on the Turkish migrant workers without empathy for the great loss they have suffered not only in terms of social and economic standing but culturally as well.

The well-intentioned project to familiarize these people with the West Berlin museums and German culture leaves unanswered the question as to how these migrant Turks are ever to come to know and understand their own substantial heritage.

Schrübbers describes the project as one of working with volunteer visitors in their own native language, in three museums of different genre and using various methods. By pursuing a more personal approach—inviting adults through contacts made in their children's schools—the project organizers tried to provide motivation for the participants. In fact, the participation of the parents "was bolstered by the expectation that their children would learn more." One wonders whether parents of American students would be similarly motivated, with the expectation that going to a museum might have a consequence not only for them but for their children as well.

The three museums offered a blend of art, culture, and history: Charlottenburg Castle, the seventeenth-century residence of Prussia's first queen; the Berlin Museum, a museum of the history of the city housed in an eighteenth-century building; and the Georg-Kolbe Museum, the former studio of the early-twentieth-century cubist sculptor. This was an ambitious selection, offering the prospect of evaluating visitor response across a spectrum of different kinds of institutions and exhibits.

Interestingly, the minor reflection of Turkish history in the Castle was expected by the project managers to produce a feeling of identification and interest among the migrant workers, but this did not prove to be the case. This is less surprising when one discovers that the "little bit of Turkish history" was that Turks had lived in the castle 300 years ago as servants!

Other early assumptions about the Turkish audience's reactions proved correct, such as the fact that the Georg-Kolbe Museum, with its presentation of the naked human figure in sculpture, presented an insuperable taboo. Schrübbers's contention that difficulties might have been anticipated because of the lack of a general sculptural tradition in Turkey rings less true than the obvious cultural barriers presented in dealing with an audience from a Moslem country. Yet the project still included exposure to Georg-Kolbe.

In the selection of museum educational methods, the "personal care" dimension was emphasized, not only in the form of the invitation but also through one-on-one conversations in the galleries and the encouragement of mutual play activities between the parents and the children who accompanied them.

Certainly we could all learn something from this close attention by the project team to cultural differences. Yet Schrübbers admits that the investigators' sensitivity to the Turks was incomplete. While it was important to work through the personal aspect, this in itself was insufficient. For example, when it came time for participants to share their personal observations, it was difficult for the Turkish workers to do so with strangers. But when they were asked to play with their children and get down on the floor to use a board game and do plaster modeling at the Berlin Museum, the activity went very well, even though the Turks are not accustomed to playing with their children, according to Schrübbers's report.

Other methods used by the museum educators to enhance the visitor experience included "analysis of objects and ensembles" (about which Schrübbers tells us nothing, assuming we all know what form such presentations took) and "narrative projection" (the autobiographical reactions).

Through qualitative observations and documentation, the art educators concluded that their job turned out to be every bit as difficult as they had originally envisioned. There were no real surprises. For example, "the children had difficulty comprehending the large, dark colored, and badly illumi-

nated paintings." Not only the children! And despite the information provided that Turkish citizens had lived in Castle Charlottenburg, "it did not
cause an attachment that could lead to intimate conversations."

Findings at all three sites confirmed that it is difficult to get people to
look at that with which they are unfamiliar and have little sense of connection,
especially when one begins with a fairly disinterested (i.e., non-museum-
going) group. One can lead visitors to the gallery (and they may look) but
one cannot make them see (or think!). In fact, Schrübbers concludes that the
museum project was "seen more as a stress than recreation."

If little was learned from the project about the visitors that might not
have been anticipated, what was learned about evaluation of museum art education programs? Here I think the paper yielded some rich information. First,
Schrübbers indicates that some measure of success can be directly attributed
to developing visitor motivation through personal and multicultural sensitivity. This is a large area to be explored by educators in museums as well as in
other educational institutions. It is one thing to be filled with good intentions,
but none of us knows enough about how to deal with the diversity of peoples
who are now visiting our museums. All of us need to be better schooled in cultural traits that affect communications, attitudinal change, and avocational interests. Assembling a data base of such information cannot be left solely to the
demographers. Art educators and museum professionals will need to continually update and readjust the templates or lenses through which they view a potential audience (exotic or otherwise, such as the Turkish migrant workers).

Second, the Schrübbers report demonstrates the extent and complexity
of evaluation that is required to adequately assess programs of multicultural
outreach. Dealing with different languages both literally and figuratively, the
project team was pressed to make all of their inferences from observations.
The report does not indicate that questionnaires, sustained interviews, or
other methods of data gathering were used. Nor did they follow up the Turkish workers' visits to see if people returned to the museums, purchased art
materials for their children, or over time showed changes in attitude about
art or German culture.

The goal of the project—to interest Turkish migrant workers in any or
all of the three institutions and what they had to offer—was difficult to meet,
and the evaluation was compounded accordingly. Indeed, Schrübbers writes
that even the "energy we had given to personal care of the participants" by
the museum professionals was too much of a burden, and that "we developed
no standard program out of this pilot study." But "Turkish Families Visiting
Berlin Museums" does show us that a fundamental belief in the accessibility
of all cultures to all people remains a worthwhile and productive basis for
further efforts by museum professionals.

COMMENTS ON PITMAN'S PAPER

Many of the major art museums in the United States and in other nations were established in the nineteenth century, during an era when universal education was being rapidly advanced by the Industrial Revolution. In North America the accumulation of enormous amounts of capital by individual industrialists led them to emulate the European aristocracy in the building of great art collections, almost all of which would eventually find their way into the museums of the large metropolitan cities.

The founding charters of many of these institutions pledge access for the masses to the kinds of cultural riches previously reserved for the very wealthy. Therefore, the educational role of art museums has been a fundamental one, at least in the United States, throughout their history, although for a long time this was given only lip service by trustees and museum professionals. In recent decades, however, the growth of museum education and its concomitant functions has been impressive, with the simultaneous development of a professional guild of museum educators that pursues advocacy, research, publications, and other professional activities.

However, as Pitman and other investigators have made clear, we are far from the millennium. Museums still know too little about their audiences and how to make the learning experience more effective. The majority of visitors go through galleries alone, without a gallery tour or other educational aids. How visitors learn to understand and appreciate works of art in such circumstances has been the subject of some recent work focused on "silent pedagogy" (Eisner & Dobbs, 1988, 1990).

The ultimate value of the various studies described by Pitman is that these add valuable insight to our understanding of visitors and the needs of different audiences; they provide an opportunity for art educators to test various hypotheses about how people can learn effectively in museums; they adopt a variety of approaches in the effort to come up with alternative solutions and avoid finding "right answers"; and they reinforce the trend among art museums to conduct or attend to such studies in the firm belief that changes in practice can and will be thereby achieved. We can say at the outset that perhaps the most hopeful news from Pitman's paper is that in virtually every case where evaluations were conducted, museums made decisions to change in ways based on the findings. No greater validation of the processes of evaluation can be offered than this putting one's money where one's mouth is.

In her opening pages Pitman recalls that museum education has become more firmly established as a priority as the value of public access to institutions has evolved. Recent reports of the American Association of Museums affirm the fundamental importance and principles of museum education and provide agendas for future actions, including a greater emphasis on research and evaluation so as to better integrate museum education across the range of museum activities. Pitman delineates the difference between this challenge and learning in other educational environments: "Museums communicate messages not only through objects, but through accompanying interpretive resources offered in the galleries and in public programs." Furthermore, access to these objects for diverse audiences involves making choices about resource allocation that make it incumbent on museum professionals to know more about visitors and how they learn or might learn. As Pitman reports, "Evaluations help to identify specific ways to improve service to visitors" by asking two basic questions: Who is (or might be) the audience? How can the quality of learning experiences in art museums be improved?

The paper begins with a "brief history of visitor evaluation in the United States," indicating that such studies have taken place since the early twentieth century. However, other than the mention of pioneering work by Benjamin Gilman at the Boston Museum of Fine Arts, there is no further elucidation of that history except a reference to Ross Loomis's 1987 book, which "gives a fine summary of the development of this field." Perhaps Pitman felt that this history did not require description in the paper, but most readers are unfamiliar with the threads of the evaluation tradition that do exist. Perhaps the next iteration of this paper will exceed acknowledgment. What did early pioneers discover about audiences beyond Gilman's findings about visitor fatigue, which led to the redesign of exhibit cases? How did museums in the first half of this century respond, if at all, to what research was telling them about their visitors? Pitman's bibliography emphasizes work of more recent vintage but might be expanded to include landmark studies of earlier times.

The core of the Pitman paper is the description of evaluation studies in four settings, all of which share the basic value that "visitor research and evaluation result in an improved understanding of the museum's audience." More important, "the research . . . suggests to staff strategies to improve the quality of learning that occurs in exhibitions and programs." However, this assertion of a link between empirical investigations and actual practice in museums is offered cautiously. There is no claim made that throughout the past 2 decades a growing tide of such studies has resulted in widespread changes. Rather, the participating institutions in the cases reported by Pitman have given evaluation efforts their due and acted upon their findings. A large job remains to persuade administrators and museum educators themselves to use the wealth of data that are available and that may have application to their respective situations.

The project that receives first billing and the most space in the paper is the most ambitious of those reported. Focus groups of both museum professionals (consensus groups) and visitors (external groups) were organized in 11 American art museums under the sponsorship of the Getty Center for Education in the Arts and the J. Paul Getty Museum in a study completed in 1989. Under the direction of Alan Newman, some 220 visitors and 115 professionals participated in focus groups that were documented in 132 hours of transcriptions. This was a systematic evaluation program on an unprecedented scale. It not only looked in depth at visitors and their attitudes and reactions, but also stimulated communication among museum professionals about their educational responsibilities and how best to fulfill them. The focus group method recalls a familiar theme, that of educational institutions borrowing from the world of commerce, in this case advertising. Madison Avenue has used focus group research for decades to better understand (and take actions in reliance on) the perceptions and attitudes of consumers.

What came out of this 2-year study? Again, as in the Schrübbers report, the results are not surprising, but are valuable for the validation they provide to the building of a theory base about museums, visitors, and exhibitions. For example, Pitman reports that "staff want visitors to have a positive, meaningful, and educational experience and to leave with a desire to return." Equally predictable is the consensus of the visitors that museums are reflective places, that objects are attractive and that emotional bonds can be formed with particular items, that many visitors still think of museums as the preserve of the upper or elite classes, and that galleries are not particularly conducive to outings with children.

But the most important finding of the external focus groups (including participants who were regular museum visitors as well as those classified as non-museum goers) was that "art museums must improve the educational quality of the museum experience and that this can be achieved through better orientation, information, and direction." This finding squares with those of a previous study, also sponsored by the Getty Center, which strongly recommends the development of the art museum's educational functions to offer additional assistance to visitors (Eisner & Dobbs, 1986). The same investigators, in the reports cited earlier, looked at museums' efforts in orientation, layout and installation, and signage to suggest ways of making visitor experiences more meaningful by strengthening access to the works of art.

As one reads through Pitman's report of the findings of the Getty focus groups, some familiar bogeys raise their heads.

> The focus groups expressed dissatisfaction with the type of information presented on labels because it frequently provided insufficient data about objects. Often, instead of providing data about an artist's life, or facts concerned with the historic or artistic significance of an object, labels offered donor information.

In other words, people wanted labels that would help them understand salient facts about the work and its meaning, a demand that probably would disqualify a large number of labels in American museums today.

The productive outcome of the focus groups for the participating art museums appears to be such ongoing changes as reorganized admission desks, new and more helpful labels, and reinstalled galleries. Equally important is the recognition by museum professionals that they can learn from listening to their visitor-clients. Furthermore, through mutual exchange among museums, good ideas can be taken from the drawing board to the galleries for enhancing access and learning effectiveness. Still, one wishes that Pitman had given a bit more of the flavor of this side of the project, for it would be helpful to know why and how curators, directors, exhibition designers, and others who were not always on the side of the museum educators have been thus persuaded. Paeans to the art museum's public responsibility do not tell the whole story; there is a story too in the rising expectations of the museum professionals themselves for their institutions to survive and hopefully prosper in a competitive world. Cultural institutions, like all others, have been driven to re-examine their purposes and methods of operation.

Pitman also does not deal with the specific problems of evaluation or any shortcomings of the focus group method as they emerged during 2 years of study involving hundreds of participants. The method may not be feasible in all cases, but even if it is very helpful we should know what its pitfalls are.

The second half of the paper runs quickly through the other three settings in which exemplary projects in art museum evaluation are featured. The Institute of Contemporary Arts in Boston, led by Abigail Housen, pursued a visitor study that featured identification of the visitors (demographic study), their preferences in art and type(s) of interpretive materials (attitudinal study), and their level of understanding and comprehension (aesthetic or developmental study). Outcomes are reported similar to those of the Getty study: "Respondents requested additional educational information to aid them in their understanding of contemporary art." This led to changes in the orientation resources and in the outreach to high schools, where students frequently expressed confusion in attempting to decode modern art.

A third study, at the Minneapolis Institute of Arts, examined visitors' reactions to an exhibition titled "Beneath the Surface." An exit questionnaire was used to determine which of seven interpretive resources had been helpful to visitors. Some 88% said they depended primarily on the labels, confirming signage's important and ubiquitous place in nurturing audience understanding. But in a comparison of "novice" and "expert" visitors, the difference in ratings on understanding of content attributes in the works was not significant. After treating these first three reports as "evaluation studies of exhibitions," Pitman's paper then shifts to "evaluation studies of interpretive resources" and introduces a fourth study. The difference between these sections is not quite clear in the paper as there is considerable overlap in the phenomena surveyed.

The Denver Art Museum, the fourth study, is presented as an institution that has embraced evaluation in wholesale fashion to provide feedback to its policy and decision-making structure. Led by Patterson Williams, Director of Education, the Denver Art Museum has dedicated considerable attention to evaluation, working with professional evaluators and training staff to work as evaluators on a modest scale. Related achievements at the museum cover a broad range of activities, but Pitman focuses primarily on the label studies that have resulted in a stronger sense of "human connection" for visitors with the exhibits.

The paper concludes with a reaffirmation of the awakened sense of public responsibility that has apparently driven museums to want to know more about their visitors and how to improve visitor experiences. Pitman mentions the older traditions of collection, preservation, and, by implication, scholarship and connoisseurship. It might be interesting to pursue a study of the impact on these dimensions in a strong educational climate. Such traditions are not, in fact, expunged by research, evaluation, and consequent change. Rather, collection, conservation, and connoisseurship are likely to be strengthened as art museums strive to provide a spectrum of interests and experiences to an increasing range of audiences, from the specialist collector and art historian at one end to people like the Turkish migrant workers at the other. As Pitman concludes, "The need to provide a historical, cultural, and aesthetic context for the artist and artwork is transforming the types of resources provided to visitors."

SOME FURTHER OBSERVATIONS

Despite the hopeful prospects adduced by the reports by Christiane Schrübbers and Bonnie Pitman, it may still be strongly asserted that neither the resources nor the skills necessary to conduct research and evaluation in art museum education have been well developed. As a consequence, art museum educators continue to depend largely on others to carry out such work.

These issues are increasingly important to the formulation of policy and practice in the fulfillment of the educational mission of such institutions. Even if such skills are developed in the course of a museum education degree program, they are unlikely to be sufficiently advanced or comprehensive. Thus, a first step toward empowering museum educators to carry out systematic and rigorous evaluation in art museums would be to strengthen the research and evaluation component of their professional programs, and provide inservice assistance for those who lack such training. A variety of manuals, self-learning computer units, tapes, and publications are needed to address this need. The alternative was described by Eisner and Dobbs (1986) in *The Uncertain Profession:* "Because the research base is small and evaluation skills scarce, programs are appraised on an ad hoc, informal basis. Evaluation is done . . . by walking through the galleries to see who is there" (p. 59).

A second priority is that a greater variety of methods are needed to nurture the skills of those individuals who evaluate museum education programs. Focus group research can be time-consuming and expensive. Visitor surveys can never be absolutely complete. Experimentation needs to take place so other methods can be developed and alternative educational strategies explored.

Considerable information is available about various audiences, about how to make school programs more effective, and about the public relations in a community that helps draw people to an exhibition. But what of some of the remaining basic questions that are generally unanswered, perhaps because they are so prosaic, but more likely because few, if any, museum educators are in a position to pursue them? For example, questions remain about layouts and installations from an educational point of view. What is the relative difference in comprehension and enjoyment between shows that feature chronological, stylistic, or thematic organization? Exhibition designers, installers, and curators have as much at stake as museum educators do in exploring such alternative arrangements.

A third priority might be to determine codes of conduct for evaluation of museum art education programs. For example, administrative support is not especially consequential if mere bean-counting is the primary outcome. Evaluators also need to conduct their work with regard for the subjects who are under study. The Getty focus group research points up this issue. It is important that the participants knew that they were being observed and documented. In art education degree programs throughout the United States, students must observe ethical standards in working with human subjects in the course of their thesis and doctoral research. The sensitivity of the museum educators reported in the Berlin museum project also indicates the importance of dealing openly and honestly with those upon whom scrutiny settles. This is an operational dimension that is not peculiar to evaluation in art museums but should be observed there as well. The growing interest in multicultural studies reinforces this ethical concern.

A fourth and final priority suggested here is that art museums need to further institutionalize resources to professionalize the field of museum education. This is not only to support the efforts at evaluation but also to facilitate the other kinds of research that can be of such material assistance in carrying out a comprehensive museum education program. Because there is much in common that institutions could share, better networks of information sharing and exchange also are required, not only to disseminate good concepts and practices but also to bring the fruits of research and evaluation to a wider professional audience while that information is helpful. Too often the research is dated by the time it is retrieved. A system of information sharing using computer-based technologies would be as desirable for art museum educators as it is becoming for art historians, who have made considerable progress in developing such resources.

The evaluation of museum art education programs presents numerous professional challenges and opportunities. Some of these are being addressed by the cutting edge of museum professionals, persons whose interest in furthering their field as well as their own work leads to broader visions of application. The development of evaluation must go hand in hand with the professional growth of museum education as a specialty discipline and as an important component of art museums. Credibility for museum education and initiatives to help bring museums closer to the educational institutions they are intended to be, can be powerfully advanced by the confidence that is the just yield of effective evaluation programs.

REFERENCES

Eisner, E. W., & Dobbs, S. M. (1986). *The uncertain profession: Observations on the state of museum education in twenty American art museums.* Los Angeles: Getty Center for Education in the Arts.

Eisner, E. W., & Dobbs, S. M. (1988). Silent pedagogy: How museums help visitors experience exhibitions. *Art Education, 41*(4), 6–15.

Eisner, E. W., & Dobbs, S. M. (1990). Silent pedagogy in museums. *Curator, 33*(3), 217–235.

BONNIE PITMAN

It has become clear that the role and responsibilities of art museum educators in the United States are different than in other parts of the world. In the United States, art museum educators in small to medium-size museums are often part of a very small team of people working together to serve an entire population in a community.

Art museum educators are generalists, responsible not only for presenting diverse periods in art history, preparing text labels for the gallery, and drafting brochures and publications, but at the same time for presenting lectures to connoisseurs, training docents, or perhaps even giving tours to groups of school children. Art museum educators in the United States serve as members of a team composed of curators, exhibition designers, and editors. The team works together to interpret an exhibition and develop programs to serve the broadest audience. However, in some museums, the museum educator remains isolated from such group interaction, which results in the educator having responsibility for interpreting an exhibition without the research, support, and guidance from other colleagues on the professional staff.

Effective art museum educators are gifted teachers and talented public relations experts, and have to develop excellent skills in fund raising, since most of the money necessary for their programming must be raised either through fees or through grants. Thus, a large portion of the museum educator's time is spent doing things other than education or evaluation. The role and responsibilities of art museum educators have created circumstances that are important to understand in relation to the context of current museum evaluation and interpretation programs.

Since the presentation of my paper at the conference in the Netherlands, a number of truly excellent publications have become available and should be noted, as I would have used them as important resources. These publications are

1. *Insights: Museums, Visitors, Attitudes, Expectations: A Focus Group Experiment* (Walsh, 1991). The focus group program sponsored by the Getty Center for Education in the Arts and the J. Paul Getty Museum has been published. This resource unit includes a video tape that summarizes the findings of four of the museums that participated in the group; there is also an excellent publication that summarizes the entire findings and provides

information about activities that some of the museums are undertaking as a result of the focus group project. This important publication is a key resource for anyone interested in learning more about the focus group process and in understanding the importance of this comparative study of visitors' responses to art museums.

Dobbs requested additional information on the activities that resulted from the museums' understanding, gained from the focus group program, of visitor needs. The Getty publication *Insights* includes a one-page summary from each of the 11 museums, outlining specific activities that the museums are undertaking at the time of the publication. Examples include the following:

- *The Art Institute of Chicago* is developing a project to create a coordinated art information system for the permanent collections. The project will include 15 illustrated gallery guides for various areas, including impressionism and postimpressionism, American art 1650–1900, as well as other areas of the collection. The texts were written for a general audience and include 15 illustrated works from the collections that are normally on view. In addition, the museum produced color-coded maps to help visitors locate exhibitions in the museum.

- *The Brooklyn Museum* has a program for older adults (35% of their current audience), who are generally less physically and financially independent. The program seeks to overcome existing perceptions of the museum as being formidable and inaccessible. It addresses the specific physical and logistic barriers that discourage these visitors, and develops engaging programs and materials for this audience. Working with an advisory committee and conducting focus groups, the museum learned about the programmatic interests of the audience and developed appropriate programs.

- *The Seattle Art Museum* has redesigned the lobby and public information areas, which were described by the museum visitors in the focus group as "austere, pompous, and uninviting." This project will include a new, redesigned entry area with new maps and the hiring of professional staff to coordinate and offer services to visitors.

- *The National Gallery of Art* designed information on the permanent collection to help visitors understand the historic, geographic, and aesthetic context, and the reasons for the installation, of the permanent collections. This collaborative project includes a team of people from the education, design, and editorial departments to develop new systems that provide information to the public without aesthetically intruding on the works of art. These new interpretive materials will be part of the museum's fiftieth anniversary program.

2. *Art Education and Human Development.* The Getty Trust also has published an important new book by Howard Gardner (1990). He surveys what psychologists have discovered in the past about principles that govern the development of human beings. Special attention is given to studies that suggest principles at work in artistic development and to studies that provide lessons for educators in the arts. Considerable flexibility is revealed in the options available to human societies in their educational and socializing practices. Gardner provides important background information that helps us to frame our understanding about policies and programs in art education.

3. *The Art of Seeing: An Interpretation of the Aesthetic Encounter.* Mihaly Csikszentmihalyi and Rick Robinson (1990) provide an insightful analysis of Csikszentmihalyi's work and interest in art and artists during studies conducted at the J. Paul Getty Museum. The authors discuss the characteristics of an aesthetic experience and what can distinguish the levels of these experiences. This important book helps us to understand the characteristics of the perceptual dimension and the quantitative and qualitative analysis of aesthetic experiences, and offers ways of facilitating such analysis.

4. *The Denver Art Museum Interpretive Project.* Finally, a publication produced by the Denver Art Museum describes the 2½-year research program funded by the Getty Grant Program and the National Endowment for the Arts. *The Denver Art Museum Interpretive Project* by Melora McDermott-Lewis, interpretive project manager, in consultation with Patterson Williams, Director of Education, was produced in 1990. The Denver Museum's staff developed a conceptual framework for creating interpretive materials for novices, or lay visitors, and created 13 experimental label and gallery guide projects based on the framework, directed at understanding how to effectively provide interpretation to gallery visitors. This important book carefully documents a number of specific studies of labels and brochures and indicates what the visitors' responses were and how they improved the materials. The Denver Art Museum is committed to creating quality interpretation that is specific to the visitors who utilize their exhibitions. This project is important because it shows the results of collaboration among curators, educators, and editors, and provides insightful examples of specific wording for labels and gallery brochures. It includes comments by visitors as well as specific evaluation forms.

5. American Association of Museums' report, *Excellence and Equity: Education and the Public Dimension of Museums*, provides recommendations that support three key concepts: Education is the primary mission of museums; the changing communities in which museums exist are resulting in new

multicultural programs and ethnically diverse staffs, boards of trustees, and volunteers; and leadership is required at all levels of the museum profession and within communities to embrace the rapid changes that museums will face in the next decade. The report provides the museum field with an important document to support the expanding public service role of museums in the next decade.

Since its publication, over 40,000 copies have been distributed to museum professionals, trustees, and educators. *Excellence and Equity* has been used by many museums to help prepare their strategic plans, and by foundations to develop new funding programs to support art museums' educational initiatives.

6. *The Audience for American Art Museums* by J. Mark Dandson Shuster (1991) summarizes a research study conducted by the National Endowment for the Arts. It provides interesting data on the number and diversity of people who attend art museums.

Recent literature in the museum field indicates an increase in the number of studies conducted by both museum evaluators and consultants. These studies have helped art museums to understand a range of issues regarding the effective presentation of information to their visitors.

REFERENCES

American Association of Museums. (1992). *Excellence and equity: Education and the public dimension of museums.* Washington, DC: Author.

Csikszentmihalyi, M., & Robinson, R. E. (1990). *The art of seeing: An interpretation of the aesthetic encounter.* Los Angeles: J. Paul Getty Trust.

Gardner, H. (1990). *Art education and human development* (Occasional Paper No. 3). Los Angeles: Getty Center for Education in the Arts.

McDermott-Lewis, M. (1990). *The Denver art museum interpretive project.* Denver: Denver Art Museum.

Shuster, J. M. Dandson. (1991). *The audience for American art museums.* Research Division Report No. 23, National Endowment for the Arts. Washington, DC: Seven Locks Press.

Walsh, A. (Ed.). (1991). *Insights: Museums, visitors, attitudes, expectations: A focus group experiment.* Los Angeles: Getty Center for Education in the Arts & the J. Paul Getty Museum.

CHRISTIANE SCHRÜBBERS

In his response to my paper, Stephen Dobbs remarked that I omitted to set out the point "regarding the objects." During the course of our talks, I recognized that this indeed was a fault and the point was not at all self-evident. Our discussions led me to put it into the following short notes:

Looking at objects is the central method of museum education, unlike in any other learning situation. In the museum, we confront an original, while elsewhere we deal with pictures and texts of and about originals. This museum educational method is, in my opinion, not yet worked out sufficiently. What matters is the development of its specificities in contrast to school methods.

Very often the term *education* is linked with *information*. My concern is to link it with *Bildung*. By this I mean not the didactic, but the pedagogical-anthropological dimension. As references I would like to call *eruditio, cultura, formatio*. I stress not the transitive but the reflexive part of the act of *Bildung*.

In relation to our museum work, *Bildung* means that visitors must relate objects to their own life. They succeed when they are able to recognize an object as a fragment in a certain associated sociocultural area, which they can compare with their own. They see a so-called masterpiece (whether of artistic or technical nature) in relative terms and draw personal pedagogical benefit from it.

Bildung, in my opinion, is one of the most eminent pedagogical tasks of our time. The range of information transmission—personally and most of all technically—is diverse and in all of its parts perfectly developed. The museum is possibly one of the few places, one of the few media, in our society in which *Bildung* is possible. It is a chance to arm people with autonomy against the electronic flood of information and of all its severe consequences.

The attitude of learning that schools teach is reflected in inquiries about the effects of lessons in physics: When pupils cannot give the correct answer to a question on a multiple-choice test, they often choose the most absurd of the given answers since it corresponds to their image of the subject and "sounds most like physics." That means for other academic disciplines as well as for information in general, explanations are accepted as given, and not tested for their truth by the pupil (reader, listener, visitor). Accordingly, pupils quickly forget the content of their lessons. If my description of this type of learning and information is generally valid, this learning is not education, but conditioning.

I feel the effects of this conditioning in the museum as well. For 2 years, I gained professional experience in my work with visitors to the Berlin Museum of Communication and Transport. This museum claims to present a network of technical, economical, cultural, and social phenomena; to show their effects in human life; and to help the visitors to define their own position in relation to our technical surrounding. In my work I stress how difficult it is to undermine wrong thinking, to dissolve the misconceptions visitors bring with them.

Last summer I worked with pupils in the museum's history of photography department. Most of them were not able to

1. Regard an object so closely that they could describe it afterwards
2. Make a comparison between two objects
3. Relate an object to their preknowledge
4. Relinquish their existing constructs in favor of new knowledge

Let me illustrate my points with this example: The technique of photography is known by every amateur as pressing the button, bringing the film into a lab, and getting back prints on paper or slides. Introducing our project, I described deliberately and extensively how the pioneers of photography had produced their photo-plates. I experimented with photosensitive substances and pointed out that metal, glass, leather, and paper were used as bearers of these substances.

When a person points to a ferrotype (a photograph on metal that in its round and shiny form resembles a button) and asks how the picture gets onto "the round thing there," I infer that the model: lab delivers paper pictures, is not yet destroyed and that the historical dimension of our topic has not been understood. An attitude that withstands a historical conscience is dangerous for our political constitution.

These pupils were a good example of those who may be called visually dyslectic—persons who typically regard pictures as the explanation of foregoing pictures—who lack the ability to use language for the explanation of pictures. They live now in a society inundated by pictures. They are made by this society. What they need is not extra information, but a real pedagogical intervention.

CONCLUSION

Chapter 14

Evaluating and Assessing Art Education: Issues and Prospects

DOUG BOUGHTON
University of South Australia

The discussions in this book are broadly focused on the evaluation and assessment of art education in museums and schools. The purpose of this chapter is not to summarize those discussions, but to highlight key issues and point to some prospects for improvement in art education. I will discuss four themes that appeared in each part, identifying the different manifestations of each as the focus shifts from schools to museums. I also will suggest some prospects for evaluation and assessment implied by each theme in the context of various ideas raised during the 3 days of discussion in Bosschenhoofd. The themes are

1. Ideology and cultural relativism
2. Methodologies for evaluation and assessment
3. The relationship of art learning and intelligence
4. The art and science of evaluation and assessment

IDEOLOGY AND CULTURAL RELATIVISM

Not surprisingly, much of our discussion was spent defining context. In order to understand evaluation and assessment practices, concepts of curriculum and art, and assumptions about cultural values, we were forced time and

Evaluating and Assessing the Visual Arts in Education: International Perspectives: © 1996 by Teachers College, Columbia University. All rights reserved. ISBN 0-8077-3511-6. Prior to photocopying items for classroom use, please contact the Copyright Clearance Center, Customer Service, 222 Rosewood Dr., Danvers, MA 01923, USA, tel. (508) 750-8400.

again to return to discussions about ideologies and cultural differences. To my mind, of the many issues discussed in the Netherlands, there were four that brought matters of ideology into sharp focus. Three of these reflect different cultural practices and assumptions about art education in different countries, and the fourth is a universal problem of ideology experienced by museum education staff.

The first issue emerged, oddly enough, as a misunderstanding about the meaning of the term *assessment*, which is central to much of the discussion in the preceding papers. It was something of a surprise to conference participants that taken-for-granted language used by colleagues on different sides of the Atlantic (and the Pacific) did not have a universally recognized meaning. Gardner's rejoinder to Steers's response paper provides a clue to the kinds of misunderstandings experienced during these discussions. To come to grips with this problem requires more than a clarification of terminology. If we peel back the layers of meaning attributed to the term *assessment* in different countries, we see that an apparently minor difference in terminology masks a larger ideological variance in the intentions and practices associated with educational evaluation in different cultural contexts. *Assessment* and *evaluation* are terms that are frequently substituted for each other by American writers; Gardner (Chapter 7) and Rush (Chapter 4), for example, appear to use them interchangeably. Schönau (Chapter 8) and Steers in his response use assessment in a much more specific way. Eisner (Chapter 5), in his discussion on the evaluation of teaching, distinguished among *evaluation, measurement, testing*, and *grading* in order to clarify discourse about evaluation. It appears to be appropriate to note the way in which the British, Europeans, and Australians use the term *assessment* as rather like Eisner's definition of grading: "a data-reduction process that uses a symbol to represent the results of an appraisal or evaluation." However, assessment in the British, Australian, and European context carries with it a good deal more taken-for-granted conceptual baggage than does Eisner's definition of grading. Assessment typically refers to the procedures used to translate student art learning (outcomes) into a value represented as a letter or numeral. Such procedures have been agreed to within the community of educators who employ them and are consistently applied to the work of all students of a given educational level who offer their work for a comparative judgment of its merits, usually in the context of an examination or a summative assessment system.

This kind of assessment process is used by educational bodies in which the procedure for judgment of student learning is controlled by state or national systems. The intention of these systems is to achieve a degree of equivalence between students in normative terms. A student's work that is judged as a 75 in school X should be equivalent to the work of other students who receive a 75 (relative to the same criteria) in schools Y or Z. Further, the expression of student learning as a value facilitates moderation[1] and statistical comparisons between groups of students, and between the distribution of art scores and those of other subjects. In some circumstances (such as the South Australian state system), the assessment process is incomplete until statistical moderation has adjusted the distribution of art scores relative to the achievement of students in other subjects.

Assessment is a term that also is applied to teachers in the context of credentialing procedures, or scrutiny for promotion. Agreed-upon procedures, such as criteria for performance standards, are applied equally to all teachers in similar contexts in the belief that objectivity will be guaranteed. (In Chapter 6 Sharp El Shayeb referred to instruments for teacher assessment and teacher appraisal in her discussion of the evaluation of teaching.) Different conceptions of the term *assessment* are rooted in the particularity of educational ideologies employed within different countries. In the United States and Canada, ideological pluralism is rampant. In the United States, each of the 50 states has its own programs, and it is not rare to find that little commonality exists among schools, often within the same state. Individual teachers are usually the sole judges of their students' work, with the result that some universities do not include grades received in the arts when calculating students' grade point averages for university entrance. Although standardized testing is used as an assessment procedure for most school subjects in the United States, this practice has not been used widely in the arts, partly as a consequence of a general disregard for the arts as a worthwhile intellectual activity, and partly due to a lack of confidence by universities in art achievement scores supplied by schools. Short-answer, pencil-and-paper style testing has been regarded by teachers as inappropriate for the arts, causing the status of the arts to be diminished, at least in terms of university entrance.

Standardized testing has not been used widely in Britain, Holland, or Australia, allowing the development of assessment procedures that are more consistent with the manner in which judgments are made about studio products within the art professions. Pressure from universities to produce codified statements that equate with other nonart subjects has resulted in elaborate and, at times, very complex state and national systems for moderation of achievement scores in several countries.

What is the significance of all this for the evaluation of the outcomes of art education programs? First, it would seem to be useful for evaluators to sharpen their terminology in order to more clearly define a context for the purpose of international comparisons. *Assessment* and *evaluation* do not mean the same thing. Second, and more important, a more unified or centralized approach to assessment is viewed as desirable in an increasing number of countries.

Gardner's rejoinder to Steers indicates his conviction that a more coordinated national effort in art education in the United States is desirable and would be likely to lead to assessment that is capable of codifying current practices. In two recent studies, MacGregor (1990a, 1991) compared art assessment practices in England, Wales, Scotland, the Netherlands, two Australian states, and New Zealand. The purpose of these studies was to advise the Ministry of Education in British Columbia on the possible introduction of a province-wide assessment system for art education. Such a signal from an important Canadian province heralds a major ideological shift regarding art assessment practices in North America.

The assessment criteria and protocol of the International Baccalaureate also points to widespread acceptance and development of centralized assessment procedures. It is noteworthy that the I.B. assessment system is accepted by universities in more than 70 countries. With an increasingly mobile population of students anxious to ensure that their educational achievements have meaning in different countries or different states in a single country, an increase in the development of centralized systems seems more than likely. In the case of student achievement within school art education programs, there may be some sense in developing at least a degree of comparability in assessment practices so that students may move from school to school within a state or province, or even between states, provinces, or countries, knowing that their achievements will be understood and recognized at certain basic levels.

A second ideological issue is apparent in the research reported by Schrübbers in Chapter 13. Selecting a target audience of Turkish migrant workers who were largely unskilled laborers with little schooling and possessing little facility in German language and limited competence in their own native Turkish, the research team at the Museumspädagogischer Dienst Berlin attempted to "discover new ways . . . to generate interest" by confronting them with the products of German artistic culture. The difficulties encountered by the Moslem Turkish audience in accepting a naked human figure in the Georg-Kolbe Museum highlight the role of culture in artistic encounters. A national ideological problem in German museum education was illustrated by the action of the researchers conducting this experiment, who anticipated potential difficulties with the sculpture, yet decided to proceed anyway. This problem was described by Schrübbers in her rejoinder and linked to the effects of the Western European educational concept of *Bildung*.

The notion of *Bildung* has to do with "the reshaping of individuals" as a consequence of educational experience. The idea had its origins in the late nineteenth century and was rekindled in the early 1970s. The aims of *Bildung*, in the context of museums, demand that museum educators "change society" in desirable ways as a consequence of programs that expose people to good art. Although the impetus of the *Bildung* philosophy diminished in the mid-1980s, Schrübbers indicated some of the difficulties of museum educators who have tried to interpret the concept in their programs, and this is certainly supported by the outcomes of the Turkish migrant worker experiment.

That the project failed to achieve its objectives, largely because of the insuperable cultural barriers between the two groups of people, is noteworthy for art educators in the rest of the Western world. As Dobbs pointed out in his response, many nations have experienced a flood of immigration in recent decades. Continuing industrialization is likely to change the demographics of previously stable nations even more rapidly in the years ahead. It is a reasonable prediction that the future of evaluation in art education will need to take account of massive population shifts and an increasing consciousness of multicultural concerns. Dobbs's observation points to the need for both art educators and the evaluators of art education programs to increase their understanding of cultural and ideological differences.

A third issue, which has more to do with artistic ideology than with cultural relativism, appears to be an almost universal tension between museum art educators and the curators of the museums in which they teach. Typically, museum educators regard the objects within a gallery in terms of their potential to generate an educational impact. Curators typically assume that good art speaks for itself and that the processes of acquisition and installation have more to do with aesthetic considerations than with educational potential. Museum educators hold the view that curators are loath to believe that multiple interpretations of their installations may be appropriate, or even possible. Generally they do not readily seek input from educators, are unconcerned about what visitors may learn from the display (or whether they learn anything at all), and, worse, may be more interested in cataloguing and preserving objects than making them available to the public. The power structure of museums invests curators with considerably more influence than educators. As MacGregor said in his response to Vallance and Haanstra, van der Heijden, and Sas, the status of docents is such that they experience a situation of absolute powerlessness with respect to any decision about the work they teach from. The result is a high degree of tension between educators and curators in the conception of both the form and function of galleries.

While this kind of ideological difference exists, the foremost concern for a museum evaluator is to define what it is that constitutes a teaching program. Traditional art education programs in galleries, designed for relatively homogeneous audiences such as school groups, are not problematic in the sense that aims can be identified, teaching strategies examined, and outcomes assessed. Evaluation methodologies based on traditional practices can be employed in more or less the same way as they are in any short-course or school-based assessment, recognizing the particular difficulties of once-only visits, finite time, imperfect instrumentation, and limited generalizability.

But the real difficulty of museum evaluation lies in the twin problems of defining a conception of "teaching" for the occasional visitor, and identifying those "learners" (other than easily identified target groups). Is the organization of a display, the lighting, the text support material, and audiovisual information to be regarded as a teaching program? Who are the people who come to galleries? Do they come back? Why do they come to galleries? Do they learn anything? If they do learn something, what do they learn? How should one define "learning" in a museum? Does "enjoyment" of the experience constitute useful learning? Whose aesthetic judgment should be considered in the acquisition and installation of artworks? Should "Western aesthetic values" prevail in museum education programs in Western countries? Is the long-term effect of museum experience more or less important than short-term measurable effects? If they are important, how does one determine long-term outcomes of museum education? These and other issues were raised by the conference participants and reflect a veritable minefield of ideological issues for the evaluator.

It is encouraging to note the evaluative research efforts, documented by Pitman (Chapter 12) and Haanstra and associates (Chapter 10), that provide different lenses through which some of these questions can be viewed. The central ideological issue remains, however, and it is the fundamental tension in point of view between educator and curator. Some resolution of this tension as a consequence of effective evaluative studies in several institutions in the United States was reported during the museum discussions.

One promising prospect for museum evaluation was discussed. In Chapter 12, Pitman reported that focus group evaluation studies in 11 institutions were effective in changing the opinion of gallery administrators, thus leading to more effective installations. This strategy carries exciting implications for the practice of museum evaluation.

METHODOLOGIES FOR EVALUATION AND ASSESSMENT

Many readers of this book may be hoping to find new ideas with respect to methods of evaluation and assessment. While certain principles of methodology are discussed in many of the papers, none of the procedures is outlined in quite enough detail to satisfy the practitioner who might be anxious to try out a "shiny new model." There is, though, a very rich mosaic of ideas to provide the basis for development of new strategies, enough to sustain practically minded evaluators who might be searching for alternative directions.[2] Appendices and tables within several of the papers offer illustrative examples sufficient to provide a flavor of the methodology used in different situations. For those interested in school assessment, Gardner, in Chapter 7, delineates the criteria used in the processfolio assessment system for ARTS PROPEL; Schönau, in Chapter 8, outlines a sample of the criteria used for the judgment tasks employed in the Dutch national exams; and Steers, in his response, provides a sample of the domain descriptions and draft grade criteria for the British GCSE assessment.

It was clear from the conference that enormous effort has been expended in many countries, on a national scale, to develop assessment strategies suitable for school art education programs. (By comparison, institutionalized museum evaluation efforts are rare.) I will discuss some views about the development of "successful" assessment practices as they are reflected in countries using centralized procedures to judge the products of student artwork in schools. The United Kingdom, the Netherlands, and New Zealand are countries in which national art assessment systems have been developed for schools. While Australia utilizes centralized moderation practices, different models are employed on a state-by-state basis rather than one agreed-upon model on a national scale. Fascinating differences exist between these countries (and state by state within Australia). Although "difference" appears to be the defining characteristic of assessment systems within different countries, there are some important commonalities.

One of the most critical preconditions for effective development and implementation of centralized assessment systems is acceptance and support of the community of teachers who are affected by them. John Steers described the recent British experience that comprehensively involved teachers at all levels of development of the current assessment scheme, resulting in widespread national acceptance of the principles employed. Evidence from MacGregor's (1990a, 1990b, 1991) recent studies of assessment in Britain, the Netherlands, Australia, and New Zealand supports Steers's view that the success of centralized assessment depends on a perception by teachers that there must be something in the process for them: They should feel they own the assessment!

The second area of agreement is that an effective assessment model must meet the three criteria described by Steers. Although there may be some slight differences of interpretation, these are validity (do the methods of assessment reflect the aims and objectives of the course?); reliability (does the methodology produce similar results for similar students under similar conditions?); and utility (is the assessment process convenient and cost-effective?). This is where agreement ends. To provide some sense of the many other questions that have been resolved differently in different countries, we can consider the following issues raised at the conference. In one sense these constitute a basic, practical checklist of questions to be resolved in the development of a centralized assessment system.

- Who judges the students' work?
- Should the students' work comprise studio material only, or should written work be included?

- If written work is included, what should be the character of this work?
- Should the teachers' judgment be counted and, if so, to what extent?
- How many judges are required to provide the best compromise between reliability and cost-effectiveness?
- How should benchmark standards be established?
- Should work from previous years be employed for benchmark purposes?
- How should new judges be initiated?
- Should judges generate the assessment grade, or should teachers provide grades to be moderated by judges?
- Should statistical moderation be employed?
- Should judges travel to schools, or should the work be sent to a common assessment center?
- Should teachers be present at assessment?
- Should students be present at assessment?
- Should criteria be used for judgment, or will global judgments do?
- Should a whole year's work be shown, or should an examination period be set?
- Should class teachers be permitted to provide advice for work submitted as part of a studio assessment portfolio?
- If an examination period is set, how long should it be?
- If a whole year's work is shown, how does one ensure that all the work was done by the student?
- Should the judges and moderators themselves be checked, and how should this be done?
- How should the assessment process itself be evaluated?

It is interesting that centralized assessment has developed in Britain, Holland, and Australia within a similar time frame spanning the past decade and a half, but the decisions made relative to the above questions have resulted in very different procedural patterns in each country.

Clearly, these questions, and others, present very difficult agendas for negotiation, but the territory must be traversed if centralized assessment schemes are to be put in place. What is missing from the decision-making process in almost all cases is a clearly defined theoretical basis to shape and support the developmental process. The basis for decision making typically has been grounded in the collective practical wisdom of teachers. Decisions of government to assess student art learning in a centralized way have pushed practice well ahead of theory in most countries.

In recognition of this problem, the Dutch have engaged in a systematic effort to provide answers to some of the questions listed above through the research efforts of Cito. The results to date have provided only a few pieces of the puzzle and are not a great deal of help in terms of the development of assessment criteria. So far, in Holland, the use of distinct criteria for the evaluation of studio work appears to increase judge disagreement in comparison with global judgments, although hope is held for the future development of more effective judgment tasks. While the Dutch research shows little difference in the reliability of two judges compared with three or five, in his response Steers raised some questions about the context of this research.

One of the most interesting polarities to emerge from the conference was in the contrast of assessment practices in North America, Australia, New Zealand, and Europe. A relatively long-established tradition of research in art education in America, in concert with recent financial support from private foundations, has engendered pockets of research effort among a constellation of otherwise idiosyncratic assessment practices in schools. In contrast, the European, Australian, and New Zealand experience has been one of more broadly agreed-upon sets of practices based on little or no systematic research, but on a custom of assessment derived from the practical experience of those directly involved.

The work of Gardner (1989) and the ARTS PROPEL team is widely known for its contribution to the literature on curriculum and assessment in the arts. The intellectual roots of ARTS PROPEL come out of a long history of research into the nature of artistic development. Interestingly, there is an apparent similarity between the assessment vehicle of ARTS PROPEL, the processfolio, and the studio evidence that constitutes the basis for judgment (and moderation) in Britain, Europe, Australia, and New Zealand. It is an exciting prospect to speculate upon a convergence of pragmatically and theoretically based assessment practices, although the similarity may be somewhat superficial. One important and inescapable observation is the value placed by educators from both research and pragmatic traditions on the evidence of long-term studio practice supported, in many instances, by both visual and verbal documentary evidence. The kind of support material that serves as an intellectual trail to enable an assessor to understand the path traveled by the learner appears to be a central concept in the assessment of studio learning irrespective of the origins of ideas about methodology. At the point of agreement between practical wisdom and the indications of research, one can take some comfort in the assurance that practice is well founded. Despite Steers's view that the ARTS PROPEL model would not meet the criterion of utility, for the purposes of application within the British national scheme, there is great potential for exploration of the relationships between existing national models and the directions indicated by the research of ARTS PROPEL.

Much less is available to readers of the previous papers in the way of specific advice about evaluation methodologies for museums, but some infer-

ences can be drawn from the papers and discussions. The first is that evaluation methods should be directly related to the purpose of the school program,
or exhibit in the museum context. The challenge, once that purpose is identified, is not so great as the identification of the purpose itself, a point made
previously in the discussion about ideologies and cultural relativism.

Despite the lack of specific descriptions of methodology for evaluation
in museums, many possibilities for research may be interpreted from the papers and discussions. One of the most pressing needs of museums is to identify the nature and expectations of their visitors. Some of the unobtrusive
methods borrowed from sociology hold excellent promise. Beyond the pedes-
trian "head counts" and "audience surveys" lies a more sophisticated research
potential in the imaginative use of participant-observers (Vallance's "guard
for a day"; Chapter 11); surveillance cameras; belief inventories; and case
studies, narratives from long-term visitors, and similar ethnographic studies.

The technique of focus group assessment described by Pitman in Chapter 12 held some fascination for conference participants. This technique, borrowed from the advertising industry, is a useful device to sample consumer
preferences. More intriguing than the technique itself was Pitman's description of its linkage with museum installations that were conceived of almost
like a commercial product. In all cases where this technique was employed,
curators and administrators were convinced of the necessity to make changes
to the installation in order to improve its effectiveness. It appears that the
problem for education staff in museums is not so much in designing evaluation procedures, or even in achieving the changes indicated by the evaluation
itself, as in convincing gallery administration of the need to evaluate in the
first place.

THE RELATIONSHIP OF ART LEARNING AND INTELLIGENCE

A fundamental difficulty encountered in any debate about evaluation or
assessment methodologies is the potential confusion of the reliability and
utility of assessment methods with the validity of what is assessed. Criteria
may be developed to enable judges to reach a high degree of agreement about
the standard of student studio work in a cost-effective manner, but it does not
necessarily follow that the work being judged is an appropriate indicator of
authentic art learning. Nor does it follow that the criteria themselves are
helpful, simply because a group of educators agreed to use them.

What *is* authentic art learning? What is the best evidence to indicate that
it has occurred? These questions represent two of the perennial issues in the
literature of art education and, not surprisingly, are the subject of much discussion in the foregoing papers. A full exploration of the complexity of these

questions requires another book, but there are some important leads indicated in the exchanges between several authors.

It has long been argued by some in the field that although visual aesthetic experience lies at the very heart of art education, its character defies objective measurement because it is a highly personal, tacit, complex, affect-laden, and often ephemeral sensation. Any attempt to describe the visual aesthetic experience will misrepresent it, due to the inappropriateness of other symbol systems to adequately encapsulate its complex and subtle form in a (necessarily) holistic way. For the pragmatic evaluator, this argument is no help at all because it does no good to know that the most important objective of the art education program cannot be observed, measured, or represented without contamination from misleading reductionism.

On the other hand, some in the field argue the opposite: The products and practices of artists are manifestly evident, their visual qualities can be analyzed and defined, and programs can be constructed to enable learners to emulate these forms of behavior and expression. It is also possible to learn how to engage in informed discussions and exercises with text material leading to the acquisition of knowledge about art. While the pragmatic evaluator happily may develop instrumentation and judgment tasks to efficiently measure the degree of skill and concept acquisition demonstrated by students, such practices are disquieting to art teachers. The problem in this case is the converse of the first. An overly reductionist approach does violence to the subtlety, complexity, and unpredictability of artistic experience.

While these positions are put forward as something of a caricature, they illustrate the polarity of views about the nature of art learning that drive much of the evaluation debate in art education. At one extreme is a mystical conception of artistic learning yoked to aesthetic experience that cannot be demonstrated by any observable behavior; while at the other extreme is a mechanistic view of skill and concept acquisition, clearly demonstrated by observable behaviors and systematically aggregated to culminate in artistic learning.

The exchange of views among Haynes in Chapter 3, Rush in Chapter 4, and Parsons in his response exemplifies something of the landscape between the polarities just described. It is evident from their rejoinders that neither Haynes nor Rush sees herself as representing one or the other of those extreme positions. However, the contrast of their views with Parsons's, and with Gardner's in Chapter 7, highlights the following key issues.

First, if evaluation or assessment is to be done at all, we must be prepared to accept that the map drawn by the symbolic representations of the evaluator is not the whole cognitive territory. An element of selection and consequent reductionism is inevitable in any description of learning. This problem is not unique to art education.

Second, without behaviors or products there can be no useful judgment.

One cannot determine mind-states without evidence. The trick is to determine the best compromise position between mystical and mechanistic definitions of art curriculum content. An appropriate position might be one that
does not tightly constrain the learner, is designed to promote independent
problem definition and exploration of visual qualities, enables the student to
work with meaningful tasks in ways related to the artist's life-world, offers
flexibility of expressive pathways, and results in both "process-products" and
"end-products" for the purpose of assessment.

Third, there are two fundamental things students do to demonstrate art
learning: They make "studio products" and they engage in dialogue, written
or oral, about artwork. But are making and talking equally important? What
is the role of language both as art curriculum content and as an evaluative
tool? Rush favors the studio product as the richest source of evidence of art
learning, while Haynes favors discourse (provided the agreed-upon conventions for talk about art are observed). There was a general consensus among
those at the conference about the value of art history, criticism, and aesthetic
learning, but the relative balance of these ancillary art activities with studio
production as an indicator of art learning remains to be further debated. In
fact, there is strong evidence that the assessment results of students' studio
work and art history may bear little relationship to each other if they are not
connected organically within the curriculum.[3]

A critical point made by Parsons about the role of language in evaluation
is that the studio product requires interpretation. Language performs a role
equally important to perception in the evaluative act—it provides the framework of meaning that enables the context of the work to be understood. Gardner's description of the processfolio values critical or historical writing by
students as important indicators of their art learning (see also Gardner, 1989).
The practice of folio assessment in Britain and some Australian states also
regards written comments about students' work as valid interpretive information for assessment purposes. In New Zealand, students are invited to submit
written comments or tapes of their reflections on the work, while the I.B.
assessment invites students to be present at assessment to interpret the work
and respond to questions (MacGregor, 1991).

There is no question that in the art museum, language is a central focus
for the evaluator. Although some curators may believe art speaks for itself,
this is simply not the case. Many artworks are cryptic, obscure, and require
interpretation, particularly for the new visitor. The important questions for
museum evaluators to explore are those that tease out the effect and significance of different kinds of text materials, their locations, their suitability for
different audiences, the distraction or enhancement they provide to the work,
the level of language, the appropriate amount of text, the best style for text,
the effect of portable tape recorders, the appropriateness of lectures delivered

by docents, and so on. The effect of all these facets of a museum experience cannot be determined by examining portfolios. Language is a crucial interpretive medium.

Standardized testing was universally rejected by conference participants as a means to determine art learning. Short-answer, pencil-and-paper responses simply do not reflect the complex character of art learning, bear no relationship to the kind of tasks associated with artistic performance, and, most important, do not reveal the intellectual footprints of artistic thinking that may be captured by examining a portfolio compiled by a learner over a substantial period of time.

Gardner's work provides some new notions about the nature of intelligence and the way in which intelligence may be regarded in relation to domains and fields. The first important idea from his work is that linguistic, logico-mathematical, musical, bodily-kinesthetic, spatial, interpersonal, and intrapersonal intelligences may be employed in aesthetic or nonaesthetic ways; in other words, there is no singular conception of "artistic intelligence." Performance of an individual on any given task could require the use of one of these intelligences or, more likely, blends of different intelligences.

A second idea of some consequence is that intelligence is conceived as a biopsychological construct manifested through action in a social context. This idea is Darwinian in the sense that the survival of a species is dependent on the successful application of intelligence in relation to survival tasks. A biopsychological construct of human intelligence has two main characteristics that differentiate it from earlier psychological theories. It is contextualized because it locates intelligence within a culture—particular forms of intelligence cannot be actualized in the absence of an appropriate context. And it is distributed in the sense that individuals rely on social interaction and instrumental support to perform tasks within a social context. Intelligence is not wholly contained within the individual, but relies on a network of interactions.

The third idea is that intelligence should be regarded as separate from domain and field. While intelligence is a biopsychological construct, domain is an epistemological notion representing the accumulated knowledge of the discipline, and field is a sociological concept used to describe the community of judges who determine the quality of ideas related to the domain. While the distinction between domain and field may not be strictly justifiable epistemologically, it is useful for a better conception of the way intelligence is related to the performance of tasks in a social context.

From this set of ideas come two very important implications for assessment. First, assessment of art learning must be done in an "intelligence-fair way" that respects the abilities and concepts central to the art form. A student cannot adequately demonstrate the ability to translate ideas into sensitive artistic form by responding to a standardized pencil-and-paper test. The learner must be given the opportunity to paint and to reflect upon the painting. Second, assessment should be based on meaningful projects that are structured over a significant period of time allowing for feedback and interaction, and the process should facilitate the recording of ideas and reflections about the progress of the project.

THE ART AND SCIENCE OF EVALUATION

The issue of scientific versus artistic methods of research and evaluation has been debated in the literature for about 2 decades. Although most readers will be familiar with the argument, I would be remiss if I did not make brief reference to it in this chapter. It is an old issue that does not appear likely to go away.

The field of evaluation has long been influenced by the methods of educational research, which were themselves derived from the natural sciences. The interests of science are prediction and control, and they result in the reduction of complex information to simpler quantitative data for the purpose of generalization. While numbers are enormously useful in many contexts and for many purposes, they do not tell the whole story, particularly in terms of human engagement with artworks. Educators who employ scientific methods seek predictable outcomes, while those involved in artistic endeavor place more emphasis on quality of experience and action, leading to relatively unpredictable consequences. The spectrum of human action viewed from the perspective of artistic vision is a different panorama from that revealed through a scientific lens.

In the late 1960s and early 1970s, art educators took a defensive stance against traditional evaluative inquiry methods, regarding scientific research with a high degree of suspicion. The assumptions of science were thought to be largely inappropriate for the arts. Alternative research paradigms were generated by adapting methodologies from social phenomenology, ethnomethodology (Sevigny, 1988), and the arts themselves (Eisner, 1988).

In recent years scientific and artistic methods have had a happier coexistence. There is now a general acceptance by art educators of the complementary views of the worlds of science and art. Research and evaluation problems may best be answered by selecting the most appropriate methodologies from the variety of quantitative and qualitative procedures available. This view was reflected in Bosschenhoofd. If museum educators are interested in identifying the demographics and return rates of museum visitors, use of quantitative methods is appropriate. If determining participants' views about a museum education program is desired, then a belief inventory may be a good choice.

If highly contextualized information describing fine-grained distinctions regarding the quality of certain aspects of teaching performance is sought, then
educational criticism may provide the answer.

What became evident at the Netherlands conference is that the maturing
relationship of scientific and artistic methods is producing an interesting interface with respect to centralized assessments of both student learning and
teacher performance. On the one hand, the character of artistic performance,
whether art making or art teaching, can be described and judged in a richly
descriptive way using the methods of connoisseurship and criticism described
by Eisner in Chapter 5. Such a description is highly contextual, complex, very
personal, and congruent with the nature of performance. On the other hand,
art making or teaching can be codified for the purpose of comparison with
other similar performances using reductive techniques derived from the sciences; there are different benefits to be gained from each procedure.

If the evaluation problem is to identify performance for "gatekeeping"
purposes in which individuals must be compared with each other, such as
teacher credentialing, or promotion of students to the next grade, then reductive techniques are necessary. If the evaluation problem is to reveal *subtleties*
of performance, to make fine-grained distinctions of quality, or to provide
sensitive feedback to teachers or students regarding their achievements, then
artistic methodologies must be used.

The techniques that have been developed over the past 10 to 15 years in
countries employing centralized assessment systems for purposes of judging
studio performance have drawn scientific and artistic methods closer together. Judgment procedures that do not constrain the notion of art too
tightly, consider cognitive trails, are sensitive to context, and accommodate
long-term performance on meaningful tasks, hold much promise for the future of assessment in art education. The apparent convergence of theoretical
developments from ARTS PROPEL and the current assessment practices of
several nations is encouraging to say the least.

CONCLUSION

No discussion about the evaluation of art education can ever fully canvas
the entire spectrum of issues the topic deserves. One notable omission in this
chapter is the issue of program evaluation. Nevertheless, the themes I identified touch on some continuing issues, identify some new agendas, and point
to several exciting prospects for the future of evaluation of art programs in
schools, museums, and community centers.

For schools, the key issue lies in the development of assessment practices
that reflect authentic art learning, given an international context that points

toward increasing coordination of programs and centralization of assessment. A secondary issue is the problem of evaluating teaching. A tension still exists between definitions of adequate teaching performance, using reductionist methods derived from the sciences, and workable models of richly descriptive interpretations of teaching derived from the arts.

Museum educators face the problem of defining a workable relationship between curators and educators that will engender a productive program of evaluative effort. Once the decision to evaluate is made, museums first must define the nature of the curriculum and second identify the nature of the learners.

The ideas articulated in the various papers in this book provide enough to sustain the imagination of any practical-minded researcher or evaluator who might be interested in defining productive pathways to follow. The issues admittedly are complex but, with the benefit of international comparisons, we now have a view of the way forward and a few signposts along the way.

NOTES

1. Moderation is the process used to adjust the grades or marks achieved by students in one educational context in order to attain equivalence with similar work of students in another context. Procedures used to do this include panels of moderators who refer to common benchmark or exemplary works, and judges who use global judgments or detailed criteria (or both); in some instances, statistical procedures may be used.

2. For a description of British, Dutch, Australian, and New Zealand assessment practices, MacGregor's (1990a, 1991) reports to the British Columbia Ministry for Education provide a much more detailed comparative analysis than is possible here.

3. Analysis of Year 12 results of all students undertaking the Public Examination in Art in South Australia demonstrates a low relationship of studio achievement scores with art history scores. The theory syllabus bears no necessary relationship to the studio work undertaken by students.

REFERENCES

Eisner, E. W. (1988). On the uses of educational connoisseurship and criticism for evaluating classroom life. In G. Hardiman & T. Zernich (Eds.), *Discerning art: Concepts and issues* (pp. 633–648). Champaign, IL: Stipes.

Gardner, H. (1989). Zero-based art education: An introduction to ARTS PROPEL. *Studies in Art Education, 30*(2), 71–83.

MacGregor, R. N. (1990a). *Art assessment in Britain: Structure content and administra-*

tion. Unpublished paper submitted to the Ministry for Education, British Columbia, University of British Columbia, Vancouver.

MacGregor, R. N. (1990b). Reflections on art assessment practices. *Journal of Art and Design Education, 9*(3), 315–327.

MacGregor, R. N. (1991). *Art assessment in South Australia, Victoria, and New Zealand: Comparisons and contrasts*. Unpublished paper submitted to the Ministry for Education, British Columbia, University of British Columbia, Vancouver.

Sevigny, M. J. (1988). Triangulated enquiry: An alternative method for the study of classroom life. In G. Hardiman & T. Zernich (Eds.), *Discerning art: Concepts and issues* (pp. 614–632). Champaign, IL: Stipes.

About the Editors and the Contributors

Doug Boughton is currently Professor of Art Education at the University of South Australia, and was Head of the School of Art and Design Education from 1985 to 1993. He has a Dip. Art Education from the National Art School, Sydney; a B. Ed. and M.A. from the University of Calgary; and a Ph.D. from the University of Alberta. He is the author of *Evaluation and Assessment of Visual Arts Education* (1994) and has had various articles published in books, journals, monographs, and newsletters in Australia, Canada, the UK, New Zealand, and the United States. His research interests include art curriculum policy, curriculum development, and evaluation. He established the National Research Council of the Australian Institute of Art Education and was its foundation Director from 1991–1994. He is a World Council Member of the International Society for Education through Art (InSEA) and Convenor of the Research Board of that Council. He was appointed Chief Examiner Art/Design for the International Baccalaureate in 1994. He is also Principal Researcher of the Art Education Research Group at the University of South Australia.

Elliot W. Eisner is Professor of Education and Art at Stanford University and was World President of InSEA when the Conference on Assessment and Evaluation was held in the Netherlands. He is past president of the National Art Education Association in the United States, and of the American Educational Research Association. His current research interests focus on the role that artistic modes of thought and aesthetic forms of experience play in the conduct of scientific research. He is the author of many books, including *The Educational Imagination* (1994); *The Enlightened Eye* (1991); and *Cognition and Curriculum Revisited* (1994).

Johan Ligtvoet lectures in education and art education at the Academy for Art Education, Tilburg, the Netherlands. He has special responsibility for the development of international exchanges and programs, and is currently in charge of the European Masters in Arts and Humanities cooperatively offered by the Tilburg Academy for Art Education, De Montfort University (Leicester), and the University of Granada (Spain). Ligtvoet earned his degrees in art education and education at Tilburg Polytechnic. His research interests include curriculum, evaluation, multiculturalism, and international art education.

Stephen M. Dobbs is currently President and Chief Executive Officer of the Marin Community Foundation. He has previously held positions as Executive Director and Chief Executive Officer of the Koret Foundation, Senior Program Officer of the J. Paul Getty Trust, and Professor of Arts and Humanities of San Francisco State University. He earned both his B.A. and Ph.D. from Stanford University. He has written, edited, and co-authored a number of significant books, including *Arts Education and Back to Basics* (1979); *The Uncertain Profession: Observations on the State of Museum Education in Twenty American Art Museums* (with Elliot Eisner, 1986); *Research Readings for Discipline Based Art Education: A Journey Beyond Creating* (1988); and *The DBAE Handbook: An Overview of Discipline Based Art Education* (1992). He has been awarded honors including the Meritorious Performance and Professional Promise Award from San Francisco State University and the Charles D. Perlee Award for Distinguished Contributions to Humanities Education from the California Humanities Association.

Howard Gardner serves as Professor of Education and co-director of Project Zero at the Harvard Graduate School of Education, as research psychologist at the Boston Veterans Administration Medical Center, and as Adjunct Professor of Neurology at the Boston University School of Medicine. Gardner is the author of 14 books, including *Frames of Mind* (1983) and *Creating Minds* (1993).

Folkert Haanstra is senior researcher at the SCO–Kohnstamm Institute for Educational Research of the University of Amsterdam. He studied psychology and fine art in Groningen and has carried out research into art education and museum education. He is a member of the board of InSEA (Netherlands) and lecturer in the psychology of the arts on the Faculty of Education of the Hogeschool Amsterdam. His publications include *Creativity Centres in the Netherlands: Policy and Practice* (1986), *Museum and Public* (with Harry Ganzeboom, 1989), and *Effects of Art Education on Visual-Spatial Ability and Aesthetic Perception: Two Meta-analyses* (dissertation, 1994).

Felicity Haynes is currently Head of the Graduate School of Education and Dean of Education at the University of Western Australia. She has been Chairperson of the Committee of Deans and a member of the University Senate. She has been president of two national professional associations, the Australasian Philosophy of Education Society and the Australian Institute of Art Education, and served on many professional and administrative committees. She received a B.A. (Hons) in English and French, a B. Ed (Hons) in Philosophy of Education, and a Masters in Creativity, Mysticism and Insanity from the University of Western Australia, and was awarded a Ph.D. from the University of Illinois for a thesis on *Reason and Insight in Learning*. She has won the Cameron Prize in Education for the best research in education, a Hackett studentship from the University of Western Australia, and a 2-year fellowship from the University of Illinois. Her interests, in which she has published widely, include art education, epistemology, conceptual change, and ethics in educational administration; she is the author of a book, *The Art of Argument* (1987).

Ronald N. MacGregor is a professor in the Department of Curriculum Studies, and former Head of Visual and Performing Arts in Education, on the Faculty of Education at the University of British Columbia, Vancouver. He taught at elementary and high school levels in England, South Africa, and Canada, before being appointed to the Faculty of Education at the University of Alberta. He joined the Faculty of Education at the University of British Columbia in 1982. MacGregor has a diploma in Art from Gray's School of Art, Aberdeen, Scotland; a B.Ed. from the University of British Columbia; an M.Ed. from the University of Alberta; and a Ph.D. from the University of Oregon. He has published more than 60 articles in major art education and education journals in Canada, the United States, Australia, Britain, and Holland. He is the author of three books. He is a former editor of *Studies in Art Education* and is currently editor of *Art Education*. MacGregor has lectured extensively, including the Leon Jackman Memorial Lecture, Melbourne; Gaitskell Memorial Lecture, Montreal; and Tacon Memorial Lecture, Toronto. He is a Distinguished Fellow of the National Art Education Association and an Honorary Life Member of the Canadian Society for Education Through Art, and was the Pacific Region Higher Education Art Educator of the Year for 1994–1995.

Rachel Mason is Reader in Art Education at Roehampton Institute, London, and was formerly Head of the Centre for Postgraduate Teacher education at De Montfort University, Leicester. She trained as a fine artist at St. Albans Art College and, after teaching art in British secondary schools for 10 years, gained an M.Ed. from Manchester University, England, and a Ph.D. in Art Education from Pennsylvania State University. Mason has taught art education at universities in Australia, England, and the United States and is well known for her publications and research on multicultural art education. Her book *Art Education and Multiculturalism* was first published in 1988, with a second edition in 1995. She was Vice-President of InSEA from 1989–1993 and President of the National Society for Education in Art and Design

(NSEAD) from 1992–1994. She is currently project director of the National Survey of Craft Education in British secondary schools.

Michael J. Parsons received a B.A. in English Literature with Honours from Oxford University and a Ph.D. in Philosophy and Education from the University of Illinois. He taught philosophy of education for many years at the University of Utah, where he became Associate Dean for Teacher Education. He is now Chairperson of the Department of Art Education at Ohio State University. Two recent books are *How We Understand Art: A Cognitive Developmental Account* (1987) and *Aesthetics and Education* (1993).

Bonnie Pitman has been the Executive Director of the Bay Area Discovery Museum (Sausalito) since 1995. She served as Deputy Director of the University Art Museum and Pacific Film Archive, University of California, Berkeley, from 1990 to 1995, and as Associate Director and Acting Director of the Seattle Art Museum from 1980–1990. In addition, she has worked at the New Orleans Art Museum and the Winnipeg Art Gallery in Manitoba. Pitman has been a consultant to the National Endowment for the Arts and the National Endowment for the Humanities in Washington, DC, the Pew Charitable Trusts in Philadelphia, as well as more than 100 art, history, science, and children's museums. She earned her M.A. in Art History from Tulane University, New Orleans, and her B.A. from Sweet Briar College. Currently Pitman is the Chair of the American Association of Museums Accreditation Commission, the national accrediting body for American museums, and is a member of the National Advisory Committee for the Getty Center for the Education Arts. She was the Chair of the committee that wrote the national policy statement on the educational role of American museums, *Excellence and Equity: Education and the Public Dimension of Museums*, published in 1992 by the American Association of Museums.

Jean C. Rush is Professor and former Chair, Department of Art, Illinois State University, and Professor Emerita, University of Arizona, Tucson. She earned her B.F.A. (in painting) from Illinois Wesleyan University; her M.F.A. (in painting) from the University of Iowa; and her Ph.D. (in educational psychology) from the University of Arizona. Her primary research interest is the experimental investigation of children's art learning and perception. She has published numerous articles in journals such as *Art Education, Studies in Art Education*, and *Arts Education Policy Review*. Her honors include Senior Editor, Studies in Art Education, 1981–1983; Council for Policy Studies in Art Education, 1981–present; June King McFee Award, National Art Education Association, 1985; and Distinguished Fellow, National Art Education Association, 1991–present. She has accepted visiting appointments to the Getty Institute for Educators in the Visual Arts, 1983–1985; Western Australian College of Advanced Education, 1985; and the Andalucia Department of Education, Granada, 1990.

Jan Sas studied linguistics and social psychology at the University of Amsterdam and the University of Utrecht. He has worked in several museums, including the Maritime Museum in Rotterdam as Head of the Department of Education. Currently he is senior lecturer of museum communication and museum public relations at the Reinwardt Academy, Department of Museology, of the Amsterdam School of Arts. He has published in the fields of visitor behavior, museum education, and museum public relations.

Diederik W. Schönau is employed by the Dutch Institute for Educational Measurement (Cito), in Arnhem, the Netherlands. As a subject specialist for the arts, he works on test development for the national curriculum in secondary education. From 1981–1993 he did similar work related to the construction of final examinations in the visual arts on all levels. He was a researcher in the Department of Art History at the Catholic University of Nijmegen from 1979–1981. Schönau received postgraduate degrees from the State University of Utrecht, with a major in the history of art, and the Catholic University of Nijmegen, with a major in psychology. His current research interests include the psychology of art, child art, assessment problems related to the visual arts, perspective, and Franciscan art. He has published a variety of articles related to those fields in various international journals.

Christiane Schrübbers currently serves as museum educator at the Berlin Museum of Communication and Transport. She earned her Ph.D. at the Berlin Freie Universität (Free University). Her research interests include psychoanalysis and psychoanalytical education. She has published several articles in German publications.

Pamela Sharp El Shayeb is Professor of Art Education in the School of Art and Design at San Jose State University. She gained a B.A. and an M.A. from California State University at Los Angeles, and a Ph.D. from Stanford University. Her research interests focus on narrative drawings and stories. This interest, supported by work in Egypt as a Fulbright Senior Scholar, has resulted in the development of the *Children's Journal*, a periodical of drawings and stories by and for Egyptian children, published in Cairo. Besides her regular teaching responsibilities at San Jose State University, she is the principal investigator of two externally funded projects, the Bay Area site of the California Arts Project, a teacher inservice project, and Artpath, an artists-in-schools project. She continues her interest in teacher evaluation as a consultant to the Far West Laboratory on the development of measures for the identification of highly accomplished teachers of art for the National Board for Professional Teaching Standards.

John Steers was appointed General Secretary of the principal British art teachers' organization, NSAE (now the National Society for Education in Art and Design), in 1981 after teaching in secondary schools for 14 years. He is the 1993–1996 President of the International Society for Education Through Art (INSEA) and has served on its executive committee in various capacities since 1983. He has served on the Art Committee and Technology Committee of the School Examinations and Assessment Committee and, more recently, as a consultant to the School Curriculum and Assessment Authority. He currently serves on the National Council for Vocational Qualifications Art and Design Advisory Committee. He is a trustee of the Art and Design Admissions Registry and of the National Arts Education Archive, Bretton Hall. He was granted a fellowship and honorary membership in the NSEAD in its centenary year, 1988, and he has been a Fellow of the Royal Society of Arts since 1984. He completed his National Diploma in Design at Goldsmiths' College, University of London, having previously studied at Stourbridge College of Art. He was awarded his Art Teachers' Certificate, also from Goldsmiths' College, and was awarded a Research Diploma in Art Education by Bristol Polytechnic. He received his Ph.D. from Liverpool University. He has published various articles in professional journals in England, Canada, the United States, Germany, and New Zealand.

Elizabeth Vallance has been Director of Education at the St. Louis Art Museum since 1984. Before that she ran credit outreach programs for Kansas State University and was Director of Curriculum Planning at the University of Mid-America, a distance learning consortium. She earned her B.A. in Psychology from the University of Michigan and her Ph.D. in Education from Stanford University. She was Vice-President of the American Educational Research Association for Division B (Curriculum Studies) from 1991–1993; her vice-presidential address, "The Public Curriculum of Orderly Images," on art museum education was published in *Educational Researcher* in March 1995. She was co-editor, with Elliot Eisner, of *Conflicting Conceptions of Curriculum* (1974). Her research interests include aesthetic education, museum education, museum visitor behavior, and the hidden curriculum. She is a photographer.

Pieter van der Heijden has a degree in art history from Utrecht University. As a curator of education and presentation, he was employed by the Rijksmuseum and Tropenmuseum, both in Amsterdam. Currently he combines an educational curatorship at Leiden's Municipal Museum with a freelance career as consultant, writer, and editor in the field of art and museum education. He regularly teaches at Reinwardt Academy and is an editor of *Museumvisie*, the Dutch Museum journal, in which he publishes articles on museum presentation and education, and book reviews. He is co-author and co-editor of *ARTI*, an innovative method for art education in secondary schools. Current research interests include narrative structures in exhibitions, visitor behavior in museums, the sociocultural function of museums, educational multimedia, and curricular approaches in art education.

Index

Accountability, 3–4
Acheson, K., 109, 110
Aesthetic development grid, 31, 33
Aesthetic judgment
  Aspin on, 31–35, 55
  medium-specific versus interpretive
    views of, 58–64, 71–72
Aesthetic scanning, 42, 59, 60
Africa, 132, 203
Aggregation of performance scores, 192
Agricultural model, 80
Allison, B., 114
Alt, M. B., 212
American Association of Museums
    (AAM), 249, 250, 263, 280–281,
    289–290
American Bicentennial, 223
American Psychological Association,
    76–77
Andis, M., 213
Anti-intellectualism, 114
Apple, M., 13
Apprenticeship systems, 131–132, 140
Arai, I., 125
Aristotle, 80
Arnheim, R., 44, 87, 97
Art Education and Human Development
    (Gardner), 289
Art education in schools
  assessment as term in, xii–xiii, 2–3, 75,
    179–180
  criteria for assessment in, 7–16
  evaluation as term in, xii, 2–3
  form and content of programs in,
    7–11, 17–20, 42–73
  functions of assessment in, 4–5, 179
  mediation by teachers in. *See*
    Teaching

need for assessment in, 3–4
outcomes in, 6–7, 13–16, 17–18, 23–
    25, 55, 131–196
problem solving in, 20, 43–52
subject matter of assessment in, 5–7
testing in, 2–3, 6–7
Art Institute of Chicago, 288
Artistry in Teaching (Rubin), 121
Art of Seeing, The (Csikszentmihalyi and
    Robinson), 289
Art production, 45
ARTS PROPEL project, 24, 25, 35, 36,
    38, 55, 65, 141–145, 146–147, 177,
    179, 186, 194–196, 298, 301, 307
  domain projects in, 24, 142–143, 182,
    195–196
  processfolios in, 24, 143–146, 152–
    153, 182, 195–196
Aspin, David, 31, 33–35
Assessment. *See also* Standardized testing
  and accountability, 3–4
  authentic, 2–3, 138–140
  concept of, xii–xiii, 2–3, 294–296
  criteria for, 7–16
  in different educational contexts, 131–
    133, 194
  environment for, 146–147
  of form and content of programs,
    7–11, 17–20, 42–73
  functions of, 4–5, 18, 62, 76, 179
  of human mediation, 6, 11–13, 75–130
  and inner state of knowing, 38–39
  intelligence-fair, 23–24, 135–137,
    305–306
  methodologies of, 298–302
  need for, 3–4
  "new" processes for, 24, 36, 137–147,
    177–183

319